with lov
best wish
your birthday
and happy adventur g
in the year ahed.

ONE PEOPLE

ONE PLANET

Minnie xox.
3x191

BY THE SAME AUTHOR

Le Prisonnier de Saint-Jean-D'Acre (Libraire Séguier)
La Route (Librairie Séguier)
Les Chemins de la Paix (Librairie Séguier)

ONE PEOPLE
ONE PLANET

THE ADVENTURES OF A WORLD CITIZEN

BY

ANDRÉ BRUGIROUX

ONEWORLD
OXFORD

One People
One Planet

The Adventures of a World Citizen

Oneworld Publications Ltd
185 Banbury Road, Oxford, OX2 7AR, England

Originally published in French by Laffont under the title
La Terre N'est Qu'un Seul Pays © André Brugiroux
This English edition © Oneworld Publications 1991
All rights reserved. Copyright under Berne Convention

A CIP record for this book is available from the British Library

ISBN 1-85168-029-2

Printed and bound in Great Britain by
Biddles Ltd, Guildford and King's Lynn

To 'Albéré', my Congolese cook : A MAN
To Jacques who was Friendship
To Sigrid and Mirella, Love
and
To all those who are searching

"The earth is but one country, and mankind its citizens"
Bahá'u'lláh (1817-1892)

CONTENTS

Chapter 1

THE END OF THE ROAD

I had vowed to hitch-hike all the way, until my last ride dropped me off at my own front door. Now, as I waited under an overcast sky, I wondered if I was going to find that car. It was October and there was an autumnal chill in the air. I was cold, but it was probably for the last time.

The streets of Troyes were damp and deserted - except for a policeman who quickly zeroed in on me. He was the fourth one since Strasbourg.

'Let's see your ID.'

What a depressing home-coming! After so many years on the road all over the world, I was a suspect in my own country, only 100 miles from home.

'The main road is over that hill and across the bridge. You can't miss it.'

Clearly he did not want me hanging about in Troyes.

Arriving at the main road, I realized instinctively that it was a hopeless place to pick up a lift, so I walked for another twenty minutes. My backpack singled me out as a vagrant, a suspect; but I had forgotten its weight along with the policeman and the cold. I was nearly home. That was all that mattered.

Grey factories on the edge of town were calling their workers back from lunch. The road made a wide curve and headed downhill. Soon I had passed the last fence, the last building. Before me stretched barren fields awaiting the winter.

I dropped my pack on the ground. Here was the strategic spot where I stood the best chance of getting a ride. After hundreds of thousands of miles I had learned to recognize such spots. I was sufficiently far out of town for the cars passing by to be heading for Paris - slowly, because there was a speed limit. There was plenty of room on the side of the road, I was clearly visible and it wasn't even raining. Everything was ideal. It was only a matter of time before someone would pick me up - one hour, two hours, maybe longer.

With each passing vehicle I stuck out my thumb automatically, but the cars sped by. I hoped I wouldn't have to spend the rest of the day there, or the night for that matter. I had slept the previous night in an abandoned shack near Chaumont. It had been so çold that I'd kept my shoes on till the very last minute before sliding into my sleeping bag. In the middle of the night, I was woken by the cold and a sharp pain in my back. I was shivering violently. Unable to stand it any longer, I had hiked for hours through the fog in an effort to warm up. Suddenly, against all my hitch-hiking principles, I had put out my thumb in total darkness, not even knowing what time it was. It had been quite a while since I'd had a watch. A Cambodian had stolen my last one in a school in Phnom-Penh and I had never tried to replace it. It had just meant one less worry.

I had stood in the darkness on a steep hill while heavy trucks passed by with their blinding headlamps, their motors roaring as their drivers changed gear. I was jumping up and down and rubbing my shoulders and chest to keep warm. The late hour, the narrow road and the steepness of the hill had all been against me; nevertheless, I had managed to 'take off' just before dawn.

Today I was more optimistic. As each driver passed, I looked him in the eye and smiled to inspire trust. I was sure someone would stop, but I didn't know when. After six years' experience, I knew only that there were no rules to the game. You just had to find that strategic spot, and then wait, wait, and wait - hours or even days if need be. It was simply a question of time.

Time: I realized I didn't have more of it at my disposal than any other mortal, but perhaps I thought of it differently. I never wasted my time, least of all when waiting on the side of the road. I had acquired the patience and relaxed attitude of a fisherman, putting out my arm, waiting, and pulling it back in from time to time. Meanwhile, I would gaze at the sky, the racing clouds, the beauty of the trees and fields; and the endless spectacle of nature would fill me with wonder. Clear, joyful thoughts would swim into my mind and I would ponder them one by one. Thinking and dreaming - or not bothering to think at all - were to me a marvellous luxury. Other people went fishing. I preferred to hitch.

A small Citroën pulled over. Patrick, the driver, was heading for Paris. I got in and took out my notebook. On one of the last pages was written the word 'France'. Underneath it I made a little tick. It was my twelfth lift since Strasbourg and my 1,978th since I'd started my trip around the world six years earlier.

From November, 1967 up to October, 1973, I had covered over 210,000 miles all over the world in a total of 1,978 cars, trucks, planes and other assorted vehicles. I never took it for granted that a driver would stop, and I never blamed the ones who chose to pass me by. But the miracle had happened 1,978 times and every time it came as a surprise. In my own way, I had always tried to return the favour. If the driver seemed responsive I would tell him stories about my trip. I would ask him about himself and his family and sometimes listen to his problems. Even when I felt tired, I would still make an effort. It was the least I could do. Often I'd had to resort to mime to communicate with drivers whose languages I didn't know, but eventually we would understand each other and laugh, and both of us would feel better. A simple step on the brakes, a touch on the indicator, had opened the door to friendship.

At first I had regarded hitch-hiking as simply a way to travel, but it turned out to be an incomparable means of maturing, of learning about myself and my limitations, and developing my character to the full. By hitching round the world I had also made a painstaking journey into myself. Friends from throughout the world had helped me out, and to all of them I owed my thanks.

Patrick had spent a few months in Auroville, India, and we established an immediate rapport. He talked about the great gurus and spiritual masters, past and present, and also about Pondicherry where I myself had stayed in a neighbouring ashram. Our conversation flowed effortlessly. We were so enraptured by the subject and by the harmony between us that we scarcely noticed the miles go by. Patrick's stay in India had left its mark on him.

'Where exactly are you headed?' he asked.

'Brunoy.'

'Where's that?'

'Just south-east of Paris near the National Highway. If you drop me off in Brie-Comte-Robert when you go through, I'll be only six miles from home.'

'None of that - I'm taking you all the way to your front door! After hitch-hiking for six years around the world, you're not going to wait for another lift! I want to be your last one. Really, it's my pleasure.'

At Brie-Comte-Robert we left the main road. Périgny: three miles to go. Mandres-les-Roses: two more. Brunoy: I'd done it! I had hitched to the very end! No one was out to cheer me home, but the village signs I had known as a child all said the same thing: Arrival and Victory. I felt increasingly dizzy.

'This is Brunoy', I heard a stranger say. Then I realized I was talking to myself. 'I'm home in Brunoy. I'm back. It's all over . . . I'm in Brunoy!'

That familiar name came drifting out of my childhood and echoed strangely in my ears. Since leaving home I had heard so many names; exotic, unpronounceable, mysterious, mesmerizing names. But this was simply Brunoy, my own home town.

Nothing was as I remembered. Ominous high-rise flats had invaded the hilltop at Mandres. Fields of wheat and roses had disappeared under cement and asphalt. The plain of Epinay where I had camped with the Scouts no longer existed; a cold new town had taken its place. Trees, grass and bird-song all belonged to the past.

'Route de Brie', 'La Point à Chalène', 'Rue du Plateau': we were getting closer. The street names, the walls, the houses, the gardens dredged up memories from the past. This was Mardelles, my neighbourhood. I had arrived.

'Let me out by the cemetery. I can walk the rest of the way.'

I pushed open a large, very new gate and passed through a dark screen of cypress trees. Just as villages had turned into cities, the cemetery too had also grown, becoming just that much more impersonal and unfamiliar. I had the distinct impression of never having been there before, and yet, nine years earlier . . .

I had to ask the caretaker's help to locate my mother's grave. Everything was different. The stone itself had been changed. The new one was unpretentious, just as my mother had been.

She had passed away in February 1965. On that day and for a long time afterwards I had felt lonely, lost, shattered. The umbilical cord had been cut for the second time. I did not cry - I never cry - but the world of my childhood had suddenly collapsed. A terrifying void had surrounded me, intensifying my solitude.

I thought very often of my mother. It soothed me to recreate her gentle image in my mind. She had possessed the three qualities I most admired: courage, kindness and a keen mind.

My mother had had a unique philosophy of life in which acceptance had been the leading principle. In those days I would laugh at what I called her 'roof-tile theory'. She had maintained that if a tile fell on her head on a windy day, she wouldn't curse the Lord but rather thank Him for not having sent the whole roof crashing down. Today I was no longer at odds with her reasoning. Indeed, her philosophy had been of immense support during a long, challenging journey. My mother had taught me to welcome my fate. What she had called 'acceptance' had become for me an essential condition for happiness.

Standing by her grave nine years later, I was no longer the same. I felt calm and serene, even happy at being close to her again. I had forgotten the crushing distress, the suffocating funeral, the shock of irrevocable separation. A new person back from a long quest stood looking at a grave, and the grave was no longer a frightening place. I had discovered those ineffable truths which enabled me now to speak to my mother - joyfully - in the middle of the cemetery.

I had visited and closely observed the entire world. In every clime I had met people whom I had come to love, who had taught me the innumerable things that made me a different person today. Now I knew that death meant nothing. When the cage was open, the bird flew to freedom; it didn't die. Our bodies were only cages that death would shatter, freeing us to soar to brighter, wider horizons.

I was 'in prison'; my mother had escaped. Still, we weren't separated. I knew she was happy. Throughout my long adventure she had been present, helpful and supportive. I was indebted to her and my first duty on returning was to see her, thank her, and tell her of my joy. Lovingly I stoked the smooth stone. For the past six years I had reaped what my mother had sown all through her life, and surely the harvest was not yet complete.

The tramps who showed up on the steps of our modest home were never sent away empty-handed. On feast days and birthdays my mother never forgot to take a piece of cake to our neighbour Mrs Julien, a White Russian living in the utmost poverty. Shortly after the war, with France lying in ruins, my mother unhesitatingly welcomed young German visitors. She had been incapable of hatred and had instinctively treated everyone with the same warm-heartedness. Whether they were my old classmates or new African friends accompanying me home from the Congo made not the slightest difference to her. During the Algerian War, we had kept two Algerian boarders and never a word had been said against anyone. Her single aim in life had been to serve with love, and she had taught me to love people the world over regardless of race or religion. Each time she opened her door to a stranger, she had unknowingly opened a door for me on the other side of the world. In that way she had continued to watch over me.

If the rest of the world has a soft spot for France, it is not so much for her cultural and technological achievements as the fact that she no longer poses a threat. Only the powerful are envied. It was merely by chance that I happened to be born in France with the privilege of being white, Catholic, and French. Nevertheless such privilege pays. I am convinced that a trip around the world remains the prerogative of the white man; I doubt whether a Black would make it. As for being a Catholic, I had always been told that there was no salvation outside the Church. With France a pillar of the Roman creed, I was clearly in luck! In the past I had actually felt sorry for those unfortunate beings born under foreign stars, those barbarians!

In time I realized that the Roman Catholic Church was simply another sect with rites unsuited to the rest of the world and a doctrine that actively discouraged the mind from expanding its horizons. It was a sectarian sect. Certain of its concepts that I had retained from Catechism and Sunday sermons actually shocked me later: the idea of Muhammad and Buddha being charlatans, for example, or the impossibility of canonizing Gandhi.

Innocent and gullible, I had first left France in 1955 at the age of seventeen. My ideas had been shaped by the official line taught in the classroom. Temperate France was the ideal mother country; she had enlightened the world and continued to hold high the torch of civilization. In 1955 (the date is significant) I also believed that policemen were honest, priests saintly, and doctors miracle-workers. I took it for granted that men urinated standing up and women sitting; that flowers were presented wrapped in cellophane; that it was good manners to keep one's hands above the table during a meal; and that there was nothing shocking about kissing a girl on the street. I was on my way to questioning it all when, for the first time, I slung my backpack over my shoulders.

During my trip through Senegal, the local newspaper *Le Soleil de Dakar* billed me in its headline as 'The Ulysses of Modern Times'. In Greece, I was dubbed 'The Modern-day Marco Polo'. While I couldn't reject outright such flattering titles and articles since they were often actually helpful to me, they still did not convey what I had wished to accomplish during those six years. Certainly my trip was both a physical achievement and a financial one, but that is not what made it a success. Those years on the road were my education. In San Diego, California, an

American professor praised the exceptional merit of my 'studies'. He explained to me that 'certain of our universities attribute increasing importance to student travel, attaching ever more value to such experience'. I was no Ulysses or Marco Polo, but I wished to break new ground in another sense - to prove that a trip around the world was possible and that it could be the best university of all.

Westerners who take time to travel in the East are inevitably transformed by the experience (and probably vice versa), but Westerners who stay home have an unfortunate tendency to believe that their technological prowess confers both knowledge and wisdom. They have forgotten that the great spiritual masters came from Asia, from the East. After all, Christ wasn't born in Marseilles or Manchester or Chicago. The human race as a whole has the potential to create a civilization based on true happiness. The key is to unite Western technology with Eastern wisdom. The only thing missing is the will to do so.

Nobody ever discussed such things back in school, but I learned an enormous amount on my travels among the peoples of the world. I learned, for example, that each of our actions generates waves of energy which come back to us like a boomerang. If we act in perfect harmony with our conscience and our heart, we emanate positive vibrations which, in turn, create an atmosphere of peace and generosity. In other words, we create heaven here on earth. But people tend not to see things that way, and the large cloud hovering over mankind is heavy with the negative energy of racism, violence, hatred and prejudice. Our accumulated wickedness threatens humanity like an approaching electrical storm. Whereas man takes shelter at the first signs of storm, he remains oblivious of the black clouds glowering on the horizon.

One day in Australia, I had been marooned on a desert road for four whole hours. The Queensland sun was scorching hot and there wasn't a drop of water in sight. In fact, I didn't even have a water bottle, having preferred to keep my pack as light as possible. Thirst was torturing me when a man suddenly emerged from nowhere with tea and food.

'Hey mate, you must be thirsty, what with all the time you've been standing there! I've been watching you for quite a while.'

I knew from past experience that hot tea was the best remedy for thirst. The man had granted my wish.

I thought of my mother . . .

My mother had never encouraged me to travel. On the contrary, each departure broke her heart. In her day, people did not travel abroad, and although she had visited most of France - a faded picture album gave mute testimony - her greatest desire had been to keep me near her. Actually, we had never spoken of such things; in fact, we had not really talked much to each other. Although our relationship had been one of deep affection, it had remained that of a parent and child - nothing more. There had been no deep intimacy between us, but that could hardly have been expected. Still, I owed her everything, especially the strength I had found in her example.

Now, standing before her grave, I felt I had come full circle. My course in 'humanities' was complete. All in all I had been gone eighteen years. I had meditated, searched, suffered and accepted. At times I had even accepted too much, but I had never given up, never abandoned my goal. An irresistible urge had propelled me along the hard, tortuous path which, I now knew, was the way of truth. I wondered how an individual could grow without walking that path of self-discovery at some point in his or her life. It was a strenuous, unmarked route that I had unknowingly chosen back in 1955. Quite unaware of the boldness of my course of action, I had pledged myself like a knight-errant to a long quest that was to take me round the world and ever deeper into myself. I had observed and contemplated and immersed myself in the lives of men. I had taken time to gather the flowers of what I believed to be ultimate happiness. Now I placed them, tied in a bouquet, at my mother's feet.

An icy wind sent shivers down my spine. The sun was hiding behind thick clouds. I reached for my backpack and, with an action I had repeated a thousand times before, slung it over my shoulder. It hung low, pulling at my back muscles. My pack was also on the verge of collapse, its straps stretched as far as they would go. Both of us were at the end of the road. But what did it matter? We had seen the job through.

Cerçay Street looked narrower. I suppose it is always like that after a long time away. Our minds, our imaginations, our memories all distort things, altering their real proportions. I was home, yet everything was different. Some of the name-plates on the doors had changed, and there were several new houses, several new stores.

A few more feet, a few more steps. I felt weary and strangely dazed as I turned into the Rue du Chemin Vert. The house stood in the same place, unchanged, just as I had remembered it. I could see someone bent over at work behind the fence. My father was weeding the garden. As if seized by some inexplicable intuition, he suddenly drew himself upright. Catching sight of me, he froze, dumbfounded. His eyes showed no sign of emotion. He seemed stunned.

Immediately I saw how much he had aged. He had never got over my mother's death. She had been his entire life, and with her death he had lost everything. I felt a deep sadness as I waved mechanically.

'Papa, Papa, it's me!'

He came painfully towards the gate. Then, leaning on the iron bars, he put his hand to his heart and began to cry. He sobbed, a sick and broken man. Sadness welled up inside me. 'But Papa - it's me!'

Once inside the house, I glanced about the dining-room. Everything seemed smaller, but nothing had changed, nothing had been moved: the same wallpaper, the same furniture, all in the same places. My head was empty and my heart sinking. I felt weak, on the verge of fainting. The inevitable had happened. I had finally come to a halt and six years of accumulated fatigue were bearing down on me. I felt crushed, as if the entire sky had fallen on me. My back continued to ache and an excruciating pain tore at my sides.

Slowly I climbed the small wooden staircase. Spread out on the floor of my room were all the packages, bundles and oversize envelopes that I had sent home from the four corners of the earth. There were sculptures, paintings, and an immense variety of objects; stacks of maps, brochures and newspaper clippings describing my odyssey; dozens of letters with rare and marvellous stamps: a fabulous feast to my eyes.

My final instinctive action was to take out my journal - the seventh - and jot down the date. Then, realizing it was all over, I put down my pen on the desk where I had done my homework as a child. I lay down on my bed. Tomorrow there would be no need to get up and take to the road.

Without a word about my trip, my father had returned to his garden.

Chapter 2

"READY GUYS? LET'S GO . . ."

It all really began for me in Canada on Saturday, November 25th, 1967, at around four in the afternoon. The hour of the great departure had finally arrived. Actually, though, I had been on the move for a good twelve years already, ever since June 30th, 1955, to be precise. At that time I had just finished my third year of hotel management school in Paris, and without losing a minute I had packed my suitcase and headed for Saint Lazare station. Today I waited, feeling so much more confident. How long ago that morning on the platform seemed when, jaws clenched and eyes constantly watchful, I had taken my first step towards the great unknown. How terrified I had been.

On that occasion my destination was Scotland. The opportunity to work abroad was the school's reward for coming top of my class, and all through my last year I had dreamed of nothing else. To cross the Channel and learn English on the spot was my greatest ambition. Once my passport and work permit had been issued, I was ready - except that I was terribly afraid. I was all alone. At the age of seventeen, I had imagined myself as a fairly confident young man. I had even thought I might pass for an adult. But deep down inside, I still felt like a child. Twenty-five years ago, young people didn't travel around as easily as today, and I was convinced that Scotland was the end of the world. As I climbed aboard the second-class carriage, my legs were numb, but nothing would make me turn back. That was simply the way I was. Scared or not, I had to see my decisions through so that later I would have no regrets.

My debut as a globe-trotter was none too brilliant. I only had a couple of pounds in my pocket that I had earned working as a cook in

Brittany. Never in the world could I have imagined the eighteen years that were to follow that first shaky, hesitant step. During my first six months in Scotland I felt miserably isolated, an experience that was repeated every time I encountered a new language. In such moments of difficulty, I retreated into myself to await a future flowering. With that resolve, I found my patience and will-power greatly increased, and eventually I learned to speak English, Spanish, German and Italian.

In Scotland I quickly learned that despite the language barrier 'foreigners' had the same needs that I had: the need to laugh, the need to relax. They had concerns and attitudes similar to my own, and I soon felt close to them. I found this feeling of a common bond was essential for learning a new language. For me it was also important to make some friends in the country - it meant a faster integration into the society. In particular, I had found that girls were a valuable means of getting to a country's heart.

Unfortunately, I soon came to despise my job as a waiter, feeling a complete fraud in my penguin costume. Through sheer will-power I managed to stay on until I had learned to speak English, but already I was devoting all my free time to discovering new places. I took to travelling at once and realized that I had a powerful urge to move, explore, see things for myself. My curiosity was insatiable. There was always something new further down the road.

After fifteen months I left for Spain with no official papers or backing, and without any friends or a place to stay. Money? I had barely enough to last a few days.

'You think you're so clever. You'll be back in a week!' my father had muttered in disbelief.

My family environment (was it different from other people's?) had never encouraged me to widen the narrow circle of my childhood thoughts and dreams. Nor had it encouraged the idea of travel. Making ends meet at the end of the month had been the sole objective in life, much more important than the splendours of Siam or the mysteries of Papua New Guinea. My father had come from Auvergne, a rural province of southern France, and lived like an exile in the suburbs of Paris. He wore down his health working in a railway yard, but all his thoughts were centred on the miniature farm he had created in Brunoy with its grazing goats, its hens and ducks, its vegetable garden. A victim of meningitis at an early age, he had not received much education, and his horizons stretched no further than his own backyard. He also had a theory: 'I didn't eat my first banana until I was twenty, and I see no reason why my children should do any differently.' For him, life had to be simple and to respect tradition. My own aspirations were entirely beyond his understanding. Although he never gave me any encouragement, he did inspire me with a sense of craftsmanship and honesty and a certain sobriety of life.

My great-grandfather had emigrated to Canada at the turn of the century. Back in France, secure on their farm in Langeac, my aunts seldom spoke of him. He was the black sheep, the skeleton in the family cupboard that no one liked to talk about. You had to be completely off your rocker to drop everything and go to live in some strange country thousands of miles away!

'André, stop reading all those books! You'll give yourself a headache. Just look at yourself! You're wasting away from all that reading. Go and watch the cows. At least you'll be getting some fresh air!'

Dear Aunt Jeanne, I can see you in the farmyard. You never did like to see me reading, but the travel bug was bigger than both of us, bigger than everything. In spite of you all, I left.

As a teenager, leaving my childhood behind, everything seemed confused. I felt the need to go off on my own to discover the key to life. Conventional education was too biased. It taught us about the religious conflicts, the Inquisition and the Crusades without ever mentioning Christ. How strange! On the maps in geography books, France and her possessions were shaded in pink as if life there were sweet and rosy! I remember a sentence in my history book that almost had me in tears: 'Every man has two homelands: his own and France, the land of freedom.'

Later, I was to learn in Germany that Charlemagne had been a German. I discovered that many 'French inventions' had also been invented elsewhere. When I got to Mexico, the *peones* didn't even know where my country was!

What finally made me leave? Like many children, I had day-dreamed over the uninspired photographs in my geography book showing water buffalo in rice paddies, a Congolese climbing a coconut tree, a Tuareg in the desert, an Eskimo in front of an igloo. I had been enraptured when a missionary came from foreign parts to preach at the church of Saint Médard in Brunoy. But all those dreams led to the bitter conclusion that there was no way to travel without lots of money. Furthermore, I had no idea how to go about it, since no one ever talked about travel at home.

The lives of famous men fascinated me more than anything else, but great adventures seemed to be reserved for heroes. In my Bible I kept the photograph of a man whose glowing eyes and radiant smile had always impressed me. How could this man, Charles de Foucauld* give out such radiance when the picture showed him shabbily dressed and lost in a desolate landscape? He must know the secret of some happiness that I was unaware of. Had travelling helped him to discover that secret?

I was also fascinated by Saint Francis of Assisi. He had given up everything - his family, friends, and fortune - to live humbly among the poor, to talk to them with infinite compassion. He also impressed me because he had been able to throw off the materialistic fetters of his environment. He was radiant in his poverty and seemed to share a secret with Charles de Foucauld, the Hermit of Tamanrasset. It was a secret which I had yet to discover.

The very night of my arrival in Spain I got a job as a desk clerk in the best hotel in Cordoba. Fortune favoured the brave: such was the lesson I was learning. Without luck I would never have managed a trip around the world. Indeed I was going to rely on luck. How could I do otherwise?

A year later conscription interrupted my Andalusian romance. Other young men anticipated military service as some sort of adventurous expedition. To me it seemed a cosy retreat, a dreary bore, a sort of holiday camp for older children with no worries and no need to take the initiative. And room, board and laundry service were thrown in for free! It was laughable.

I had always hated wasting time. Whereas most of my comrades in arms wanted only to return to their families and sweethearts, to the nostalgia of the Saturday night dance in their old home towns, my own great ambition was to escape - to the ends of the earth if possible. That is how I came to spend the next two years in the Congo, as manager of the Officers' Mess on the air base in Pointe-Noire. I had gone one better than my celebrated Uncle Paul who, as the family's one 'great traveller', had dazzled us with tales of Moroccan *spahis*!

The kitchen of the Officers' Mess was Albert's kingdom. He was a man in the true sense of the word, and it is to him that I have dedicated this book. African and proud of it, 'Albéré' as he pronounced his name, had adapted to French colonization but had never tried to act like a white man. He was too intelligent, too shrewd, to get hung up on that

*French explorer and missionary (1858-1916), author of books about the Tuaregs.

kind of thing. I thought he was marvellous. Endowed with a great heart, strong determination, a keen sense of justice and honesty, Albéré was extremely conscientious in his profession. His dedication won my respect and admiration. He was illiterate, yet philosophical - in his own way, of course. Basically, he had common sense. One time he pinched my arm and then his own, looking very absorbed.

'White skin, black skin, don' mean nothin' at all. The Lord God made us all!'

As an old man who knew about life, he treated me like an inexperienced child. I was his '*piti moana*' (little kid). We worked as close colleagues in the Mess, and dear Albéré broke down and cried the day I left.

Although it was forbidden to leave town, I spent most of my free time visiting African villages or venturing into the jungle. I even visited Dr Schweitzer at the leper hospital in Lambaréné in April of 1959. Africa was now in my blood. I vowed to return one day.

'Of all the places in the world, why do you have to go to Germany?' one of my aunts protested, but that was to be my next stop. She had lost her husband in 1914 and both her sons in 1940. But paradoxically, it was in that 'enemy' country that I fell most deeply in love. My love for Sigrid was absolute and sublime - and luckily occurred at a moment in history when our two countries were at peace.

Then on to Italy. I started out as a shoeshine boy for want of anything better. There I met the lovely Mirella who taught me the meaning of the stars guiding my heart. There, too, I completed nine years of apprenticeship that toughened me and fostered my desire to travel. So far I had followed my luck through highs and lows. I had learned about Love and Friendship - with capital letters - and had discovered thousands of other things. But my initial question remained unanswered: what was the secret of human happiness?

I had to find out. I felt compelled, so I set out once again. This time I chose Canada even though it was the middle of winter: February 14th, 1965. I was pleasantly surprised to find salaries much higher in North America, and I soon realized that I could save enough money to carry out my impossible dream of a trip around the world. My three years in Toronto provided me with a unique opportunity to prepare my budget and lay my plans.

I had a job as a translator. It was honourable work, it paid well and, most importantly, it was something I enjoyed doing. My boss was pleased with me and, like other bosses before him, was training me in the hope that I would eventually take his place. To complete the picture, I was in love with a charming girl from Quebec named Charlotte. To all outward appearances, I had it made.

Yet, in the final analysis, that cosy, orderly life meant nothing to me. Despite appearances, something was breaking down inside me. From a crumbling inner husk a seed was emerging that needed the sunlight of adventure to grow to maturity. An instinct, a deep and urgent imperative, goaded me towards the road - a road I was destined to struggle with, day after day, for the next six years. I had no choice. I had to go, to leave - this time for good.

I mentioned earlier that a man can get to know a country best by making friends and getting to know its people. Unfortunately for my friendship with Charlotte, I wouldn't rest until I had known a great many more countries. Neither Sigrid nor Mirella had been able to hold me back from my wandering, and now Charlotte found herself in the same position.

I carefully drew up an itinerary that would take me across the Americas. I wasn't thinking beyond that, one challenge being enough for a start. Strongly influenced by the Western social system, I decided to make the trip by car in the company of a few friends. I was also sufficiently influenced by the typical North American fear of disease that I endured so many injections I was like a pin-cushion. During the previous twelve years, I had learned to fend for myself, to take risks, but considering the scale of my present plans I didn't feel capable of doing the trip alone. The unknown still frightened me even while it attracted me. Only at the last minute did I find two young Canadians planning to leave in a week on a trip round South America. They were going by car and were looking for a third person to share costs. Later I would regret my decision to join them, but for now there was only excitement. One week: the delay seemed like an eternity. I had been ready for such a long time!

I had just turned thirty.

'You thoughtless young fool, you'd better start thinking about your future . . .' Jacques' last letter had stabbed me like a knife. I was angry with him for his lack of understanding; he of all people should have known how I felt. Since the Congo, our friendship had grown stronger. It was a marvellous bond, a rich exchange of thoughts and feelings, which in Italy had led to a perfect communion of the spirit. Jacques had taught me to question things, analyze them, reason them out. He had given me the best tool for my quest. But now, on the verge of my departure, he was letting me down.

Saturday, November 25th. I stood for a couple of minutes on my doorstep, gaping in sheer astonishment. My backpack and a modest suitcase lay on the ground at my feet. I felt at a loss, dazed by a sense of approaching disaster. The Austin was waiting, black, shiny, almost dragging on the ground. It was a grotesque sight. A bright red canoe was strapped to the roof. Attached to the rear was a trailer containing two motor cycles . . . Whatever for?

I felt trapped. The sky suddenly seemed as low as the suspension on the black taxi.

'Good God! I'd swear you were leaving for a weekend jaunt to Algonquin Park!'

Gary, aged twenty-three, installed telephones for the Bell Company. George, twenty-four, called himself a teacher, although of what it was hard to imagine, given his lack of knowledge. They looked thoroughly pleased with themselves: they had even remembered the fishing rods. In Ontario, as soon as one left Toronto, there was nothing to do except fish from a canoe. Gary and George had never been out of their own neck of the woods and firmly believed that from north to south the Americas were paved, air-conditioned and lined with hamburger stands and drugstores.

They were literally going by taxi, since their Austin was nothing other than an old London cab fitted out for the occasion. In front, next to the driver, the empty space traditionally reserved for luggage now contained a seat. The interior separating window had been removed as had the back seat and the jump seats facing it. In their place, at mid-level, there was now a wooden plank supporting a foam mattress. The back of the car was thus divided into two areas: sleeping berths on top, and a storage space for luggage and equipment below. All that equipment was apparently 'necessary': a movie projector (goodness knows what for, since they had neither movie camera nor film), a slide projector, loads of developing accessories, a huge barbecue with an electric spit, not to mention a generator as bulky as it was useless. I found myself looking around for a colour T.V. or golf clubs. On the other hand, they hadn't thought to bring jerrycans for drinking water or fuel, rope, or a fire extinguisher. They weren't even carrying a first-aid kit, let alone a shovel.

The car was nearly collapsing under the weight of their inexperience. As I walked around it, my apprehension increased second by second. The tyres were bald, the suspension on its last legs, and the weight of the trailer behind forced the car's nose into the air. On the first bump we would surely lose the exhaust pipe. And what about my belongings? Where would I put them? With all their paraphernalia I could see no room to squeeze them in.

'Throw 'em on the bed. Let's go!'

Dumbfounded, utterly bewildered, I took my place in front. I slid between the two seats and perched on the transmission hump, crossing my legs sideways so as not to hinder the driver's access to gears or handbrake. I had no backrest and the bedboard dug into my shoulder blades. My head completely blocked the rear-view mirror, rendering it useless. Since I was a last-minute addition, there had been no time to rearrange the seating. We had two seats for three and 50,000 miles ahead of us. Even if we changed places, it would hardly be a joyride.

'Ready, guys? Hit the road?'

'Let's go!'

George, the owner, took the driver's seat. Various electric wires of different colours stuck out from the dashboard. Joining two of them at their bare ends, he started the motor. He squeezed a fat horn which honked happily, and we were on our way. Yonge Street, the commercial street of Toronto, was thronged with people. Soon the outskirts were passing us by. So long, lousy city.

'Hey, André, what do we do now? What are your plans?'

'I'm for driving as far as possible. How about heading straight for Washington? I've never been there. I'd just as soon skip New York.'

'O.K. We're game!'

I had intended to follow the East Coast first, then drive along the Gulf of Mexico to reach Central America. They had no plans at all. I hoped they would trust me as navigator.

After a while I took the wheel, and both of my companions fell asleep. A thick fog covered the snowy Allegheny Mountains. The taxi pulled continually to the left, and the brakes seemed inadequate. Silently I pondered: 'This car's never going to make it on the rough and ready roads of the Andes or the Pampas. With luck we'll get to Mexico! And even if they know how to make repairs, where on earth will they find spare parts? In England?

Baltimore, Maryland: eight in the morning. After a quick wash at the bus depot, we set out to stock up our food supplies in a supermarket. Being French, I thought of buying bread, cheese, salami and butter - but not George and Gary! They didn't bother to ask my opinion before stocking up on eggs, bacon, hot dogs and relish, pancake mix and some white, sliced bread that tasted of

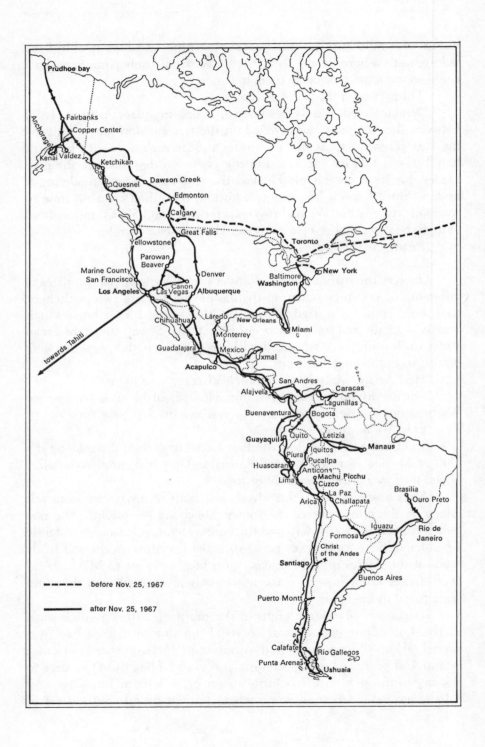

- - - - - before Nov. 25, 1967

─────── after Nov. 25, 1967

blotting-paper, which no self-respecting Frenchman would eat. How far apart we were.

Around noon we reached Washington, a white and spacious city. We parked near the Mall, and my companions unloaded their motor bikes. While they roared off to sightsee, I went to visit the Capitol on foot.

We spent the night in a park beside the imposing Lincoln Memorial. We got into our pyjamas on the sidewalk and slid, one by one, into our 'beds'. For the first few days - until we got the hang of it - it wasn't easy. We had to hold on to the roof or the car door and edge on to the bed-plank feet first. Then we had to get into our sleeping-bags, a feat that required a certain amount of agility. The last one in closed the door. The sleeping space, planned with two people in mind, was extremely restricted for three. Fortunately, we were all on the thin side. Our feet dangled in mid-air, suspended over the dashboard. Of course it was impossible to move, roll over or, especially, to sit up, since the ceiling was only a foot above our heads. But this forced intimacy did not bother me nearly as much as their crass indifference to the world and other people. Face to face with our basic incompatibility, I already regretted my hastiness in throwing in my lot with them.

The next morning I visited the FBI. On the wall of the lobby there was a map that showed the world divided into two blocs, one white and one red, the goodies and the baddies. Overhead in gigantic letters was written: 'Beware of Communism. You are being listened to. Take care.' In the US, Communism was the bogeyman, a hideous devil with a forked tail whose deadly bite excluded you for ever from respectable society. I was sure they held exactly the opposite opinion on the other side of the earth. This trip around the world promised to be instructive!

Virginia, the Carolinas, Georgia, and at last Florida! With omnipresent advertising, sun, sea and palm trees, Miami seemed a vision of paradise American-style. We suffocated in our taxi while powerful, glittering monsters swept by in air-conditioned silence. The string of luxury hotels on Miami Beach extended as far as the eye could see. Hotels, limousines, and pavements were packed with those little old ladies who flourish in white America. They were everywhere with their white hair streaked with purple, their rhinestone-encrusted glasses, their flashy rings weighed down with gems, and - of course - their hair-curlers. After all, this was Florida, where merry widows came to squander their husbands' life insurance.

George and Gary, overcome by the heat, squandered more of their savings on cans of beer. I wondered how long their money would last at the rate they were going. No doubt about it, trouble loomed ahead.

Palm trees, hibiscus, orange trees and pines: the landscape was changing as we crossed Alabama, Mississippi and Louisiana. Already you could smell the tropics. We followed the road that led towards Mexico, driving for many hours at a stretch and stopping occasionally at a drive-in just long enough to order fried chicken. The average American seemed to be born without legs. He drove to the bank, to the movies, to the store, to church and to restaurants. Everything was done by car. There was even a saying that sex education began with a kid's first Chevy.

The puffed-out cheeks of the black trumpet players seemed ready to burst as jazz filled Dixieland Hall. Bright brass throbbed in the smoky air. When the musicians paused, tap dancers with hats in hand took to the floor. When they stopped, it was to pass those same hats around the crowd. Amid gales of laughter, they stuck the collected dollars on to their sweating foreheads. The music would start up again, flowing and rolling down Bourbon Street.

The old French quarter of New Orleans lent a certain charm to what would otherwise be just another American city. Bienville Street, Toulouse Street, Saint Louis Street, Royale, and D'Iberville were echoes of France that faded away in the smoke-filled air of gambling houses and strip joints. Glowing purple in the neon light, go-go girls strutted and stripped with obvious boredom - either on the bar or right on your table! 'Oh là là, mademoiselle . . .' That little 'Frenchie' side brought out the best and the worst in the minds of Americans. On the positive side were the charm, the art of loving with tenderness, the deep emotions. On the other the idea of obscene jokes and activities the Mayflower pilgrims would never have dreamed of.

At two o'clock in the morning I tugged at the sleeves of my Canadian friends. Their eyes were red and popping out of their sockets. God knows how many beers they had drunk.

Again there was a strip-tease to a background of jazz, but this time it was on the street as we groggily undressed and slithered into our sleeping berth. A few minutes later a policeman knocked on the window. Illegal parking or indecent exposure?

'Excuse me, but there is a better place a little further on. I'll show you. It's quieter there.'

The next morning my two partners wanted to go canoeing on the Mississippi. Only the cold discouraged them. While they were getting their act together, I took a last walk down Bourbon Street under a grey sky. The tiled roofs, the wooden balconies and the flower-bedecked porches all conveyed an air of nostalgia. Only a passing carriage interrupted my brief pilgrimage. The black man holding the reins was wearing a fruit-decorated straw hat identical to the one perched on the head of his horse. He was singing and his voice echoed strangely in the silent street. I quickly retraced my steps, leaving behind the aroma of fresh-ground coffee, the antique displays in shop windows and the tiny restaurants. Still I found a few moments to visit Saint Louis Cathedral. The paintings and stained glass reminded me of country churches back home with Saint Louis departing for the Crusades and Joan of Arc liberating far-off France.

When I arrived back at the taxi, the Canadians were sulking. They were champing at the bit to get back on the road, and I was obviously holding them up. But all the travelling without stopping, without being able to really see anything, was making me miserable.

On Friday, December 8th, 1967, we crossed the Rio Grande at Laredo, but only after abandoning the trailer, the motor bikes and the generator. My pals were finally learning. Once into Mexico, everything seemed suddenly different, more alive. It felt like a homecoming again after a long absence. Loud voices, colours, smells, tanned faces (smiling, expressive and picturesque), a musical language, friendly crowds; it was a new, vibrant world and it did my heart good. The Mexican sun was warm and welcoming. On the horizon we could see the Sierra Madre mountains. Nearer at hand were small huts with thatched roofs, little sad-eyed donkeys and gigantic cacti of all shapes.

We arrived in Monterrey at nightfall amid chaotic traffic. Thick dust covered the streets and hung in the air, enveloping the pedestrians and their sombreros while goats and mules vied with noisy trucks and buses and battered 1920-vintage Fords. Amidst the lively, joyous market crowd, we stopped to eat *tortillas* and *frijole* soup but were wary of the hot sauces offered us. I immediately seized the opportunity to talk to men and women. Their expansive gestures and laughter found perfect expression in Spanish. I felt myself unwinding as hawkers plied us with green peppers, fruit, and all manner of merchandise. George and Gary, on the other hand, seemed very uncomfortable. Away from their own lifestyle and familiar surroundings, they felt totally out of place. Their expressions reflected their unease. To them, these peasants jostling us, speaking a strange language and revealing mouthfuls of bad teeth when they laughed seemed repulsive. They both wanted nothing more than to return to the car to drink imported beer. I felt rather sorry for them.

Suddenly I realized how right French Canadians were to fight for their language and culture, to preserve their identity. My two English-speaking companions were at a complete loss as to how to deal with anyone who didn't speak their tongue. Poor creatures! Nothing seemed to interest them except their car and their beer. Now I realized the folly of having thrown in my lot with them. But I had only myself to blame. My own abject fear had compelled me to seek travelling companions in the first place. Nevertheless, we would have to put up with each other until we reached Brazil. In any case, I wanted to see Rio and the carnival. After that I would weigh up my choices.

On December 12th Mexico City commemorated the apparition of the Virgin of Guadalupe. Throngs of people gathered before the Basilica of Villa Madero amid fire-crackers, marching bands and hymns. The celebration had been going on for a week already, but today the people were singing, dancing and feasting as enthusiastically as ever. It surprised me that they could express deep piety in such a manner, for I had been brought up on a much more austere brand of Catholicism. All this simple and exuberant joy seemed somehow superficial. The joy I was seeking would be a peaceful and radiant one, which would draw its strength from an inner flame, not from the warmth of the surroundings.

For four days we did the rounds of the consulates of Ecuador and the various Central American republics to obtain the necessary visas for continuing our trip. It was difficult and time-consuming, but I also managed to slip in a visit to the Archaeological Museum. I left Mexico with the firm intention of returning some day for a longer stay.

A border a day! Olé! We notched up 1,516 miles on a frantic cross-country race down through Central America. The only stops on our mad dash southward were for border formalities. After leaving Mexico we didn't pause to see a thing. My companions drove as if they were in a car rally. In Puerto Arrista I glimpsed the Pacific Ocean for the first time - an immense, dark expanse glittering in the moonlight. At dawn I saw a flock of pelicans swooping over the majestic waves, while thousands of crabs scuttled across the wet sand.

We crossed the Guatamalan border in a torrential rainstorm on December 18th. We were instructed to stop at all six sheds for control of our finances, territorial security, customs, immigration, health and so on. We ran back and forth between check-points. The last shed was reserved for the hippies: it was a barber's shop! The controls lasted hours. Finally an official tongue licked an official yellow sticker and slapped it on our windscreen: we were free to leave.

On the 19th, it was El Salvador. Again there was a six-shed control, but this time it went faster. Condors looked on while our belongings were inspected.

On the 20th, Honduras. Two extra customs control points. A hairy, unshaven man sat behind a rickety table, mechanically swatting flies. As he questioned us, a group of youngsters gathered around the door to gawk, calling out to us and barely concealing their laughter. The man got up and chased them away, but as soon as he sat down again they were back. As we left, the kids offered us cigarettes, dollars, fruit juice . . . and their sister.

On the 21st, Nicaragua. The 22nd, Costa Rica. There the customs office was clean and, furthermore, efficient. We even took showers.

In theory the Pan-American Highway stretches from Alaska to Chile, but here it was already showing serious signs of deterioration. In places the asphalt had disappeared altogether. While hump-backed oxen pulled overloaded carts along the winding road as it climbed through fields of sugar cane and around banana and coffee plantations.

On the 23rd we arrived in Panama. It was a hot, humid, exhausting day. I felt sticky and the dust clung to my skin. We had just gone over a 10,000-foot pass, the Cerro de la Muerte.

'Can you give me a lift?'

A tall guy with long hair and a dusty backpack approached us with a friendly smile. We learned that he was American and that he had left the States at the same time as we had. The difference was that he had hitch-hiked. I could hardly believe how fast he had been able to travel, and I admired his courage in travelling alone. He had just crossed the same seven borders and yet was perfectly relaxed. He slept anywhere, even in the open, and did not seem to be at all afraid. It was something entirely new to me. Meeting him made me forget all my own problems with the bulging taxi and the heat. He had hitch-hiked from Atlanta to Panama and seemed ready for more. I didn't think I would ever have the guts myself, but I had to take off my hat to him.

I felt extremely sorry to refuse him, but with the best will in the world we simply had no room for him in the car. We gave him some oranges and he sat down again at the side of the road, seemingly unconcerned. Where there's a will there's a way, but a lone traveller certainly needed a measure of bravery that I felt I would never possess.

Panama City was nothing but an enormous slum with a stench that made me gag. The people were pitifully poor. Stray dogs and children rummaged through overflowing dustbins. Above their heads colourful patched-up clothes dangled limply from rusty balconies. Nothing moved, for there was no wind, not even the slightest breeze. The heat was unbearable. Curious Blacks, Mestizos and Indians peered at us from windows and balconies while blaring transistor radios echoed from house to house. The atmosphere was like a travelling circus. For the first time the poverty and squalor shocked me, and I had no desire to dance or sing, even though it was Christmas.

We started inquiring about a boat that could take us to South America. Panama was a dead end. The Pan-American Highway petered out completely, and there was no other land link to Colombia. The Americans had apparently judged it undesirable to continue the road, preferring instead to keep a span of ocean between themselves and the South American Third World. But even in Panama City there was an American colony. They had a virtual city of their own on the northern shore of the Canal complete with paved streets, private villas, lawns and flower gardens. The world of the suburban residential neighbourhood had been re-created. It was nauseatingly clean and neat. There wasn't a single fly and even the heat seemed bearable.

'Hey! It's the other ramp for the crew.'

A handsome young man sporting a cap and gold braid had mistaken us for sailors. Obviously we didn't look very respectable. Our car had been put aboard the boat the day before, and we had been reduced to sleeping on benches in the railway station. We straightened out the misunderstanding and moved into our air-conditioned three-star cabin on the *Santa Mariana*. I was furious at having to spend $132 for three days on a boat, especially when I knew that without the car we could have flown for half as much. I made up my mind that this was the last time I would give in to the whims of my Canadian companions.

All the same, I took advantage of the luxury to treat myself to a long shower. Since meals were included, we then went to the dining room and gorged ourselves in the presence of some very dumbfounded American tourists. They were all old and well-off, the sort who spend their retirement taking cruises and pretending that they are seeing the world. To them we were clearly an embarrassment.

Our boat was lifted like a toy through the three canal locks of Gatun, Miguel, and Miraflores. By nightfall we had reached the level of the Pacific and passed beneath the Bridge of the Americas. We made a stop at Buenaventura, Colombia. It was exhilarating being able to pull on my jeans and disembark at last for a stroll around the port. Actually there wasn't much to see, but still I felt better than aboard the Santa Mariana.

The ceremony when we crossed the equator seemed to me rather grotesque and revolting. Mustard, ketchup, dozens of eggs and pounds of spaghetti were thrown around amid much hilarity, while people in the surrounding countries were starving.

Seagulls, pelicans and dug-out canoes escorted us into the port of Guayaquil, Ecuador. We unloaded our car at low tide and surveyed the damage: a flat tyre and a missing exhaust pipe. Then we had to wait through several tides before we could leave the port. The tangle of red tape in Latin America lived up to my worst expectations. It took endless tips and palaver, since the customs officials seemed to positively enjoy being obstructive. Trailing from one shed to another, from office to office, we filled in countless forms. Whenever we refused to pass banknotes under the table, things suddenly became difficult again and the pile of forms grew taller. It was only after forty-eight hours of 'procedure', of covering endless miles along dingy corridors and up and down dozens of stairways, that we were finally allowed to depart - but not without passing out cigarettes and dollars one last time.

The equatorial jungle was dense and filled with huge fiery-coloured flowers. Birds jabbered and shrieked incessantly as we crossed over into Peru. I was enthralled.

In Piura we made the acquaintance of Glaedy and her friends. They took us to the village of Catacaos on the sparsely inhabited coast. A white flag flapping above a mud hut meant that inside there was *chicha*, a fermented juice made from corn. We sat around a table for hours on end, but with such spontaneously friendly people it was time well spent. Two guitars strummed in the background. The poverty-stricken interior was cloaked in dust, and clods of dirt fell from the thatched roof through which rays of sunlight filtered. Dogs, cats, chickens and rabbits scuttled about between the rickety tables and across the earthen floor. The *chicha* was fermenting in clay pots decorated with crudely-drawn figures. A large, painted *calabash* was the only drinking cup available and was passed from one person to the next. Hunks of meat and fish dangled high in the air, safe from the dogs but not from the flies. A cloud of blue smoke lingered over our heads. In a corner on the ground, the crackling flames of a wood fire licked big black kettles resting on stones. All the tables were occupied and a cheerful camaraderie filled the air.

Everyone ate from the same plate and soothed his burning palate with the abundant *chicha*. Raw fish marinated in lime juice, sweet potatoes, roast kid, pork steeped in hot red peppers and raw onions: it was the best, most succulent meal I had had in a long time. Tender boiled corn-on-the-cob called *choclo* served as the Indians' staple food, taking the place of bread.

Fighting cocks scratched about outside the door. A light sea breeze cooled the air. I could have stayed for ever, but my Canadian friends were anxious to drive on, always to drive on.

Chanchan, Trujillo, Lima, Huancayo: it was all too fast, like a conducted tour of a museum. As we left Arequipa, Peru's second largest city, the pavement gave way to a rough dirt track full of pot-holes, rocks and mud-filled ruts. It would have been a cinch in a Land Rover with a high axle, but in our taxi it was a different story. We forded rivers, and kept getting stuck in lakes or sludge, often having to wait long hours until a passing truck could haul us out. The 'road' stretched on listlessly, nonchalantly, at an altitude of 12,000 feet. At the foot of an imposing mountain range permanently crowned with snow, thousands of llamas grazed on the short, parched grass. Watching over them were Indians wrapped in red wool capes. Each of them wore a white bowler hat decorated with a black ribbon. Puna, the Andean mountain sickness caused by lack of oxygen, tormented us. At Puno, on the edge of Lake Titicaca, we left our car and took the train to Cuzco. The road had become a torrent of mud.

Panting, meandering, the train crawled onwards, clinging to the mountainside. The trip took all day. Sitting in one of the wooden carriages, I studied the slightly flat, earth-coloured faces around me. Each stop was like a festival with food trolleys trundled up and down by ruddy-cheeked women, all sporting the same bowler hat. The next morning we changed trains, and after another half-day trip we reached Machu-Picchu.

I was overwhelmed with happiness, feeling I had truly reached one of the high points of my trip. It was a moment of pure magic when I gazed at the sheer beauty of those majestic, silent, ominous ruins. The experience was lost on the two Canadians, who had practically had to be dragged there kicking and screaming. They were impervious to the atmosphere of the place and wanted to leave almost immediately. I persuaded them to spend the night so that we could witness the setting and rising of the Incas' sun god. More than four centuries earlier, human habitation here had ceased, yet I felt a strange spell falling over me. I almost expected the sun-worshippers to emerge from the ruins at any moment. The night beneath the stars was one of indescribable beauty. I was filled with a deep calm. In a sort of communion, I shared in the peace of that Andean peak whose secrets we may never discover.

In La Paz I met one of the most beautiful girls I had ever seen. Marianella was a rich heiress - her father owned a sulphur mine - and we immediately struck up a rapport. But her beauty was no match for my ambition to see the world. As a token of friendship she gave me a roast chicken when I left. I shared it in the car with Gary (who of course didn't think it was anything special) while George slept in the back.

We drove day and night as the rains became heavier, threatening to block the road to Rio. We took turns at the wheel. One black night as Gary drove, the headlights of the car were reflecting off a wall of shiny wet rock to the right, but to the left there was only darkness. I didn't dare allow my imagination to dwell on how deep that ravine might be. Anxiously I watched Gary, whose eyelids seemed to be closing. As the road climbed higher, we suddenly came upon a boulder blocking our way. Without a flicker of reaction, Gary drove directly into it, totally immobilizing the car whose nose now pointed skyward. The immediate result was that both the brakes and the clutch were ruined, and we were beginning to slide backwards.

'Damn, damn, damn! Gary, what the hell are you playing at? Look out! We're gaining speed. We're going to go over the edge!' . . . The car is rolling backwards faster and faster, and Gary isn't doing a thing about it. There he sits, hands frozen on the wheel, mouth agape. I panic. I will have to jump out. It's the only way. Why isn't he steering away from the precipice? As the first wheel goes over the edge, I leap out through the door.

I fell heavily. I felt groggy, my head ached, and a warm liquid was running down my forehead and nose. Blood!

'Hey, André, what's the matter with you?'

Silence.

'Where do think you are? At the beach? First of all, you don't go diving in a sleeping-bag.'

I had been dreaming. After we had hit the boulder, we had fortunately managed to steer the car back against the rock face. George had returned to La Paz on foot in the hope of getting a spare cylinder block. In my dream I had relived the entire experience. Asleep with Gary in the steeply sloping taxi, I had slid off the shelf and right out of the back door which had given way under my weight.

That afternoon a military convoy came upon us. We were blocking part of the road.

'*Señores*, you must clear the road. But we will help you. We'll tow you all the way to our camp in Challapata. There maybe you can get your car fixed.'

We tied the front end of the taxi to the back of a truck with a long tow-rope. Then we chained the rear end to a jeep which would follow and help us brake on the long downgrades. In that manner we headed back in the direction we had come from. Sitting in their truck, the Bolivian troopers with their shaved heads laughed as they watched us.

Suddenly the brake lights flashed on. The truck had stopped and our taxi was charging towards it. What was the jeep behind us doing? Not a lot. With a tremendous din of crashing metal, we smashed in our front end: headlights, bumpers, bonnet and all.

Eventually, we limped into Challapata. While George and Gary indulged in their favourite pastime in the bar, I went over to join the soldiers. They invited me to participate in their training session. I accepted and did a little target-shooting.

'You know, Lieutenant, you seem pretty well equipped. This rifle is American, isn't it? Not bad. Has it ever been fired in anger?'

'Of course, *Señor*! We're a company of Rangers. Our speciality is anti-guerrilla warfare. Just three months ago we shot down Che Guevara - with these very rifles!'

In Aguas Blancas, Argentina, we must have been the first tourists to pass through the customs office in a century. There seemed to be no administrative procedure to cover us. True enough, we had taken short cuts by using the kinds of roads never mentioned to tourists. As a result the official at Aguas Blancas sent a policeman to accompany us to the nearest border check, some 180 miles away! Long discussions and negotiations took place concerning the taxes we should be asked to pay. In the end we wasted more than a day but managed to escape for the sum of 1,000 pesos handed over to a corpulent, perspiring officer who was playing tough. We quickly slipped away before he could ask for anything more.

Since leaving the Andes the weather had been beautiful. The ground had been hardened by the sun. With a bit of luck, we would make it to Rio in time. Otherwise, goodbye carnival!

We drove non-stop in a race against time and the rain. For the

moment the road was fairly dry. Come on, old cab, roll on, roll on! Alas!
Every thirty miles we had a new problem. We lost another exhaust pipe,
and the wings were dragging on the ground. We had six or seven
punctures, including one at night. And then there were the two hours we
spent trying to drag the car out of a mud-hole. Yo heave ho! Barefoot and
naked except for our shorts, we pulled and tugged in all directions for two
whole hours. Yo heave ho! My two chums were exhausted and kept
collapsing against the sides of the Austin.

'Come on, you guys! Now you see why I wanted to travel as light as
possible!'

I think they finally saw the wisdom of this, at least after getting
stuck in the mud another ten times.

The pampas stretched out for ever, an endlessly flat landscape of
scrubby vegetation broken by an occasional *lapacho*, a tree with a thick
trunk that tapered at the top like a Perrier bottle. Perched on the trees
were parrots and sleepy birds of prey who seemed to be sizing us up. We
suffered from chronic thirst. The old cab wasn't making as much progress
as I would have liked, but we just kept on driving. Our only goal was to
burn up miles, to leave this empty land, to escape the rain which sooner
or later would drown us in mud.

In the city of Formosa we were stopped by a policeman of the
Transito, the highway patrol. With a cap set sideways on his unkempt hair
and a cigarette glued to his bottom lip, the man looked entirely baffled.
Obviously our taxi, still sporting the red canoe, intrigued him. With a
doubtful frown he scratched his unshaven chin. Foreigners at this time of
the year! He muttered something. I decided to pretend I didn't
understand the language. He motioned us to get out and looked us over
contemptuously. We were dirty and dishevelled. Lack of sleep had
furrowed dark lines into our faces, accentuated all the more by six-day
beards. As he stared at my cap, his eyes narrowed. He had decided I was a
'*guerrillero*'. Ordering us to move aside, he climbed into the car and eyed
our belongings suspiciously: cameras, movie equipment, tape recorder.

'So what's this, huh?'

He had found the two telephones which in London had been used
by the cab driver to talk with his customer. My two clever friends had
ignored my advice when I had warned them to remove the phones. Too
bad, for they were going to give us a lot of grief now. The policeman was
getting on my nerves. I took one of the receivers off the hook.

'Hello, Brigitte? It's Brigitte Bardot', I said, staring at the poor man,
who was even more convinced that he was dealing with three spies.

George and Gary burst out laughing, but the policeman did not flinch. He called to a colleague and then, pointing his machine-gun in our direction, motioned us to get back in. Guns in hand, the two men took their places one on each running board of the taxi.

'*Vamos.*'

A sign over the gateway indicated that we were entering the premises of the Office of Regional Security. But under the heavy weight of the taxi, the soft ground beneath the gate gave way and we found ourselves stuck, unable to go forward. Both of the guards started shouting for help. One, two! One, two! Half the uniformed men in camp surrounded the car, whose condition was looking more and more terminal. Standing a bit to the side, I took out my movie camera and filmed this comical scene that was evocative of silent film comedies. An officer, red in the face, rushed towards me gesticulating wildly.

By the time the gates closed behind us, the courtyard was packed with people. All the offices and barracks had been emptied and the entire crew was waiting to see the spies. The Chief motioned us to follow him and gave orders to send the bystanders packing. No one moved. Standing still, swinging our arms, we scanned the surrounding buildings while someone went to get an interpreter to facilitate the interrogation of the '*gringos*'.

The sky was growing dark. Good God, surely they weren't going to keep us here for ever! In stumbling bad French, a student translated questions and answers. They finally understood that the telephones were useless, but the tape recorder . . .

'Play this tape . . . yes, that one!'

Impassively Gary took out the recorder and placed it on the bonnet of the taxi. He pushed the 'play' button. An amplified buzzing sound, turned up as high as it could go, filled the courtyard followed by a superb concert of croaking frogs taped two or three days earlier on the night of the full moon. The crowd burst out laughing. Fuming and furious, the chief hurriedly scribbled a safe-conduct pass and pointed to the door.

As we slammed the car door, the first raindrops were making dark splotches on the dusty road. We didn't have a minute to lose.

On February 14th we were refused entry into Brazil because we were unable to meet the requirements for the automobile security deposit. All other South American countries had demanded the same amount - $5,000 - but Brazil wanted six times as much. Forced to leave the car behind, George and Gary were worried for its safety and went hunting for a good garage to store it during our absence.

Meanwhile I headed for Iguaçu where I witnessed one of the most beautiful natural phenomena in the world. Higher than Niagara, wider than Victoria, the Falls of Iguaçu were practically unknown. And yet, in its setting of virgin tropical forest, the foaming giant, measuring two miles across and some 300 feet in height, was truly fantastic. Situated on the Parana River, where Paraguay, Argentina and Brazil meet, it could be seen twenty miles away, so dense was the cloud of spray it created. The noise was absolutely deafening.

After a veritable marathon by bus, we arrived in Rio at night during a torrential rainstorm that gave the city an air of deep sadness. Visiting places that have been endlessly described and enthused about can often turn out to be an anticlimax. Fortunately, Rio was an exception to that rule. The city was tucked in between sugar-loaf peaks clothed with tropical vegetation, and the amazingly blue ocean contrasted strongly with the dazzling white of the beaches.

The women of Rio were very attractive and flamboyant. Miniskirts were the rule, and so were brilliantly coloured sweaters, huge earrings and sequined shoes. Each detail, taken separately, seemed in atrocious taste. When put together, however, the effect was wonderful. The girls were full of life and spontaneity and had the habit of taking your hand while flooding you with chatter. I was captivated!

By chance, I met a *Carioca* who offered to take me to his *favella*. He mentioned a voodoo ceremony that I might be able to watch. I hesitated. The *favellas* were shanty towns built of wooden planks, ramshackle slums clinging to the mountainside, with a bad reputation. However, my natural curiosity got the better of me and I accepted. My guide led me through dark, muddy alleyways where shadowy makeshift huts stood outlined against the starry sky. From inside the houses came soft lamplight and sounds of life. My guide lifted a board and motioned me to stoop down. We had arrived at his home, a sort of shack with walls made from cardboard cartons. Two children were already sleeping in the one and only bed.

His wife prepared us a scanty meal and by the time we took our leave, my guide was very drunk. I placed a few *cruzeiros* on the cardboard box which served as a table. Then we left, but a moment later I found myself entering a second hut, this time covered with palm fronds. A lamp gave off a flickering light and the air reeked of *quinchasa*, the rot-gut alcohol made from sugar cane. I suddenly found myself missing my Canadian mates, for four colossal men were coming towards me, looking thoroughly threatening. I refused the glass they held out. That was a mistake, as immediately a fist slammed into my eye.

I could see nothing but showers of falling stars. My guide - where was my guide? I barely had time to turn around in search of him before another hard blow hit me. I was groggy and felt the ground giving way under my feet. I had to get away. With one leap I was outside and racing down an alley. I couldn't see a thing and risked breaking my neck at the slightest obstacle, but I hardly had a choice. By chance, safer residential areas were not far away. With a pounding heart and a taste of blood in my mouth I emerged breathless into the well-lit streets and saw with relief that my assailants had turned back.

The carnival began like an explosion, igniting the city and the *favellas* with an electric current that started bodies vibrating. On the first evening, I found myself in a local club in the Flamengo neighbourhood. As usual, my two Canadians were rather ill at ease and stuck close to my side.

With the first note of music the tables emptied. Arms flew up, hands shook violently, shoulders and necks convulsed, and the dizzying samba poured out its endless joy, its brisk rhythm, its invigorating warmth. The merrymaking would continue non-stop for three days and four nights.

Everyone danced alone, just as in Africa. The crowd of *Cariocas* was dense and intensely alive, a swirl of colour and light. Most of them were dressed in swimsuits or loincloths and garlanded with bright flowers. Bodies were soon shiny with sweat and glittering with gaudy jewellery. After four hours I could no longer feel my legs. George and Gary called it quits and returned to the youth hostel.

The festivities continued all through the day. The crowds in the street no longer walked: they seemed ready to launch into dance steps at any moment. A mere kick at a tin can or the clatter of a dustbin lid could set them off again. Samba was in the air, and bodies would burst into motion on the slightest pretext.

In the shadow of the skyscrapers on President Vargas Avenue, grandstands had been set up for the parade of the samba schools. This was the biggest popular festival in the world. For the next seventeen hours there would be a non-stop spectacle buoyed by the unflagging music. Not even a tropical downpour could dampen their spirits; the crowd and the dancers were utterly oblivious. Oh, the magic of the samba!

The following day around noon, I finally gave up, drunk from the music and fatigue. My head full of colours and noise, I left as the last group of samba dancers prepared to go on parade. The sound and rhythm of the bands stayed with me until I had finally crawled into my sleeping-bag.

'Where have you been?' asked the two Canadians.

'I was watching the samba schools' parade. It was fantastic.'

'Oh, well, we decided to get some sleep. You know this carnival thing gets kind of monotonous.'

As soon as I woke up, I headed out again to Copacabana and the beaches. I spent an entire day on top of Corcovado where there was a splendid view of the bay. For hours on end, I followed the progress of the sun. Gazing down at the city, I located its parks and museums. My eyes took in every inch of the spectacle.

'Are you guys coming with me to Brasilia?'

'Where's that? You think it's worth it?'

In silence I got up, grabbed my toothbrush, toothpaste and movie camera. I packed my kit and put it in a corner.

'Dear God, you're both hopeless. I think I'll go on to Brasilia alone. We can meet up in Buenos Aires in ten days, the 16th of March. Okay with you? So long!' I had had just about enough of them.

Brasilia was a gigantic building site, an artificial city, which nevertheless possessed a strangely seductive beauty. It was a monstrous symbol of tireless human creativity, a curious mixture of failures and stimulating successes. What it lacked, however, was a soul.

It took me twenty hours to reach the city by bus, and then I spent another hour trying to find my way out of the labyrinthine bus depot. Already my first problem was rearing its head: how and where would I spend the night? I decided to wait and see. It felt so liberating to be on my own for a change that I wanted only to breathe freely and not worry for a while.

A tall building under construction caught my glance. There was a sign, 'Touring Club do Brazil'. Why not sleep there? Surely there would be some corner to hide in. On the third floor I found a suitable spot behind some sacks of cement. Several newspapers were scattered about the floor. I had heard that cyclists doing the Tour de France wrapped themselves in newspaper to keep warm when racing through the Alps. Since I'd left my sleeping-bag behind, this was the perfect opportunity to see if the technique was effective. I lay down on the cement floor placing my movie camera under my head. My first attempt at roughing it was not a notable success. At the slightest noise I would leap to my feet. Between being scared and being cold, I ended up not sleeping at all, and in the morning my chest was smeared with newspaper headlines.

I spent an entire day strolling along the straight avenues, gazing admiringly about me. The architecture was daring but the colours were warm, and the city as a whole had a charm of its own.

Around noon I chatted with two guys who were leaving for Recife in the north and offered me a seat in their car. What tough luck! If only I had made a firm decision back in Rio to part ways with George and Gary! Sick at heart, I declined the invitation for I now had only eight days left to get to Buenos Aires. It made me furious to think that I had all the time in the world, yet still remained a prisoner of the Canadians. In any case, my decision was made: from Buenos Aires I would go my own way.

I made my first serious attempt at hitch-hiking. For a while I had no luck, but late in the evening an old American car finally stopped for me. Three glum, unshaven heavy weights motioned me to get in. Hesitantly, I slid into the back seat next to a man who proceeded to stare at me. As a mere beginner I did not feel very safe. Maybe I should have waited till daylight before taking a risk.

'Give me the gun.'

Right under my nose, the driver passed a large pistol to the man sitting next to me. The latter grabbed it, checked the cartridge clip and then, bending back his arm, pointed the barrel to the ceiling. He looked to the right, then to the left. Was he checking to make sure that no one was around? That there would be no witnesses? Witnesses of what? They couldn't be planning to murder me! Fear gripped me. Although it wasn't the first time I had been really scared, my previous experiences did not help much. I decided to give them everything - my movie camera, my traveller's cheques, toothbrush, shirt, trousers, everything, if only they would let me live.

The guy cleared his throat noisily and spat out of the window. This was it! The end was near!

'M . . . Mister! Please!

He looked at me, surprised, and suddenly burst out laughing.

'So, what's the matter, my little Frenchman? Something wrong? Yeah, I get it, you're scared of my gun! Bet you thought I was a gangster, eh? Well, the gun's in case we spot any game around here. The place is full of wild animals!'

He fell about laughing and immediately seemed friendlier. I was going to have to learn some self-control if I wanted to continue alone.

Right now I was much too emotional. Then, too, I was on edge because of Gary and George.

They dropped me off in Ouro Preto, a typical small town that still retained its Portuguese-colonial character. Indeed, it was where the movement for independence had originated. Walking down a cobbled street, I noticed a young man sweeping some steps beneath a sign reading 'Republica'.

'What is this "Republica"?'

'It's the student centre.'

'Sorry for asking, but would you perhaps have some little corner where I could sleep the night? I don't know where else to go.'

'Sure. Come on in . . . but on one condition!'

'Yeah?'

'That you come dancing with us tonight. We're having our annual ball.'

'But I don't have any clothes except what I'm wearing.'

Half an hour later, I was fully dressed for an evening out. One student had lent me his shoes, another a shirt and tie, and a third a pair of trousers. I was thrilled. Everything was going so beautifully! Increasingly I regretted my obligation to join the other two in Buenos Aires.

On March 19th, 1968, I caught up with Gary and George at the home of Margarita, an Argentinian girl we had met in Machu Picchu. The two of us had spent hours together, and she was delighted to see me again. Clearly the other two were not. Indeed, they were furious because I was three days late. I had done my best, but 2,000 miles by bus had been a long way to come. Yet another concern seemed to bother them more. After going over their finances, they had realized that they were overdrawn at their bank! Ah yes, credit was not a rubber band that could be stretched indefinitely. Tired from the long journey, I lost my temper.

'I'm fed up to here with you both', I retorted, 'and I don't give a damn about your financial problems! Go on without me! I want to be free, do you understand? FREE!'

I had spent ten days preparing my little going-away speech and now it dropped with a thud. The other students who had joined us at Margarita's looked as taken aback as the Canadians. A heavy silence fell over the room. What were they going to do? Beat the hell out of me? They knew I still had some money.

'Hey, listen! You owe us money for the trip here from Rio.

After all, we had to drag along your pack and suitcase.'

'You must be joking! Nothing doing! I paid enough already getting here by bus. And enough is enough! I warned you not to waste your money, but you simply didn't listen. You wanted to play at being rich Americans, so now you can accept the consequences. I'll help you look around for new tyres, but that's all.'

That Saturday night we took part in one of the most popular Argentine television shows, the Mansera Show. Since I spoke Spanish, I answered the questions of the interviewer and at the same time managed to slip in a few words about our tyre problem. Mansera promised to find us some new ones. We even pushed the taxi on to the stage (since it wouldn't start) and gave a demonstration of our agility in climbing into our sleeping berth. Our performance was a great success. Mansera picked up the receiver of one of the taxi phones, and applause filled the air.

Outside, Margarita's friends were waiting. A few of us decided to stroll through the streets of Buenos Aires, parts of which reminded me of Paris. Around four in the morning, I left them to return to the taxi. As I opened the car door, a hand grabbed my wrist. It was Gary, armed with a large spanner. George, just behind him, glared at me with hate in his eyes.

'Either you pay or we bash your face in! Your choice!'

'Let go! I'll pay. Just give me my belongings.'

For four months I had staggered along under their dead weight. Now, day had not yet dawned as the Austin pulled away. Left behind, I felt nothing but relief.

My apprenticeship was over, once and for all. I was going to carry on alone, somewhat poorer, but at last I would be free to do as I pleased, to go where I wanted. I felt as though I was coming out of prison, bag in hand. The doors to the world stood open before me.

Chapter 3

INCORRIGIBLE 'FRANCÉS'*

'Say, André, have you thought about going to Tierra del Fuego?'

'Of course, but it's 2,000 miles away and I doubt if there are many cars going down through Patagonia. No, I really don't think it's possible.'

'Well, I might have a lead for you. It's quite possible that my friend Irma could get you a free ride on a military plane.'

Without wasting a minute, I dashed over to see Irma. She had worked as a secretary for the Argentine Congress until the military coup.

'I hate soldiers', she told me. 'I'll do whatever I can to help you take advantage of them.'

For hours we waited in the offices of the LADE (the military travel service). Thrilled at the idea of wringing something out of the military, Irma tirelessly confronted every man in uniform she could find in the halls of Congress. On the evening of April 14th, Irma met me at Gilles' place. Gilles had been putting me up in his kitchen since the beginning of the month.

'Here it is, folks! I managed to swing it. Here, André, fill in this form. That's not all, I also got a letter of recommendation to the commander of the Rio Gallegos Air Base. Here's another one for Ushuaia. You never know. They might come in handy.'

I never did find out who had signed my letters of introduction, but whoever it was, they worked like a charm. In Rio Gallegos, Captain Medici gave me a personal welcome and flew me in his own fighter plane south to Ushuaia.

*Frenchman, in Spanish.

It was a beautiful day. Leaving flat, desolate Patagonia, we passed over the southernmost peaks of the Andes where they leaped the Strait of Magellan to die in Tierra del Fuego. Once past the last snow-covered ridge, we came in over a bay and landed in Ushuaia, the world's southernmost town. Dear God, was it ever cold!

Seeing me enter his office, Commander Padilla burst out laughing. He was a short, chubby, amiable man, and my Don Quixote silhouette amused him. He pulled up a chair for me and without further ado produced a bottle of three-star cognac from a drawer. The real stuff.

'Ha-ha-ha! That's a good one . . . "un francés" (a Frenchman) hitch-hiking in my planes! Ha! This cognac's not bad, eh? Ha-ha-ha! So you're going round the world with your little bag!'

I had left everything behind in Buenos Aires except a small backpack, my sleeping bag and movie camera. Paring down my belongings to the bare minimum - in order to travel as light as possible - would become a permanent obsession. In the best of spirits, he filled up his glass for the third time and emptied it in a gulp or two.

'Where are you going to sleep?'

'I was just about to ask you, Commander. I was hoping that you could show me a spot where I wouldn't be in the way. All I need is to be out of the cold. The autumn is none too warm around here.'

'In other words, you're relying on me, yes? My officer's mess, how's that for you?'

'Really?!'

'Tell me, "Francés", I've invited the admiral and a few other officers to have dinner with me tonight. Wouldn't you like to come? I'm sure you've got plenty of good stories to tell, eh? I live a hundred yards from "your" mess. I'll send my chauffeur to pick you up. Yes, you'll go down a treat! Ha-ha-ha! I like you and your little bag.'

After a magnificent meal, we moved into the drawing-room which overlooked the bay. A small wood fire crackled cheerfully in the fireplace. The admiral came over to me.

'Tomorrow morning I'll give orders to the fleet to welcome you on board. You can eat in the wardroom during your entire stay here. OK?'

Ushuaia consisted of four modest little streets lined with prefabricated houses built of logs and corrugated iron. Nestled at the foot of the last Andean peaks, the town seemed to stare out at the countless islands of the archipelago at the end of the world.

'My little "Francés", just listen! Thanks to me, you are about to make the trip of the century. You see - over there in the port - those three battleships from our admiral's fleet? Just behind them there's a small boat, red and white. You see it? That's the *Polargas*. She comes here once a month from Punta Arenas, Chile, to supply us with fuel, and she's leaving again tomorrow. If you feel like wandering among the islands of Tierra del Fuego, through the Beagle Channel and the other Fueguino channels . . . Ha-ha-ha! After plane-hitching, now boat-hitching! That way, at least, you won't forget Commander Padilla. Yes, "Francés"?'

That evening I told my story to the local TV cameras and managed to slip in a few words of thanks to my host.

Alone, leaning on the rails of the *Polargas*, I gazed at the islets and rocks drifting by. I was leaving the cold, desolate end of the world in which the laughter of Commander Padilla echoed so strangely. Rain, sun and violent winds roamed at will through the barren maze of islands. The grey waters of this southern ocean were coldly impressive and evocative of Antarctica itself. Trees with tortuous trunks bowed before the wind. They shared their rocky reefs with ducks, penguins, seals and sinister vultures.

At night the Southern Cross glittered majestically overhead. Not for anything on earth would I have changed places with any other man. In the wheel-house Captain Albarran was surveying the channel with a pair of binoculars, while behind him a young couple laughed and whispered. Catching sight of me, the young man called out:

'Hey, you! Give me back my gloves!'

'But these are my own gloves. I bought them second-hand at an army surplus store in Buenos Aires. I also picked up my boots, long-johns, and jacket there. They sold everything - even used toothbrushes!'

'That wasn't at Chinche by any chance? That's exactly where I got fitted out too! Here, this is Jenny.'

We all three stared at each other and simultaneously burst out laughing. We looked exactly alike: the same jackets, the same gloves, and no doubt the same long-johns, courtesy of the Argentine army.

Jenny was an American student from Atlanta and had met the young man in Rio. He was broke and she still had a few hundred dollars left. Now he had taken to managing the finances and everything appeared fine. He was Mexican and I liked to call him Mex, but his real name was Juan-José. He came from a wealthy family and had left a few months earlier on a chaperoned Grand Tour of South America. He had met Jenny during the carnival. Right then and there, he had abandoned everything - planes, hotels and chaperone - to hitch-hike south with her.

'I get it! You're the guy who was on TV! Yeah, that's it, you're the one who was sleeping in a cab. So deep down you're a bourgeois too!'

April 26th, 1968. The monotonous drone of the engines had stopped. The *Polargas* had docked at Punta Arenas. The red sun was shining weakly on the cold waters of the Strait of Magellan. In twelve days we would be taking a boat to Puerto Montt. Meanwhile, we decided to take a look at the Ventisquero Moreno Glacier which spilled down from the Andes into Lake Argentino, some 400 miles to the north. We would go '*a dedo*', by thumb.

The wind was blowing violently. The track ran between the blue waters of the Strait and the yellow flatness of the Patagonian plain bristling with dusty bushes. On the horizon the summits of the Andes stood outlined in eternal whiteness. To make better time we split up. Rain was falling, adding to the desolate aspect of the landscape. *Gnandus*, small ostriches, raced alongside the car, scaring·away the *caiquenes* (wild geese) and frightening the thick-fleeced sheep that grazed in their thousands. Sun-blanched skeletons lined the track.

In Rio Gallegos I found shelter and a rug to sleep on at the end of a hotel hallway. I shared my humble lodging with a Colombian who astonishingly had come all the way from Toronto on a bicycle! William Arcila Gonzalez, thirty-five years old, had been pedalling across the Americas for five years. To finance his odyssey he gave talks along the way, illustrating them with some of the 4,500 slides that he carried with him on his bike!

I slogged my way through muddy streets, going from café to café in the hope of finding a truck bound for Calafate. Rio Gallegos was flat and grey, and a freezing wind swept through the empty streets. Inside the small bars, men drowned their boredom in gallons of alcohol. I met their empty gazes.

Jenny and Mex had caught up with me. Together we wasted a whole day and most of the next waiting for any vehicle that might offer us a ride. The cold was so paralysing that we sparred with each other to stay warm. Finally, as we were heading back to town discouraged, a car stopped and backed up. It was going to Calafate!

'Eh, you guys, come give us a hand.'

Without paying much attention, I had noticed the smoke from far away. Sitting in a circle in front of their shack, a group of *gauchos* were watching a sheep slowly roasting over a wood fire.

In Argentina meat was more than the national dish: it was often the only dish. In the north, beef was the usual fare. It was either grilled whole on a *parilla* or sliced into thick incredibly tender steaks which overflowed the plate. In Patagonia the *gauchos'* principal food was lamb. We quickly learned that when hunger struck, the thing to do was to look for a thin column of smoke rising above the wide spreading Pampas.

Arming ourselves with huge knives, we willingly attacked the dangling barbecue. Raw tomatoes, a loaf of bread and a large jug of wine were passed around. When the meal was finished, our hosts gave us a large share of the left-over meat for our trip.

Calafate was a dead end located on the edge of ninety-mile-long Lake Argentino. The glacier merged into the lake's waters some sixty miles from the village. Six days had passed since we had left Punta Arenas. The first day we had covered 120 miles, the second day none at all. Three miles had been our total for the third day, fifty-five for the fourth, and finally 120 miles yesterday, getting us to Calafate. In the afternoon, an ancient truck offered us a lift to the glacier. Practically an antique, it hardly looked as though it would make it.

The wooden bridge had been washed away, which compelled us to walk the last seven miles in the dark. The weather was very cold and snowflakes were melting on our faces. Total darkness enveloped us. We found our way only from the sound of our footsteps. When our feet made a sucking noise and the ground felt soft under foot, we knew we were on the muddy track. From time to time we whistled to make sure that we were all still together. Finally we could tell we were getting closer by the rumbling noise of the glacier echoing through the still night air. Suddenly, Jenny tripped.

'Jenny, make sure you fall on your face! Don't forget you're carrying the remains of the barbecue on your back!'

Mex's words eased the tension. Our morale was high and rightly so, for we had reached the shelter. In the one and only room, illuminated by the dim light of an oil lamp, we organized ourselves for the night. Juan-José and Jenny lay down fully dressed, their heads resting on their packs. I was the only one to have a sleeping bag, but it was so thin that it didn't prevent me from shivering all night long. I bitterly regretted not having anything warmer. The cold was becoming really painful. For the last two days, I had lost all feeling in my fingers and couldn't even manage to zip up my sleeping bag.

'Mex, how many fingers can you still feel?'

'Don't even mention it. Riding in the open air on those trucks is killing me. I can't even stand up when we stop.'

It was raining outside. Hurled by violent winds, the rain pounded on the windows of the shelter. More distantly, the glacier continued its ominous rumbling. It sounded as if the night itself was being wrenched apart.

At dawn we were rewarded with a sublime vision: a wall of ice towered above us, 360 feet high and over half a mile wide. A gigantic frozen river some seventy-five miles long, the glacier fed into the dark green waters of the lake. The Ventisquero moaned continually, emitting long, plaintive wails. Towering over our three tiny silhouettes, the spectacle suddenly reached its climax. In a deafening outburst, an enormous slab of ice broke away from the glacier and crashed into the lake. The iceberg danced and rolled, creating monstrous waves that broke at our feet, and a thunderous echo roared and reverberated among the surrounding Andean cliffs. Mesmerized by the sight, we remained there the rest of the day, our eyes fixed on the turquoise mountain of ice.

Returning from Calafate, we spent three days jumping up and down round a fire as we waited in vain for a car to pass by. It gave us the opportunity to sleep in the local prison on damp, stinking mattresses. The walls seeped water and the floor was oily. In neighbouring cells, a handful of prisoners coughed and spat all night long. Yet I thanked God and the prison guard for having provided us with this shelter, for outside the temperature was still dropping.

On the third day, Mex and I attempted to horse-hitch. One of our jail buddies, having slept off his drinking bout, was heading back to his *estancia*. We tried to ride one of his horses bare-back, but immediately we found ourselves sprawled on the frozen ground.

'*Señores*, you should have asked me first. These horses aren't broken yet. I've just bought them.'

Once again, we spent a memorable night, this time in a shack built of loose-fitting boards through which the wind whistled at will. After a welcoming cup of *maté* (the bitter tea of the *gauchos*), we made an attempt at sleeping, covering ourselves with stiff, untanned, foul-smelling sheep skins. Since there were lots of them, we piled them on: ten or so to serve as a mattress, and seven or eight more as blankets.

'Well', remarked Jenny, 'you can say that sheep are both bed and board to us.'

'Perfume too . . .'

In the morning the wind was so icy that at one point we had to lie down close together on the frozen track to protect ourselves from the cold. When we finally arrived back in Punta Arenas on May 9th, we had nowhere to go except the prison. It was our third night in jail in only ten days.

'The girl stays in the women's cell, and you two sleep here in the office', a guard announced.

'Too bad they aren't better organized', commented Mex. 'They might have sent us two to sleep in the cell with the girls!'

A few minutes later the guard informed one of his journalist friends of our arrival. As a result we appeared nicely photographed on the front page of the local newspaper with the headline, 'The first Authentic Hippies in Tierra del Fuego'. We were instant celebrities, and the three local radio stations clamoured for us to make statements. They even had Jenny sing a Joan Baez hit on the air. In a matter of hours we had become the town's star attraction. That Saturday night we were thrust on stage. Jenny sang for a second time, and when the master of ceremonies came on after her number, the entire audience rose to their feet demanding an encore.

The boat we were to take to Puerto Montt had been immobilized by a strike, forcing us to extend our stay in the penitentiary. While trying to arrange a 'plane-hitch', I had all my cash stolen and Jenny nearly got raped.

During the three weeks spent in Tierra del Fuego, I gradually adopted Mex's attitude to life. He was consistently in the highest of spirits and possessed a natural zest for life. Charming, shrewd, witty and relaxed, he was the living proof that everything depended on one's own attitude and that things really did work out in the end.

'Keep the faith', he repeated continually, 'keep the faith'.

For a few weeks I had been getting a lot of pain in an inconvenient spot: pain that the cold weather and adventures of late had only exacerbated. I knew I could no longer put off a visit to a doctor, so I took the train from Puerto Montt to Santiago and went straight to San Salvador Hospital.

The building was huge and terribly depressing with endless corridors and massive walls. The vaulted ceilings made it look more like a fortress than a hospital, and the large waiting room with its forest of thick pillars was reminiscent of a monastery. Impoverished patients pushed and jostled for seats like a crowd scene out of the Middle Ages. Seated on the floor were frightened, moaning women and spotty children in rags. I ached terribly, and the scene before me did nothing to alleviate my pain. Swarms of people crowded round the reception desk. Selfishly, I decided to take advantage of my status as a European. Pushing open a large door, I marched down the corridor in search of a doctor or a nurse. Dr Puentes took me immediately into his office.

'You have an anal fissure. We're going to have to operate.'

I explained my situation to him, making him understand that such an operation would cost me the equivalent of a visit to two, three, or even five or six countries.

'Oh, you're the guy in the paper. Well, I'll put you on the paupers' list. Come back tomorrow, and I'll have a bed for you.'

The old hospital was cold and filthy. In the bathrooms cockroaches and woodlice fought over the rubbish. The stench was unbearable. Cats scavenged in the dustbins that stood about, and blood-stained bandages lay strewn on the floors of the hallways. The one and only bathtub was ancient and lined with a black ring as thick as tar. The sheets were torn, and the discoloured mattresses a mass of holes and bumps. The food would have put even the healthiest person on the sick list. I accepted my fate because this way my trip around the world wouldn't be cut short. Furthermore, the staff were exceptionally kind and competent.

'While I'm at it, I think I'll cut your hair', said Dr Puentes as he prepared me for the operation.

Many of the staff took to parading past my bed, eager to chat with the 'French hippie'. My nurse Luzmaria, an Auraucan Indian, took a fancy to her patient, spoiling me with little steaks, egg sandwiches, fruit and quince jam. Although visiting hours were strictly observed, I never felt lonely or bored, for Mex was always beside me. I don't know how he did it, but he managed to get past all the staff.

'You're cured now', announced Dr Puentes after ten days. 'You must give up your bed now, my little "Francés". I need it for someone else. Where are you off to now?'

'Well, actually, I don't know. I still don't feel too good. You couldn't maybe recommend me for a bed in the fire station or something? I don't know . . .'

'With the firemen! You're out of your head! You'll never be able to rest there. To convalesce . . . wait, let me discuss it with my Czech colleague. She's fond of you.'

At around five in the afternoon, all the patients in the room were on their feet, clustered around the large window. They couldn't believe their eyes. An incredibly long Cadillac was arriving to pick up 'the pauper'. The Friedmanns, American citizens representing the US government and friends of the Czech doctor, drove me to their home in Barrio Alto, a residential neighbourhood of the Chilean capital. A large garden with a swimming pool, old master paintings, stylish furniture and a profusion of flowers awaited me. A bed had been prepared in the library, and I quite wondered how I would ever manage to fall asleep in sheets so silky.

'Madam, I'm terribly embarrassed for all the inconvenience this is causing you. And to cap it all, you're getting ready for a party.'

'Party? What are you talking about, Andrew?'

'All these candelabras, the silver cutlery, the fine porcelain . . .'

'But, my dear boy, this is only our everyday tableware. Now, come with me. Let's put a log on the fire.'

Once again I took up my pilgrim's staff and returned to my travels. I couldn't wait any longer, even though it was hardly the most rational plan of action. I was still obliged to bathe my bottom twice a day in boiled, permanganated water. When the need arose, I would knock at random on doors in Andean villages. It wasn't easy, and I was often taken for a madman. But I had to follow Dr Puentes' orders.

The Christ of Las Cuevas brought back distant memories of a film I had seen as a child in Brunoy. Now, fifteen years later, here I was in Las Cuevas. 'He' was up there, 3,000 feet over my head. The statue of Christ the Redeemer had been erected at an altitude of 13,150 feet on the summit of an Andean peak. His outspread arms kept the peace between Argentina and Chile. The border passed over the mountain, and symbolically Christ had one foot in each country.

The access road was closed by ice and snow, but I found an alternative route some two or three miles long. The least one could say of this path was that it ascended steeply. But I was stubborn. I wanted to reach the statue and to reach it that very day, for I had to return to Santiago the next day for a check-up.

I started climbing even though my scar hurt. Looking up towards the summit, I could see a huge stone arm that would serve as a landmark. I progressed slowly. The snow was deep, and I sank into it with every step. That only meant that I would have to redouble my efforts. I had barely covered a third of the distance when the sky suddenly darkened and snow began to fall. In a matter of minutes my visibility was reduced to zero. Thick snowflakes swirled about, forcing me to keep my eyes half-closed. I had lost all track of the path I was following, and common sense was warning me to turn back. Still, I refused to give up. I had gone through so much to get this far that now I was determined to go all the way. Risk or no risk, I would continue. For a brief moment during which the sky seemed to be clearing, I caught sight of a road a few yards higher up on the right. Although the road took the long way up, I wondered if it wouldn't be wiser to follow it after all. I turned to the right, not knowing where I was stepping, yet I felt confident because the road was there.

I placed my foot on a large rock, but realized too late just how precariously balanced it was. I fell over sideways. Good God! What could I hang on to? There was nothing but crusted snow, pebbles and a steep slope below me. I stretched out my arms to get a better hold, but no use; I had started to slide. I tried digging my feet into the snow, but the ground gave way beneath me and I slid faster than ever. I didn't know where I was going: I couldn't see a thing. My sweater snagged on something, exposing my skin to the rock, mud, and snow. I lost a glove; my trousers tore. Damn, a cliff! My camera bag was banging over my head, its strap was searing my neck, and all the time I was slipping closer to the precipice: I could feel it, dark and gaping, beneath me - at least a 300-foot drop. Oh God, if only I had turned back! Twice my head hit hard against some rocks. The second one tore my ear open. I was certainly bleeding. My body began to bounce. It was horrifying. At full speed I saw a mass of rocks approaching . . . Crash! I fell in a heap against them. Slowly, I regained my senses. Only ten yards further down, the fatal chasm yawned.

I walked for another three hours along the icy road until, staggering, I reached the summit. At the foot of the statue were two weather stations: one Argentinean, the other Chilean. Without really choosing, I collapsed in Argentina.

I was not to see anything of Christ the Redeemer of the Andes. It was useless to anticipate any end to the storm. One of the weather men accompanied me back down. To keep warm, he offered me some peach brandy before taking the opportunity to down several shots himself. Soon he was drunk and I was exhausted.

We tripped and fell countless times. I didn't have the right shoes, my guide could hardly stand up straight and neither of us could see ahead. At times I collapsed right on top of him. A memorable descent! On reaching Las Cuevas, I was so utterly drained that I slept in his bed for fourteen hours without even having thought to ask his permission.

'I can't actually congratulate you for prowling around like that in the Andes, but I guess you didn't do yourself too much harm. Everything is fine, incorrigible "Francés"!'

In a matter of seconds, I had slipped on my trousers. Then, without a word, I shook Dr Puentes' hand for a long moment. As I marched through the corridors, people turned round to stare; my confident stride intrigued them. I didn't dare run, but it was almost as if I had. Not only was I completely cured, but everything was, truly, fine.

This time nothing could stop me. I was ready to spend the rest of my life on the road. I felt too free, too happy to consider anything else. I had proved to myself the extent of my mental and physical resistance. I was an 'all-risk guy', as Charlotte used to say. I felt as strong as an ox. With what Mex had taught me about life, hitch-hiking, and handling money, plus my own will-power and tenacity, I now felt ready to take on the whole world.

June 23rd, 1968, six o'clock in the morning: Carlos was waiting for me. Standing in front of his shiny new truck, he puffed on a cigarette. We were going to Peru together. It would be like three days in a luxury coach with my own personal guide. We experienced torrid days and freezing nights as we crossed the driest desert in the world. Burning up 1,400 miles in a single run, I was becoming a professional hitch-hiker. Not bad! When we reached the Peruvian border at Arica, Carlos sang me the *Marseillaise* as a farewell gesture.

Two hundred and twenty miles in nineteen hours! A record! Sitting in the front seat of a Fiat 850, I watched the landscape go by. At each turn of the road the motor screeched. One by one, the gears were changed down. Then we'd pick up speed again. The motor, however, belonged to the truck, because the car I was sitting in was riding piggy-back. Time didn't matter - not for me or for the copper-skinned Indians that I glimpsed from my perch on this 'auto-immobile'. But I was anxious to meet up with Mex and Jenny who were waiting for me in Lima.

When I arrived, I found that Jenny had already left. She had had to go back to university. In the meantime, Juan-José had managed to obtain letters of introduction to visit two mountain *haciendas*.

'Before going any further', said Mex, 'we absolutely must see Huascaran, the second highest peak in the Andes. At that spot the range is split into two majestic ridges, the White and the Black. It is one of the most amazing places in the world.'

At 13,000 feet up, breathing became more difficult. Beneath a full moon and a frigid sky, we rode in the back of an uncovered Mercedes truck. For seven hours we shared the fate of the twenty Indians riding with us. Together we were jolted around at the mercy of the pot-holes and thrown against each other at every turn. Unfortunately, the thick wool of their ponchos and short pants gave off a strong smell of sheep. If only Jenny had been there!

The Indians spoke Quechua, the Inca tongue, and were very friendly in spite of the language barrier. As a token of friendship they offered us a few coca leaves. In chorus, we all chewed rhythmically during the entire trip. Without saying a word, they taught us the ritual of coca. Using a nail, usually a rusty one, they extracted from the *poroncito*, a kind of gourd, a white powder, used to sweeten the sour taste of the leaf. A ball of leaves and powder was formed and stuck in a corner of the mouth, increased in size from time to time by the addition of a few more leaves. The leaves produced from often mysterious pockets were not always very fresh, but . . .

Soon, from the waist to the roots of the hair all sensation disappeared, including Andean mountain sickness. I had the distinct feeling that my body was made of boiled cardboard. Yet my feet were cold, and that only accentuated my sense of numbness.

The coca leaf cost next to nothing and was sold everywhere in stacks. The poor man's drug, it quenched thirst, staved off hunger and killed pain, thereby replacing any need for a doctor or dentist. It also dulled the intellect and so prevented the disinherited from thinking too much. As a makeshift solution to appalling poverty, it was thus a social balm. In the final analysis, the easy availability of coca served to guarantee the privileges of the handful of wealthy families who divided the country among themselves. While the *peones* subsisted in unimaginable poverty, the Peruvian army had just taken delivery of the first supersonic Mirage jet in all Latin America.

As I bounced along in that truck, I felt shame for myself, for the country's leaders, for all those people who didn't give a damn about the poor Quechua Indians looking at me with such simple smiles. They were no doubt sorry that they had nothing else to offer us.

We crossed the first ridge, the Black Range, the one on which it never snowed. In the shade of eucalyptus trees were small groups of low white houses climbing the mountainside. The atmosphere was gentle and peaceful. Indian women sat on their door steps spinning wool. They were dressed in bright colours and wore twin bowler hats, one placed on top of the other. On their backs they carried children crawling with flies who were never, ever washed ('It protects them from the cold, *señor*'). The young ones slept, unaware of their misery.

'*Gringo, plata!* White man, money!'

A little girl, protecting her face from the sun with one hand, looked at us out of the corner of her eye. Her other hand was extended towards us and she defiantly blocked our way. She was cute enough but her determined air and filthy rags gave her the look of a sad and pitiful doll. For the hundredth time, we would refuse to give alms to a child. For the hundredth time we would be taken for Americans, undoubtedly because of my movie camera. I felt ill at ease, but what could I do? I had to be able to pursue my travels. To interrupt them would do nothing to change the fate of these poor people. It would certainly not change this little child's fate or that of the circle of children surrounding us now, shouting in unison:

'*Gringo, plata!*'

'*No hay centavos!* I don't have any small change', Mex tried to explain. He was as embarrassed as I . . .

They had an answer to that.

'We also accept banknotes *señor!*'

She looked me straight in the eye. Her gaze was gentle and sincere, but the rest of her face was tense, her mouth tight. She was accustomed to this battle of wills and knew exactly what to tell the *gringos* who tried to sneak away.

A swarm of urchins tagged along behind us, jumping and turning about as if playing a game. We climbed up through the streets of Yungay towards Huascaran that dominated the horizon. Our intention was to reach the two small lakes that lay at the foot of the mountain.

Dance and laugh, poor little ones: mischievous children, fearless, mocking . . . and condemned. Neither you nor I knew it, but fate was looming over you. In three years, death would descend upon this valley. An earthquake would empty the lakes of Huascaran. At Yungay and on the plateau there would be 16,000 victims. Little girl, with your hand outstretched, the shadow on your face which I took to be that of poverty may in reality have been the shadow of death.

It was cold. Concealed by the mountain, the moon lit up the clouds from behind, giving Huascaran an uncanny resemblance to an erupting volcano, an impression reinforced by the rumbling of a glacier. We walked for five hours, covering eighteen miles and climbing 6,000 feet. The humble huts of the mountain hamlets were built of mud and thatch and were surrounded by little fields that looked almost like suburban lawns. Donkeys and cactus dotted the landscape. The effect was desolate without being dreary. Through every village we were escorted by ragged children and sniffing dogs. The inhabitants of the Andes knew only two words of Spanish and harassed us with their vocabulary born of poverty:

'*Gringo, plata!*'

At the end of our marathon, there was only a simple hut. A fat

Indian woman brushed aside old cans and rags and offered us a space on
her dirt floor to lie down in. Next to us was a large decrepit bed in which
her five children were already asleep. The hut was located at a strategic
spot through which caravans of mountain-climbers had to pass and from
where they launched their assaults on Huascaran. The woman watched
over the base camps and salvaged whatever was left behind, canned food
in particular. From the thatched ceiling hung corn cobs, onions, and
smoked meat. The woman closed the door after letting in the chickens,
pigs and dogs.

On our way back we followed the Cañon del Pato where the two
ridges divided. The path was hewn from the rocky cliff-face and wound
through some forty low tunnels. I felt as if trapped in the jaws of a
gigantic vice. We walked for hours.

'I've had enough', complained Mex. 'We've tramped fifteen or
twenty miles. Listen, do you hear that? It sounds like a car engine.'

A beat-up blue truck was coming down the road behind us. Mex
stepped out in the middle of the track and waved to the driver to stop,
but the guy drove right past us with a monstrous roar that echoed against
the cliff face. We remained seated at the side of the track until the dust
had settled.

'The bastard! He didn't even slow down. What rotten luck! That
was the first truck all day!'

Half an hour later I noticed some long blue streaks on the side of
the cliff. The rock had recently been scraped.

'Mex, look!'

Six hundred feet below us, the foaming waters of a swift stream were
covering and uncovering a jumble of metal . . . with tyres. The wreckage
was blue . . .

After the arid desert of the Pacific coast and the cold peaks of the
Andes, we descended into the steam bath of the Amazon Basin. Nothing
better for the health than abrupt climatic changes! From Pucallpa we
decided to head up the Ucayali River, one of the Amazon's major
tributaries.

At Huanuco, half-way, we stopped to rest. The one and only track
had been reserved that day for climbers going to the Andes. A fat, bald-
headed pig of a man, the police chief, put us behind bars. Motive: our
long hair meant we were vagrants, and vagrants belonged in jail until
they learned how to live better.

'Open those up!' screamed Old Piggy, pointing to our bags on the
floor of the dungeon-like cell.

After one night, Mex managed to spring us from jail. Among his belongings, he was carrying a cup-and-ball game and what looked like a sort of miniature TV set in which one could view pictures of scantily-clad Danish girls. Mex gave a breathtaking demonstration of cup-and-ball. When Old Piggy tried, he made a fool of himself in front of his subordinates, nearly knocking himself out in the process. Then, for a long time, he leered with delight as he held the Danish gadget up towards the room's single weak light bulb. Before we left, we got back the 'viewmaster' and game that had saved us. They might come in handy again.

We took to the road, heading downhill amid breathtaking scenery. The narrow, muddy track dropped from the Andean coolness to the tropical forest. The 9,000-foot plunge meant an interminable ride aboard a truck inching down at six miles per hour. At Death Pass the trucks edged slowly around the wreckage of a fuselage. Two planes had crashed on the spot, and their remains had become a permanent part of the landscape.

I dreamed of the Congo where I had first come to love the tropics, with their orgy of green, wild, primitive life. When I thought of the many roads I had travelled since fearfully approaching those first African huts, I realized how much I had been a victim of the reticence and repulsion inculcated by my own civilization.

We returned to Pucallpa, a collection of flimsy huts with a rickety wooden bridge spanning the Ucayali and a little boat rocking on the water. Everything was bathed in a strong smell of rotting vegetation and muggy, suffocating heat.

'The trip down river costs 170 *soles* in the third class. But, *señores,* you certainly cannot travel third class.'

For six days we navigated through tropical forest for just a dollar a day, everything included. A dream! The *Adolfo* was picturesque, to say the least - particularly in the third class. We were living in a menagerie, and the stench emanating from this lowest deck explained the captain's surprise at our insisting on the cheapest fare. For travelling companions we had five bulls, several caged boa constrictors, chickens running about loose, cockerels that crowed constantly, stray dogs, indefatigable parrots, and donkeys that fought over the bananas piled behind the toilets.

I took my first shower in a filthy stall. The door did not close, and the lukewarm, murky water dripped down between two big rocks on which one had to stand. It was difficult to keep one's balance, and the situation became all the more critical when the rocks started rolling. Yet the boat was not moving at all. Suddenly a head emerged from under one of the rocks. How bizarre! Then I realized that I had climbed on top of two tortoises which had sought shelter in the shower stall, which was after all the coolest place on the boat!

We shared our 'meal' with the crew and the few Indians who had managed to sling their hammocks in the menagerie. The cook, frighteningly thin, dished up some rice, beans or a few noodles garnished with skimpy pieces of doubtful-looking meat. The meal was served on a sheet of wrapping paper. I slept on a pile of smelly, untanned tapir skins that I shared with several dozen maggots. Next to me were stacked bags of onions and dry salted fish. In the morning the 'chef' gave us almond water and dry bread for breakfast.

On July 28th, the *Adolfo* stopped over in Flor de Punga. It was the Peruvian national holiday. To the sound of flute and tambourine, we danced on the bank of the river at the edge of the monstrous forest. Sugar-cane brandy flowed generously. I was very thirsty, so how could I avoid drinking it? How could I refuse the cups that were handed to me? There was nothing else to drink . . .

When I regained consciousness, I found myself stuck head first in the bowl of the first-class toilet. How had I found my way back to the *Adolfo* and walked up the plank used as a gangway without falling into the piranha-infested river? Even Mex was at a loss to explain it.

Iquitos marked the end of the line for the *Adolfo*. We got ready to disembark. The PIP (*Policia Investigaciones Peruana*) was watching the landing.

'You two, over here!'

Once again it was the police and the routine questioning. Where did we come from? Why were we travelling like this? Who were we spying for? It was becoming amusing. We left fingerprints like other people handed out autographs. Police station celebrities, we again posed for pictures, face and profile.

'We're going to check with Interpol. Meanwhile, you wait here. If you don't misbehave, we'll let you go in two or three days, but you'll have to leave the country. We don't need any revolutionaries in Peru, understand?'

Getting expelled was a godsend, since it was in the right direction. To the amazement of the police, we were overjoyed by the news. The trip was a police initiative; therefore it would be free. That evening we were summoned to the station. In reply to innumerable questions, Mex delivered a full speech about our trip. As a future lawyer who had interrupted his studies, he excelled in his 'Address to the Court':

'Dollars, dollars: that's not all there is to life. No, friendship is the real treasure, and believe me, people need it more than money. Friendship and understanding are precisely what we want to show you. We wanted to learn to love your country. You see, luxurious hotels for foreigners don't interest us; they only create an obstacle to true knowledge and prevent the peoples of this earth from coming to understand one another . . .'

On August 2nd, we were deported *manu militari* and conducted aboard the tugboat *Victoria Regia*.

We spent an interminable week in Leticia, the southernmost city of Colombia. The city was located on a strip of land that separated Peru to the west from Brazil to the east. The heat, which the daily rains did nothing to alleviate, and the extreme humidity made our wait all the more nerve-racking. We were anxious to go down the Amazon to Manaus, and a boat chartered by some Frenchmen showed up as the perfect answer. Once unloaded, it was returning downstream to Manaus, its home port.

It was a beautiful cruise. The *Cidade de Natal* skimmed slowly over the muddy waters of the Amazon, already a mile or two wide. Every sunrise or sunset was an unforgettable sight, and I didn't miss a single one. Just as memorable was the sight of one of the ocean liners which plied their way into the heart of Amazonia. Whenever one of the innumerable islands came between us, we would see only the ship's funnels gliding above the curtain of tropical forest.

Amidst all the delirious profusion of nature, I experienced an overwhelming sensation of well-being. More than ever, I felt at peace. I understood the exhilaration of pilots when they feel in complete control of their machines. I was firmly in command of my machine, and it was running smoothly. I was living in harmony with the earth. While discovering the world I was also delving into myself, an adventure that increased my desire to go further and deeper.

Manaus, which half a century earlier had been a rubber capital, was now a ghost town. The elaborate stucco opera house which had once been filled with world-famous voices stood mute, evidence of vanished splendour and now a refuge for bats.

The climate made us hopelessly sluggish. We dragged through the day, overwhelmed by the sultry heat and torpidity that only increased as the hours went by. I spent my time drinking countless *guaranas*, a cheap fizzy drink made from local fruit. The abundant vegetation seemed on the point of swallowing up the entire indolent city. We crashed out on the sidewalk in front of the Law School.

'*Para voces*. It's for you.'

Two beautiful coffee-coloured creatures with caressing eyes drew us out of our sleep. The sun was already high. Next to us on the ground they had placed a tray holding two breakfasts: china cups, aromatic coffee, orange juice, soft-boiled eggs, toast and marmalade. VIP service! Maria and Elvira, who had also brought us soap and a couple of shirts, began singing a beautiful, bewitching Brazilian song that I could have listened to for ever.

Our two friends led us into the kitchens of the Governor's Palace. There we were provided with meals that unfortunately were always sprinkled with detestable *farinha*, a ground manioc root which tasted like sawdust. Each night in front of the Law School, our circle of friends became larger and the party went on longer. Mex had everyone singing and laughing, way into the wee hours of the morning.

Terça-Feira 27 Agosta (Tuesday, August 27th): Mex left to use up his Mexico City-Rio round-trip ticket that he had booked a year before. He would be waiting at home in Mexico City where I would join him for the Olympic Games.

I wanted to go up through Venezuela along the Orinoco River, just as in one of my adventure books, *Orénoque-Amazone* by Gheerbrant. Impossible! That part of the world was in the hands of all sorts of guerrillas, and I could imagine the complications that might arise. I had spent enough time in jail as it was. Besides, there was another obstacle. The smug, self-satisfied Venezuelan consul wanted me to slip him thirty dollars under the table in order to obtain a free visa. Fat and conniving and glistening with sweat, he had utterly repelled me. Instead, I decided to leave Venezuela for later.

Back in Leticia I made another try at plane-hitching. The livestock of southern Colombia had been decimated by foot-and-mouth disease. An air lift from Bogota had been set up to bring in healthy cattle. I decided to camp at the foot of the airport control tower. On the fourth day an army Hercules unloaded its shipment of livestock and was ready to return empty. The crew agreed to take me on board. The cabin, a genuine flying cattle-shed, smelled of cow-dung. It reminded me of Langeac, of my Aunt Jeanne's farm.

The Amazon jungle is the largest wilderness in the world, but in Bogota the man of the wilds inevitably rediscovered 'civilization'. For one thing, it was impossible to sleep under the stars. It just wasn't done. So once again I was treated to the damp floors of prison cells - except for a single night when I slept in a genuine bed as the guest of the foreign minister's son.

Time was flying, the date for the Olympic Games was drawing nearer. I did not want to miss them, but I was desperate to visit Quito first. Being in a hurry, I decided to take a bus even though the cost far exceeded my daily allowance. In the jungle of Santo Domingo I took a moment to visit the Colorado Indians. I was sorry to be in such a rush, since I had been invited to spend a full week on horseback. At that time of year the cattle muster was beginning. And then, too, I was attracted to pretty Adriana and her two equally pretty sisters in Quito.

Caracas was already North America, or almost, with its skyscrapers, flashy neon signs and horrendous traffic. I took up hitch-hiking again. It was an uncontrollable urge, and besides, in this country of oil and highways, my French *'pouce'** worked admirably. San Felipe, Barquisimeto, Agua Viva, Lagunillas near the forest of derricks on Lake Maracaibo . . .

'I'll have to lock the door', said the prison guard. 'It's the rules. But don't fret, I'll warn the guy on the next shift. So, good night Francés.'

Previously, on my way south, the Republic of Panama had granted me a visa. At the time I had been a respectable tourist, along with the two Canadians. Our taxi had served as a kind of guarantee. This time I was a tramp and Panama didn't want anything to do with me. I was advised to re-enter Central America via San Andrés, a Colombian island in the Caribbean, located off the Nicaraguan and Cost Rican coasts.

As I boarded the Avianca plane, I had no idea what lay ahead. I did not even think about it, having become accustomed to constant harassment. Why wasn't the plane taking off? There was nothing on the runway. What was the hold-up? We were already twenty minutes late . . .

---

*The vocabulary of hitch-hiking: the French Canadians call it *faire du pouce - un pouce* is a thumb. The English and Americans say *hitch-hike, thumb a lift* or *hitch*. Venezuelans say *cola*, Germans and Israelis *trampen*, Mexicans *de aventon*. Chileans say *a dedo*, Brazilians *boleia* or *carona*. *Auto-stop*, often abbreviated to *stop*, is used everywhere else and pronounced variously otostop, aouto-stop, auto-sitop, etc.

Chapter 4

ACAPULCO GOLD

'Alajuela' had a cheerful ring, and yet it was the name of a
penitentiary eight miles outside San José, Costa Rica. For once I hadn't
volunteered but had been picked up at the airport on the pretext of not
possessing a round-trip ticket. Costa Rica was one of several countries
that required visitors to show a ticket for departure before being
admitted. Great.

'*Señor*, you must purchase a ticket immediately. Otherwise I will
have to deny you entry.'

'But they don't sell train or bus tickets here.'

'You must buy a plane ticket.'

'Why a plane? I want to see the regulation that says I have to go by
plane . . .'

That's how I wound up in jail at Alajuela, whose name resounded
like a cry of 'hallelujah', but which bore no further resemblance to
anything joyful. It was now up to the authorities to get me out of the
country!

At four o'clock someone shouted my name: it was the last call of
the day. I tugged at the arm of a fellow prisoner to show him I didn't have
a bowl. He answered by handing me the old tin can he used himself. I
rinsed it out in the urinal. Then I went to the hole in the wall that
communicated with the kitchen, passed the can through, and pulled it
back out dripping with an indescribable juice in which rice and black
beans floated. Having no cutlery, I slurped up the food with my fingers,
taking great care not to cut myself on the rim of the can.

I was starting to get tired of prison life. A few days earlier, as I had been leaving Colombia, two policemen of the DAS (the secret police) had literally kidnapped me from aboard the airplane just minutes before take-off. The nervous pilot had suspected me of being a hijacker. Fearing a forced landing in Cuba, he had immediately contacted the control tower and I had ended up being booked for forty-eight hours. My pack had taken off for San Andrés without me, but fortunately I had kept my papers on me. Now I had received a similar welcome in Costa Rica!

It was my sixth day in jail. The capital's penitentiary was a huge square building of yellow stone. The double-barred cells were clustered along arcaded corridors opening on to an inner courtyard. It was a prison with no vacancies. The beds were simple wooden planks without mattresses and were shared by two cell-mates. I decided to make do with the stone floor, except that it was deathly cold, for I didn't even have a blanket. An old convict named José rented out pieces of cardboard to lie on. When I told him my story, he let me use one for free.

I thus discovered the prison world, a world of coping and surviving. One elderly gentleman, fat and simple-minded, had a flourishing business renting out a battered deck of cards. Another prisoner rented out his newspaper, and still another a game of draughts. Some of them mended clothes or repaired shoes. Victorio was an artist who salvaged bones from our morning soup to carve into 'jaguar teeth'. He polished them on the rough walls of the latrine while chatting with the men squatting alongside. Dissatisfied with his most recent 'tooth' he gave it to me. He had been working on it for three days.

I was stuck. I had nothing to keep me busy. Sitting, standing or squatting, I could only contemplate the misery around me. The hours dragged by, gradually eating away at my morale. Every five minutes the cone-shaped toilet reservoir tipped, spilling its water down a filthy drain with a flood of noise. The guards beat up a prisoner who had lost his wits and dragged him off to solitary confinement. How could people live like this? How could they endure it for seven or eight years? A few of them confided in me:

'I stole nineteen bicycles . . .'

'I swiped four cases of oranges . . .'

'Me, loads of cloth . . .'

'I raped a young girl . . .'

In a neighbouring cell, a respectable-looking young man told me candidly: 'The Judge gave me the choice between marrying the girl I'd made pregnant or spending eighteen months in jail. As you can see, I chose jail.'

He stopped talking as voices rose and faces clustered behind the bars. The guards were 'escorting' into the courtyard an old veteran who was waving happily with both hands.

'He's a regular. This is the third time he's been back.'

As the days crawled by, one came to forget the stale smell of urine, the dampness, the cramped cells, the walking in circles for exercise, the pallid faces and blank stares. It was a strange world where no one bothered to say 'Good morning' or 'How are you?' Goodness was hard to come by.

My main concern was to get expelled in the right direction. At dawn, on the seventh day, I left Alajuela in style - with a machine-gun jabbed in my ribs. I was being deported. I had won! Aboard the plane that flew me to Nicaragua, an attractive and sympathetic stewardess named Elda did her best to comfort me. The plane had very few passengers, so Elda slipped a couple of spare meals into a big paper bag.

'For your journey.'

I was in Managua, Nicaragua, the Olympic Games were only two days off, and the Mexican Consulate was getting on my nerves. In order to obtain a visa, I had to buy a plane ticket from Managua to Mexico City. The price was ninety-two dollars, the equivalent of three months of travel. And that wasn't all:

'I am sorry, Sir, but I cannot give you a visa.'

'What the hell is this? You just made me buy a plane ticket! I've got money, traveller's cheques and a valid passport. Listen, I'm a professional translator; it's written right here. What do you think I am? This is incredible!'

With an air of contempt, he motioned me to step back.

'Get your hair cut!'

There they were! The famous words I had been waiting for! Little did it matter that men had been wearing their hair long since the beginning of time. For with the appearance of the crew cut in the twentieth century, short hair had quickly conquered the world as a symbol of strength, virility, morality, and superiority. Today it was harder than ever not to conform. We were becoming a society of shorn sheep!

'Is there an official style? Any particular cut recommended by the regulations? Have you any preference?'

'Don't try to be clever with me, sunshine! And shave off that beard and moustache! *Comprendido?*'

As the curtain fell on my South American travels, my black curls fell as well. I had loved that continent passionately; Latin America drew me; the Latin temperament appealed to me. In spite of the multitude of contradictory regulations, in spite of the dubious 'welcome' at certain borders, in spite of the exaggerated zeal of many officials, I retained fond memories tinged with nostalgia of my South American brothers. *Cariocas*, *gauchos*, Andean Indians, how can I ever forget you? You who, despite your dire poverty, spoke to me of joy?

I threw my arms around Mex. Good old Juan José! How had he managed to keep his hair long? He was furious at having missed the student revolution.

The welcome I received at his house was distinctly cool. Horrified at the idea of having a 'Che Guevara' for a grandson, his grandmother was no longer on speaking terms with him. His lawyer father and his mother both held me responsible for their son's transformation. They greeted me coldly, but at least they greeted me. In barely three weeks their opinion had changed in my favour, thanks to my culinary talents. Snails *à la bouguignonne* did the trick: they adored French cooking.

Their villa was luxurious, complete with two maids and three cars. It was my first real stop in ten months, and I must admit that the time was ripe.

Mexico City was in festive mood and I let myself be carried along. I attended the Games with unremitting zeal and even broke one of my own records: I saw everything without spending a single peso. I applied the methods I had learned from Mex and with particularly happy results. Of course, I was still on Latin ground. I doubt that I would have had as much luck in Munich or Tokyo, but in Mexico I was still in the Kingdom of the Hard Luck Story . . .

'I'm sorry, *Señor*, but you need a ticket to watch the cycle racing.'

For fifteen minutes I had been trying to talk my way past the guard, and now I was face to face with his superior. How was I going to manage this? Eureka!

'Listen, my dear Sir! Try and see it my way. Last night Aguastibias won a smashing victory in the 400-metre breast-stroke. Bravo for Mexico! The entire country is flying flags and rightly so. You must admit that this gold medal makes you happy, especially since it's only the fourth Mexican gold medal in the entire history of the Games. Now imagine me, a poor little Frenchman. How I would love to see my country's flag waving from that centre flagpole! Today I've got a chance to hear the *Marseillaise*. Please, Sir, let me in! I know

France is going to win. Cycle racing is our national sport.'

'All right, go on in - just this once!'

I was also in the Kingdom of the Deal . . .

'Hey, you there! Yes, you! Let me see that picture . . .'

Blast! For a few days now, I had been getting in by using the ID card of a French coach who was dating Mex's sister. This time I was about to be caught red-handed. The photograph showed a guy past fifty with silver sideburns and a narrow moustache.

'It's, ah . . . well . . . this picture was taken in a supermarket, in one of those instant photo booths, so you know, the quality, the details . . .'

'All right, go ahead. You're skinny but you're smart! Eh, *gringo?*'

And I myself was the King of Curiosity. I had a compelling desire to visit the Olympic Village, but it was closely watched by both the police and the army. At the entrance a guard armed with a bayonet looked me over casually. I decided to wait. Soon a bus pulled up and the guard sauntered over to check out the driver. I had been waiting for just such an opportunity and lost no time in dashing around the back. When the bus moved off, I trotted along beside it right into the Olympic Village.

After wandering around for a while, I ended up in one of the four restaurants. The food on display was appetizing, real first-class stuff. Why not give it a try? After all, they no doubt threw lots of it away. I observed the ritual: tray, silverware, a kind of cafeteria in other words.

'Your ticket, please.'

Whoops! I hadn't noticed that the cook was asking for tickets. My tray was filled with succulent roast beef. It was impossible to turn back. I felt an idiot.

'Sorry, but I've forgotten it.'

It was embarrassing to admit it, but I was becoming more and more skilful and glib in coming up with white lies.

'Well, go and get it!'

'But I'm late already, and I've got to go into town. There's a whole group of us. Please . . .'

The head chef stepped up, suspicious.

'That's against our policy. What team are you with?'

My mind flew at the speed of light. Let's see, which athletes would be known as champion smooth talkers?

'Italian.'

'That figures! And may we know what sport you're in?'

'*Luchador*! Wrestler!' I blurted out.

My skinny silhouette wasn't going to be much help in convincing them, but I had said it and I was stuck with it. Then, miraculously, the chef waxed enthusiastic.

'Say, *luchador*, you've got to eat, buddy! Are you sure you took enough? If you want seconds just come and see me!'

At times I wouldn't have minded being a wrestler - especially outdoors at night. I would wake up at the slightest noise, not knowing what sort of man or beast might be lurking, ready to pounce. In the dark my imagination ran riot. I never slept soundly, for I never felt completely safe. Only exhaustion would force my eyes to close. I never really got used to it.

One evening on the outskirts of Puebla, at the foot of Popocatepetl, I decided to sleep in a garbage dump in order to have some peace and quiet. I stumbled about in the dark, tripping over tin cans and bedsprings in search of a place to crash out. The place stank and was infested with rats, but at least it was quiet. I crawled in under some bushes, looking forward to a good night's sleep . . .

A noise directly above my face jerked me from my sleep. Instinctively, I grabbed for my pack. Dawn was breaking, yet fifteen inches in front of my face there loomed a pale moon! For lack of a public toilet, an honest old *campesino* was in the habit of squatting on this spot in the morning before going to work.

'Not on me! *Miseria!*' I yelled, suffocating.

The poor fellow leaped into the air, his trousers still around his ankles. Trembling, he turned and peered through bleary eyes to see what sort of devil had howled at him from out of the bowels of the earth.

For three months Juan-José was my guide, showing me his country's natural beauty and artistic wealth, teaching me about its pre-Columbian and colonial past. I visited village libraries, town halls, trade unions, hospitals, power plants, police stations and churches. I witnessed there the nation's history, especially that of the 1917 Revolution as represented by the three great artists, Siqueiros, Diego Rivera and Orozco. What strength was contained in their frescoes! What truth in their simple, didactic paintings!

I had some difficulty getting to the Yucatan. The region had long been inaccessible and had different traditions from the rest of the country. The houses were white with thatched roofs and contained a single oval room. Instead of windows, there were two doors opposite each other, between which the hammocks were strung. The inhabitants of the Yucatan had aquiline noses and skin the colour of honey. They seemed to have stepped out of the frescoes and bas-reliefs of Palenque.

In school I had learned all about the Egyptians and Greeks. But when it came to the New World, the books stated simply that Columbus had discovered only savages. Yet, at a time when classical Greek sculpture was disappearing in favour of the flat representations of Byzantium, the Mayas were creating bas-reliefs of amazing fluidity. Each portrait conveyed a different mood and filled me with admiration. I realized how limited my history books had been. By restricting themselves to our own cultural 'grandeur', they did a grave injustice to the rest of the world's magnificent heritage. Why didn't such books present the history and artistic wealth of *all* humanity? By failing in their task, they only perpetuated arrogance, misunderstanding and estrangement among the world's peoples.

With its sculpted skulls, giant tortoises, phallic gargoyles, and 450-foot stone serpent, Uxmal fascinated me. The fortune-teller's pyramid caught my fancy in particular. What if I were to spend the night up on top? Romantic? My strange request was peremptorily dismissed by the guards.

'They worked hard to build a hotel for you *gringos*. And besides, it's dangerous in the ruins at night. We shoot at anything that moves to discourage vandals and thieves.'

The risk appealed to me. I decided to give it a try. The sky was aflame as the sun sank behind a curtain of trees. Stars appeared, and crickets, toads, and a thousand other nocturnal creatures began their evening concert. The adjacent hotel had a magnificent pool and, since I felt dusty and sticky, a bath seemed particularly inviting. I climbed over the low surrounding wall and slipped quietly into the cool, chlorinated water. A hotel customer joined me and asked what I thought of my room. I replied that I was immensely satisfied.

Carrying my sleeping bag under my arm, I walked back to the ruins and the 'free-fire zone' where I had chosen to spend the night beneath the stars. During the day I had already planned my approach: first the nun's house, then the pelota court, and finally the graveyard. Slowly I crept forward. At the slightest noise I froze in my tracks, and then continued, bent double. The pyramid stood in the middle of an open field, not far from the sentry-box. Crawling across it would take too long. So I broke into a sprint. A moment later, panting, I was pressing my back against the bottom step of the pyramid. The climb was difficult, for the sides of the pyramid were extremely steep. I had a hard time getting over each step, especially since I had to crouch to avoid being seen. The sound of voices warned me of the approach of two soldiers. I remained motionless and held my breath, waiting until they had gone before continuing my climb.

I lay down at the foot of a red jaguar adorned with seventy-two pieces of jade: the throne of the high priest. The air was warm, the moon not quite full. The stars shone more brightly than ever. I dreamed that the city was coming to life again, just as it had been over 1,000 years ago.

The capital of Mexico was a monstrous city bristling with skyscrapers and devoured by a gangrene of concrete. However, it did retain one charming custom: 'Aay, ay, ay, ay . . .' The *mariachis** were groups of strolling musicians dressed like cowboys in their Sunday best: black skin-tight pants embroidered with silver curlicues, gaudy jackets with white sleeves, extravagant hats and leather boots. They congregated around the Plaza Garibaldi where they enlivened the late evening hours with their guitars, violins, trumpets, tambourines and flutes. For a dollar they would dedicate a serenade to your sweetheart, friend or relative, either on the spot or at your home. As a welcoming gesture Mex took me to hear Las *Mañanitas* and *Las Golondrinas*. The singers were not always in tune, not did they have flawless voices; but the ambience more than made up for that. It was a joyful, sparkling fiesta. The *mariachis* roamed the streets until just before dawn, singing in the shadow of apartment buildings. Sometimes two admirers would have the same idea at the same time; the sweetheart would then be obliged to listen to two competing serenades.

The *mordida* (literally 'bite' or 'mouthful') was as much a part of Mexican folklore as the *mariachi*. Indeed, the *mordida* had evolved into an institution in its own right. Here is an example:

A policeman whistles, approaches nonchalantly and asks for my papers.

'Actually, this car isn't mine. It belongs to the friend I'm staying with, a lawyer. I'm simply a tourist . . . from France.'

'Sorry, but you don't have a licence and my job is to enforce the law. You'll have to come with me to the police station.'

'But, you see, I'm in a hurry. Here . . .'

By now we have strolled around behind the car where I slip him a ten-peso note. He unfolds it and frowns.

'Listen, *señor*, driving without a licence is a serious offence . . . and

*The word was derived from the French *mariage* ('marriage') during the reign of Maximilian.

the cost of living is high in Mexico!'

Theoretically, considering the situation as a whole and especially the luxurious car I am driving, I should give him two or three times the amount I have offered.

'Try to understand! If you ask for more, I'll have to give up eating. My only real means of transport is my thumb.'

He is a kindly soul.

'OK. Beat it!'

Juan-José's father explained that it was not really advisable to get out of your car, that you could simply put the note inside your papers.

'Assuming you have plenty of cash, how much mordida do you give?'

'That depends on the seriousness of the offence, but considering my position, I usually give fifty pesos.'

The mordida eked out the monthly salaries of los grises, the grey-uniformed officers in charge of traffic. It also saved traffic offenders from having to go to court, a welcome reprieve since, paradoxically, Mexico's penal code was severe and involved lengthy court procedures. The inevitable result was a kind of racket in which the mordida became more or less automatic. A truck driver explained to me one day how he paid before the officer could blow his whistle:

'In this country, no one really obeys the law anyhow. So, like everyone else, I stop and hand over my five pesos even before they check up on me. That way, I never have any problems.'

Thus I understood what was happening one day on the road to Villahermosa as I watched truck after truck pull to a stop. Each time, a kid would run up to the truck and then return to a police Chevrolet parked off in the shade. The mordida kept everyone happy. The truck drivers got off scot free, the policeman slept in the shade, and the kid got his commission.

Every night for a week Mex and I slept on the fine sand of the Acapulco beach. The hotels, numerous and luxurious, lined the emerald bay. Almost every evening we had visitors who offered us 'Acapulco Gold', cheap 'grass' grown illegally in the area.

Mex first taught me how to smoke an ordinary cigarette properly, how to inhale the smoke. I coughed and choked, but practice gradually made perfect. I was determined to learn about everything.

Soon I was ready to try my first joint of marijuana. It looked like a fat cigarette, inexpertly rolled and pinched at both ends. I inhaled slowly and, following Mex's advice, held the smoke in my lungs as long as possible. I pressed my lips together to block my breathing. A few minutes later, my body began to defy the laws of gravity. I felt euphoric and calm at the same time. I looked at Mex. His head seemed enormous and his body tiny: he resembled a foetus. He smiled, revealing teeth that seemed to swallow up his face. I burst out laughing. I felt like laughing endlessly for no reason. The longer I watched his open mouth, the more I choked on my riotous laughter. He, too, began to chuckle.

Time passed imperceptibly, the minutes dissolving into space. Our voices sounded loud and fragmented. My ears picked up sounds I had never heard before. In a daze, I looked at the beach, the ocean, the waves that thundered with a new crashing sound. I was stoned. I had forgotten everything - Mex and the rest. I was flying. The landscape had become a theatre stage, a succession of painted sets. I felt as though I were looking through an old-fashioned stereoscope. I immersed myself in every detail, one by one, each time forgetting the picture that had gone before.

We went to a fair. The people there seemed like wax figures in slow motion. Each new sensation lasted an eternity, obliterating all previous sensation. I revelled in a vanilla ice-cream cone. Never had ice cream tasted so ambrosial! Every delectable mouthful bathed my palate in a completely new, fresh sensation before gliding ever so gently down my throat.

Smoking exhausted me, and very soon I wanted only to sleep. As I returned to Condesa Beach, the walk seemed to go on for ever. I felt as if I was moving my feet without going forward, as in a nightmare. The next morning I had no headache, nothing at all. But one week had been enough. I had had the opportunity to see what smoking pot was like, but it did not really interest me. It was more congenial in a group and certainly less painful than a boisterous night of drinking. Yet, all in all, the mirage of drugs didn't attract me any more than alcohol did. In future I would 'smoke' a few more times when the occasion arose, but without really deriving any pleasure or benefit from it. The experience had been solely part of my education.

Drugs? No thanks! You believe you are getting 'high', even 'flying', but after each 'trip' you come right back down to earth. From everything I had seen, the secret of joy was not to be found in drugs. In any case, I much preferred a clear mind. I understood the desire of many people to escape, to dream, to forget a reality that depressed them, but running away was no solution. My first encounter with genuine drug addicts rapidly convinced me of that. I was sure that something existed which would enable people to live intensely and to the full without coming down with a bump. I had to discover that 'something', and to that end I would continue on my way. My 'way', which as in a dream had no end, would take me ever onward, towards stronger sensations, towards more and richer joys, towards unforgettable friendships.

Chapter 5

ALASKAN HIGHWAY

'Hey, get out of here! You're bad for business.'

Habits and customs had suddenly changed. In Mexico all I needed to do was stand by a petrol station in order to find a driver willing to take me along. But on crossing the big border bridge spanning the Rio Grande, lost among hundreds of Mexican commuters, I had entered America the beautiful where everything was different. I felt I had entered the jungle.

In the past, hitch-hiking had been easy here, but today people were afraid. Isolated in their mobile shells, they no longer knew anyone. Thus I would be forced to walk more, wait longer and play hide-and-seek with the local cops. The situation wasn't really critical - there were still some friendly truck-drivers, students, hippies, and even understanding soldiers - but the mood was no longer the same. In South America I had been a *gringo*, a White. I had even been 'rich'. Now in the North I was a reject, a pauper in a society which officially had no poor. I was going to have a tough time of it, and my enemies would be legion: indifference, selfishness, inflexible laws and a cold winter would be the major ones. At the outset I accepted the hard facts of my American adventure. In the kingdom of the dollar, I would be challenging the highest standard of living on earth. I would have to count each coin, each banknote; and if I succeeded in North America, then the whole world would be my oyster.

I wanted to get further than Albuquerque but the tougher hitch-hiking was slowing me down. The city itself was perfectly anonymous, overly clean, too well-kept. The silent traffic moved as if programmed by a computer. Pedestrians had almost disappeared from the scene. Those remaining were in a hurry, their faces pinched shut. I longed for the crowds of South America with all their joyous festivity.

Feeling somewhat lost, I instinctively headed for the police station. The police were neither friendly nor hostile. They simply made it clear that their work was to deal with traffic, security and order, but certainly not with hand-outs. Without any further ado they sent me to the Salvation Army.

At six in the morning a psalm coming over the loudspeaker dragged me from my sleep. I would just as soon have slept in but to complain would have been ungrateful. At least there had been shelter for the night, and the mandatory shower had done me good. Standing by the beds which had been assigned us for three days, we listened to a couple of verses from the Bible. Other biblical quotations lined the walls of our six-bed dormitory.

The 'captain' would not believe me when I told him I was going to Alaska. Then, still dubious, he gave me a voucher for the clothing store.In mid-winter, even in the southern states, shorts and tee-shirts were not seasonal wear. With a moth-eaten scarf, sturdy boots and a stained leather jacket, I was equipped. I thanked the captain and took off on my trip.

In Denver a freeway went through the heart of town. I had barely been dropped off when a cop was on to me. I was in a fix, for hitch-hiking was illegal. I played dumb, pretending not to understand the language. He ranted and raved, talking faster and faster in an effort to make me understand. Finally he exploded:

'Fine, fine! Understand? You'll get fined! Money, money!'

Rubbing together his thumb and index finger, he made me the sign: *money*.

I felt indifferent, distracted. I was simply travelling through. I was going to Alaska, so I couldn't care less about fines or money. Suddenly I had an idea.

'Oh money! You give money? Me eat. Thank you.'

Disgusted, he returned to his car, made me climb in beside him, and drove to the nearest snack bar. As soon as the car had disappeared I left and walked for a long time through the poorer neighbourhoods of Denver. Without being really discouraged, I still didn't feel very happy, especially about hitch-hiking. I hated the frustration and futility of having to hang around endlessly, wasting my time. Having lost my bearings, I could not find the strategic spot. Of course I knew I would find a lift sooner or later, but for the moment I was wasting time. I had wanted to cross the States in one stretch.

'Hello, man! Are you hungry? If you want to eat for free, you have to put up with an hour-long sermon at the Baptist Mission, just a block from here. But the soup's on the house!'

I hesitated for a moment. Things just weren't working out right. No cars were stopping, and now this guy had mistaken me for a tramp. It all seemed to spell defeat. Good God, I couldn't give up so easily!

I felt a wave of nausea on entering the hall. Another Skid Row: how many were there on this earth? I was young, they were old, and my first instinct was to turn around, to leave. All the riff-raff of the city had congregated here, out of sight, hidden behind the rich façade of American society. Suddenly, Denver struck me as nothing but a luxurious and fragile screen behind which was shoved the city's misery. Eventually I went in after all.

I stood in a corner waiting for something to happen, scrutinizing the faces of these outcasts. Their skin was spotted, scarred, pock-marked; their eyes were sad and glassy, watery; their eyelids weighed heavy; their bare heads displayed dirty, dishevelled hair; their mouths were twisted in the bitter grimace of poverty. They were the dregs of an opulent civilization. They waited without really waiting, still alive but shunted away from the living, struck from the rolls of this model nation's citizenry, rejected for not conforming to the official norms. With unexpressive faces - in Mexico, the poor still had the strength to smile - they attended without listening, but without refusing either, the sermon given by the Baptist minister. Hands braced on the sides of a lectern, shoulders square, the preacher didn't have a particularly angelic look about him.

'Jesus Christ came to save us . . .'

'Yeah, yeah, yeah', answered a voice from the back of the hall, 'yeah!'

The minister stopped, his finger pointing towards heaven. Solemnly, he stepped down from his platform and walked with a heavy and determined step to the back of the room. With a forceful gesture, he grabbed the vociferous soul, who had obviously celebrated too enthusiastically the announcement of the good news. The unfortunate drunk was dragged to the door, and the freezing wind that for a few seconds invaded the hall made everyone understand that the reverend didn't trifle with the law of the Lord.

'No food for you tonight!' he announced, closing the door. Then he returned to his pulpit and continued in a loud voice: 'Jesus came to save us.'

The assembly settled back into a deep torpor, rocked to sleep by the plaintive tune issuing from the harmonium. The minister finally clapped his hands.

'Six o'clock, soup-time.'

Instantly, everyone rose and formed a line. My neighbour nudged me with his elbow.

'Say, if you don't have a bed for the night, go across the street to the Citizen Mission. There's room there. Just follow me.'

At the shrill sound of a whistle, everyone stripped naked. The pot-bellied, the emaciated, the crippled and the hunchbacked all placed their ragged belongings in numbered baskets along a wall covered with religious pictures. We numbered at least thirty. In silence we marched into the showers. As we emerged we were handed enormous cloth sacks with holes in them for our heads and arms. Balenciaga had certainly not designed these nightgowns, which rubbed uncomfortably against the skin. Again the whistle blew and everyone climbed to the second floor. Metal bunk beds awaited us. The weak rushed as best they could to grab the bottom bunks. The light was switched off, only the dim light of the bathroom remaining on throughout the night.

At five-thirty, the whistle blew once more. The snoring ceased, immediately replaced by the sounds of coughing, spitting and clearing of throats. Outside, it was still just as cold.

Little by little my feelings of abhorrence faded away, and I no longer regretted this experience of being a voluntary vagrant. I know that it taught me something new about people and was sure that some day everything would fall into place. Already my South American adventure had enabled me to throw off the fetters of habit inherent to the 'system'. I slowly withdrew from the cult of appearances, learned to master my reactions and to slough off pre-conceived ideas. It was not easy, for social conventions are imbued in us in our earliest years. Fear of the poor and of poverty was part of the heritage that many of us received in the cradle.

Physically, all was going well. I was living on next to nothing, and my body was of little concern to me. I wanted only to carry out my plans. I had made my choice to forget about luxury, comfort, good food and soft white sheets.

In Montana I worked my passage by helping two truck drivers unload twenty tons of poultry. When we had finally unloaded the last crate, they presented me with two chickens which a cook roasted for me at a truck stop in Great Falls. It was also in Montana that it began to snow. This was the start of a time of great hardship.

Before long I was back in Canada. The temperature in Calgary was -30°F and I didn't have nearly enough clothes. Night had already fallen and I no longer felt human, with cheeks as hard as marble framing a trickling nose.

'Sorry, but here in Canada the Salvation Army asks for a one-dollar contribution for the night. It's the rule.'

What else could I do in this icebox? I was exhausted and, after all, one dollar wasn't so very much. I could make it up elsewhere. All I had to do was turn over a dollar and I would be able to lie down in a warm place.

The snag was that I was stubborn, and I had made a decision never to pay for the privilege of sleeping. One dollar wasn't very much - true - but it meant one day less somewhere else. It was that first dangerous compromise. I knew that if I gave in this time, I would do so again, and each dollar that slipped from my grasp would make my trip just that much shorter. It was therefore out of the question.

'Please, just let me spread out my sleeping bag on the floor. I don't want a bed.'

'Sorry, it's a dollar or nothing!'

I walked across the city to the Welfare department where I needed a few minutes to recuperate. I had lost all feeling in my limbs, and the sudden heat of the office almost knocked me out.

'Can I see your unemployment card, please.'

'But I told you, I've just arrived from the US. I'm hitch-hiking. All I want is a little corner for my sleeping bag.

Behind me a man, obviously unemployed, who had come to register, whispered in my ear, 'Here, I'll lend you my card.'

'Too late. The secretary already knows I don't have one.'

My last resort was the police. Freezing, I showed up at the station but again there was no possibility. Everywhere the rules were strictly enforced and soon I was outside again. For two hours I trod the streets of Calgary, which were as shiny as a skating rink. I was utterly exhausted but still found the strength to continue my struggle against surrender. If I gave in I knew that it would all be over, that I could kiss goodbye to my trip around the world.

'Sorry, it's against the rules!'

The night watchman at the bus depot refused me a place in one of the buses.

'Rules, rules! They'll kill me with their rules! Damn it all, doesn't it occur to anyone that it's -30° outside'.

'What's the problem, man?'

Saved. A young man with locks of hair protruding from under a weird little cap offered to help me. He was American, worked in the theatre, and had left the US to escape military service in Vietnam. He was sharing a hotel room with two other Californians. Smiling, he took me by the arm.

'There's still space on the rug', he said. 'Come on.'

This time I was sure of it: nothing would ever defeat me. Of course, I had felt this same light-headed sensation before - when I had checked out of the hospital in Santiago, for example - but now I felt a kind of confirmation. As the days went by, I felt increasingly in control of myself. Most of all, I had a burgeoning faith in luck and in my guiding stars.

I continued my trek towards the north. In Edmonton my feet were so cold, I felt as if I were walking barefoot on the ice. The temperature flashing on the outskirts of the city read -40°F I didn't need to write it down in my journal, for without even gloves on my hands, I would have no trouble remembering.

I was looking for the home of my cousins whom I had met once before on a brief visit. It took me two hours to locate their house, so large was the city. I arrived looking as frosty as Santa Claus; my eyelids were practically frozen shut.

'You look a lot better than when you came here from Toronto!'

Toronto was far away, two years behind me. At the time I had been living the life of a bureaucrat with fixed working hours, three meals a day, a warm and comfortable bed - in a word, routine. Now they found me in better shape, which hardly surprised me, for travelling suited me and it showed.

We had a real celebration. I had been the first to renew the family ties that had been broken at the time of the departure of 'Crazy Grandpa'. I first spent ten days with Georges and then went to Antoinette's. The members of this older generation, born on the farm, were very different from their children whose lives were essentially ones of comfort and ease. The older ones had grafted for a living; the third generation spoke only English, lived in the city and seemed to be ashamed of the past. Antoinette laughed as she told me a story about Grandma Brugiroux. One Christmas Day the old lady had heard the postman shout, 'Merry Christmas!' and had answered, 'Marie Chrismass?

Don't know her, but there are some new people livin' a bit further on. Might be them!'

It hadn't been so cold in Edmonton for over a century. Yet, in spite of my cousins' entreaties, I decided not to extend my visit any longer.

'You're mad, completely crazy, to go to Alaska at this time of the year! In the summer it's feasible, but in the winter! Won't you at least take the bus?'

'Come on now, don't worry about me. I've got four times as many clothes as before. Look at my feet: four pairs of socks, my Salvation Army shoes, and fur-lined boots! I've got two pairs of gloves, a leather cap with felt-lined ear flaps, several sweaters, two parkas, two pairs of long-johns . . .'

Feeling like the Michelin Man, I took the highway at the northern edge of Edmonton. It was a beautiful morning with a temperature of -35. Even with my face hidden inside a ski mask and my thumb muffled in nylon and wool, hitching involved a dangerous degree of exposure. I had spent the previous night in a 'Husky' (truck stop), trying to hitch a lift in one of the gigantic trucks heading for Alaska. I hadn't succeeded, so now I had no choice but to get out on the road. The biggest gamble had begun.

The pale sun was struggling up into the fleecy sky, as the Saskatchewan River smoked in a prison of ice. The silent landscape was majestic, stretching in its pristine whiteness as far as the eye could see. The trees were covered with frost and seemed more beautiful and more solemn than ever. I enjoyed hearing the crunch of my boots on the snow. At all costs I would have to keep moving, walking, jumping, running, just to keep my blood circulating. Each time a car door opened, it seemed like a miraculous salvation.

Grande Prairie, Pouce Coupé: the highway was like a mirror on which the cars had difficulty staying in line. Even less reassuring was the sight of several overturned vehicles in the ditches. Some of the wrecks looked very recent . . .

I was becoming more and more tenacious. My folly and recklessness were paying off. The first day's results weren't too bad: four lifts for a total of 375 miles. I had reached Dawson Creek, the starting point of the Alaskan Highway. Only 1,500 miles separated me from Fairbanks at the other end.

After a good night spent in the Welfare House with my buddies - vagrants, alcoholics and the unemployed - I again hit the white road, little used at this time of year. There were only three or four cars a day. I had already figured out one trick: all the petrol stations offered piping hot coffee as a bonus. I gulped down three or four cups at each stop in an effort to keep a little warmth inside me.

The best method of getting a ride was to wait patiently in every café or garage. There was one open about every sixty miles, and the few drivers on the road at that time would be sure to stop there too. I always took good care not to get dropped off in the middle of nowhere. Otherwise I risked having my lungs burned by the bitter cold. In such extreme temperatures it was possible to lose the skin on your fingers by simply touching a car door, and any driver who stopped too long could have his tyres freeze to such an extent that they were no longer round. Therefore I didn't dare make the slightest miscalculation. Each step in the outdoors was like a slap in the face. Once I got dropped off at a café that was closed. I thought I was done for! During those three hours of waiting, I sprinted back and forth over a hundred-yard course. God knows how many times! Finally an old Oldsmobile filled with black people came to my rescue, even though it was heading back south.

'Ah, so you're French, and you're hitch-hiking. You know, last year we met another French hitch-hiker like you. Well, that one disappeared, and about four months later they found just his hand. No one knows what ever happened to him. Yep, in this very spot and in mid-winter, just like you!'

That was all I needed! The image of that hand lost in the snow would haunt me for a long time as I travelled through Alaska - especially since everyone I met was more than happy to repeat the tale.

The sky was cloudless as we crossed the Rockies. The mountains were spacious; I found them less oppressive than the Alps. The trees, the rivers trapped in ice, the lakes covered with mist: everything seemed gigantic. Brown moose crossed the road oblivious of the traffic, creating an additional hazard for the drivers, who already had enough trouble following the road through its dangerous curves and constant ups and downs. The scenery, however, was so enthralling that I even forgot my fear of accidents. I felt fit and at ease, in a permanent sort of way. I was finding endless pleasure in admiring the landscape and observing people. Both continued to amaze and delight me.

The full moon was bathing the night in a silvery glow as I dozed in a tanker at Iron Creek in the Yukon. Hitching had become almost impossible when, on the verge of giving up and taking the expensive bus ride, I had encountered that rare bird: the offer of a lift all the way to Fairbanks! A thousand miles in one hop! And to top it off, the offer had come from a young man who said he never usually picked up hitch-hikers!

The scenery consisted of endless plains, white and seemingly infinite. Above the thick blanket of snow protruded the tops of trees. The trunks themselves were buried beneath. It seemed totally unreal.

The last part of the journey began to take on epic dimensions. Every twenty-five miles Dane, the driver, had to empty a can of anti-freeze. Then we ran out of petrol in the middle of the night. Luckily the next petrol station was only some two or three miles away. As Dane headed off into the darkness, I shivered uncontrollably. He should never have gone; he was taking a terrible risk.

At milepost 1314, I had arrived. Alaska! Ouch! They asked me for $2.20 for an ordinary hamburger, a few French fries and a cup of coffee! I was certainly going to spend more in Alaska, but I couldn't afford to be too stingy. I had to think of my health. I could do without luxuries or even any real comforts, but I had to be careful to consume a minimum of calories. Dane informed me that refusing hospitality to travellers was a punishable offence. That was good news! A fine law! But the same one also prohibited hitch-hiking in winter, he added, smiling and winking at me.

In Fairbanks the temperature was -28°F. What a Godsend! It felt like the French Riviera compared to the more usual -75! Fairbanks reminded me of a Christmas card. I was pleased with my accomplishments. I had made it to Fairbanks as fast as the bus from Edmonton. Just five days! Without a doubt I was the first person to hitch the Alaskan Highway in winter. When I realized that I'd come all the way from Tierra del Fuego without spending a single night in a hotel, I couldn't help feeling pleased with myself.

The Salvation Army had put out a 'full' sign, the Centre for the Rehabilitation of Alcoholics decided I was too sober, and the chapel was locked. I decided to try the police station. Even though Alaska was still the US, considering the severe cold I didn't dare overlook any possibility. Sergeant McClughn was an old hitch-hiker and took a liking to me. Laughing, he locked me up in an overheated cell and poured me coffee in exchange for an account of my adventures. I had told the same stories a thousand times before, but it was my way of thanking people. So, I started over again.

'Aren't you lucky, Andy! If only I could have done that myself . . . Say! Tomorrow I'm patrolling with the Piper. Want to come along?'

That short trip in a light aircraft gave me the idea of going to the

Arctic Circle - hitch-hiking, of course. In Alaska one family in four
owned a private plane, the roads being so few and far between.
Unfortunately, I quickly learned that in winter, traffic was considerably
reduced by the extreme cold and the bad weather in general.

Transport agencies, company hangars, offices: every day I went back
and forth between Fairbanks and the airport, trudging two and a half
miles through the snow in the hopes of getting a seat for Prudhoe Bay, an
oil-prospecting area in the northernmost part of the state which received
its supplies by cargo plane. For a week I was sent on one wild goose chase
after another. Refusing to give up, I continued patrolling each and every
room of the airport to the point where the pilots and mechanics no
longer paid any attention to me.

When I showed up towards noon on the seventh day, a Hercules
was sitting on the runway, it's engines roaring. Its captain, a friendly fifty-
year-old man named Ray Boland, was preparing his check-list. It was the
first time I had seen him.

'Cap, I'm that crazy Frenchman that they were talking about on the
radio the other day. I'd like to go . . .'

'Yes, I remember. Well, come on and climb aboard. And hurry up
about it. You know, this is strictly against regulations. Now, hide in there
and don't you dare move. Okay? You're lucky; the weather is good.'

The plane was loaded with salt for drilling wells. At 1.45 p.m. the
engines were revved up, making the plane vibrate. Then we were
airborne.

The Yukon River, sinuous and still, unfolded beneath our eyes. At
2.30 p.m., sixty-four degrees North, we reached the Arctic Circle and
began crossing the Brooks Range: a thousand white, jagged peaks. The
sun was very low and would be setting in less than an hour. It tinted the
mountainsides with a delicate pink, while the valleys were shaded a
steely blue. The wind swirled clouds of snow which made the mountains
look as if they were smoking. The glowing sun sank in the west. At 2.45
p.m. the plane banked and began circling over the ice-packed Beaufort
Sea which was barely distinguishable from the coast. Only an occasional
patch of blue hinted at the ocean's presence.

At 3 p.m. it was already twilight as the Hercules came to a stop on
the icy gravel-strewn runway of Britpet (British Petroleum) Camp
Number One. At the end of the runway, which in the summer was a
swamp, a wrecked aircraft remained as a reminder to the pilots of the
Great North of the perils of landing.

A derrick pierced the immaculate sky like a church steeple. At its foot, huddling together to conserve heat, were a dozen prefabricated houses designed like mobile homes. There were also twenty or so enormous trucks every bit as big as the houses.

Unfortunately I could not get off the plane, since my presence there was unofficial. I would have liked to have had a look at the houses and the faces of those pioneers of the 'black gold' who spent six consecutive weeks on the job before enjoying two weeks of rest and recreation in Fairbanks. They were apparently well paid. Were they happy?

As consolation for having had to stay on the plane, Ray Boland handed me a certificate testifying that I had crossed the Arctic Circle.

In Anchorage, the Pacific Ocean tempered the polar harshness of the climate. The thermometer showed 14°F, leaving me with the distinct impression that spring had come. I arrived in the middle of the World Dog Sled Championships which had been organized as part of the Fur Festival. The sled teams were impressive and, even if the sport of 'mushing' had been introduced by Europeans, the entire spectacle had a certain charming authenticity. The presence of Inuits (as the Eskimos prefer to be called) among the twenty-two 'mushers' reinforced that impression. Harnessed together in lines of between eight and sixteen, the dogs had thick, glossy coats of fur. Some had light-coloured eyes. They howled impatiently and tugged at their harnesses; the staggered departures only increased their agitation.

At the end of the first twenty-five mile relay, the teams crossed the finishing line in a state of extreme fatigue. The dogs, drenched with snow, panted clouds of vapour. Their muzzles and chests were covered with ice; their mouths were often bloody. Exhausted, some had collapsed midway and had finished the race sitting on the sled. They came in covered with frost but looking grateful for their musher trudging behind them. At times a musher was even forced to drag the exhausted team himself. The races lasted three days. I never got tired of gazing at those sleds silently speeding through a wilderness of white.

There was very little to do in Anchorage, and it did not take long to explore the city. I spent part of my time at Merrill Airport, always on the look-out for a lift elsewhere. I wanted to visit the Inuit in their own environment, away from the tourist circuit. Alaska was a country of superlatives. Everything was on a larger scale than anywhere else: ninety-pound cabbages, for example. The majority of the people were Indian, but no one really lived in igloos. The only one I saw was in Anchorage and had been built by Boy Scouts so that tourists with bulging wallets would not be disappointed.

Each day I waited at the airport . . . in vain. Promises were broken,one after another: Little Diomede in the Bering Strait, five miles from its Russian twin; a bear hunt at the North Pole; even Bethel, which was where Liz came from. Liz was a pretty girl with a round, sweet face, almond eyes and wide cheekbones. With her long, fine black hair, she looked beautiful dressed in a squirrel parka and sealskin mukluks decorated with coloured beads.

I made friends with some Vista Volunteers who insisted on introducing me to another Frenchman. Why not? We could always reminisce about home, and the exchange of a few banalities would hardly create any obligation.

The guy showed up looking quite elegant with a camera slung over his shoulder, but as he removed his hat and dark glasses I was struck speechless. Indeed, the astonishment was mutual, for Michel Villon was an old friend from Brunoy. Like me he had itchy feet, and had once gone from Paris to Jerusalem on a motor scooter. Now he packed me into a big shiny car filled with gadgets and whisked me off to his home where he fixed a gala dinner washed down with champagne. He had been a cook at the Westward Hotel for the past six months, and I was afraid that his trip around the world must be ending right there. He had fallen into the classic trap of money: a job to earn it and a girl-friend - I would almost say - to spend it. There is no doubt about it. For someone with the urge to travel, falling in love can be a danger.

'Your trip around the world is all very nice, of course. But young man,what about your trip to eternity? It's the great journey towards our Good Lord that counts. Personally, I know where I am going after I die. Can you say as much?'

'You're very lucky, Ma'am!'

What else could I say to a charming old lady who had just served me with a succulent mushroom soup at the end of a long, trying day hitching through a gale? It wasn't the first time that I had listened to a short sermon in exchange for a bowl of soup. I was not against the idea, and the homilies of this good-hearted woman on the subject of the First Assembly Church of Kenai were not entirely missing their mark. It was simply that, in the light of all these years spent in Europe, in Africa and on the roads of the two Americas, I had come to believe that such questions, fundamental though they were, could not be resolved by any one group claiming to have a monopoly on the truth.

'Jesus Christ, our Saviour . . .'

It was one sermon after another. By chance I had met a pastor of the First Church of Christ, and the dear man had offered me his son's bed to sleep in, since he was in Vietnam. The first day I endured the ordeal with good humour. After all, I was imposing on them and listening was a way of repaying my debt. But alas, during the three days that I stayed in that little town of Valdez (nicknamed the Switzerland of Alaska), every movement, every mouthful was seasoned with a 'Jesus Christ, our Saviour'. In the end I was unable to stomach it. The pastor's wife, Mrs Cousart, was continually preaching at me and gave me a small book which tore Roman Catholicism to shreds. She wanted me to stay on with them, perhaps in the hope of converting me. Grace before each meal, Bible study and prayers for dessert: it was hell.

'André, you missed the service yesterday. That's not good. And what's more, I don't like the people you associate with. The Van Brunts, especially, are not for you. They are Bahá'ís. That's a funny religion, so steer clear of them!'

I had met Don Van Brunt at Copper Centre, an Indian village.

'If you happen to pass through Valdez, come and have dinner with us.'

What hitch-hiker would refuse such an invitation?

I liked the Van Brunts. They welcomed me naturally, without formality. Their inner peace and calm intrigued and pleased me. We talked about travel and about Paris which they knew well. One evening before leaving I ventured a question about their 'funny' religion:

'We are working for unity in the world.'

They didn't say anything more.

I continued on my way southward, parallel with the Pacific coast and criss-crossing the narrow strip of Alaska so aptly called the Panhandle.

Ketchikan was a small fishing port into whose harbour an occasional curious whale would venture. The area was inhabited mainly by Indians. In front of their small houses stood imposing sixty-foot totem poles carved out of cedar trunks from the nearby forest.

My first stop was at the Salvation Army. Unfortunately, I arrived too late. The building had just been destroyed by a fire; the charred ceiling beams were still smoking. Across the street in the City Hall, the welcome matched the climate. The secretary refused to let me see the mayor and wouldn't hear of my dossing on the floor. Just at that moment a quiet young man who had been working nearby came over to me.

'Wait for me outside. I'll be right out.'

Fred and Sherane welcomed me like a brother, and I shall never forget them. I was a guest of honour, yet I felt completely at home. Fred lent me his car and acted as my guide. When I was ready to leave, they gave me a present accompanied by these words:

'Thank you for coming to see us, André. Thank you for accepting our hospitality. It made us so happy. Come back whenever you like. Our house will always be open to you.'

In the package they had handed me, I found an inscribed postcard of Ketchikan, some cheese and a bottle of rosé wine from California. How thoughtful! 'Thank you for coming to see us.' I will never forget those words. Never.

'In the garden of thy heart plant naught but the rose of Love . . . The earth is but one country, and mankind its citizens . . . Let not man glory in this that he loveth his country, let him rather glory in this that he loveth his kind . . . Of one tree are all ye the fruit, and of one bough the leaves . . . Man must be a lover of the light no matter from what dayspring it may appear . . . the strife between religions, nations and races arises from misunderstanding.'

For the first time ever, the most inaccessible, most sensitive chord within me had been struck. I read and reread those words of Bahá'u'lláh, the founder of the Bahá'í Faith, and they resounded like music that until this moment had gone unheard. A pure joy overwhelmed me. A secret fire had been kindled in the very depths of my soul.

I had first glimpsed the book at Fred's, had bought a copy and read it in a single session.* It had been a revelation. In the dead of the Alaskan winter, after fourteen years of what I now recognized as a quest, a bright and burning flame was lighting my path and shaping a single itinerary out of the many roads I had travelled.

Suddenly the pieces of the jigsaw were falling into place. The men and women, black and white, that I had met along the way were all inhabitants of the same earth, the same country. Separated, isolated, they were like the thousand pieces of a puzzle, devoid of any significance. Brought together the assembled pieces took on a single shape, radiating a clear, crystalline beauty.

Every religion claimed to hold a monopoly on truth, the exclusive right to exploit the Divine Word. Each one accused the others of being

Bahá'u'lláh and the New Era by J.E. Esslemont (Bahá'í Publishing Trust: 415 Linden Avenue, Wilmette, Illinois 60091, USA and 6 Mount Pleasant, Oakham, Leistershire, England.

infidel, heretical. Today, throughout the world, there were as many
Christians or Buddhists as there were Muslims, and certain pagodas or
mosques were every bit as wonderful as the cathedrals of the West. It was
hard not to admit that a single, unique force animated these hundreds of
millions of beings. 'A *sincere study of these different religions of the world
shows that, under different names and terms, their truth is essentially one.*'
The fervour of Muslims, their foreheads touching the ground as they
prayed in the streets of Niamey, Niger, had strongly impressed me at the
time of my return from the Congo. That memory now resurfaced in my
mind . . .

Not only did I know that I was pursuing my own way, but I would
also feel from now on that I was following the right path, the only one
that held true meaning. The more I encountered different varieties of
men separated from each other by religion, lifestyle or custom, the more I
understood, the more I was going to understand, the teachings of
Bahá'u'lláh. '*It is clear seeing and free thinking, not servile credulity, that will
enable them [people] to penetrate the clouds of prejudice, to shake off the fetters
of blind imitation, and attain to the realization of the truth of a new Revelation*'
(J.E. Esslemont, *Bahá'u'lláh and the New Era*, p 71).

The man had both hands clamped on to the steering wheel and jerked it
back and forth in a totally useless manoeuvre. His head wobbled, his
eyelids dropped, and his eyes seemed barely to be focusing. He looked on
the verge of collapsing, nose to the horn. The car reeked of alcohol, and
his incoherent mumblings were punctuated with loud belches. I gripped
my seat, the door handle, the dashboard. I no longer knew how to steady
myself. He would slump on the brakes, sending the car into a tailspin on
the black ice, and then accelerate violently. How was it going to end? My
eyes danced back and forth between the speedometer - where the needle
was flirting with the hundred-mile-an-hour mark - and the icy road on
which we were zigzagging dangerously. Fortunately at sunrise there was
almost no one on the road.

I am convinced that hitch-hikers run a much greater risk than
drivers. Only a week earlier, in Haines, I had ridden with a raving
maniac. This time it was a drunkard pickled to the gills.

'Here, I'll drive a while. We can take turns. After all, it's only
sensible to share the strain of driving.'

Phew! He agreed to let me drive, turning his attention to polishing
off a bottle of whisky, some of which dribbled down his shirt front. He had
a habit of sliding down on the seat; I kept having to shove him back up.

Damn, I couldn't help skidding either.

'You're a real idiot. Give me back this jalopy. It's not made for little punks like you. Give me the wheel, I tell you.'

It was snowing heavily. I was the innocent victim of a madman who passed every vehicle in sight, spitting out streams of invective. Twice we skidded violently on the ice. What could I do? I was stuck. Get out? It was impossible in this weather. I would catch pneumonia with my so-called parka that absorbed the tiniest snowflake! I could only hope that he would make it to Guesnel, the next village, where I would at least find shelter.

Seven miles further and an hour later, having drunk a cup of coffee in Guesnel and found another lift, I noticed the blue flashing lights of an ambulance and heard the siren of a police car. A group of curious bystanders forced us to slow down. My nose pressed against the steamed-up window, I recognized my drunkard's station wagon. I could barely make it out, but the car appeared to be on its side, twisted around a pylon in the middle of a field on the opposite side of the road.

Chapter 6

I'LL NEVER SEE JACKIE AGAIN

'André, why don't you take a hot shower?'

The words had an odd, familiar ring. I had heard them somewhere before. A few days earlier, a guy had picked me up along the road and when we arrived at my destination he had invited me over to his place for a drink.

'Why don't you take a hot shower?'

Mechanically, I had refused. It had not been the right time of day for 'ablutions'. With a touch of humour I had added:

'No, thanks. You know, I'm like the hippies. I never wash'.

My previously friendly and obliging driver, feeling no urge to laugh, had actually scowled in displeasure - and to such an extent that he had practically thrown me out of the apartment on the spot. At the time I had not made the connection between the idea of a 'hot shower' and my precipitate departure . . .

'Excuse me?'

'I was saying that if you wanted to take a hot shower . . .'

Dressed in a sumptuous bathrobe of transparent silk, undeniably perfumed and holding a glass of red wine, Daniel had just welcomed me into his pleasant apartment on Greenwich Street. The place was decorated with subtle good taste; each object was displayed with meticulous precision. Daniel's three rooms opened on to a terrace on the top floor of an old building which looked out over San Francisco Bay. The view was fantastic. Daniel had served as my guide all day, along with Michel, a painter, and had invited me to stay with him for as long as I liked.

The soft music of a zither filled the room. Daniel was already stoned and was automatically rolling a joint for me.

'Daniel, I've been delighted with my first day in San Francisco, but if you'll excuse me, all the walking has worn me out. I'd just like to brush my teeth and lie down. I can hardly feel my legs any more.'

Leaving the bathroom to return to the living room where a stylish sofa awaited me, I passed by Daniel's room. The door was wide open; he was reclining on the bed. His pose was surprising, to say the least. With a wave of the hand, I mumbled a vague 'g'night'.

'Andrééé . . .'

I came back towards the door. His voice was unnaturally suave.

'André, I'm disappointed . . .'

'Oh? Why?'

'I admit that I thought the two of us . . . uh . . . I would like to spend the night with you. But I get the idea that you're not too interested. Am I right? It's not your scene?'

In place of the 'hot shower', I felt as if I'd been doused with a bucket of ice water. All of a sudden I understood Michel's undulating stride, the dimly-lit restaurant, their shared indifference to the beautiful Californian girls.

I lay down on my bed fully dressed. But either from fear of a surprise intrusion or from the after-effects of shock - I am not sure which - I was unable to sleep.

In Richmond the door at John and Deon's was always open. Gently, calmly, they welcomed me as if we had always known each other. Deon was pregnant but did not seem to regard my presence as an imposition.

'You are most welcome. We're delighted to have you here', she said.

John and Deon were trying to put into practice the two great hippy principles of peace and love. I immediately felt at home, and we all got along marvellously well. Two days later, Jim and Lee joined our group and made manifest their respect for the famous slogan, 'Make love, not war'. Even with the necessary intentions, it would have been impossible for them to wage war due to a simple lack of time: they never got up off the spare mattress!

The apartment was simple and inviting. Friends and strangers, all sharing a similar outlook, dropped in constantly. Seeking human kindness or wanting advice, they took comfort in the presence of John and Deon who were always ready to give of their time and friendship or, at the very least, to offer a cup of coffee. On the carpet were laid out a row of sleeping bags, one of which was mine.

'John, aren't you afraid that some of your things will get swiped? Like your stereo or your books? People parade through all the time. You seldom even know who's sleeping here.'

'You know, André, somebody "borrowing" something may well have a greater need for it than I do, and most likely he will make better use of it.'

The walls were covered with paper flowers and posters, arty or humorous. Books were piled in every corner. Light from coloured bulbs mingled with the rock music which filled every room to create the characteristic mood of well-being. In the hallway near the entrance, a sign asked visitors not to 'smoke'.

'For more than a year we tried just about everything', John explained. 'Marijuana, LSD, acid. But now that we've finally found what we were looking for, drugs no longer hold any attraction.'

The birth of the 'hip' movement in the USA was not a mere accident. The first hippies to settle in Haight Ashbury came from well-to-do families. The age of immigrants and pioneers, of the daily struggle to make a home or build a fortune, was long gone. People had begun questioning their own roles in a society of opulence and waste. The hippies were not outcasts ejected from the great 'Made in USA' machine. Rather the movement can be considered as a natural phenomenon, a sort of safety valve which might, for a while, head off the dangerous over-consumption feared by many today.

Materialism, carried to extremes, could no longer satisfy them. They wanted to break out of the vicious circle of production and consumption, and go back to man's roots to find there the life that they lacked. They dropped out of the mainstream of society and attempted to put into practice Christ's words about love. They were inspired by the first Christian communities, but also by the gurus of India and by the earlier beatnik movement. A few outward signs served both to identify and unite them: flowers, sandalwood necklaces, the smell of incense. Perceptive and sensitive, they picked up on the 'vibrations' of universality and unity radiating across the world over the last century.

Thousands of young people rushed to California and founded numerous communities where happiness seemed to reign. At first, the children of non-violence and planetary brotherhood were well received. Their ideals of love, even if prompting some indulgent smiles, made people stop and think. The movement spread rapidly throughout the country, but unfortunately the enthusiasm of those young people, pure and confident by nature, soon got out of control. Little by little the principles got swallowed up in the new fashion of letting it all hang out. From the cult of individual liberty, which was becoming ever more exaggerated, a variety of abuses were born.

The use of drugs, which at first had been treated as a new experience or a path to self-knowledge, degenerated into a relentless habit fuelled by the desire to go ever further. The taste for experimentation pushed curiosity to the level of genuine risk. In Haight Ashbury young delinquents, who had never been exposed to the original ideals, took over centre stage, relegating the flower children to the periphery. The pipes and tambourines disappeared from Golden Gate Park, and Hippy Hill was no longer the paradise where young dreamers could watch the flight of the seagulls or gaze at the beauty of bare-breasted girls lying on the grass, offering themselves to the California sun.

When the Hell's Angels' motor bikes roared through the streets of Haight Ashbury, rattling the windows of the psychedelic shops which were closing down one after another, violence had appeared on the scene. At the time of my visit (April-May, 1969), drugs had become a scourge. People who didn't use them were looked down on. The more potent the drug, the more devastating the 'kick', the more the user gained respect. Soon everything was good for kicks: breathing fumes from exhaust pipes or smoke from ovens, sniffing heated glue or acids of all kinds. But drugs - the initial effects of LSD, for example, last twelve hours - exacerbate feelings of anxiety along with those of well-being. Disturbed by increasing sensations of fear, the user has nothing else to turn to except more drugs, and thus becomes all the more ensnared. To the relief of much of America, the great 'hip' movement was dying out. It had been an outburst which had threatened the tranquillity of those people who preferred their fellow countrymen not to think too much. Drugs did a lot of harm to American youth, but even more harm was done by the new image being spread throughout the land. Those who had given up everything in order to breathe more freely were now being stifled.

The movement was on its last legs, but John and Deon never lost hope. They took me to listen to Steve, who spoke every Monday night in the antiquated hall of the Ashbury theatre to two or three hundred young people - Blacks, Whites and Asians dressed in bright, showy, always unexpected attire. Steve talked about God, love, non-violence, and also about drugs. How I had changed! In Toronto I had distrusted and belittled, even feared, the hippies concentrated in the neighbourhood where I had gone to teach French. Now here I was among them, without fear or second thoughts, trying to understand them.

At the end of the talk everyone embraced and chatted, arms linked fraternally or thrown around each other's shoulders. Then they formed a circle, chanting in unison as each one gently swayed his head and then his body. When the entire circle was moving as a single unit, each person breathed in deep fulfilment.

'You can't get lost when you don't know where you're going', whispered my neighbour, visibly happy to have communicated this message to me.

On our way home, I noticed that John had a slight limp.

'It's an awful story, André. It happened very near here. My wife and I were taking a walk with some friends of ours, a black couple. Suddenly a car stopped alongside us. Two white guys got out, grabbed our friends and stabbed them. They must have been on a bad trip, freaking out on acid. Our friends died almost immediately, right here in front of this shop, on this pavement. When I tried to defend them, the men stabbed me as well and left me bleeding on the side of the road. I had my liver and colon damaged and lost a kidney.'

With tears in his eyes, John spoke calmly, without any sign of bitterness. He said nothing more about his aggressors. On the knee of his blue jeans a patch decorated with daisies hid the hole torn by the knife. However, there was no way for him to undo the wound in his knee. He would be lame for life.

In silence, we paused for a moment. Then John proposed that we go on to Point Lobos, where I often went to breathe the invigorating sea air. It was night time, and the cries of the thousands of seals who spent their life slumped on tiny islets had ceased. We talked about my trip, and on returning to the house John said, 'There's nothing more I can wish for you, because you're really "living" already. I think that real life inside society today is no longer possible.'

In Marin County, on the other side of the bay, spring with all its greenery had arrived. Dwarfed by the gigantic arch of the Golden Gate Bridge, enormous ocean liners passed underneath looking like humble fishing boats. But America was like that; everything was on a grander scale. A modest country road was as wide as one of our highways back in France, and a minor stream quickly took on the aspects of a major river. The ocean wind was sweeping across the waves, whipping them up into foam. I loved to watch it; that was why I had taken up my position at the entrance to the Golden Gate Bridge.

Michel and his huge Oldsmobile jerked me from my reverie. Michel's only aim was to spend his entire day in the sun. He ran on LSD, and his euphoric look was a sure sign that he'd had his daily ration. As he drove around, he had come across other uplifted thumbs and had taken their owners on board. Two of the hitch-hikers, a girl and a boy, were visibly tripping on acid. And then there was Jackie, seated up front next to me. Jackie's head was tilted upwards and her eyes stayed fixed on the ceiling as we swayed gently back and forth with the motion of the car. She was rather pretty and appeared very young. I would have said about twenty, maybe twenty-two. Her thighs, her bare arms, her skin looked almost like those of a child, but her face looked older. Her features and what little I could see of her eyes made me suspect she might be ill.

A marijuana joint was passing from mouth to mouth. There was nothing shocking in that here, where the opposite would have been more surprising. The views from the car windows were beautiful, ever blossoming and boundless, but my eyes kept coming back to Jackie. Abundant brown locks of hair hid her from me, and her indifference towards me, towards the others, towards her surroundings intrigued me more with every passing second. I wondered if she, too, might be in the middle of a 'trip' like the others, but I immediately rejected the idea. Jackie was so pretty and seemed to have everything going for her.

At Point Reyes we walked along the beach. On one side there was the deafening crash of surf breaking on the sand; on the other there was the forest, a green refuge from the wind and clamour of the Pacific. Leaning against a tree trunk, I let my eyes follow the swell of the enormous waves. Jackie had come over to me. Melting her sad eyes into mine, she rested her head on my shoulder. Without thinking, I took her hand and with that gesture discovered the hopelessness of her situation. Disgust and pity wrenched at my heart for her wrists were pitted and scarred with a thousand small brown marks. Puffed and bruised, they bore the signs of a slow death. Jackie was a heroin addict. I was completely overwhelmed by my discovery.

As the sun set she was still there, leaning against me. I hadn't let go of her hand. I could not find it in my heart to push her away. I had even decided to try to help her. She yawned more and more frequently and often touched her stomach. Suddenly her hand tightened in mine.

Gently, she raised her eyes and murmured without looking at me, 'Please, don't leave me alone'.

Michel had understood and signalled our departure. Once back in town,behind Buena Vista Park at the end of the black ghetto, he stopped. Jackie got out and walked rapidly away.

'You get it?' said Michel. 'This one is serious, not for laughs. It's heroin, the real stuff.'

When Jackie returned, she was like an automaton. She sat down mechanically and seemed on edge. She explained that she hadn't been able to find her usual contact, but only some bastard who had taken advantage of the situation and demanded double the price. She had paid ten dollars for a tiny pouch that she now slipped into her mouth, ready to swallow it if we met a policeman.

Michel dropped us off - Jackie and me - in North Beach near Broadway, the most disreputable street in the city, at the corner of Greenwich Street and Jones Street. I decided to accompany Jackie home and to give myself two or three days to see if I might be able to do something for this girl who looked as lifeless as a rag doll, scrambling up the stairway to her room in a flophouse. The room was narrow and dark. In the dim light given off by a single red-painted light bulb hanging from the ceiling, I looked about me. A broken-down, unmade bed with dirty sheets, a chair, a white wood table: everything seemed to give off the stench of despair. A few crumpled garments lay untidily on the floor.

Jackie threw her sheepskin coat on the bed. Already she held in her hand the small rubber pouch, still glistening with saliva. Opening it, she poured the fine white powder into a teaspoon, then picked up an eye-dropper to draw water out of a dirty glass that had been lying under the table. Frantic with agitation, she tipped the contents of her handbag on to the threadbare carpet and rummaged about for a match. Then, with a mechanical gesture, she passed the flame under the spoon.

My presence obviously troubled her. She was losing time and her agitation was increasing. What was she looking for on the dusty floor? She had found a filthy piece of cotton wool. Pushing a syringe through the cotton, she filled it with the awful concoction. Then, ready at last, she sat down on the bed, rolled up her sleeve and bound her arm with a rubber tube, one end of which she clenched in her teeth. Her veins bulged, and her skin looked even bluer and more bruised. With a sudden gesture she attempted to pierce a vein which disappeared as the needle twisted askew. I was both repelled and fascinated. She was certainly in pain yet continued to plunge the needle angrily into her sickly flesh.

'I usually get it in one . . .'

It was awful. Motionless, tense, I scrutinized her face, which all of a sudden lit up. Blood flowed into the syringe . . .

For fourteen months she had been sliding towards annihilation.

'I realize what I'm doing to myself, but I can't help it. I knew I risked getting hooked fast, but somehow I thought I'd be stronger.'

For much of the night we were visited by a variety of callers - strange people to say the least. They were all more or less 'high' and had come there because Jackie was gentle and knew how to listen with a smile. Among them were a dealer in heroin and a gun maniac who never stopped playing with his revolver. Bewildered by this encounter with the dregs of society, I wondered if along my way I would ever meet worse. At seven o'clock the following morning, Jackie got up slowly and slipped on a sweater and a miniskirt. That was all.

'Where are you going?'

'I need dope. I need heroin. I can't store it here. It's too dangerous. I have to go out every time. Wait for me. I'll be right back.'

We spent the next day in Muir Woods in a forest of 300-foot sequoia pines. Affected by the atmosphere and also by the harmony existing between us, Jackie had been able to hold back for a few hours. However, as soon as we returned to her room, her first move was to shoot up.

The plunger in the syringe slowly pushed the poison into her vein. As I watched, Jackie untied the rubber strap and her eyes came back to life. Suddenly there was a heavy thumping on the unlocked door. She barely had time to hide the syringe before a man was standing in the doorway. His face unshaven and heavy with sweat, he made a grimace. He didn't look like a cop. Reassured, Jackie motioned him to come in. For a few long seconds he stood motionless, slightly hunched over, out of breath, holding the door handle in one hand and hanging on to the door frame with the other. Jackie seemed to know him. He was probably one of the multitude of night visitors.

'I've just killed a sailor. The fool tried to defend himself. I must have fired four times. And God damn it, he only had thirty-five dollars on him . . . I thought he had 800. The cops are after me . . .'

Jackie tried to comfort him. She told him how unlucky he was, how the bad things always happened to the same people, but that she could probably help him escape. Her 'friend' with the itchy trigger finger had just noticed me. On the other hand, I had had my eyes on his gun ever since he'd arrived. Opting for discretion, I mumbled with a slightly constricted voice words like, 'Well, I think I'll be leaving you two now . . .'

Once outside, I regretted my cowardice. Maybe Jackie was in danger. I went to see her brother who refused to have anything to do with her 'as long as she messes around with that shit'. Around noon the following day, I ran into her again. She was adorable, in great shape.

'You see', she said, 'the fact that I can go out with a guy like you proves there's still hope for me. André, I like being with you. Promise you won't leave me . . .'

'Just listen to me, Jackie. I'm the last person to take an interest in you. If from now on you don't make an effort to get out of the mess you're in, you're done for. Finished, you understand?'

I took her hand. Her wrist was swollen; she had just shot up again and had done it badly.

'Jackie, promise me you'll try methadone.'

'Okay, I'll give it a try. But you know, I'll have to go to the hospital for that. They won't keep me more than a week, and a week isn't enough. The last time I left the hospital, I think I slipped down one step further . . . Anyway, never mind, let's not think about it any more.'

For the next three days, I hardly saw her. I wanted to keep my distance a little, having no desire to get mixed up in some drug scandal. Once a day, I dropped by to see how she was, but there was no one home. On the third day I finally found her. It was almost time for her fix, and I realized she wouldn't talk much until she had finished . . .

'On Monday night, three guys jumped me in the ghetto and dragged me into some room. The bastards raped me . . . sons of bitches! You'd think at least they would have given me back my coat. But wait, that's not all. I was hitching last night when a plain-clothes cop picked me up. After a few minutes, he caught sight of my arms, and announced that he was going to book me for forty-eight hours. You can guess the rest. Going to jail once was enough for me. He took me to one of those pleasure boats in the harbour. At least he brought me home in the morning. Actually, I might just as well have stayed, since my pusher had given me sugar again instead of dope. What could I do? I went back to the ghetto.'

I had now known her for several days, but was still unable to get used to her way of looking at things, and especially her way of putting up with them. She almost seemed to have worked consciously at reaching such a state of depravity. She spoke of it as naturally as if she had spent all her life striving for this moral decay. At this point in her recital of the events of the past seventy-two hours, I tried to intervene. I wanted to make her admit that it was all ludicrous and that with a little courage she could still get herself out.

'Don't waste your breath, André. I think it's already too late. But then again, it might simply be a bad patch, an unlikely series of coincidences. Really, I haven't gone through a bad patch like this for quite some time. On Tuesday afternoon it all started up again at my dealer's place. There were three of us - him, me, and a sort of friend - when two guys with guns burst in. They tied up the other two and robbed them of $2,500, a whole week's profits. For keeping my mouth shut, I got $400 and a roll in the hay in a noisy motel nearby. To top it off, I came back home to find that my room had been burgled. Here, take a look . . .'

She took my hand and led me out along Broadway. Without thinking, I followed her. We went first to Gigi's, where she worked from time to time as a go-go girl. For twenty-five dollars she was expected to wriggle her body from six in the evening until two in the morning, naked, in front of a crowd of poor fellows who wouldn't notice that their drinks were being constantly replaced. They already had all the girls they needed for that night. Too bad. We wandered on to take a look at a new apartment located in a slightly better neighbourhood, but there was nobody around. In the ladies of a snack bar she shot up for the fourth time that day. I felt that she was out of my hands, and that from now on there was nothing I could do for her. In the black ghetto, our tram tore off the door of a car that was changing lanes recklessly. Jackie's attention was riveted on the three black occupants.

'You see those three guys? They're the ones who raped me the other night.'

That was the extent of her reaction. In truth, her self-respect was such that she no longer reacted at all. And all the time I was holding her hand - her poor, bruised and swollen hand - I felt that she was draining away my enthusiasm, my vitality.

'Jackie, we can't go on like this any longer. I'm going to have to leave. Won't you at least make an effort? Look, if you want, I'll take you to Tahiti but you know on what condition. No more heroin, ever. What do you say?'

She stared at me with her sad eyes. In vain I tried to find in them some kind of message, if only a silent cry for help, some shred of life or will-power. Nothing.

I would never see Jackie again.

Parowan, Utah. The sky hung low and a fine mist blurred the countryside into a uniform shade of grey. I had been waiting three-quarters of an hour alongside the shiny asphalt. Two lesbians had dropped me off in the middle of a barren landscape. I would have preferred a little shelter, yet I was glad in the end to have left the company of those two crazy women. It would have been ungrateful to complain.

In theory, I never hitch-hiked in the rain. I had soon learned that drivers didn't take pity on you. Quite the contrary: 'He's wet through already, he can just as well wait a little longer; I won't let him soak my car seat.' But for the moment I had no choice.

A pink Chevrolet pulled to a stop. The car's young occupants did not inspire much trust, but it was raining.

'Where are you going?' I asked.

'Oh, around . . . we don't really know.'

'You must surely know if you're going north or south. I'm heading for Salt Lake City.'

'Well, get in, we'll take you a bit further. But I warn you, we don't drive very fast.'

The driver was an unappealing young man of twenty or twenty-five. Next to him sat a young woman with a world-weary look. She was blond and vulgar. In the back next to me a man with long greasy hair, Elvis Presley sideburns and a short-sleeved sweatshirt, puffed on a cigarette. From time to time, the ash fell on to the baby sleeping in his lap.

The driver looked at me in the rear-view mirror.

'Say, buddy, we have some money problems. Like we haven't eaten for three days. If you can give us five bucks, we'll fill up with gas and everyone will be happy. What do you say?'

I had been expecting it. They had taken me for a real sucker.

'Listen, you guys, if I'm hitch-hiking it's because I don't have a dime. If you're out of gas, you can drop me off right here.'

'Hey, what do you take us for? We're not going to leave you like this. In Beaver there's at least a truck stop. We'll drop you off there.'

Beaver was in fact filled with huge container lorries. Unfortunately, no one would pick me up. After twenty minutes, the guy in the pink Chevrolet came over to me.

'You can stick with us. You won't do much better here. But first come and have a bite.'

Apparently he had found some money. His wife was holding two ten-dollar bills in her hand. We took to the road again, driving slowly.

The woman nervously surveyed every passing truck, following each one with her eyes.

Suddenly we stopped. A container lorry was parked on the other side of the road. The woman got out, crossed the highway and spoke briefly with the driver who had stopped for a snack. His mouth full, the man answered with a shake of his head and then took another bite of his club sandwich. The woman returned. When the baby started crying, she glanced at him vaguely and then took up her search once again. In front of us, a tanker was labouring along. As we passed it, the woman rolled down her window and hung half-way out. With her whole arm she signalled broadly to the driver. The car lurched to the right, forcing the truck to stop. It was downright dangerous! A few seconds later, she had hauled herself up, not without difficulty, to the level of the cab and was talking with the driver. Returning to our car, she leaned through the window.

'They've agreed, but only for five. It's not much!'

'Listen, the way things are we can hardly refuse. Five dollars each, that makes ten. It's better than nothing. Go ahead!'

This time the woman climbed into the cab. One of the two drivers pulled the curtains shut, while the other got out and smoked a cigarette behind the truck. Disgusted, I left them on the spot. A few seconds later I was picked up by a circus manager to whom I related my encounter with the travelling prostitute.

'Now I understand', said my new driver. 'I spotted that pink Chevrolet some time ago. So, the guy at the wheel is the pimp and his lady does the trick . . . How much does she charge?'

'In general, if I understood right, it's ten dollars for about five minutes.'

'Do you think that for twenty or thirty she'd agree to spend the night with me?'

'What!'

'You think she would? You know, she's not a bad-looking doll.'

There were days when I despaired of the human race. But I couldn't let that alter my determination to experience life to the full. I would surely have to plumb many depths if I wished, some day, to reach the heights.

Every day I wrote a few lines in my diary as an aid to memory. All I needed was some quiet corner to sit down in and a table to write on. Whenever I had a little extra time, peace and quiet, I liked to linger over a blank page. I would try to stand back, to get a different perspective. In the margin I would scribble a few drawings or paste a picture. I would reread my previous entries, often written in haste, and sometimes add to them a new reflection or two. In Los Angeles, at Gérard's house, the setting was perfect for this type of meditation. For hours on end, I sat alone gathering my thoughts and reaching new conclusions.

Gérard, a Frenchman, worked as a waiter at 'La Grange', one of the city's chic restaurants. He was not the best of all possible acquaintances; as a matter of fact, Gérard was not very interesting at all. He was like countless other Frenchmen throughout the world: a smooth talker and a womanizer. He was particularly obsessed with the latter, bringing home a different girl each night or sometimes even a pair of girls. However, when a hitcher arrives in an unknown city as vast as Los Angeles - which stretches on for miles and miles - any address is as precious as gold.

'Howdy! We've come to work here. Gérard has rented us his place for the day.'

I had been busy writing when a black man, stocky and muscular, arrived bristling with cameras and carrying two or three leather bags. Three girls and two other men were with him. Speechless, I watched the photo session unfold. It was unbelievable! Everyone stripped naked. One of the girls, a blonde, was fairly pretty, but the other two were almost repulsive with heavy thighs and flabby stomachs. The black guy snapped shot after shot. The flash, plugged into the wall, went off every five seconds. Soon they were ready to move on to group pictures. The blonde refused, claiming that she only posed for calendars, and then only alone. The photographer was unimpressed.

'Well, you could have stayed home, then. You didn't have any objections to pocketing twenty-five bucks. So, come on now, turn this way . . . yes, that's right . . . move your head a bit. Put some feeling into it! What a dumb broad! Hey, you two, wake up! Tickle yourselves; it's good for the close-ups!'

The whole affair was sordid and nauseating, but with the exception of the blonde and myself no one seemed at all disgusted. Even this had its routine! From time to time, one of the actors in this nightmare would come to the kitchen for a drink.

'You're a fool not to join in', one of the men told me. 'For ten dollars an hour, it's worth it. It brings home the bacon!'

California was also the beauty and grace of Eurina, a young black woman with whom I got along marvellously well. We were both oblivious to any

notions of race or skin colour. But California for me was first and foremost
a small apartment in San Francisco on Dolores Street. Some Bahá'ís had
invited me one evening to take part in their meeting. In a room with
simple and modern decor many people - individuals of diverse races and
backgrounds - had gathered. Immediately I felt the mood was positive, the
vibrations exceptionally strong. The group formed a unit with more than
usual cohesion. Travelling had gradually taught me to feel out other
beings and to perceive certain 'waves' more quickly and intensely. *'That*
which the Lord hath ordained as the sovereign remedy and mightiest instrument
for the healing of all the world is the union of all its peoples in one universal
Cause, one common Faith', wrote Bahá'u'lláh. I had before my eyes vivid
proof of the truth of his teachings. Seeing Blacks and Whites, Jews and
Christians, believers and atheists living together in harmony and
radiating visible happiness, I could no longer doubt the divine nature of
the message being transmitted to me by my Bahá'í friends.

A young Chinese was speaking: 'Jesus said to love one another.
Bahá'u'lláh tells us how to do it. He has not come to abolish Christ's
teachings, but rather to fulfil them.'

Everyone listened to him with unfailing attention, unusual
emotion. Seeing these people assembled here in a single faith made me
think back to the early Christian communities and their religious zeal.
The modern apartment had taken the place of the catacombs. Hearts
were open wide; I wanted to embrace them. I felt free. I was filled with
joy and felt certain that I had discovered the path of truth.

Hadn't history proved that the Holy Word was the most powerful
binding force among peoples? Swords and cannon had brought only
suffering and oppression; the Word had brought love and unity. Hadn't
Christianity triumphed unarmed over an all-powerful Roman Empire
proud of its brutal legions? And hadn't Muhammad unified endlessly
warring tribes with the breath of his revelation to create a civilization in
which caravans could trade in peace from Damascus to Cordoba, from
Cairo to Baghdad?

Today, nevertheless, the spirit of the teachings of Jesus and
Muhammad is rarely heeded. Their example of love is no longer getting
through. Over the years, their original message has been obscured with
dogmas and conflicting interpretations, so that it is very difficult for a
person seeking the truth to know where to turn or how to understand the
ancient Scriptures. Bahá'u'lláh says that it is for this reason that God has
'in every age and cycle . . . sent forth a divine Messenger to revive the
dispirited and despondent souls with the living waters of His utterance'. He

explains this phenomenon of spiritual renewal by saying that *'every age requireth a fresh measure of the light of God . . . Every age hath its own problem, and every soul its particular aspiration. The remedy the world needeth in its present-day afflictions can never be the same as that which a subsequent age may require.'*

Just as it would never occur to anyone to build a new house with old materials, so nobody can expect to build a new world with outmoded human beings. Bahá'u'lláh taught that humanity could, with love, create happiness on earth. The task is not to change society as a whole by applying this or that political principle or 'ism', but to change every individual, one after another. After all, a pyramid cannot be built from the top down. A better world depends on the will of every individual, and with the help of God such a world is possible. Only the transformation of individuals can result in the transformation of society; the two stages are indispensable to the realization of that Golden Age which we are all awaiting.

To help change mankind and society, Bahá'u'lláh addressed each of us individually, but he admonished nations as well. In our sick world, universal peace and social justice are ever more imperative. Our radically new conditions of life - ultra-rapid transportation and worldwide communications - no longer leave us any choice. The new technology has reduced the earth to a global village, to borrow MacLuhan's phrase, and only a world administration, with people whose sole concern is to promote the well-being of mankind, can push our tortured planet out of its rut.

The true revolution is yet to be accomplished, a revolution in our hearts and minds. Human happiness - and that is what it all comes down to - will be found by integrating our physical and spiritual natures. Today, thanks to Bahá'u'lláh's teachings, we possess the means to realize that harmony towards which he aspires. We simply have to understand that creature comforts, the harnessing of energy and the achievement of material progress are not in themselves sufficient.

During my trip around the world I met more smiling poor people that happy rich ones. Because of the imbalance between scientific progress, which has made huge strides, and spiritual development, which barely limps along, our century is one of instantaneous but ephemeral pleasure. The spiritual underdevelopment of the human race is the real reason for our unhappiness.

Incredible but true! I had landed a job as ship's boy aboard the *Thorsgaard* and would thus be hitching to Tahiti! Before the date of departure, set for June, I had several weeks in which to visit as many places as possible. In Los Angeles I went around the world twice - if briefly - thanks to Walt Disney and his Disneyland and then to the innumerable sets of the big movie companies whose studios were open to the public.

Luxury didn't interest me, but I didn't want to neglect any part of my education. It was my aim to have as complete a vision as possible of the world and its people. So, I traipsed around Beverly Hills on foot, an activity that approached the absurd in a city ruled by air-conditioned automobiles resembling miniature luxury liners. Every house was indeed a castle surrounded by a riot of trees, shrubs, flowers and fountains. The swimming pools were as immense and inviting as they were ubiquitous. Dazed by such a spread of wealth, I covered eight miles on foot without meeting a single pedestrian. It came to the point where I began to feel thoroughly out of place. Dependent on my two legs, I felt ridiculous and outmoded. I ended up hiding whenever I caught sight of a police patrol. On foot in such a neighbourhood, I could not help appearing suspicious.

The day I made the decision to leave Los Angeles, I made a second equally momentous decision. I wanted to hitch my way out of that monstrous city starting from the very centre of town, a project which presented considerable difficulties (in general, it is preferable to take a bus to the outskirts). I just wanted to see if it could be done. First, I spent a long time looking for the road to Las Vegas, no small matter. Then, within the framework of what was permissible, I waited. Hitch-hiking was technically illegal in forty-eight of the fifty states. Nevertheless it was tolerated under certain circumstances which varied from state to state. That fact meant I had to go to great lengths to find out what was acceptable in each new state.

In California I could not step beyond the road sign indicating the entrance to the freeway, and I had to be careful to keep both feet on the pavement. I waited from 9 a.m. to 6 p.m., time enough to get a good taste of carbon monoxide and California dust, and to attract the attention of an all-powerful cop on a motorcycle who gave me a ticket simply, he said, because he felt like it. I refused to pay and gave him a fake address in Canada. I became quite proud of that California ticket and kept it in my diary as a trophy, a kind of hitch-hiking diploma!

On the road to Las Vegas I was reluctant to sleep out in the open desert. The wind was strong and I didn't want to get my eyes and sleeping bag full of sand. And then, too, there was no way I would be able to talk my way around a snake or a scorpion. At the edge of a small town, I spotted a children's playground, and its green carpet of grass, so surprising in that part of the country, attracted my attention. With the complicity of darkness, I slipped into the playground, and made my bed on top of a big metal slide where I was hidden from view and would not be disturbed. Around four in the morning I was woken up by a steady, rhythmic puffing sound. The wind? I poked my head out of my sleeping bag, and received a spurt of cold water from an automatic sprinkler which had just started up. That green lawn! I should have guessed! I quickly slid down the slide to find refuge inside a giant hot dog. That didn't last long either, for the hot dog was perforated with holes through which came intermittent showers propelled from a second sprinkler. Soaked, I returned to the side of the road and waited for the kindly sun to rise and dry me out. Puffy-eyed and shivering with cold, I was still able to laugh at my latest misadventure.

Las Vegas: all night I wandered back and forth along the four-mile strip of neon-lit hotels and casinos. Men were killing each other in Vietnam and Indians were starving in the Andes; yet here they threw hundred-dollar bills right out of the windows amid the din of brass bands and the smoke of high-class cigars.

I was able to breathe again once I reached the Grand Canyon. Carved from the rock by the green Colorado river, the great gorge is a mile deep, ten miles wide, two hundred and twenty miles long. Nature is still the most beautiful sight in the world, and here in America it was also the most imposing. The phantasmagoria of colour, the thousands of peaks like fairytale castles and the strange lunar landscapes filled me with a desire to dance, to sing, to pray.

A night in a pine forest gave me a tremendous scare. Half asleep, I heard a scratching noise very close by. An armed marauder? Not at all. It was a coyote, come to sniff me out. My abrupt awakening had surprised him just as much as his presence was worrying me. A full moon was shining brightly. His open jaws revealed a mouthful of glistening teeth and his thick, furry tail waved almost imperceptibly. I could feel the tension in his body as he stood solidly planted on four sturdy legs. Motionless, we observed each other for several long minutes. From time to time the coyote would howl, and my heart would beat harder. Was he calling to his friends to join him? I didn't have so much as a twig to defend myself with. Aaaoooh . . .! Aaaoooh . . .! The mournful cry sent terror ringing through the pines and shivers tingling down my spine. Frozen with fear, I didn't make the slightest sound except, perhaps, for the chattering of my teeth. It was neither the first nor the last time that I would be frightened. I was emotional by nature, but I never let such sensations, even though frequently felt, alter my decisions or plans. Once the coyote had gone, I pulled my sleeping bag tight over my ears and slept as deeply as before the beast's intrusion.

And then the Rockies. Yellowstone Park had just opened its gates; patches of snow showed that winter was only very slowly slipping away. I had been riding with a Vietnam vet who used a heavy-calibre gun to take potshots at the billboards lining the road. Now I was being calmed down once again by the park's serenity and natural beauty. I got myself organized: a patch of snow would serve as a refrigerator - assuming that the park's predators did not have too keen a sense of smell - and the geysers would be perfect for heating up some of the canned food I had just bought. At a turn in one of the forest paths, I entered a clearing which opened up on to a plateau full of smoke and whistling steam. It brought back memories of old railway stations in France.

In Yellowstone the earth's crust is very thin. The magma, being close to the surface, finds its way out through thousands of openings. Old Faithful, named for the regularity of its performances every sixty-five minutes, was the park's main attraction. Invariably the geyser shot boiling water and steam 300 feet into the air for five minutes. Elsewhere, hot water from underground springs gushed and steamed, ejecting sulphurous or ferrous matter that created a beautiful palette of colours. I placed a can of ravioli in the Minerva fountain; one hour later my meal was ready. This is the life!

The nights were cold, so I slept in the heated lavatories.

'You're better off sleeping here', said one of the rangers who discovered my sleeping quarters in the morning. 'The bears are dangerous. They could kill you.'

With twelve miles of hiking each day, clean air and regular meals, everything was great. The only thing missing was a socket for my electric shaver. Leaving the park, I found a supermarket with a rotating rotisserie grill and decided to give the chickens a short break. Pulling out the plug, I took my shaver and used the stainless steel sides of the oven as a mirror. I must admit that the procedure was quite novel, but my efforts met with success. By the time staff and customers noticed what I was up to, I had already finished and quickly plugged in the rotisserie again and disappeared.

I had enough time left to consider a detour southward. I had a strong desire to see my friend Mex, to tell him my adventures and of my encounter with the Bahá'ís. Most of all I wanted to show him that his student had learned his lessons well.

In Chihuahua I did some train-hitching along with the poor inhabitants of the border region who, lacking both money and legal papers, travelled back and forth between the scorched earth of Mexico and the world of the Yankee. They taught me the skill and tactics of the *mojados*, the wetbacks, who swam across the Rio Grande by night and then walked for days before finding a ranch that would hire them. Frequently they were caught by the American border patrols as they emerged from the waters of the Rio Grande, hence their nickname.

In the slowly-plodding train overloaded with sundry goods, I shared the company of these *tramperos* and felt once again the allure of the Latin way of life. In my own way, I was every bit as comfortable as the *gringos* who passed us in their air-conditioned, first-class compartments. The journey seemed endless. At each stop one or two *tramperos* would jump out and run over to the closest shack to chop some wood in exchange for a tortilla and a few black beans. When the train got up steam again, they would run and leap aboard the already-moving wagons.

In Mexico City the cruellest of disappointments awaited me. I had made a 3,750-mile round trip for nothing. At a time when I was feeling on top of my form, I found in Mex a poor soul who was no longer interested in anything. The brilliant law student who had dreamed of becoming a champion of the poor was now little more than a lifeless shell. Mex had given himself over to drugs; he could think only of marijuana. We had nothing to say to each other. It was a bitter blow for me, almost a bereavement. I had lost my friend, my mentor.

Barely arrived and already terribly disheartened, I fled. Goodbye, Mex. You were a true friend.

Chapter 7

PIRATE, WATCH YOUR STEP!

For three hours I had been pounding steadily on a winch, trying to dislodge the rust and flaking, salt-corroded paint. The hammer was getting heavier and heavier, and my hand was so numb I could no longer stretch out my fingers. My arm ached and my muscles were stiff and tense - on the verge of cramp. Each passing second was marked by a blow of the hammer, by a flying chip. It was hot; I felt I needed a break.

'Hey, what are you doing? I see our *monsieur* isn't used to hard graft. Come on now, get back to work, you laggard. We'll make a sailor of you yet!'

I had six huge winches to do. If only they had given me a nice quiet job painting, it would have been easier to wrangle a break. Indeed, no one would even have noticed. But with this job, as soon as the hammering stopped, Boxy would come over and bawl me out. Boxy was a South African and bore a strong resemblance to Popeye. Actually, he wasn't a bad guy, and the ten or twelve others who made up the crew had also been very welcoming.

For two days now I'd been on the *Thorsgaard*, a Norwegian merchant ship transporting cargo and a dozen passengers to the islands of the South Pacific. I had signed a rather peculiar contract: it stipulated that in exchange for my work I would not receive any sort of remuneration. But by working aboard the freighter, I obtained free passage. That meant saving $380, equivalent to a whole year's living expenses, my average expenditure during my six-year world tour being a dollar a day.

We had left Los Angeles two days ago. By now the seagulls had abandoned our wake, and we seemed to be all alone on the vast Pacific. Despite the blisters swelling on the palms of my hands, I was in great shape. I felt intoxicated by the sea air, by the wind of liberty that blew freely across the world. When my eight-hour shift was over, I lay back on a deck chair, basking in the last rays of the sun and watching the amazing performance of hundreds of flying fish with their endless silvery leaps.

At supper time the crew assembled and, for the third time that day, resumed their quarrelling over eating habits. The Norwegians provided us with a sweet goat's cheese that looked like a bar of laundry soap, and fish shaped into little balls and every bit as sweet as the cheese. The East Indian from Samoa pushed away his plate and asked for rice. The American wanted bread to make a sandwich while I dreamt of salami and Camembert cheese. The Chinese from Singapore had found a solution: he had a small hotplate in his cabin on which he simmered long, transparent noodles. We were all a long way from home, and we all missed home cooking. Every man is conditioned to this, and instinctively seeks out familiar foods. To indulge such a desire, no matter how legitimate it might be, was totally impossible for me. French cuisine was unfortunately far beyond my slender budget.

There are hundreds of islands in the Pacific. Unable to visit them all, I decided to concentrate on Tahiti and some of the islets of French Polynesia. This seemed a logical choice: being French I would feel at home, for Tahiti played a part in every Frenchman's fantasies. Polynesian women, leis and shell necklaces, the warm and affectionate welcome: they were the very stuff of dreams.

'I'm sorry, but I cannot let you disembark if you don't have a round-trip ticket. Yes, sir, you must show a return ticket to Paris.'

'You're kidding! This is my country! We're part of France here. And first of all, where are the women with their leis?'

Tahiti did not want to encourage dreamers seeking the idle life, sunshine and fresh air. On the pretext of closing their doors to beachcombers, the authorities refused to let anyone disembark without making sure of two things: the traveller had to be wealthy, and he had to 'promise' to leave again.* My American tourist visa, valid for five years,

---

*Besides possessing a round-trip ticket, a traveller also had to show proof of sufficient funds. In general, one had to keep at least $350 (in 1969) in revenue in order to make a trip around the world - $350 that would never be spent but merely displayed at the various borders where such demands were made.

reassured the customs office henchmen that I could return to the US without any problem. Thus I was allowed to disembark, provided I left a deposit of $280 to cover the cost of a plane ticket to Los Angeles. Yet when I was ready to leave Tahiti, suddenly I became French and therefore subject to the local law - including a stipulation that prevented me from getting back the full amount. We're in the zone of the French franc. 'You can't exit with more than $180. The rest will be refunded in Pacific francs.' Worthless anywhere else!

On July 15th, 1969, I made a personal appearance in every hut in Polynesia, thanks to the French Radio and Television Service. It was the day after the national holiday and, since there was very little news, the local station put me on the screen for a quarter of an hour. The chance interview turned out to be a tremendous boon. Between two traveller's tales, I explained my problem. Tahiti was beautiful, but there was water everywhere. How could one hitch-hike round the eighty-odd islands of French Polynesia? Nevertheless it would be fascinating to see examples of all three types of islands: volcanic, coral, and volcanic-coral combined.

The newspapers spread my appeal, and the following morning the results exceeded all my expectations. In the streets of Papeete everyone recognized me, and offers came from all sides.

'Just tell me where you want to go and which day, and I'll have a boat ready for you.'

'No problem, we have room for you . . .'

'Your interview on television was very good. I agreed with everything you said. Ah, it's a beautiful world, *monsieur*. I have been waiting for you . . .'

'Come and see me at my office . . .'

That day I was the number-one topic of conversation in all the *fares* (houses) and cafés on the island. In the newspapers I shared the front page with the famous navigator Bernard Moitessier and the Queen of England . . .'

Christian, a sailor from the *Aunis*, recognized me and took me on board. The crew of the ship were glad to break the monotony and came to talk to me. Meanwhile, the cook cut me a magnificent sirloin and tossed it on the grill.

'God damn it, you guys! Look lively!'

It was too late, for the officer had already spotted us. He came over but did not seem angry.

'Relax, gentlemen. My dear Brugiroux, rest assured that you are most welcome on board and that you may come back whenever you wish.

Don't worry about the food either. We throw plenty of it overboard for the sharks; it might just as well go to you instead! Very good, this round-the-world trip of yours. It takes guts to do that sort of thing! Don't make us beg you to tell us more about your adventures. On TV last night it was all too short.'

The invitation had come at exactly the right moment. Life in Papeete was hopelessly expensive: three oranges cost a dollar! Inflation dated from the filming of 'Mutiny on the Bounty' when Marlon Brando wrecked the local economy with his dollars. Since then every visitor was assumed to be an 'American' and rich with it.

'Pirate, watch your step!'

Captain Oliver had seen me on television and received me with full honours aboard his ship, in his cabin and at his table. A great drinker, he also fancied himself as a great lover; he delighted in recounting his exploits, laughing loudly all the while. His mate on the *Meherio* was a chubby man nicknamed 'Chicken-fat' who never stopped telling jokes. With the help of the Chinese cook and a few sailors, they caught a 175-pound tuna and bludgeoned it to death on the deck amidst great commotion.

Maupiti, remote and hard to reach, was ringed by a coral atoll. The waves crashed against the reef which was unbroken except for a small gap. The *Meherio*, an old barge formerly used during war-time as a lighter, slipped through the passage with infinite care. A curtain of coconut trees along the coral reef still hid the island itself from view. I caught only a glimpse of the Protestant church whose white walls and red sheet-metal roof stood out against the sheer cliff.

The barge, loaded with breeze-blocks and shrubs, manoeuvred slowly, responding to the orders of Oliver who was slightly tipsy from the effects of *hinano*, the local beer. When we finally docked, the small jetty was swarming with happy, shouting children. I quickly realized that I was the principal attraction. The arrival of a *popaa* (white man) in Maupiti was a rare occurrence. Mr Varoo, a watermelon planter, decided to celebrate the event and gathered together several friends in my honour. As I refreshed myself with the inevitable *hinano*, he slipped a shell necklace over my head. He did not speak a word of French, but this made his welcome seem all the more touching. We immediately felt like old friends. Mrs Varoo grilled some red mullet that we ate with our fingers. Children came and crowned us with fragrant garlands of flowers, and at the end of the meal the grandmother brought some large, very sweet grapefruit found only on this island. Mr Dupont invited me to spend the night in his *fare*. When I was ready to leave, he dusted me with talcum powder and perfumed my neck in accordance with local custom.

'*Iorana*. Hello!'

Everyone was smiling. In the morning, the sun shone brightly; only the ocean breeze could temper its ardour. Two rows of modest wooden dwellings stretched along the edge of the lagoon at the bottom of a cliff. I spent all my time in bathing trunks.

One day I explored Maupiti on foot for two hours. I had to cut across the mountain through tangles of manioc, coconut palms and mango trees. Thousands of tiny crabs scuttled away at my approach and from time to time a coconut fell to the ground with a thud. Along the way I encountered a Maupitese harvesting copra. To help me quench my thirst, he split open a coconut. Its milk was delicious.

'*Maruuru*. Thank you.'

That was the extent of my vocabulary, but it was enough when combined with a warm heart. He pointed out the path to the *marae*, which were the island's primitive stone monuments, now in ruins. Later on, as I completed my tour of the island, I met another *popaa*, Alain. A physiotherapist from Nice, weary of civilization, he had found this remote corner of the world to make a new start in life. He arranged for us to meet later so that he could teach me about deep-sea diving.

With a steady, practiced motion, Etienne sent his light pirogue with its graceful outrigger gliding across the water. With us was his sister Mariela, whom Alain wanted to marry 'Tahitian-style'.

The lagoon was a fabulous world. The water was crystalline; the white sand diffused the sunlight and enhanced it. The coral reefs were veritable gardens of paradise with the most beautiful flowers I had ever seen. It was an exquisite sensation to feel my body floating in this world of silent beauty. White anemones and sea urchins with long black thorns swayed gently, animating the lacy coral with their graceful movements. Thousands of fish with unusual shapes and psychedelic colours passed back and forth, up and down, through light that seemed ever more dazzling. Red, orange, vivid yellow, phosphorescent blue, velvety black: gazing in awe, I almost forgot to breathe. Alain and Etienne were growing tired of harpooning. In the bottom of the pirogue, red and grey mullet, parrot fish and *carengue* flipped about in their final convulsions.

Mariela's mother, who had learned English at the time of the American occupation of Bora Bora during World War II, allowed her daughter to come and cook the catch in Alain's *fare*. Meanwhile, Alain went back to her house and asked her mother's permission to keep Mariela during the entire course of his stay. Tahitian-style marriage was just a matter of a few words.

'She's about as lifeless as a log', he told me the following morning, 'but she's an honest girl, and her skin is softer than I had ever imagined.'

It was now my turn to become the subject of gossip on the island. Why was this white man still a bachelor? What ridiculous convention could he be observing? Occasionally some respectable, matronly *mamae* would grab my arm and ask point-blank, 'You're not sick, are you *popaa*? Don't you want to try a Tahitian girl?'

I didn't have the heart to answer that, since Alain had taken the best one, the others did not appeal to me at all. Where were all the gorgeous, slender, dark-haired girls of the travel brochures? It seemed that they were actually Eurasian (of Chinese-European parentage) or mixed-blood, and not true-to-type Polynesians at all. Gauguin's paintings of Polynesian women, with their heavy features and thickset, well-rounded figures, are far more accurate. I wondered how Tahitian women, the famous *vahinés* of every Frenchman's dreams, could have acquired their reputation. After months and months at sea, the sailors of the Cook and Bougainville expeditions would have been ready to fall head over heels in love at the first sight of *any* woman. Moreover, coming from straight-laced Europe to these islands, where women were allowed a great deal of freedom, they must have felt they were in Paradise - and gave glowing accounts of their experiences on their return. *Voilà!*

With patience and the help of Alain, I was initiated into the mysteries of deep-sea diving and underwater harpooning. The lagoon swarmed with prey that was easy to catch. Nevertheless, it was preferable to be able to differentiate - beyond any doubt - between the edible and inedible species, as the latter were often very poisonous. I also had to learn to be careful of the coral which bristled with deadly spikes as sharp as razor blades. Under the sea beauty and danger were intimately entwined. The manta ray, which could measure as much as five feet across, looked graceful when sliding over the water or kicking up clouds of sand on the ocean floor. However, it was also capable of enveloping a diver once and for all.

I also learned to watch out for the powerful, streamlined sharks. Alain told me that on sighting one of these ash-grey yellow-edged fins, a diver had only to slap the water noisily and the shark would be frightened away. Nevertheless, it was still terrifying to glimpse those menacing jaws heading straight for me. Immediately I would beat the water violently, hoping to God that the trick would work. One elementary precaution was to pull a harpooned fish out of the water without delay. If one didn't, the blood might attract the sharks who paid regrettably little attention to detail. Having very poor eyesight, a shark might grab an arm or a leg instead of the dead fish or bloody spear which was its original target. I could not get used to the idea that I actually risked being eaten by one of these monsters, and each fishing trip was consequently also a time of apprehension. It was simply the price I had to pay to feed myself.

I grilled my catch over a charcoal fire along with pieces of breadfruit. My daily menu also included grapefruit, coconuts and an occasional can of corned beef bought from the Chinese. As a special treat, I sampled sea urchins, lobster, *parhuas* and winkles. The ocean was a good provider.

There were no cars on the island for the simple reason that there were no roads, and neither was there any electricity, running water, books - nothing. Maupiti was far removed from the world and the chaos of civilization.

I was often invited out. Roiti, Mr Dupont's gentle companion, taught me the secrets of the Tahitian oven, the *himaa*, that I had never heard about on my hotel management course. One day I took part in a genuine *tamaraa* (feast) prepared for some forty guests to celebrate a marriage. On a table covered with banana leaves were dishes of lobster, raw fish with lemon, tomatoes and onions, and papaya preserved in coconut milk. Then there were the culinary marvels of the Tahitian oven: sucking pig with vegetables, manioc, *taros*, *ourou*, breadfruit, bananas and sweet potatoes. Sweet and sour seasonings were freely combined.

I watched Roiti out of the corner of my eye. With consummate ease, she dug into each platter with both hands and invited me to do the same. To the soft background music of an accordion and a guitar, the guests grew mellower as glasses of beer and wine were emptied and replenished. When the adults got up from the table to dance, the children rushed to gobble up the leftovers intended as their meal. An empty barrel fitted out with a bamboo cane and nylon cord served as a double bass.

One beautiful day a motor boat came to the island to pick up two army recruits, and I hitched a ride with them. Thereafter I continued to island-hop wherever my luck might take me. From Bora Bora to Moorea, from

Raiatea to Huahine, I roved the seas of the Societé Archipelago. The southernmost islands were off limits because of the atomic bomb, and the Marquesas Islands were too distant. There remained the Tuamotou atolls.

An atoll resembled a white buoy floating on the surface of the water. The sand beaches, immaculate as icing sugar, and the emerald-green waters of the lagoons stood out clearly against the deep blue of the ocean. The palm trees, the flowers and the tranquillity were even more beautiful and impressive than elsewhere. The clean, cheerful villages surprised me with their Protestant churches, well-swept paths and low white walls. I felt small in this vast world of water, but I also felt very good, for it was a world based on kindness, naturalness and simplicity.

In Manihi, kids interrupted their playing to shout, 'a plane, a plane!' Nonchalant adults, curious nonetheless, quickened their pace. Everyone converged on the runway fashioned from crushed coral and tar. Tilting their heads upward they saw, for the first time in the history of their island, a twin-engine plane which circled to display itself to the best advantage. The *popaas* were taking over, building runways and jetties, installing generators . . .

Rangiroa was the largest atoll in the world. There the hours drifted sweetly by and I devoted a lot of time to my journal. In its pages I sketched the pink and white flowers of the frangipani, the wide, blood-red petals of the hibiscus, the fragrant *tiaré*, the bougainvillaea, the smooth-skinned papaya, the parasitic vanilla plant. I even sketched a plump *vahiné* doing her laundry and the crudely carved wooden divinity called a *tiki*.

Tenini, the son of the *Tavanaa* or village chief, taught me how to dive to depths of thirty feet, something I was not yet accustomed to. One morning he dragged me along without either spear or mask.

'Come on, we're going fishing!'

'What with? Don't tell me you're planning to fish with that ridiculous piece of wood!'

'Come on, you'll see for yourself.'

I followed him to a small fish trap that he had made for himself. With a piece of coral, he smashed the end of the stick before plunging it into the water. A milky liquid spread from the crushed wood and turned the water cloudy. A few minutes later, anaesthetized fish floated to the surface. All we had to do was pull them out of the water.

'You mangy old swine. Get the hell out of here, you filthy pig!!'

The high-pitched screams, followed by a string of obscenities that would turn a sailor's ears red, echoed clearly down the street. Mami Fatia was in the store belonging to the Chinese, and the man whom she had addressed so crudely had either insulted her or simply jostled her. It didn't matter which; Mami Fatia was never fussy about details.

'You know', she went on, 'thank God there were children present. Otherwise I would really have let fly, the bastard!'

I was unable to fish any more. I had stepped on a poisonous coral, and my foot was swollen and painful. Since I had difficulty in walking, I spent my time chatting with this truculent matron whose gossip was unbeatable. Past fifty, she lived alone in her *fare* situated in the middle of a courtyard surrounded by a low wall. Wandering hens occasionally deposited an egg in her yard, but more often she was visited by terrifyingly thin stray dogs. Tired of chasing them away, she had taken to fixing poisoned meat balls.

'The dirty brutes! They come and wreck my frangipanis. Whoever owns them should keep them under control.'

Mami Fatia told me all about the island, its inhabitants and their peculiar vocabulary: When a young man and woman eloped to a *motou* (small island) to hide out until their parents let them marry, that was called *tapouni*. When a young man surprised a girl at night, that was called *motoro*. *Motoro* seemed to be a particularly widespread custom.

In spite of her age and widowhood, Mami Fatia was very gay and girlish. She was planning to marry a poor, docile Chinese man who was only twenty-six.

'Why marry another old man? One like that was enough. And besides, I need somebody to look after my copra and coconuts. No, it's better to take them young and poor. The rich ones are too lazy to do anything at all . . .'

A native of the city of Papeete, she looked down on the *paumoutous* (inhabitants of an atoll), for she had learned how to talk to the *popaas* and did not like wasting time with just anybody. She adored french fries and fixed herself a greasy batch every day, which she devoured with gusto. Serving her community as a sorceress and healer, she grudgingly doled out a special ointment that she had concocted as a panacea for every minor ailment.

One morning she was in a fury as she marched over to see the *Tavanaa*. A young hooligan with a skinful of beer had been brazen enough to try *motoro* on her during the night. To defend her honour, she had had to smash her hurricane lamp over his head.

'They're just jealous because a *popaa* comes to visit' - she meant me - 'and because I like my Chinaman better than them. I'm going to complain to the *Motoi* (police officer). In my house everything is taboo. No one gets past the door. Even the old girl is taboo!'

That was dear Mami Fatia, who with her stubby yet nimble fingers could braid a *tiaré* necklace better than anyone.

To find a berth on a boat, all I had to do was hang around the port in Papeete and ask - in English since that was the mother tongue of most navigators - if there might be room for me. A Scotsman named Dick was en route from the British Isles to Australia by way of Panama and agreed to take me aboard as a cook. My ability to speak English and my status as a Frenchman made things easier, since the British liked to stick to their own language but did appreciate the culinary talents of the French. Actually, there wasn't a lot of cooking to be done on the *Reina Christina*, a thirty-five-foot sloop, and I made little use of what I had learned in college. My work consisted mainly of trying not to drench my feet when serving the coffee and securing the plates on the shelves before they could come tumbling down in heavy weather.

I was leaving Tahiti for good, having returned there for just long enough to find a passage out. I had revisited the black beach of Venus Point, Mount Diadem, and the cliff of Mahina, and I realized how different Tahitians were from other Polynesians. Papeete was an unpleasant city, featuring all the negative aspects of Western civilization whose damaging influence grew ever stronger on the 'big island'. As in other parts of the world, the *popaas* had destroyed the traditions and way of life of the local population. In the Tahiti of the past, the old and the sick were taken care of, and begging was as unknown as private ownership or the desire to work. Certainly, today, the girls were still around, children were still kings, every birth was systematically welcomed, and adoption was a common phenomenon; but the *popaas* had introduced the profit motive, driven out hospitality, and brought in the Chinese, originally to replace the naturally indolent Polynesians as workers on the sugar cane plantations. The Chinese soon put into practice their talent for business. Then bureaucracy and the military arrived . . . 'A *noa noa tiaré*, Tahiti . . .' That tune, strummed on an old guitar, was still lingering in my head. With a mechanical gesture I felt for the freshly picked *tiaré* that I had worn each day in my hair.

There were two means of transport that I didn't trust for a minute: the motor cycle and the sailing ship. It was on the latter that I found myself. Although I had been assured that the keel was loaded with lead which would automatically bring the mast back to an upright position in case of trouble, I was still thoroughly scared . . . yet again. Scared or not, however, I was determined to continue.

Another problem was seasickness. For the first three days I spent long hours hanging over the rails. Actually I didn't have much to throw up, as Dick was stingy and hid all the canned goods under his mattress. Vomiting on an empty stomach was worst of all and gave me a tremendous headache. My head throbbed so mercilessly that I couldn't even sleep a wink. Towards the end of the third day our captain had evidently had enough of seeing a member of his crew in such a state for he presented me with two small green pills. Their effect was instantaneous. I recovered my will to live. Mean old Dick had been hoping to stretch his supply of pills a little further. He was a true Scot!

After those first frightful days I felt fine. For hours on end I contemplated the lonely immensity of sea and sky, and I understood why some people sacrificed everything else to their love of sailing. Whether it was high in the mountains, in the heart of the jungle, or in the middle of a desert, the call of the wild drew people out of themselves, and towards their Creator. I loved nature, and solitude no longer frightened me. Yet, all things considered, I preferred the human heart for it was there, in that secret place, that I truly discovered the Beloved One. And it was in the presence of other people that I was beginning to feel I could serve Him best.

Dick, Richard and Dennis were my fellow sailors, and they took turns doing four-hour watches at the helm. Once I had finished wedging the dishes safely on to their shelves, I would join the others on deck for a chat. The 'vibrations' were good, and a genuine harmony reigned on board. Reclining on the varnished boards of the deck, we put the world to rights. We discussed everything from political problems, though social questions, to philosophical choices. Dick was forty-five and puffed endlessly on a pipe that seemed never to go out. Richard, the American, was twenty-five and barely out of college; he had not yet had time to make up his own mind about anything. Dennis had done a lot of travelling and gave me good advice about visiting India and Thailand.

There was no berth for me on board, so each night I bedded down with the ropes and sails in the front storeroom. I found myself a small niche in the prow where, bent double, I tried to sleep. My ear was pressed to the thin hull of the ship, and the sound of the waves was amplified - it was like spending the night inside a loudspeaker: quite a bizarre experience.

At dawn on the ninth day we were off the coast of Rarotonga, the main island of the Cook Archipelago. I happened to be at the helm and in my exuberance I doffed my hat to the captain who seemed to me a master navigator. Hitting the bull's eye after eight days on the open sea struck me as an incredible feat. But my unbounded enthusiasm proved to be my undoing, and I was forbidden to go any farther on the *Reina Christina*. Rather than feeling flattered, Dick had been insulted by my proclamation of a 'miracle'. Proud of his seamanship and of his status as a former naval officer, he was deeply hurt and furiously angry, and ordered me never to set foot on his boat again. That would teach me!

These islands were a long way from anywhere, and there was only a single link each month to the rest of the world in the form of a boat and plane going to New Zealand (the country responsible for the defence and foreign relations of the Cook Islands) on which all seats were booked weeks in advance. I refused to worry about my departure, however, for I was quite content where I was. In contrast to Papeete, the natives were very hospitable and quick to offer assistance and friendship. Even the customs officer did everything he could to help me. Another advantage, no less important, was that prices were only a quarter of those in Tahiti. As I walked about, the Polynesians greeted me like a neighbour and invited me to join them. They were worried in case I was lonely. One day a young man begged me to accept his bicycle, as he was afraid I might tire myself by walking. Ingenuous, simple, cheerful, comforting, these happy people touched me profoundly. Once again I dreamed of what the world could be if everyone would only make the effort . . .

The surroundings, too, were heaven on earth: perfect beauty and harmony. It did you good just to be there. The Minister of the Interior himself granted me a stay of three months without my even asking for it. I remembered the difficulties I had often had in the past trying to obtain visas. Here, I did not even intend to stay, yet had immediately been offered the opportunity to settle down for a while. Still, despite the inner peace and calm, a compelling urge pushed me onward. Although I was in Paradise, the inactivity weighed me down. I was a traveller, not a holiday-maker. Idle leisure wasn't my style.

By chance a plane from the New Zealand Air Force had made a forced landing on the golf course. Thus I had time to get to know the crew. Best of all, I was able to obtain a seat aboard the second Hercules which arrived the next day to rescue the first. Leaving the

Cook Islands on a Tuesday morning, I landed a few hours later at Whenuapai, the airport serving Auckland, New Zealand. It was Wednesday. I had crossed the International Date Line.

My first impressions were unfavourable. Auckland on October 1st, 1969, was decidedly ugly to behold. People frowned and fretted, jostling each other in their hurry. Nobody wore flowers in their hair, and grim expressions had replaced the smiles. Coming straight.from Paradise to the middle of 'civilization' was a rather rude awakening. At once I came face to face with all those things I had so easily forgotten: the noise, the carbon monoxide, the sick, dog-eat-dog competitiveness, the alarming news headlines. Stepping off the plane, it seemed to me that I had stepped on an anthill, or worse, a colony of cockroaches fleeing and scuttling through stinking drains. Auckland reminded me of Toronto; there was the same British-style architecture, the same feeling of a brand new country struggling for survival. In the Archipelagos, everything that was not a Pacific island was considered 'big country'. I had lost my taste for the big countries.

Standing barefoot on his doorstep, sporting long hair and a ring on his toe, Geoff asked no questions but simply offered me a place to stay. His room, bright with posters and paper flowers, the non-stop music, the smell of incense, all reminded me of San Francisco. From morning to night the loudspeakers blared out their rock music. Constantly stoned on the 'mary jane' he grew on his window sill, Geoff welcomed crowds of bizarre visitors, all more or less stoned themselves, and his companion Cherry brewed endless pots of tea.

His brother Paul was trying out a little white pill called Mendrex which effectively destroyed all physical co-ordination. Meanwhile, a tall girl wearing transparent trousers and a delicate purple heart on her forehead swayed slowly back and forth directly in front of me. After a quarter of an hour, she perched a big greenish-brown felt hat on her head and swayed her way out of the door. That was the last I saw of her. Most of the men wore earrings and their hair hung down to their waists. The girls also played out their fantasies, wearing huge, square glasses with purple lenses, granny-style dresses, torn sweaters, fringed jackets, faded jeans. The only thing they all had in common was their blank, totally vacant look.

On Sundays their colourful meetings broke the monotony of the traditional, deathly-boring British-style sabbath. Gathered on the manicured lawns of Albert Park, they talked, watched the clouds, listened to the guitars strumming soft, strange tunes or danced a wild conga. At the end of the day they grouped around a speaker who took up the favourite theme of flower power.

'Stop making war! We want to make love instead - and exactly when we feel like it, without the authorization of *your* laws. The system is corrupt, hypocritical. Legalize grass . . .'

In North America the movement had already gone astray, but that didn't prevent the new spirit from infecting youth everywhere. Some went to extremes, swept along by a movement they did not really understand. Nevertheless, I respected these young people who insisted on thinking and getting involved in the problems of war, injustice and racism.

'Pigs! Ho Chi Minh! Sieg Heil!' screamed the crowd.

The demonstration went on for three hours. Fights broke out, police dogs pounced and policemen clubbed. Caught in the crossfire (I had simply been following Geoff) I got pushed and knocked down. A cop in a torn uniform dragged me out of the mêlée by my leg, and I barely escaped taking a ride in the paddy wagon. As far back as the Kiwis could remember, there had never been such an incident in their peaceful country. The demonstration had been called to express the young people's opposition to sending New Zealand troops to Vietnam.

'This damned war has to be stopped', said Geoff. 'If they send our boys, they're only going to make the situation worse. And what's more, there's no way we're going to support imperialism.'

'I agree', I answered, 'but in my opinion you're acting in a totally negative way. You talk about peace, but you promote violence in Auckland, your own home town. In the end, all you're doing is starting a new war somewhere else. OK, there's a big black war cloud hanging over us all. Why add to it? I think you have to start by making peace within yourself, then with those around you. Then you can work on putting an end to war - in Vietnam and elsewhere.

'OK, but if we don't demonstrate, the politicians will just carry on with their filthy tricks . . .'

'I know', I responded, refusing to become discouraged. 'But nobody's forcing you to riot. Why react violently to police provocation? Politicians are hypocrites. They say they go to war so that we can all live in peace. I know they're wrong. But you can't beat them on their own ground. Stop playing their game. Be a true pacifist. Make peace with yourself first.'

Apart from Auckland, New Zealand was a good place to live. People there had remained human, and a visitor on foot received a friendly welcome whose warmth and spontaneity far exceeded mere politeness. As a hitch-hiker, I was never treated as an outcast or an oddity. I had no problems getting around, for in New Zealand hitch-hiking was considered a natural thing to do, and a man living in the wild was just as respected as any other.

At the time of my visit, apart from the Vietnam issue which unfortunately interested only a certain group of young people, the great national problem was that of the 'All Blacks' tour. The national rugby team was on its way to South Africa, and Pretoria was refusing to lodge the team's Maori member in the same hotel as his white team mates. A sport-mad country which made it a point of honour to defend one of its non-white sportsmen is a fine country.

Heaven on earth is not an impossible dream, says Bahá'u'lláh. All will become possible the day that love of our neighbour becomes as important to us as our own material well-being. New Zealand provided a foretaste of what heaven on earth could be like. The two ethnic groups - the Maori and the *Pakeha* (the whites) - lived together in harmony. Most people lived in private houses surrounded by gardens. Slums were unknown, pollution non-existent. Medical care was free and devoid of red tape; old people were not abandoned. There was work for everyone in decent conditions. Technology had been adapted to people's needs rather than, as too often happens elsewhere, the other way around.

New Zealand was a luxuriant garden in which the people had planted the most beautiful flowers and trees that the world had to offer and created lawns just about everywhere, replacing the indigenous grass. They did this in a natural setting which was already breathtakingly lovely. All the beauties of the world came together in its virgin beaches, deep fjords, volcanoes, snow-capped peaks, geysers, changeless lakes, gently rolling hills . . . I spent eight very happy weeks exploring this world in miniature. There was no exertion on my part: everyone helped me, put me up and showed me around even before I could state my wish. My feelings of wonder were as great as the beauty of the scenery perpetually changing before my eyes.

In Bluff, the southernmost city of New Zealand, I put my strength to the test. I wanted to make sure that the country's warm welcome, added to the lazy months spent in Polynesia, had not softened the tough physical shell that I had been gradually forging for myself. A violent wind was whipping the rain horizontally. Alas, I had no anorak, and my moccasins were taking in water. I was drenched and shivering from the cold in a no man's land that offered no shelter, not so much as a bush. Stoically I waited, buoyed up by my confidence and faith. The most important thing was to keep my self-control; I refused to fret about whether a car would stop for me, or whether I would find a place to sleep.

In South America, the latter question had plagued me every day, beginning at about three o'clock in the afternoon and spoiling a major part of my day. But eventually it had dawned on me that when it was time to sleep, I was always able to find the few square inches needed to lie down in. No longer was I the trembling waif awaiting my train in a Paris railway station. Gone were the days when fear of the unknown had thrown me into the arms of George and Gary, the Canadians. From time to time, the weight of my backpack digging into my shoulders reminded me how vulnerable a lone traveller could be. No protection, no comfort, no tenderness: such was my lot. But I had to add that if, indeed, I was alone against the world, I had the advantage of being healthy, all in one piece, open and receptive, entirely devoted to my quest. My body was at my command; I insisted on strict obedience. I was still a free agent.

To pass the time as I waited, I repeated to myself the names of the island's trees: *matai, miro, rimu, kamahi.* Then I made a list of the birds I had seen: *pukeko, tui, kiwi . . .* I thought of the Scottish salesman who had taught me those names the day before. He had been one of those jovial people whose infectious high spirits seem to light up the world around them. He kept a special notebook in which he wrote down the names and addresses of all the hitch-hikers he picked up.

'I'm planning my own trip around the world', he had told me with a laugh.

A Maori driving a small van made a U-turn in order to pick me up. Night was falling.

'I'm going to Tutira Lake. You want a lift?'

Was that place on my itinerary? What difference did it make? The man was a sheep-shearer and invited me to watch him at work. In this country where wool was so important, it would have been a pity to miss out on a sheep-shearing. But it would have been even sadder to refuse such a spontaneous gesture of friendship.

Before the animal had time to realize what was happening it was gripped tight and turned over and over as if on a spit. First the belly was shorn, then the flanks and backs as the electric clippers cut rapidly through the fleece. The man was on piecework, so he didn't pay much attention if he occasionally nipped the animal's skin with the cutters. The work began at dawn, and around eight o'clock the men took their first break, gathering over plates of lamb chops, potatoes and gravy, washed down with tea.

'Go ahead, eat', urged my Maori friend, serving me up three chops.

'Eat now! We're not hippies here; we have plenty for everyone. You've got to eat to keep up your strength.'

For the second time, I bought a ticket to New Caledonia without any intention of going there. In both New Zealand and Australia the authorities required an ongoing plane ticket as well as an entry visa for the next country to be visited, before they would grant a visa of their own. Since I was French I did not need a visa for New Caledonia, which was a French overseas territory. As for the ticket, I simply sold it back to an agency each time! My experience in Alajuela Prison had taught me a lesson. As misfortunes always come in threes, I would have to go through the same procedure for Indonesia.

November 25th, 1969: I first set foot in Australia. My home town and I were now literally poles apart. I had left Toronto exactly two years before. I couldn't help thinking back to that London cab, the canoe, the generator, the motor cycles . . . Sunburnt and weather beaten, profoundly marked by the long road I had travelled and by the effort it had demanded, I was also poles apart from everything I had been back in 1955 when I had left school. Yet, face to face with the immensity of this new continent, I had the feeling that my first real marathon was only just beginning.

Fringed on the north by a strip of the tropics and on the south by a temperate zone, most of Australia is nothing but an enormous desert fourteen times the size of France, and almost as vast as the USA. Although technically illegal, hitch-hiking was more than tolerated; it was not uncommon to see queues of hitch-hikers on roads leading out of town. Most of the hitch-hikers were unemployed people moving about in search of a job. Drivers were always amazed when I told them of my plans to tour the country; they could not imagine anyone hitch-hiking across Australia for pleasure. Ten thousand miles!

It was December. Summer was just beginning, but on the coast the temperature was already over 100°F. The thin leaves of the trees were as red as flames, and the flowers took on their warmest tones. There was a smell of molasses all the way from Brisbane to Cairns. The vast sugar cane fields of Queensland were being burned. As if it were not hot enough already! Apparently, the burning process facilitated harvesting. In Cairns the sun rose white-hot at four o'clock in the morning. In Tully there was no shade along the road. Sweat streamed down my forehead; I felt as if I were melting. My head ached terribly, and a black veil blurred my vision.

Someone was tapping me on the shoulder. As I came to, I realized I had fainted. Although he had one leg in plaster, the man grabbed me vigorously around the waist and helped me to his car.

'I don't drive very fast', he said, 'but my rule is never to leave anyone on the road. Once I had to walk twenty miles. No one wanted to pick me up. Ever since then . . .'

Further on we stopped to pick up two other young people without any luggage. They were unemployed workers and as red as beetroots. We had come across them just in time. The man with the cast dropped us off at a camp in the middle of a forest. I rushed to a water pump, but the water was boiling hot and burned my throat.

I travelled on by short leaps interspersed with long waits under the scorching sun. The skin on my arms was swelling up, and the slightest touch made me gasp in pain. While I was not yet totally disheartened, I was beginning to wonder if I had bitten off more than I could chew. Was it really reasonable to attempt to hitch-hike such long distances in such fierce climatic conditions? Yet even at moments of extreme fatigue, something always turned up. Someone would bring me a jug of iced water, and the simple gesture would rekindle my courage as the water quenched my thirst.

A big Australian-made Holden made a U-turn and came back to pick me up. The driver invited me to his place for a meal. I accepted a little spaghetti; I wasn't really hungry and didn't want to take advantage of him. There was a shower, and I scrubbed myself clean very quickly so as not to keep my friend waiting. A good shower, a plate of spaghetti, a cup of tea: that was all it took to make me feel like a new man, revived and ready to hit the road again. Rather than leave me on my own in Townsville, where he lived, he drove me out of the city, stopped, raised the bonnet of his car and waited. It was an effective show of solidarity, for almost immediately another car pulled to a halt. My driver introduced me to his successor, and my journey continued.

I spent an entire day in Richmond, flaked out on the steps of a garage office. I was utterly exhausted. The sun had dried me out and was slowly killing me. Longingly I day-dreamed of Alaska: the same endless wastes of virgin land, the same solitude . . . but without the heat.

Over my head, a thermometer recorded 130°F. I thought back to the wilting heat of Manaus that transformed living men into zombies. No, even that comparison didn't seem to apply. Here it was more like an oven, a dry-heat oven, that was roasting every fibre of my body. I tied a handkerchief around my temples, then buried my head in a cardboard box. The asphalt and ochre horizon danced before me. I could no longer swallow anything except a little water, milk or orange juice. Inside the office, a young girl wearing an extra-short miniskirt over pink panties eyed me constantly. I couldn't even find the energy to smile at her. If I tried to move, I was sure the skin on my thighs would crack. At the edge of the dirt road, a hundred yards away, I had planted my backpack amidst empty Coke bottles and beer cans - Australian roads were always strewn with litter. A buzzard had perched on my pack and was checking it out.

Colin, a young, bearded Irish professor, finally picked me up for the long crossing of the heart of the desert. We were passing straight through the middle of the great Australian furnace: 1,000 miles through a fiery landscape of red earth, stunted yellow vegetation, barren trees with twisted limbs. The stench from decaying carcasses of cows, sheep, emus and kangaroos made the air unbreathable. Depending on how long they had been dead, the corpses were either grotesquely swollen or reduced to bleached and disquieting skeletons. 'Willy-willies' - whirlwinds of dust - whipped across the floor of the desert before suddenly, for no apparent reason, swirling up into the sky. Fortunately there was the occasional pub, a veritable oasis where one could buy chilled beer. (When I asked for tea, I nearly started a riot!) In Mount Isa, a large mining centre, people drank in frenzied agitation. All along our route, very black Aborigines dressed in rags watched us with deep-set eyes. Sometimes they looked frightened, sometimes disinterested, but always sad . . . the saddest people in the world.

At Alice Springs I left Colin and got ready for another long, hot wait. The brightness of the desert burned my eyes, ants nibbled at my feet, flies buzzed about my face. It was no longer possible to stand by the road with my thumb stuck out: there was a genuine risk of dropping dead. Instead, I left my pack on the shoulder of the road along with a sign indicating my destination, while I hid out wherever I could find a patch of shade. I would sit under a eucalyptus tree after spreading my sleeping bag over its branches; otherwise the scanty leaves did little to block out the sun. Eventually a driver would stop alongside my pack and honk his horn until I showed up!

The town of Coober Pedy was peopled with adventurers who braved the scorching heat in search of opals, hoping to find their fortunes and then made a quick getaway. The men, mostly Greeks and Sicilians, lived underground in relative coolness. The cabins above ground were used for storage. Their lives were those of nineteenth-century gold prospectors. Poverty and disappointment were far more common than lucky strikes, but the men I talked to were not discouraged. The acres of desert were studded with opals, just waiting to be found. It was genuinely possible to get rich quick. But I was not an adventurer and large sums of money had little appeal for me. I was a student of the soul; my wealth would be knowledge.

Port Augusta. Suddenly, close to the sea, nature woke and blossomed again. Amid the fields of grain and greenery, towering trees and fertile vineyards, I felt able to breathe at last. Red brick houses, double-decker buses, zebra-crossings: once again I discovered the colonial style. Every colony reflects the style of its mother country. Sydney had a strongly British flavour.

Ann, a friend from Toronto, let me stay with her. She had lost none of her kindness, yet she disappointed me. Although I was grateful to her for putting me up when I was on the verge of exhaustion, I found no great comfort in her presence. We no longer had anything in common, anything to talk about. Our worlds were too far apart. I listened to many things which had long ceased to interest me. Money was at the centre of her new life, along with social status and success. Beer, cigarettes, easy chairs, fridges and wall-to-wall carpeting: nothing was missing, not even the gossip about the members of Toronto's Australian Club. It was all so irrelevant to a travelling life, and I sank into a stupor of boredom.

It was Christmas, and so there was a party. Pretty hands decorated with rings and bracelets plunged into a platter heaped with crayfish fresh from the bay. I felt very distant from all those people wrapped up in their narrow lives and conventional values. I despised their notion of 'class' and their attitudes and mannerisms which carefully conformed to those of 'worldly' society.

The 'world' - I now knew - was entirely different. Sadly, however, I seemed to be the only one there to have realized this. As I considered my good luck, I watched them at their 'fun', which consisted in getting drunk and doing nothing. Between swallows, they would let drop a few banalities. Eventually they took their leave, slightly tipsy and even more vapid than when they'd arrived. They leaned on each other for support as they groped uncertainly for the light switches. Aline, plump and snobbish but not bad looking, talked to me about her cruises and conducted tours before confessing, 'It's true I don't really see anything. They just lead me around . . .'

The beer party enabled me to draw some conclusions about the inhabitants of the other end of the world. The 'real men' were the big drinkers, tough guys who didn't hesitate to slap the girls on the back while guffawing uproariously. Their role model was the pioneer, the virile cowboy of dark saloons.

Men and women formed two very distinct groups. Following my natural inclination, I had homed in on the opposite sex. That was a big mistake. In Australia, anyone who showed gallantry towards women, who courted them or offered them flowers, was immediately labelled a pansy. The young ladies, as might be expected, were very ill at ease in the company of a Frenchman. Despite their ultra-short miniskirts and their swimsuits, neither of which left anything to the imagination, they were completely nonplussed at the first small compliment, the merest hint of charm. When in Rome, they say . . . but would I ever succeed in overcoming my Latin temperament?

Sydney was a fine city in a fantastic setting. The magnificent, sheltered deep-water bay, dotted with attractive islands, was a paradise for sailing and water sports. However, I didn't stay long for, all things considered, I preferred the desert.

I set off on my travels again. I passed briefly through Melbourne, where I met a young Pommy of the purest 'made in England' style: bowler hat, short hair, tie, dark suit, rolled umbrella under the arm. Without a doubt, he had never heard of Flower Power or any of the other ideas that were uniting young people across the world. He was quite pleased with himself and said that he had come to make his fortune. The Australian government had paid his air fare from far-off England on the sole condition that he stay a minimum of two years. I suddenly wished I had not chosen Canada. In Australia I would surely have saved up just as much money for my trip around the world, and in addition I would not have had to pay for the trip. But I hadn't known about such possibilities. Advertising for the 'white zones' (Canada, Australia, South Africa, New Zealand) was illegal in France. I asked him why Canada did not offer a free trip.

'Maybe it's because Australia needs more immigrants than Canada.'

'Well, in that case, why doesn't she open her doors up wide?'

'What do you mean?'

'I mean, why doesn't she let non-Whites in?'

'What more do you want! What about all those Greeks and Italians arriving by the boatload? Aren't they enough?'

The conversation ended abruptly. I walked away without even saying goodbye to my Pommy. Then, not being able to leave it like that, I turned on my heel to make a final remark.

'Your white "superior" skin: are you sure you chose it?'

I think he answered something like, 'But I'm no racist . . .' No racist. No, certainly not. He just didn't care for Greeks or Italians. Blacks were lazy, dirty and smelt bad. Arabs were tricksters just waiting for the opportunity to stab you in the back. The smaller the world grew and the closer air travel brought us together, the more individuals edged away from each other. When would people overcome their animal instincts and the outmoded idea of territory? How much longer would foreigners be looked upon as natural enemies? Were we white Westerners so narrow-minded as to lack any humility? Inebriated by our technological achievements - so very recent, after all - we believed ourselves to be superior. Where were we during the golden ages of the Hindu and Chinese civilizations?

There was only one answer to this distressing question: Love. Love your fellow human beings and abandon all prejudice. People needed friendship and security. They needed to laugh to be happy, no matter what the colour of their skin or the style of their hair.

'If you beheld a garden in which all the plants were the same as to form, colour and perfume, it would not seem beautiful to you at all but, rather, monotonous and dull. The garden which is pleasing to the eye and which makes the heart glad, is the garden in which are growing side by side flowers of every hue, form and perfume . . . Do not be content with showing friendship in words alone, let your heart burn with loving kindness' ('Abdu'l-Bahá).*

In Perth I breathed the ocean air again after crossing the southern desert. David had picked me up in Port Augusta and driven me all the way to the west coast. We had stopped only to quench our thirst. One thousand, six hundred miles in a single stretch through choking dust: it was a new record, and I had only waited five minutes for the lift! The scenery was always the same: a parched, scorched land. At night the inevitable kangaroos leaped about in all directions, posing the constant risk of an accident.

At the Automobile Club in Perth, they told me I would have to give up the idea of continuing northward along the sea. Darwin, 2,500 miles to the north-east, was now impossible to reach by the coast road. The rainy season had started and could paralyse all traffic without warning - perhaps tomorrow or the next day, perhaps an hour from now . . . I hated the idea of turning back. Cut across the centre of the country? No

*Bahá'u'lláh's son. *Paris Talks*, 1912, p53 (Bahá'í Publishing Trust - see p90 for addresses).

thanks! I decided to push forward and watch for the last northbound drivers.

By the time I reached Roeburne, the asphalt had long since given way to rough gravel. Driving became difficult, but the road was dry, which was the most important thing. How long would it stay that way? At the moment I was waiting in the shade of a eucalyptus tree. My feet were placed in a brackish puddle. My hands were over my eyes, protecting my face from the burning, wind-whipped sand.

Sweat ran down my back and legs. My body was slowly shrivelling up. My throat was dry as sandpaper. All strength had left me. The temperature was pushing 150°F in the sun. I wondered how much it would register in the shade of the eucalyptus. 120? 130? I had drunk over a gallon of water that morning and eaten nothing at all. And still I was dehydrated. Around noon the sound of an aeroplane engine jerked me out of my torpor. I rose to my feet like a corpse on Judgement Day. I hadn't even noticed the little airport. Thanks to Brian, the pilot, I made a leap 10,000 feet into the air. I was living again.

Once I had returned to earth, however, the routine began again. The heat became ever more torrid, ever more unbearable. It was like waiting on a grill. Only my dread of having to retrace my steps pushed me onward.

'Come along! You can help us push if we get stuck.'

The family crowded together to make room for me. A madman heading north was just what I needed. He tore along at top speed, for the rain clouds were gathering in the sky.

It began to rain, and soon the road was just a succession of puddles, some shallow, some deep. At each stop, I ran to get something to drink. With a metallic rattle, a machine spat out a can of icy Coca-Cola. It was so cold that it gave me a sore throat. Finally, in Kununurra we came to the end of the road. A furious typhoon had torn everything apart in a mere twenty minutes.

I landed in Darwin aboard a Cessna plane that collected milk from remote ranches. Darwin was a steam bath clamped between jungle and ocean. The monsoon had arrived. Before me, just beyond the waves, was Asia.

There were no sailing ships leaving port. Considering the weather, it would have been madness. Each day tons of water poured out of an ink-black sky. The deluge was usually preceded by a windstorm that swirled about the dust and sand. The streets turned into rivers; all the houses were perched on stilts. I found shelter under an empty house. The next door neighbour, intrigued, observed me for a long time from behind his hedge. Finally he greeted me and invited me over for dinner. I hadn't sat down at a table for eleven days. As usual, I told the story of my travels. I think he understood that it was my way of thanking him and was appreciative.

'You're lucky. I work at the control tower. It's too bad you didn't arrive yesterday morning, though. All day long a guy was pacing about the airport lobby yelling at the top of his lungs, "Anyone for Timor? I've got a spare seat for Timor".'*

I was dismayed. Was my luck running out?

'Tell me, Mr Viegas, do you think I'll find another plane today or tomorrow? Can I just go and hang around the airport?'

'No, unfortunately. Not with the monsoon. Small aircraft are grounded. That fat American who was looking for company yesterday was taking a big risk. I'm not even sure he would have been authorized to take off today. The weather forecast is awful, especially for the next few days.'

The next day, nevertheless, Mr Viegas telephoned his wife.

'Tell André to go to the Koala Motel and to ask for Mr Hutton. He's just come to pick up his flight plan for Bali. André might be able to persuade him . . .' And Mr Hutton turned out to be a great guy, understanding and generous . . .

*An island in Indonesia, half of which formerly belonged to Portugal. It was a common stopping place between Australia and Bali.

Chapter 8

I BURNED INCENSE
AT THE FOOT OF TATHAGATA

In Bali any foreigner staying in the home of a private citizen had to be declared to the authorities. How was I going to find a bed? I was very tired. I had spent the day roaming the streets of Denpasar, the capital, and had gradually felt a fever coming on. I felt very lost and bewildered in the middle of this swarming city with multicoloured chaos all around. My head ached. Even the language was entirely alien. Until now I had always been able to make myself understood, but here in Bali I came up against a wall of incomprehension which was not amusing in the slightest.

Night fell over the teeming *djalan* (street) called Diponogoro and slowly absorbed the daytime cacophony of pony carts decorated with little bells, sputtering overloaded *bemos*, the three-wheeled taxi-scooters which carried up to six passengers, and jingling bicycles, all careering brazenly through crowds of alert pedestrians. Slowing the dust settled, dancing in the halo of light surrounding the few tiny huts. Next to me a naked little child played with one of his mother's poor, sagging breasts while she held out a spicy salad of green mango floating in a kind of caramel sauce. In the darkness, I leaned against one of the flimsy supports of a street stall roofed with banana leaves, and ate with my fingers. I had a hard time finishing the bitter-tasting concoction served up on an enamel plate. And now, where was I going to sleep? I was tired, exhausted, ready to drop.

From behind me, as if from another world, a melodious voice swept through me like a caress. I turned around. An angelic face of infinite sweetness smiled reassuringly. All my aches and pains suddenly melted away. At the sight of this woman emerging from the darkness, I felt enveloped by a sense of well-being I had never experienced before. Just as in a fairy tale, she beckoned me to follow her.

Mrs Sukenashi's house was made of interwoven bamboo slats which had been whitewashed and covered with a sheet of corrugated iron. Across the earthen floor scuttled little black piglets and cheeping baby chicks. There was virtually no furniture. A few clothes hung from nails driven into the bamboo. Overturned wooden crates served as a bedstead and a mat took the place of a mattress. Two boys slept in one 'bed'; the other was now reserved for me. Mrs Sukenashi slept in the next room with her five daughters. Offering me her hospitality, she welcomed me with the musical words, '*Selamat datang*'.

Although I was beginning to feel very ill again, I repeated those words whose meaning I could guess. 'Welcome!' What a marvellous woman! '*Selamat datang!*' She had nothing, but she proved to me that it wasn't necessary to possess in order to give.

Unable to sleep, I shivered through the night. I had difficulty in breathing, and my clothes were soaked with sweat. I certainly had a high fever, and not for the first time. Persistent diarrhoea and vomiting repeatedly forced me out of bed. My benefactress, already up at four in the morning to prepare the daily rice, came over with a lamp in her hand and a worried look on her face. She knelt beside me and handed me a dictionary. Word by word, I tried to make her understand what was wrong with me. She then pointed to the word *nurse*, disappeared for a minute, and came back with an assortment of pills and coloured tablets which I swallowed with a little water. Another miracle - Mrs Sukenashi was a nurse! A few minutes later she brought me a bowl of boiling tea. How had she guessed? I had badly wanted some hot tea but had not dared trouble her any further. Soothed and calmed, I sank into a deep sleep.

When I awoke, the hut was empty: school and work had left me alone in the company of an adorable little lady with big black eyes. Seated on the other makeshift 'bed', she had been waiting for me to wake up, swinging her graceful legs like children everywhere in the world. She was seven years old. As soon as my eyes were open, she smiled and said something that I couldn't understand. I made a gesture to show her that it was hot. She got up, found a fan, and waved it gently to cool me off. All the while she continued her light chatter.

'*Tidak, tcha panas, manis.*'

With difficulty I assembled the words of my new vocabulary. I was thirsty; I would be grateful for a little warm tea with sugar. Iomate was

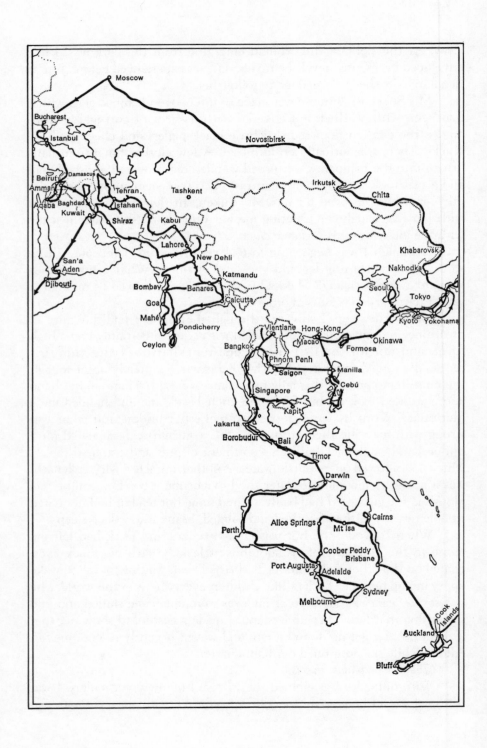

already in what served as a kitchen. Crouching on the floor, she blew on the moribund fire. I watched the embers come back to life and begin to glow red between the two stones placed on the ground. Soon, with bowed head, she was serving me tea.

Slowly I recovered. Handi, the eldest of the Sukenashi children, showed me how to sit on the luggage rack of his bicycle and then pedalled tirelessly in his desire to help me discover his blessed country. Around Mount Batur, the central volcano, terraced rice paddies reflected the brilliance of the sky. Peasants in conical hats trudged through the grey mud, using both hands to guide wooden ploughs pulled by pairs of pinkish buffalo. Rice dominated the landscape of Bali. As the staple, almost exclusive food, it gave the inhabitants the incomparable fineness of skin that I so admired.

Bali had me under her spell. I spent long hours watching the dancers move like graceful marionettes guided by invisible strings. Their movements were co-ordinated to perfection, and the play of their fingers, which seemed to obey some celestial music, aroused in me an intense emotion. Dancing, like every other aspect of life in Bali, was a perpetual offering to Shiva. I was particularly sensitive to this interweaving of the sacred and the profane, which I also encountered under the roof of the Sukenashi home as they prepared for a celebration. The eldest girl was using a pair of scissors to shape magnificent decorations from leaves of bamboo. Fashioning necklaces of fresh flowers, the mother tried to pronounce a few English words; I made a special effort to understand, for she was still worried about my health and comfort. She desperately wanted me to feel comfortable in her home. How could I make her understand that I was in better spirits than I could ever have wished?

We took little baskets made of woven coconut leaves and carefully filled them with a pinch of rice, a little saffron and some fragrant petals. It looked like a doll's picnic lunch. On trays I arranged pieces of fruit, bananas, sugar cane, *salak, blimbing, rambutan, lengkeng, djambumonet* - tropical fruits sadly unknown in the West. They would be savoured at the close of the ceremony. Everything took place in an atmosphere of peace which soothed and inspired. In a large cage placed in the courtyard, turtle-doves cooed. Time had lost all meaning. The humble home vibrated with the exhilaration of shared friendship and became, to my eyes, the most beautiful palace in the world.

The entire island was devoted to the gods, and small offerings were repeated a thousand times each day. In this country, where the buses stopped to let their passengers place a few petals at the foot of a statue by the roadside or even standing in the middle of the road, the most insignificant scrap of material, the smallest piece of wood, could become an effigy, a work of art. Bali was sculpted, finely worked; nature itself seemed to have been assembled by an artist. There were countless temples, and prayer was a manifestation of joy. Ritual was never stiff or solemn: it was filled with happiness, colour and music. Bali was all life.

I did not waste a moment but observed constantly, storing in my memory those fleeting instants of lost paradise. As the *gamelan*, the Balinese xylophone with its bamboo slats, tapped out light music in a hidden courtyard, a group of very young girls practised the movements of their ancestral dance. On the side of the road, a craftsman carved a piece of ebony which slowly came to life to the rhythms of the past. Holding a tall staff decorated with coloured rags, a peasant herded his flock of ducks, which advanced with necks outstretched. Men as erect and dignified as cavalrymen glided by on old bicycles; children with shaven heads ran merrily about; women stopped at street stalls before continuing on their way, swaying under the weight of the loads balanced on their heads. I loved the colourful patterns on the *sarongs* that both women and men wore draped to their ankles. The slight, bare-breasted Balinese women with their golden skin were a graceful sight to behold. I thought of the ironic doggedness of the local officials in charge of censorship who spent their days scrutinizing imported Western magazines and sticking small squares of white paper over any nakedness!

Every day seemed a holiday as life rolled gently along, constantly renewing itself. Old men cheered on their fierce, arrogant fighting cocks; baboons climbed up on temples; lean dogs romped about in packs.

At the end of the day, I made my way over to the 'Three Sisters' where the world's young globe-trotters assembled. I did not care for the place: it was a 'Whites Only' area. But I was able to pick up news there and get useful hints for the next leg of my journey. In this troubled and often dangerous part of the world, forewarned was forearmed. All the travellers I met there slept in hotels and had fistfuls of dollars. They spent a lot of time at the 'Three Sisters' reading *Newsweek*, drinking beer and sometimes smoking dope. But what were they seeing of Bali, the jewel of Indonesia?

I placed some halved hard-boiled eggs and some rice on the altar to their ancestors which stood in the small courtyard adjoining the Sukenashi home. The entire family was present and Mrs Sukenashi was dismayed. I had announced my imminent departure.

'You are good man', she said. 'You learned so many things'.

Maybe - but to me she was far greater, because she possessed the secret of happiness in life, the radiating love that transformed all things. With a heavy heart, I tore myself away from Bali. The children waved until I was out of sight.

Java. Hitch-hiking was becoming a problem. Waiting in the Banjuwangi truck shed, I wondered if I would ever manage to take off. Seated on my backpack, I was reading quietly among the idle drivers and the usual crowd of gaping onlookers to whom I no longer paid any attention. In the surrounding dusky shadows, a group squatted, picking lice off one another. Monkeys? No, just Javanese waiting, like me, for a ride. They asked no questions but were content to swallow a few mouthfuls of rice, spit on the ground and belch uninhibitedly.

My progress was slow. The roads were crowded with peasants transporting water and grain, *zebus* drawing high wooden carts, armed military personnel, women bowed under heavy loads. The monsoon forced me to find a roof each night, but that was not a very complicated task. Having learned certain key words that I was careful to retain, I would drop my pack in any village at random and seat myself on top of it. Immediately I would be surrounded by inquisitive people who would rush over, observe me for a few minutes and then, without any introduction, begin to question me. The questions were always kind and polite - and always the same: 'What is your name? . . . Where do you come from? . . . Where are you going?' I would wait for the fourth one that was never long in coming: 'Where do you sleep?' I would point to my sleeping bag, and without fail I would end up sleeping on the bare floorboards of some hut. Everyone slept on the floor. Even in the poorest of families, I was warmly welcomed. My needs were few, I was easily satisfied, and they gladly shared what they had. In Jogjakarta, I was offered in all seriousness the communal tooth brush . . .

The *Dharma*, the doctrine, was chiselled into the rock of eighth-century Borobudur, the largest Buddhist temple in the world. That same 'trip to eternity' that the little old lady had preached to me about in Alaska here took physical form in an imposing four-storey structure 100 feet high and measuring 350 feet on each side.

'*What is this middle path that the Perfect One has discovered, the path that opens the eyes of the spirit, that leads to rest, to knowledge, to enlightenment, to Nirvana? It is found between asceticism and worldly life . . . It is a path of purest activities unaffected by desire of the desirable or fear of the fearful*' (Sermon of Benares).

I ascended the symbolic path of salvation formed of steep and uneven steps: the *Karmadharta* where man is attached to the world; the *Rupadharta*, man freeing himself; the *Arupadharta* where man is free; *Nirvana*, represented by an enormous shrine, a *stupa*.

Djakarta was a festering wound of poverty slashed from Indonesia's overpopulated main island. A modern street proud of its luxury-class hotel, a few respectable neighbourhoods, and some vestiges of colonial Batavia (as the city was known during the years of Dutch rule) gave way to slums and yet more slums spreading out as far as the eye could see. From the midst of open sewers and endlessly teeming confusion rose gigantic monuments commemorating the revolution that had followed World War II.

The first evening I had to summon all my courage just to cross the square in front of Seneni Railway Station. The area was jammed with crowds of people dressed in rags, pressed around charmers manipulating hideous snakes, around quacks and sellers of amulets. Naked children begged and wheedled as the blind, the mutilated, and what seemed like all the pariahs on earth, chanted verses from the Qur'án. And then there was the army of *betjacks*, those bicycle-rickshaws Suharto called 'the exploitation of man by man'. Many of the poverty-stricken owners spent their nights crouched on the seats of their rickshaws. With my humble sleeping bag, I suddenly felt extremely privileged and rich in comfort. I almost felt guilty when I noticed in every corner dusty, emaciated bodies lying on shreds of coarse sacking.

After overcoming those first moments of panic, I approached the street vendors waiting for customers behind their push-carts of steaming, aromatic food. They offered a series of succulent dishes at more-than-modest prices, and I quickly realized that the crowd was not in any way hostile. On the contrary, everyone was smiling and greeting me.

Unexpectedly, I ended up sleeping in the home of a ship-owner in a fashionable neighbourhood. A liveried chauffeur, an attentive maid, iced water and pastries placed on my bedside table, smooth sheets, breakfast in bed, elegant tableware: everything was there, and it was astonishing. But it didn't last, and I didn't regret the shortness of my stay in the home of this rich man. The welcome offered me by Mr Soegkarno, who lived much more modestly, touched me more deeply. He apologized for the smallness of his house, but invited me to sleep in the adjoining shed. The humble always asked me to excuse their poverty; the rich, on the other hand, displayed their fortune without considering for a moment that such ostentation might be shocking. They never dreamed of apologizing. With the rich, one is 'treated'; with the poor, one is 'welcomed'.

The head-hunters of Borneo no longer hunted heads . . . more's the pity!
Yet, even if this fact detracted a little from the excitement of my trip, at
least I could count on continuing my travels with all my appendages
intact . . .

From Kuching, the capital of Sarawak, I followed the coast and
then travelled up the Rajang, the main river of the island. The wooden
boat, a genuine river-bus, was absolutely crammed full. It zigzagged from
one shore to the other, stopping at the wave of a hand or a hat or even a
shirt. The boat was packed with Malays, Chinese, and Dayaks (Borneo
natives), all crowded cheerfully together. Dead branches and tree trunks
floated on the muddy water. A rich, heady scent rose up from the tropical
forest beneath a scorching sun.

Kapit, the terminus and last Chinese bastion, was situated on Iban
territory. The natives only left their village hut (the entire tribe lived
under a single roof) to come and trade in Kapit. In exchange for their
rubber and pepper they received petrol for their motorized dug-out
canoes, oil for their lamps and batteries for their transistor radios. Each
shop had its own Iban clientele. In one of the picturesque stores I came
upon two head-hunters who were gazing happily at the assortment of
merchandise on display. They were naked except for the blue arabesques
painted on their bodies and the feathers stuck in their hair. The
shopkeeper, with his imperturbable, moon-like face, was tracing Chinese
characters on a slate. The Ibans were laughing. I hesitated. Would it be
easier to approach them if I first took off my shorts? They spoke no
language other than their own dialect. Eventually, after several hours of
gesture and palaver, I pulled out a few Malaysian dollars . . .

The powerful motor boat carried us upstream against the strong
current of the Rajang; then up the turbulent Paleh, and finally over the
countless rapids of the narrow, shallow Sut on which we came close to
capsizing several times. The sky was no longer visible, for the jungle
formed a vault over our heads. On the dark branches to either side,
bright yellow kingfishers with orange breasts and large red beaks
scrutinized the water's surface, seemingly indifferent to our passing. The
river provided the only link between these remote tribes and the rest of
the world, for the forest was virtually impenetrable.

A few tree trunks placed along the shore served as a jetty. Children
came running up, followed by a few of their elders hungry for news. The
'house' was built on stilts right at the river's edge and measured some 300
feet in length. The steep roof sheltered two wide corridors, one of which
was partitioned into fifteen rooms called *bileks*. Each *bilek* had a tiny

suspended kitchen attached at the rear and was intended for the use of a single family. The second corridor, the *ruai*, was a sort of covered veranda where people strolled, chatted and worked. It was also a storage area for sacks of rice, fishing rods, small rubber presses, and pestles for crushing the *padi*, the unhusked rice. In front of the *ruai* was a terrace-like platform open to the sky. Called the *tanju*, it was used for drying laundry, tobacco and pepper.

All the villagers were assembled on the *tanju* and were surprised to see a fully-clothed white man appear at the foot of the tree trunk that served as a staircase. Sensing my embarrassment, an old man picked up my backpack, pulled the straps over his forehead and climbed up to the platform. Amid general laughter, I in turn attempted to ascend the trunk. The tiny steps reminded me of the little perches on which my father's hens used to roost.

Presley, one of the two boatmen who had accompanied me to the village, introduced me to his father. The old man had long hair down to his waist and had been tattooed all over with soot. He invited me to follow him into his bilek. At the entrance I had to bow down and salute, so to speak, the four skulls hanging from the door frame. I had forgotten that I was in the land of the head-hunter. The old man sat down, rolled a little tobacco in a palm leaf, and began smoking slowly. The entire family was smiling at me, but communication was difficult. I didn't know what to say or what to do, so I simply smiled back.

The floor was made of bamboo slats, regularly spaced. The walls were made of planks and the roof was covered with *nipa* palms. There was no furniture apart from a few crude chests. The women wore sarongs that reached from their waists to their ankles; the men wore only the briefest of loincloths.

Five of us sat cross-legged in a circle on the floor. Bilang, Presley's younger sister, had bright eyes and pretty little breasts. In the middle of the circle she placed some boiled rice, greens and sliced yams. The only drink was water. It was a thoroughly frugal meal, which undoubtedly explained the amazing good health and splendid physiques of these 'savages'. I ate with my fingers like everyone else. Unfortunately, the perfectly cooked and separate grains of rice weren't making it to my mouth. I spilled them all over the place, to the great amusement of my hosts. The father then showed me how to eat. He formed a ball with the rice by lightly compressing it. Then, with his hand cupped, used his thumb to slide it into his mouth. At the second attempt, I became socially acceptable! I found this technique invaluable all the way to India.

In the evening on the *ruai*, I talked very slowly about my travels. The entire village listened attentively as Richa, a very intelligent young Iban, translated what I was saying. When night had fallen, we unrolled mats made of woven palm fronds. Couples and women slept in the *bileks*, children and bachelors on the *ruai*. I drifted off to sleep, fairly certain that nobody would cut my throat.

At 5.30 next morning, the cockerels sounded reveille - a bit early for my taste. The children were the first ones up, and their scampering feet set the flexible bamboo slats strumming like harp strings. The forest was still shrouded in mist as men and women got up and disappeared into the half-light. They left with wicker baskets on their backs to harvest the *padi*, to work on the pepper and banana plantations or gather in the latex. Lovely Bilang, who was both timid and teasing, brought me a cup of chocolate and then ran off laughing to join her friends. Richa stayed close to me, observant. Presley showed me around his 'village'. The only people remaining were noisy children and old men who were constantly busy but always greeted me courteously. I visited one after another. Each time they would unroll a small mat for me to sit on, and would smile with sincere friendship and kindness. Pigs and chickens that were being saved for feast days ran about between the stilts under the house. Their feed was pushed through the slats of the floor above. Skinny dogs, fighting cocks, monkeys, parrots, and toucans with ivory-coloured bills were all common household pets.

Armed with small guns, we left to go fishing. The pirogue headed upstream, battling its way through menacing rapids. Amid the lush vegetation and heavy scents, cicadas creaked and birds screeched in agitation. I felt happy here in the heart of the Borneo rain forest. We caught a large quantity of whiskered fish, and Presley was overjoyed. On our return, we gathered ferns along the shore and cooked them like spinach. The dish formed part of the daily menu. An Iban couple were stuffing rice and water into bamboo sticks. After blocking the ends with leaves, they heated the tubes over a wood fire and then plunged them into the river. After a week of fermentation, a rice alcohol called *tuak* would be ready for consumption.

While the adults were harvesting the *padi*, the elders hung on to straps hanging from the ceiling and used their feet to thresh the rice of the previous day's harvest. Then the women rhythmically sifted and winnowed the husked grain and spread it out to dry on the *tanju*, all the while driving the hens away with long sticks. Other old people wove baskets, made fish nets or carved tools out of wood. Two naked little girls lifted and dropped in rhythm a pestle used to pound the golden grains of rice into fine flour with which flat round cakes would be prepared. The children were kings of the long-house, and their joyful cries, or at times their whimpers, echoed throughout the day. As a background to all the activity, twangy music blared out of a transistor radio. It seemed that nowhere in the world today would a self-respecting tribe be without a radio.

At five o'clock in the afternoon everyone returned to the house. It was time for the communal bath in the river. Men and women waded in the water 'fully-dressed', keeping on their sarongs. I bathed in my swimming trunks - to everyone's surprise. I admired their bodies which, though small, were sleek and healthy. Some had light skin; all had round, very dark eyes, flat noses and finely etched lips. The women were pretty with their soft dark hair, the men fine-featured and handsome. Everyone discreetly observed the white man, and good humour prevailed. Bilang and her friend Jawaï burst out laughing as they splashed me.

As we ate, Bilang made some sweets in my honour. In silence I thought about how this little world - so close to its own origins - was threatened. Insidiously, Western civilization was worming its way in with its outboard motors, its rubber presses, its transistor radios . . . The young no longer wanted to be tattooed or to have their ears pierced. They cut their hair short, American-style, and wore tight jeans. Cigarette packets were making their appearance, and one or two plastic toys could be found on the floors of certain *bileks*. The world was becoming uniform without becoming unified.

Bilang showed me around her *makaï*, her kitchen. In huge Chinese jars dating from the Ming Dynasty, she stored rice, oil, and *tuak*. She had me chew some *pinang* (betel), the leaves of which were coated with a salty white paste. It was intended as an aid to digestion and turned one's saliva red. The older women had permanently reddened lips which, nevertheless, did little to hide their blackened, broken teeth.

Richa came to get me and took me to his *bilek*, where his grandmother offered me a pineapple. On the fire she was roasting pips from the *nangka* fruit; their seeds tasted like chestnuts. In the 'attic' were stored all the trappings for the coming feast days: panther skins decorated with multicoloured feathers, goat skins embroidered with mother-of-pearl, bonnets made of pearls and feathers. There were also the gongs of the gamelan. He proudly showed me a string of skulls - remnants of battles of the past or of the ancient nuptial custom that had required each proposal of marriage to be accompanied by the offering of a head.

Lovesick young men were particularly unwilling to risk their lives. Thus they hid in the tall grass, waiting for a child or an old lady to pass by.

The houses had been built on stilts to prevent surprise attacks by head-hunting raiders. In 1920 Protestant missionaries put an end to head-hunting, but fortunately for the survival of folklore, the legends died hard.

Official anti-Communism measures limited my stay in Borneo. I had only managed to get a one-week visa, and my time was now up. With a heavy heart, Bilang presented a papaya that had been especially cooked for me. We drank a little rice alcohol. Richa placed a string of beads around my neck, and Presley set on my backpack a small buckle that he had decorated himself.

'*Selamat tinggal, selamat tinggal* (goodbye).'

Arms were raised and hands waved as the long-house slowly disappeared from sight, sinking back into the jungle.

Singapore was an Asia in miniature, an irresistible foretaste of that largest and most fabulous of continents. It was a kaleidoscope of motion, colour, noise and light - a feast for all five senses. One of the largest ports in the world, the city was a vast, swarming marketplace overcrowded with shops and a remarkable hodgepodge of architecture. The streets were thronged with easy-going Chinese, smiling Malays, crisp, reserved Indians, and aloof Europeans. All the world's major religions were represented too: Hinduism, Confucianism, Taoism, Buddhism, Christianity and Islam. There was just as much variety in dress. There were silken saris embroidered with gold thread, black *samfus* (loose pants worn by Chinese women), long *cheong-sams* split down the side, colourful sarongs, American naval whites, smart English business suits, the inevitable miniskirts and of course the 'anything goes' of the international travellers.

Singapore was one of the culinary capitals of the world, where each could satisfy his appetite according to his means. From the modest trays on the food barrows to the counters of small cafés to the tables of the most refined restaurants, one could feast on glazed duck, Chinese noodles, peeled fruit, magnificent pastries, endless varieties of curry, balls of ground mutton, wriggling fish - all for the asking.

There was a multitude of odours: the smell of incense, discreet in the shops, heavy in the temples; the fragrance of sandalwood and of a thousand fruits and the stench of water stagnating in ditches. There was also a hubbub of unusual noises: the hammering of Sogo Lane where tree trunks were hollowed out to make coffins; innumerable bicycle bells; the siren blasts of cargo ships; Chinese firecrackers; the gongs, flutes and cymbals of parades and funeral processions . . . The city was an uninterrupted succession of colours, of the bizarre and unexpected, but it was a mosaic without cement, constantly shifting and changing.

The first obstacle for a dazed visitor like me was the language. Four major languages were spoken: Chinese, Malay, English and Tamil, written with Chinese, Arabic, Latin, and Tamil characters respectively. Malay was the official language, but not the most widely used. English, which was no longer anyone's mother tongue, served as a lingua franca. Tamil was spoken only by part of the Indian population and Chinese was divided into numerous dialects. The result was chaos, and a prime example of how easy it is to raise artificial barriers between people and prevent them from living happily together. There was an obvious need for a common secondary language and alphabet which would promote universal understanding without destroying anyone's mother tongue nor the ideas and culture that it represented.

One after another, I visited the temples dedicated to the various religions practised in Singapore. In a temple to Shiva, a naked Brahmin sprinkled me with perfumed water. Elsewhere, I burned incense at the foot of Tathagata (Buddha). In a Taoist temple I threw pieces of wood shaped like large beans at the foot of a statue whose mouth dribbled opium. My head was thick with the deafening blare of the ceremonies: firecrackers, the gongs of Buddhist processions, drumming, the chimes and trumpets of the Hindu temple. Everywhere there were special lighting effects, perfumed candles, flower petals scattered in profusion, litanies, incantations . . . I thought back to our Catholic high masses of the past with their incense, bells, magnificent robes . . . The scene was not so different. There was the same festive mockery, so remote from the teachings of the founders of the religions concerned. It had never struck me before. Rituals too played their part in dividing mankind. Moreover, if there was only one God, why were there so many religions?

Asia was a powder-keg. My trip was threatened by all the various wars, revolutions and ambushes that people were so good at starting. Travelling would be increasingly difficult, if not downright dangerous. Wherever I turned, the outlook was none too promising. Sarawak: a hunt for Communist terrorists and a daily curfew. Malaysia: guerrilla warfare on the Thai border. Thailand: the road between Bangkok and Phnom Penh had been closed for ten years for reasons of 'neutrality'. Laos: only Vientiane was accessible and relatively safe. Burma: the borders were quite simply closed. Vietnam: we all know about the war there.

On March 20th, I learned from the *Straits Times* that the Vietnamese were on the point of invading the Cambodian capital. I could have given up the whole idea but I was not in the habit of backtracking, and events in Singapore itself decided the issue for me. I had no other choice but to sally forth, for special police corps were being formed with the sole aim of hunting down hippies. All those who had found shelter in the Chinese Quarter at the Sam Leong Hotel or other haunts were being expelled. At the university where I had found a quiet bench to sleep on, I felt relatively safe . . . but not for long. An English hitch-hiker called Philip warned me that it was becoming impossible to move about the city. He had been arrested in a souvenir shop, where the police confiscated his passport and told him he would get it back only at the border.

'This is no good! Just no good. I don't want to be a monk any more.'

'But for what reason, revered Pra Boontin'?'

'Monk not allowed to touch women!'

The cell on stilts was narrow and very simple. But in an affront to the rules of monastic rigour, *Playboy* centrefolds had been pinned to the walls, and a row of naked, big-bosomed women beamed down into the room.

It was a tradition in Thailand that each family must produce a *bonze*, a priest. It was a matter of honour, and for that reason Pra Boontin' was here before me with shaven head and eyebrows. Stretched out on a board, his feet close to a fan, he puffed desperately on a strong-smelling cigarette, for he was planning to spend his entire life in this school of idleness. The vows of a *bonze* could apparently be annulled, but who would want to hire Pra Boontin' who had never learned a useful trade?

A victim of tradition, he sat in deathly boredom in his monastery, his *wat*. As a reward for good behaviour, he was entitled to the veneration of his fellow men and to the best seats on buses. Once in his lifetime every young man was expected to retreat to a pagoda for at least three months before facing up to the challenges of life. If not, he was considered unreliable and unfit for marriage. The idea in itself was not a bad one. For a man on the threshold of adult life, to draw apart and meditate in peace and quiet on what he knows and on what he ought to do in life, was an excellent notion. But the original spirit had been diluted with time and today the retreat was nothing more than a tiresome chore. The time was spent with transistor radios, Playboy magazines, dice and cards, and anything else that would speed the hour of release.

For two weeks I had been trying to familiarize myself with the sacred texts of Buddha, the *dhammapadas*. In the margin of the texts and in my journal, I had taken notes and drawn the various *mudras*, the sacred gestures. I had learned their meanings and knew by heart the story of Buddha's life. But how could I really work in such an adulterated atmosphere?

'Tonight, I go to play!'

Why not? I thought. After all, the life of a monk was not incompatible with sport; there was even a certain relaxation to be gained.

'What game are you going to play?'

No sooner had I asked the question than I realized my error. The Thais, like the Chinese, are unable to pronounce an 'r' and replace it with an 'l'. My *bonze* had actually meant to say 'pray' and not 'play'. For him, I was 'Andelé'. That 'l' gave rise to many a surprise. One morning, on awakening, Pra Boontin' told me happily, 'Today feast day. Plenty lice.'

Bewildered, I struggled to understand.

'Yes, today plenty lice, plenty lice, good lice. Don't you like lice?'

Oh no! I didn't like them at all! Then, too late, I understood that he had been trying to say 'rice'.

The Wat Huala Pong was a huge complex of cells, of *bots*, *viharas* and *chedis*. It was one of the 300 oases of silence in infernal Bangkok, a bustling, foul-smelling, polluted and over-populated city crisscrossed with fetid canals. Pra Boontin' got up each morning at six, carefully wrapped his saffron-coloured tunic about him, and left with a large black bowl covered with a copper plate to get his provisions. There were few scenes more typical of Bangkok than the daily appearance in the grey streets of all those yellow puppet-like figures begging for rice and being abundantly rewarded. With great respect passers-by took off their shoes, knelt down and bowed to the *bonze* before giving him their offering. Once the bowl was filled, any additional rice was dumped into a sack carried along by a boy servant. The *bonze* then took his leave in a dignified manner and without a word of thanks, just as was recommended by the Buddha. In the past a monk was satisfied with only a handful of rice, enough for him to keep body and soul together for another day of meditation. Latterly, however, the begging bowl had taken on family-size proportions. By offering large quantities of rice, the man in the street invested in his spiritual future, hoping thus to win a place in heaven.

Pra Boontin' had his own corner not far from the Institut Pasteur. No one dreamed of pinching it from him since he was an elder, having been a *bonze* for ten years. Sitting cross-legged, he ate with his fingers and then passed the bowl to me. The leftovers would be shared by two or three little novices who acted as his servants, running his errands and cleaning his cell. The second and last meal of the day was taken at eleven o'clock in the morning. In the evening, I was left alone to swallow the rancid leftovers, for a *bonze* ate only twice a day.

White smoke was rising from the chimney. It was a good sign. A corpse was being cremated! On such a day, in addition to the colourful spectacle, we would eat well, for cremations were an excuse for family reunions where all could eat and drink their fill. Thais were generous people, and a foreigner was always a guest of honour. The immediate family had one last picture taken in front of the red and gold coffin, which then was carefully dismantled. A second, much simpler coffin was opened with a chisel. An unbearable stench rolled out, stinging the eyes. The corpse, partially decomposed, was marinated in its own noxious juices. Its hands were joined, enclosing lotus blossoms and sticks of incense. One of the dead man's friends uncovered the corpse's head and extracted with his finger a Thai coin, a *baht*, that had been inserted into the mouth a hundred days previously. Before being placed in the crematorium, the corpse was sprinkled with perfumed water. Then each person stepped forward to light the funeral pyre. I took my turn with the rest.

These wakes were Pra Bootin's opportunity to make himself useful. Wrapped in his orange robe, hidden behind a huge oval fan, he was expected to chant for two hours at the foot of a solid gold Buddha. With ice-cold Coca-Cola, cigarettes, a fan and a spittoon, everything was ready for two hours of duty on the floor of the huge *vihara*, or prayer temple. Afterwards he would return to his cell with a present given to him by the family of the deceased. *Bonzes* could only be paid in kind; when the time came for me to leave, I took loads of soap and toothpaste off his hands . . .

Bangkok was also the home of the cheapest call girls in Asia. New Petchburi Road was lined with luxurious hotels, hamburger stands, drugstores and bars whose customers were American GIs on R & R. Raw neon light splashed the night, while inside the bars, soldiers drunk on alcohol and music danced erotically with silky-skinned girls. Once their selection was made, they paid the owner and disappeared in a cab along with their chosen companion.

I was intrigued by the excessive number of massage parlours, so I simply pushed open a door. In a display window bathed in pink light, girls were waiting in front of a TV set. They were painted like dolls, dressed in tight white blouses slit down the front, and each of them carried a number. The tinted glass prevented them from seeing the watering mouths of the ogling, over-excited male customers. It seemed a degrading and ridiculous business, and I wondered what could be going through the minds of those women. The war with its thousands of young Americans with money to burn and time to kill suddenly seemed very close.

'Well, have you chosen your number, John?' A hand descended on my shoulder, making me jump. 'It's three dollars for an hour. You get a towel over there . . . The cashier is on the right . . . And if you want *foki-foki*, it's extra. You arrange it with the young lady.'

'*Koon, koon.* You, come here!'

Pra Boontin' showed me a photograph published in the Bangkok *Daily News*. There was no mistaking the likeness; it was definitely me. The picture showed me barefoot, in shorts and an Iban necklace. I was gripping my movie camera in one hand and touching with the other the chin of a famous television dancer. The gesture had not meant anything. I had simply been adjusting her pose before getting her on film. The girl had been extremely beautiful, dressed in a silk tunic embroidered with gold and silver and a crown inlaid with precious stones. She had worn false fingernails, long, curved and golden, and orchids in her black hair. But in Siam, unfortunately, nobody, except perhaps a dollar-toting GI, touched a woman in public. I had been unaware of that custom.

My lack of *savoir faire* had earned me a disapproving caption: 'This hippie doesn't know how to behave, which is not surprising for a person so poorly dressed. Thailand does not like hippies. How did this one manage to enter the country?' I was upset by the tone of the commentary, all the while realizing that I should have been more discreet. I explained to Pra Boontin' that such a gesture was commonplace in Europe and he should not hold it against me. I also told him that I was shocked by the unfriendliness of the caption. To vilify a foreigner was hardly a step towards peace and understanding. Journalists had tremendous responsibilities. Maybe this journalist had been feeling sour on that particular day - even though it had been on the feast day of *Songkran*, the Buddhist New Year. I wanted to forget this minor incident and to remember only the extraordinary generosity and brotherhood of the people of this country in which I was able to travel everywhere. It was a country where I did not have to spend a single night in the open. At sunset, people often came to pick me up where I stood on the side of the road.

'It's late now, come to my house . . .'

It was a country where complete strangers paid a foreigner's bill in a restaurant without saying a word: it had happened to me.

In a little house on stilts, built from rough planks and roofed with thatch, I greeted my host with my hands joined on my chest and my head slightly inclined. It was a much more beautiful, more respectful greeting than our vulgar handshake. My host invited me with marvellous spontaneity to share his meagre meal of rice cooked that morning, shreds of meat, and Chinese peas. Simplicity, generosity, compassion, detachment, pacifism: all were fruits of Buddhism.

All along my route, elephants with their drivers perched on their heads trudged to work. Thousands of grey or pinkish buffalo with huge, semi-circular horns - and often with a child herdsman dozing on one of their broad backs - grazed peaceably alongside white *zebu* with undulating humps. Mountains, jungle, beaches, endless stretches of rice paddy: such was the landscape of Siam. It was hot, extremely hot, and nowhere more so than on the new bridge that spanned the famous River Kwai.

In the evenings when I was really exhausted, I had no hesitation in arriving uninvited at the nearest pagoda. With their pointed, golden roofs, pagodas were easy to spot. The scenario was the same each time. Immediately I would be surrounded by curious *bonzes* who would finger my shirt, lift my bag, play with my beads, and then start stroking my arms and legs. Thais have no body hair and were therefore intrigued by the sight of hairy limbs. It always set them off laughing. Once past that inevitable introduction, I would ask to speak with the head monk before whom I would kneel and bow deeply, my hands joined together at my forehead. Once permission had been granted, I would summon one of the young novices to show me where I might unroll my sleeping bag and mosquito net, and I would find another to fetch me some leftover rice. Then I would strip off to take my shower surrounded by dumbfounded *bonzes* who would scrutinize me from head to toe. Sometimes, exasperated, I would splash them to chase them away. But they would always return to watch the shaving session. For most of them it was the first time they had seen an electric razor and above all . . . a beard!

Phantom jets, angels of death, tore the air with their screams of terror and pain. The din of their engines and the clangour of war had long since scared all the birds away. Interminable convoys identified by a white star rumbled past loaded with bombs. Overhead camouflaged helicopters buzzed threateningly back and forth. Aboard the trucks, tanks and sundry rolling stock appeared a crowd of blond, gum-chewing giants: the Yanks were on manoeuvre. Passing Korat and Udhorn-Thani, I continued northwards towards Laos. I arrived in a country at war, a country of fear and death.

Without a word, a shoeshine boy emptied the contents of his wooden bowl into the conductor's hand. This man, barefoot and ragged, was offering to pay my bus fare. Burning with shame, I tried to make him take the money back, but he had already taken off, and the dense crowd prevented me from going after him. This humble shoeshine boy, in his noble act of self-sacrifice, proved himself to be a *bhikshu*, a true holy man, unlike the thousands that dress the part but don't have the true spirit in their souls. I shall never forget him. *Kob koon* - thank you from my heart.

In Lang Xang (Laos), the land of a million elephants, I did not catch sight of a single one, because of the war. Only the city of Vientiane, breathing slowly like a dying man, was accessible.

'They shoot at anyone with a white skin . . . How are they to know you're not an American? You don't carry a placard, do you?'

I had been warned. Nevertheless, I wanted to visit Luang Prabang, the ancient capital, located further up the Mekong River. I made inquiries, but whether by river or road the answer was always in the negative, or at the very best: 'Go at your own risk. You have a fifty-fifty chance of making it.' I felt no desire to play the hero. I preferred to finish my trip around *this* world before considering a visit to the next one. A mission of French military education corps offered me a seat on board their plane, but the date of departure was too far ahead and my visa wouldn't allow me to wait. The airport of the Royal Laos Air Force was my last recourse. Inside a huge hangar, military families squatted, waiting for flights to Luang Prabang, Paksé and Savannakhet.

For three days I sat patiently among the whining children. Only once did I get thrown out by the security patrol. The airport was buzzing like a beehive. Tiny T.28s, training planes, took off and landed, one after another. A stock of bombs had been adapted for them; their mission was to set fire to the straw huts in the bush, thus creating an exodus to the cities which were still controlled by the American-supported government. The exodus would in turn provide proof that the population wished to maintain their government, since they were 'spontaneously' seeking refuge in the cities which were still in the hands of the official power! At the controls of the T.28s were American pilots in civvies whom I ran into every day. Officially, there were no US soldiers in Laos. I continually pestered these non-civilian civilians.

'I want to go to Luang Prabang.'

The planes were overloaded, but I finally managed to get a seat. The city slumbered at the foot of the Phousi, at the confluence of the Nam Khan and the Mekong. The heat was heavy and intense, but the general air of lethargy was deceptive. The place was swarming with soldiers. This was war. Grenades went off in a cinema, machine-gun fire burst out in the suburbs, and everywhere there were refugees, the human tragedy of our century. It was a city of mute, indescribable despair.

Bendara, which in Pali, the local language, meant 'star of five beauties', was a name as light and happy as the notes of the *Lanat* (the small teak xylophone). A mere nineteen, Bendara had greeted me on my arrival in Vientiane in her tourist office in the Lane Xiang Hotel.

'Why don't you come to our place?'

In a huge wooden house on the outskirts of the city, nine children did their best to forget the war. Mr Bandasak, her father, had lived in France. I shared a large bed and mosquito net with her brother Saysana.

As soon as she got home from work, Bendara changed out of her miniskirt and undid her chignon, letting her magnificent hair fall down her back. She had a tiny body but was fragile only in appearance, for she was skilled in judo. Cheerful, frank and engaging, she was in love with freedom. Like a true Sagittarian, she had wanted to be a pilot, a profession which in Laos was closed to women. Lively and intelligent, she could already speak six languages and wanted to learn Russian and Spanish. She had applied for a scholarship to study political science in Rostov in the Soviet Union. On the application form, in the section marked 'Race', she had written: Mongrel. She felt stifled in her tourist office and dreamed of travel to far-off lands. Striving for universal brotherhood and rejecting contemporary Buddhism, she belonged to that group of young people who had moved beyond the confines of borders and nationalism. Bendara's 'star of five beauties' was a guiding light for five continents.

Smoke lingered in the room. The indolent cat waited for the transparent *marguillas*, the small fly-eating lizards to drop from the ceiling before seizing them with one swipe of its paw. Dogs romped about. Bendara took care of most of the cooking. From time to time, she would leave the fish frying in its pan and come and talk to me on the veranda. She would come and go, filling the hours with her delightful presence while the rhythmic calls of the buffalo-toads marked the passing of the night hours.

She made me forget the alarming news that reached us from neighbouring Cambodia and Vietnam. Her parents, brothers and sisters had retired for the night beneath their mosquito nets. Bendara, the only one still up, sat down next to me. Her freshness and innocence still surprised me; I wasn't used to young girls. Her utter trust baffled me. She looked at me with infinite tenderness. Yet she seemed somewhat preoccupied. After a moment's hesitation, she suddenly asked in soft, melodious French:

'André, have you ever kissed a girl?'

'All foreigners are asked not to leave the capital.' Radio Phnom Penh repeated the message every hour.

Confusion was widespread. The Communists were within firing range of Pochentong Airport - where I had just landed - and now occupied half of Cambodia.

The largest ruins in the world, the fabulous temples of Angkor Wat, were still controlled by the troops of Lon Nol. If I wanted to go there I would have to do so immediately, for the situation was rapidly deteriorating. Needless to say, Lady Luck smiled on me once again. A group of Israelis had been authorized by the Ministry of the Interior to carry out agricultural research in the Angkor region. I travelled the southern route by Land Rover in the company of Mr Roth. The direct route around the northern side of Tonlé Sap Lake had been cut off. Thanks to Mr Roth's official credentials, we were allowed past several military roadblocks without problems.

Siem Reap, the nearest town to the Khmer temples, was swarming with men in uniform. Preparations were under way to stand a siege. Trenches were being dug, sandbags stacked, crates of ammunition unloaded and machine-guns positioned at every street corner. The tourists had already cleared out except for a few madmen like myself. I found French bread, butter and black coffee in the market-place - all those things I had missed most during my travels. And yet I was unable to enjoy my French breakfast, for my heart wasn't in it. The people around me were in such distress that I couldn't possibly gorge myself, indifferent to their plight.

I rented a bicycle, bought a big pineapple for next to nothing to serve as my daily meal, and left Siem Reap by way of Général De Gaulle Avenue. Four miles ahead, the largest complex of ruins in the world awaited me in a setting of astonishing tranquillity. Suddenly, the war seemed far away.

OSLO
Home again after eighteen years of adventure. I had a dream: to go round the world - and I made it come true.
(Photo: Odd Anthonsen)

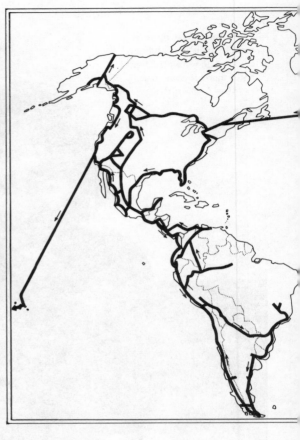

DJAKARTA
When you're hitch-hiking,
anything goes, even this
Indonesian 'betchak'.
(Photo: author's collection)

PERU
At the beginning of my trip I
joined up with two
Canadians because I was
afraid to travel alone.
(Photo: El Comercio de Lima)

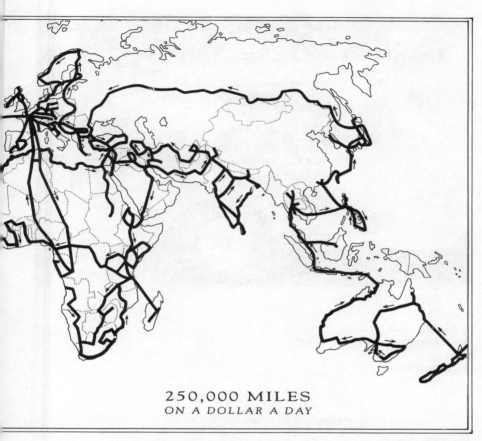

250,000 MILES
ON A DOLLAR A DAY

TEHRAN
Alone and unafraid
after thousands
of miles.
(Photo: Etalaa, Tehran)

BARRANQUILLA
(Colombia)
In jail again! This time
they suspected me of air
piracy.
(Photo: Marcel Welty)

BRAZIL
Anyone attempting a
world tour nowadays faces
an obstacle course across
consulates and borders.
Here at Manaus my friend
Juan-José and I are having
problems with our
Venezuelan visas.
(photo: Diario Da Tarde, Manaus)

ALASKA
On the road at 45° below.
In those temperatures I
could not stay out of doors
for more than half an hour.
(Photo: Edmonton Journal,
Canada)

PAKISTAN
Weakened by persistent diarrhoea, I
went down to 115 pounds and really
thought my travels were over.
(Photo: Lankadipa, Colombo, Ceylon)

BANGKOK
I sampled every food
the world had to offer.
(Photo: Thairath Newspaper)

SOUTH AMERICA
My budget of one dollar a day restricted me to eating
from food stalls in the street.
(Photo: Marcel Welty)

AMSTERDAM
I slept where I could. In Amsterdam I took refuge on a barge. Here I
am with Táhirih, the bargee's little girl, in my arms.
(Photo: author's collection)

JAPAN
In Japan it is an honour to pick up a gaijin (a foreigner),
which is rarely the case elsewhere!
(Photo: author's collection)

Everything was grandiose, immense, built to the scale of the gods who were once worshipped there. Ta Phrom was my favourite temple. French archaeologists had done a remarkable job of clearing away only the minimum of vegetation to give an idea of how the temple looked when they first saw it. Majestic kapok trees of imposing size had imprisoned the stone. Their enormous roots, like the tentacles of some insatiable monster, had wound around the pillars and lifted up blocks weighing several tons. Some had found their way up to the roofs; others pierced the surrounding walls. Inexorably, Nature had reclaimed her rights. Irreverent monkeys leaped from wall to wall, clinging to the white, furrowed trunks of the *stalaos*. On the *gopura* or gate of Ta Som, the roots of a fig tree had created a grotesque Beatles-style hairdo on top of the four giant heads of Lokeçvara. Battles and military scenes were followed by the coquettish ballets of the *devattas* and *apsaras*, celestial dancers with suggestive forms. Angkor Wat was pure, endless delight. All my senses revelled in its tranquil joy. Giddy with ecstasy, I felt utterly safe - but I was mistaken.

The war was all around me; I had to return to the capital. I had promised myself ten days of archaeological treats, but on the morning of the ninth day chose to make myself scarce, perched on top of an overcrowded truck. I was just in time. The next day (Thursday, June 4th, 1970), the ruins fell into the hands of the 'rebels' who bombarded Siem Reap and the airport. I had another lucky break. What's more, hitch-hiking saved my life: the train bound for the capital was blown up!

Barbed wire, sandbags, watchtowers, roaring jeeps, firing posts, slogans on walls and pavements, zigzag trenches, sub-machine-guns, soldiers in helmets: one spark would set the whole thing off - especially since most of the soldiers were inexperienced and impulsive young recruits. The spark soon came. A shot went off, followed by an echo. Another answered back, then two, three. A machine-gun burst into action. A grenade exploded. The war was sweeping in. Flares pierced the blackness of the night. I was sleeping in a classroom located in the buildings of the Catholic diocese. The shots were coming from a water reservoir, a heavily guarded strategic point some hundred yards away. I turned off the electric fan to listen to the whistling of the bullets. I wondered whether I could risk a look outside. I held my breath. My stomach was in knots, and my heart was pounding. I was scared. Yet curiosity got the better of me, and I crawled towards the window.Flares lit up the night.

'Oh, what a beautiful red! Look at that lovely white one!'

The entire episcopal staff was on the balcony. From the fourth floor, two or three priests made joking comments on the 'firework' display. An hour later the all clear sounded and I fell asleep as though nothing had happened.

'Down with Sihanouk! Long live Lon Nol!' 'Death to the Viet Virus!' The walls dripped with slogans inciting hatred and murder. Schools had been converted into barracks, and Phnom Penh was now nothing more than a parade ground. Having come to power, the new Head of State no longer concerned himself with details. 'We have to get rid of the Vietnamese', was the gist of his proclamations. His fellow citizens did not concern themselves with details either, but took out their age-old grudge against Vietnam by simply massacring, raping or plundering any Vietnamese they could get their hands on. Hundreds of corpses floated down the Mekong. It was all the more appalling when one realized that Lon Nol had been pointing his finger at the North Vietnamese and not at the Vietnamese immigrants who had been living in Cambodia for a long time, working hard for their livelihood. It was probably that very industriousness which the local population held against them: the immigrants worked and worked well, to the extent of becoming master craftsmen and managers of much of the country's commerce. Patriotism has broad shoulders and many crimes are committed in its name. Thousands of Vietnamese managed, nevertheless, to escape the massacre and find some sort of refuge. Many of them were huddled in the mud around the seminary; some had even set up camp on the roof. They had lost everything they had. And here I was still griping because somebody had pinched my watch and cash.

Looking at them, I remembered the war - our own - that I had lived through as a child in Brunoy: the deserted marketplace, the ration cards for bread and milk, the biscuits studded with big salt grains handed out during break at school, the air raid warnings that sent us scurrying to the basement. Words flooded unbidden into my mind: exodus, firing squad, bombing, Gestapo, hostages, death, death . . . Fear pervaded my earliest memories of life. Where I had seen nothing but suffering, hatred and hideousness, people had tried to make me understand that it was really called glory, grandeur, heroism. Patriotism was an astonishing thing. Killing became legal, a duty, a way to attain honours and medals . . . like the Olympic medallions in Mexico City. Dear God, human behaviour can be hard to understand.

'Hey, who do you think you are? A racing driver? Look at the state of the road. We're going to kill ourselves at the speed you're going!'

'Listen, buddy, you see the sun over there, just above the horizon? In five minutes it will have set, and all hell will let loose. I don't want to end up looking like a piece of Swiss cheese.'

The Korean diplomat driving me to Saigon was hardly optimistic. Expecting trouble, he pushed the accelerator to the floor. I felt extremely uneasy. Having the choice between a mortar shell and a roll into the ditch was not a laughing matter.

For thirty years Vietnam had been living in the shadow of death. War was everywhere: I was not allowed even to set foot in North Vietnam. The roads were filled with tanks, trucks, jeeps, machine-guns. For the last couple of days I had felt like a general on a tour of inspection. It was loathsome. I was no longer on a trip around the world, but on a weird hitch-hiking trip to the various 'theatres of war'.

In contrast to Vientiane or Phnom Penh, Saigon was in full swing. The war was every bit as present as elsewhere and even more murderous, because it had become a part of everyday life. Every inhabitant had suffered physical or mental damage - sometimes both. I was taken for an American and therefore assumed to have pockets full of dollars. Motor cycles, rickshaws and cars all stopped to offer their services. I felt compelled to explain that I was French, whereupon without another word I would be driven to wherever I wished to go - for free!

The monsoon was turning the streets into a mud-bath, and everything was being rotted away by the war. In the capital itself, brothers were at each other's throats. There had been a student uprising against Thieu, and in the National Assembly the delegates were tearing each other to pieces. Then, of course, there were the fist fights between drunkards, and between the bar girls and the GIs on leave. Violence went on at every level; children were being brought up on it. I was discovering man in his most primitive, most hideous aspect.

Yet some of the world's most rarefied beauty was also present, mingled in with the thirty-year-long butchery. The Vietnamese women were, in my opinion, the most angelic on earth. Like colourful, scintillating wings, their traditional *ao dais* fluttered delicately in the midst of the minefield. At the top of the side slit, just above the black silk pants, appeared a small triangle of skin. Light-skinned and fine-featured, with delicate lips, almond eyes and long, jet black hair covered by a conical hat, the slender and graceful Vietnamese women helped me understand the nostalgia that the veterans of French Indo-China felt for Vietnam. When would the sun shine again on their country, the country of *Ahiṃsa*, of non-violence?

'Hitch-hike through the Philippines? It's obvious you've never been there before. You must be out of your mind. They'll shoot you as soon as look at you. Believe me, you'd do better to give the Philippines a miss.'

The Air France pilot warned me the minute I got off the plane, but I was sceptical. I had just come from Vietnam . . . If I had listened to everybody's good advice, I would still be back home in Brunoy.

'Taxi, Mister, taxi!'

'I'm not a customer. I'm hitch-hiking.'

The taxi-drivers couldn't believe it. One of them grabbed my arm.

'But, Mister, it's impossible. Hitch-hiking is terribly dangerous, believe me. It's twelve miles to the city, and it's getting dark . . . I don't think you understand the situation . . .'

Flabbergasted by my stubbornness, he bought me a bus ticket! This arrival in Manila was none too reassuring. After the powder keg of Indo-China, here I was in the land of cut-throats.

My host Eddie took no risks at all. As soon as he had greeted me, he gave me a warning. In the Philippines, a loaded gun was a man's best friend. We were going out for a drive, so he slipped one gun into his belt and placed a second one on the dashboard of his car where it was in full view. In town, I was startled to see signs outside banks: 'Please deposit your weapons before entering.' The police were armed to the teeth, and the newspapers were brimming with stories of crime. If I was to believe my Filipino friend, all his neighbours were murderers or thieves.

If I wanted to visit this country, I was going to have to arm myself . . . with courage and a good store of peace-loving vibrations to counter the violence. There was certainly no question of my carrying a gun. We would see!

The capital, Manila, resembled a gigantic merry-go-round with its colourful carriages and *jeepneys*. These jeeps from the Second World War, converted into collective taxis, were bright with chromework and profusely decorated, hand-painted with exuberant motifs, every one a masterpiece in its own right. From here I was going to try hitch-hiking around Luzon, the largest island to the Philippine archipelago which comprises no fewer than 7,700 islands. I didn't have much luck hitching, but managed to get around just the same. On the other hand, I got asked plenty of questions. 'Why go around the world? That's insane!' In the eyes of the Filipinos, the only trip worth making was to the United States where you could soon make your fortune.

In Baguio, a small resort surrounded by mountain pines, I celebrated - in my own way - my fifteenth anniversary as a globe-trotter. The air at this altitude was fresh and invigorating. I came out of a kind of lethargy that had been with me for several months. It had been something like a coma, brought on in part by the heat of the Australian and Asian steam-baths, but also by the constant closeness of the angel of death. The mayor of Baguio was visibly pleased to welcome me to his community. He had me sign the Visitor's Book, gave me an autographed copy of a book about his city, threw a banquet in my honour, and organized a press conference. The national television network was represented as well as seven radio stations. For a long time now, I had been feeling detached from things, and I was just as indifferent to the bouquet of microphones as to the filthy ditches where I often took shelter. Nevertheless, I could have easily started believing that I had it made, that Brugiroux was on its way to becoming a household name. No, I was simply here, in shorts, a more-or-less-clean shirt and beat-up old shoes, standing in front of some people, talking about my trip.

Once again I took up my favourite themes: our modern communications were narrowing distances, but at the same time people were setting up more impassable barriers. Universal consciousness could save the world from portending chaos. But only if people had the will . . .

Following my encounter with the media, hitching suddenly became much easier. The bus and ferry companies were only too happy to give me free trips. I decided to explore the country more thoroughly, in spite of the risk of assault. Luzon, Samar, Leyte, Mindanao: the transport conditions were almost beyond description. At times I had to trudge several miles in the mud in order to change to another bus on a drier road. Bridges were often simply missing. The crowd of travellers would then pay a toll in order to cross a plank bridge on foot. I averaged only ten miles an hour, and by nightfall I was all in. I slept in a series of shabby villages swarming with hens, goats and pigs. But I didn't mind, as the scenery was always magnificent.

In Bohol, life was good: although that sounded like a tourist slogan, it seemed to me to be true. Seeing me pass by in front of his hut, Mr Cabagnot called to me and begged me to do him the honour of visiting his home. I had a hard time imagining the same sort of thing happening in Europe . . . He had only eight children, which wasn't very many for a country where a dozen was considered the minimum. And from what I saw of it, raising children was easier than raising pigs, for the latter were much harder to come by. The Cabagnot son, who imagined himself a hippy, announced what he considered to be the basic tenet of the philosophy of Western youth: 'Make babies, not war!' In the minds of these people, making love was entirely synonymous with procreation.

The affection, concern for others and peaceful atmosphere of the Cabagnot household touched me deeply. I was happy in their company and they, for their part, treated me as their favourite son. The father asked me to leave a photograph with him, as he wished to include me in the family album. Frequently, I thought about the great good fortune I had had in finding, from one end of the earth to the other, homes in which I could be surrounded by the comforting presence of a genuine family. Without such a sustaining influence, I would never have been able to continue. What a pleasure to be able to walk into a kitchen and surprise the mother of a family in front of her stove. What precious intimacy! Without it, how could anyone come to know the soul of a people? I doubted very sincerely that I could have tolerated a hotel room, even a luxurious one, 365 days a year. In spite of its comfort, a hotel room was never more than a cell devoid of human warmth, terrifyingly anonymous.

The Cabagnots took me along to the fair in Batuan on the other side of the island. In the square in front of the church, a few makeshift stalls competed for the attention of the public. The stall which was having the greatest success was that of the Three Magi.

'Come on in, ladies and gentlemen! Come and see the marvel of marvels, the most extraordinary natural spectacle in the whole of the Philippines . . . Step right up! It's money well spent . . .'

My stomach churned at the sight of three hideous monsters, living foetuses, aborted beings. The parents, first cousins, had had fourteen children, six of whom had been born with the same abnormality. After two such births, the parents had had the idea of making money out of their misfortune. Caspar, Balthazar and Melchior - fourteen, eighteen and twenty-five years old respectively - were no more than three feet or so in length and weighed between ten and twenty pounds each. Blind, they remained in the same curled up, foetal position, and their involuntary spasms provoked roars of laughter from the audience. They nauseated me; I could not bear to look at them. A few of the spectators were even trying to tickle them.

'Aren't they lucky!' said the person standing next to me. 'They must make a fortune from them!'

The spectators were having a fine time, laughing heartily, without either cruelty or malice in their eyes. In 'Westernized' societies we try to hide away our hunchbacks and mentally disabled, whereas here the reaction was natural rather than condescending. The Asian response to a disagreeable situation always surprised me, but it was the correct one: to face things squarely and good-naturedly. A Westerner would start swearing at the slightest mishap. In Asia, they laughed. It was healthier. The souls of individuals are not affected by their physical disadvantages, any more than clouds prevent the sun from giving out its dazzling brightness, according to 'Abdu'l-Bahá.

Seven weeks later, at the moment of departure, I was once again overwhelmed by the sadness of separation, and this time more strongly than before. I was leaving the most receptive country on earth. The Filipinos possessed the secret of successful hospitality: the desire to share the things that make them happy. They were ready to take to their hearts anyone who could laugh at life. A true example of the Filipino warmth and openness was Maggy, with her generosity of spirit and charm, who showed me Mactan Island, facing Cebu, where the explorer Magellan had been murdered. How could I explain the fact that these poor, deprived people could give and love with so much spontaneity?

I had armed myself with friendship only to be swamped by a deluge of affection and love. How strange to think that I had been warned to be on my guard, to carry a loaded gun (or two), and never to leave my bus for fear of death . . . and yet I had found unbelievable gentleness and friendship. With a heavy heart I walked up the gangplank of the boat. I had never been so sorry to leave anywhere.

Chapter 9

IT'S NO GO IN CHINA

Junks bristling with sails, thousands of sampans, a crowd bustling with life and activity, a booming world of business: together it spelled Hong Kong. For months I had been among Chinese people, but this time I was on the mainland itself and at the very door of the world that made so many people dream or tremble: the Red China of Mao Tse-Tung.

Although the Cultural Revolution was over, I still had little hope of entering the land of the Great Wall. I had looked into the matter much earlier. As far back as Vientiane I had gone to the Chinese Consulate, only to be taken for a conspirator if not a spy. Private door, half-closed spyhole, an interrogation according to the rules: no luck. I had another try in Phnom Penh.

'You are most welcome in China . . . but we don't issue visas!'

What was left? Trying to sneak in did not strike me as impossible, but I had a strong sense of self-preservation and no desire to rot in a Chinese jail. And yet Wendy Myers* had made it there! But that had been in 1964, and since then the Red Guards had changed a lot of things. I might just as well forget it. Nevertheless I was annoyed.

There was no consulate in Hong Kong, and yet China was omnipresent. The red star shone from the top of the tallest bank in both Victoria and Kowloon§. Elsewhere, in certain stores and warehouses,

*A young British girl who also hitch-hiked around the world (1960-67). She did her trip in two instalments, before and after a long stay in Australia and New Zealand. Her family gave her substantial financial assistance.

§Victoria, the capital, is built on Hong Kong Island. Kowloon is across the harbour on the Chinese mainland.

Mao's portrait was in full view. Ships flying the red star were docked not far from US naval submarines in a permanent show of defiance. Propaganda shops blatantly displayed their wares. An exhibition flooded with slogans and giant photographs occupied most of a skyscraper. Everything was dedicated to Mao, and the Little Red Book, published in fifty languages, was on sale everywhere. Cinemas and supermarkets distributed products from Communist China - at fixed prices, for bargaining was prohibited.

After wandering about the city, I felt disgusted by all the fantastic Maoist propaganda but also frustrated at not being able to cross the border. I finally came across the office of the China Travel Service in Victoria which also served as a consulate. It was my last hope. A gilded statue of Mao dominated the middle of the room, and photographs of menacing mobs, armed soldiers and technical achievements assailed the visitor. The brainwashing exasperated me, but I was convinced that the Chinese people were different.

'We cannot grant a visa at the moment . . . No, there would be no point in waiting. We have no idea when Peking is going to send us the next quota, really no idea at all . . . and in any case, there would be six weeks of formalities . . .'

Which all meant, very simply, that I would not be going to China. My hopes had been dashed. I had desperately wanted to get to know the Chinese people, who were not only the most numerous on earth but also possessed an ancient history and extensive heritage. I would also have liked to learn something from the Chinese political experience.

The young woman I talked to wore the typical blue uniform, short hair, and no make-up. She was extremely aggressive and very well indoctrinated. She tried to provoke me into saying the worst possible things about Americans and their imperialist 'lackeys' in Cambodia and Vietnam. In her eyes only Mao was right. I was repelled by such fanaticism. I left, but only after she had recommended me to read the book about China on sale in her office. Certainly, one could stay at home and travel the world by watching television or leafing through newspapers and magazines. But reading a beautiful love story was hardly the same as actually being in love.

Just to check if there was one final chance of my project getting off the ground, I visited the China Travel Service in Kowloon. There I met with the same reply, the same disappointment, but this time I was able to make friends with the young Red Guard on duty. Over cups of green, sugarless tea, he explained to me his ideas about Mao and China. Mao was struggling against the antiquated morals and traditional hypocrisy of Confucianism and to that end had introduced the notions of criticism, national effort and respect for women. He had stressed the need for progress and modern science and elevated work into a popular ideal. As a result, China was now in tune with the times. Bravo! It was true, and I said as much to my new friend.

'Capitalism is the enemy', he added. 'We have to get rid of it with guns.'

He seemed ready to grab a rifle at the first command! But there we agreed to differ. I made a point of explaining my theory of non-violence, of universal love, of spreading the good vibrations. We would get together again. In the meantime, he gave me a copy of the Little Red Book in Spanish, prefaced by the 'traitor' Lin Piao.

I explained to my friend Wu, whom I saw two or three times more, that Mao was one step behind. Power had been, but was no longer to be, found in the barrel of a rifle. The two principal losers of the last World War were now in charge of two of the world's most powerful economies, and since 1945, wars had resulted in nothing but shared failures, divisions, and a continuation of the status quo: Korea, Vietnam, the Middle East . . . So then, if no one could win, what was the purpose of war?

'You see, Wu, violence only breeds violence. If you seize power with a machine-gun, you encourage the next guy to do the same. You get caught up in a vicious circle of violence and you don't change a thing. You think you're bringing about a revolution, but really you're only perpetuating the violence that in the end will make you a victim, too. Making war in order to have peace: isn't that something of a paradox? Believe me, only peace will bring us peace. As 'Abdu'l-Bahá said: "*The solution of economic questions, for instance, will not be accomplished by array of labour against capital and capital against labour in strife and conflict, but by the voluntary attitude of sacrifice on both sides.*" '

I would only see Red China from a distance, from Lok Machau, a hill along the river that formed the border. From that vantage point I could see the province of Kwangtung and a green plain stretching away to the horizon. Hundreds of curious tourists were pouring out of air-conditioned buses and chasing after the hawkers of souvenirs. Little ten-year-old girls with infants strapped to their backs posed against the Red-China backdrop for one dollar.

'Hello, picture baby, chee (cheese) . . .'

Failing entry into Mao's Red China, I decided to console myself with Taiwan. Blast! They didn't have a consulate either. Once again I took up my crazy hunt for visas. On Wyndham Street, the office of Chung Wah Travel Service handled procedures.

'I'm infinitely sorry, but we don't grant visas to French citizens!'

For goodness sake! The great Charles de Gaulle had opened an embassy in China, Taiwan's sworn enemy. As a result, no visas for Frenchmen. But the official slipped me a useful hint.

'Unless, of course, you know someone in Taiwan who would like to welcome you and serve as your sponsor . . .'

Unfortunately, I didn't know a soul in the land of Chiang Kai-shek. I returned empty-handed to the home of my Bahá'í friends, twin brothers of Chinese descent who had put me up in their apartment. A gigantic American pulled open the door. A miracle! He had just arrived from Taiwan, where he had spent the last two years teaching.

'Well, it seems almost impossible to me. Even the Formosans themselves have a hard time getting passports . . . I have an Italian buddy, but . . .'

An Italian! What a piece of luck! Those people were unsurpassed at cutting through red tape; they were champion wheeler-dealers. Antonio was great. As soon as he received my letter, he went to retrieve his residence permit which he had temporarily turned over to the government in order to go to the US for his father's funeral. He was the director of one of the Pearl Buck Foundations, those institutions which take care of the numerous children fathered by American soldiers in South-East Asia. My problem was solved: I had become Antonio's brother-in-law.

While awaiting my 'invitation' to Taiwan, I paid a visit to Macao, the second tiny wart on China's immense body. As its principal claim to fame, the Portuguese colony boasted the world's largest casino. Actually, for all practical purposes, Macao and the two islands of Taipa and Coloan had been dependent on Mao ever since 1966 - to the extent of celebrating October 1st, the Red China national holiday, as if it were their own. Of course that did not prevent the residents of Macao from celebrating the national holidays of Portugal and Taiwan as well!

Back in Hong Kong I bought a new movie camera. Prices were low, and my old Ercsam had finally given up the ghost after ten years of loyal service. My movie camera was my only possession of any value and together with my diary provided me with a record of my journey. It didn't quite go with the image of a hitch-hiker and I had often felt too embarrassed to use it. In addition, I never stopped cursing the extra weight (seven of the twenty-five pounds I lugged on my back), and each day I wondered why I hadn't taken along one of those mini-cameras the size of a pen instead. But in the end, Providence knew best. Eventually I would enlarge the films to 16mm and use them to illustrate public talks, something I had never dreamed of when I left France - any more than I'd dreamed of writing a book. I had simply left to study and search for my own truth, nothing more.

In order to get used to super-8, I filmed the nightmarish reality of the 'Strait of Perfumes' which is what 'Hong Kong' means in Chinese. With its densely-packed houses, the steep-stepped streets, floating slums and crowded shops, Hong Kong was an incredible jumble which did not bear the slightest resemblance to any place in Europe. The bay was beautiful, but despite all the animation, it was a cold, reserved city. Everything revolved around business and dollars, and no one ever smiled. The girls were splendid-looking but distant, assertive and unsentimental. Like Bangkok and Sydney, Hong Kong was an American R& R post, which no doubt explained part of the problem. 'Want a date? Call K 669805 JESCORT.' All the newspapers were crammed with such ads. In Wangshai, the neighbourhood immortalized by Suzy Wong, a sign on every door read: 'Welcome US boys'. Drinking unaccompanied was out of the question, and the dollar was King. As a result, no girl wanted to be seen with a white man for fear of being taken for a prostitute.

The Cantonese language radio broadcast two hour-long programmes about my trip. Chen, a young woman with ivory skin, conducted the interview, interspersing it with the songs of Piaf, Brassens and Aznavour.

Whew! I had finally made it to Chinese China - a makeshift China to be sure, but China none the less. In order to enter Taiwan without alarming the authorities, I plastered my hair down with water and got rid of the photograph Wu had given me of the 'renegade dog' (the supreme insult: 'Mao' means cat!). I was lucky not to be sent to a barber, for only a few days previously an order had been given lifting the compulsory haircuts for foreigners. The new ruling had been prompted by an incident in which the sailors of a Danish ship had had their heads shaved by force. Furious, they had hoisted anchor without even unloading their cargo. Such goings-on were bad for business.

'Isn't it wonderful to have friends who come from so far away?' The tourist office in Taipei, the capital, had no qualms about displaying this quotation from Confucius. Never mind that the 'friends' had to prove themselves to be above suspicion, and that they risked losing their visas if their countries of origin dared make eyes at Peking.

Throughout my time among the Chinese, I had been bombarded with one surprise after another. Now in Taiwan I felt completely overwhelmed. The spectacle on the streets was ever more bizarre. Sweeping, green-tiled roofs covered little shops with utterly astounding displays. Everything was unfamiliar. I launched into a fascinating guessing game. Crushed roots, dried lizards, brightly-coloured powders: might it be some sort of pharmacy? And that vendor of greenery: was he a horticultural specialist selling to plant-lovers? Or might he be in competition with the first store-owner? What name could I give to this shop: grocery store, dime store, or drugstore? Bitter oranges, spiral sticks of incense, shredded octopus, moon cakes, firecrackers in a variety of sizes, dried fish, hats pierced with holes . . . There was no point in enumerating; the list would be endless. Yet one item intrigued me more than the rest. Piled in crates was a large quantity of clay balls, each of which contained a hard-boiled egg. If the ball was black, the yolk inside was coloured red. In the white balls the yolk was green. Finally, to keep things simple, the 'white' of the egg was in all cases black. When ready to be served, the eggs would be sliced and stuck on to skewers along with pieces of ginger.

The language problem also contributed to my feeling of disorientation. Chinese characters were certainly decorative, but they were also extremely numerous and quite mind-boggling. Still, I learned to recognize a few of them. The ideogram for 'man' had been simplified over the years, losing its head and arms in the process. Today it consisted of a simple 'Y' turned upside down. 'Sun' had also evolved to the point of becoming a rectangle with a bar in the middle. 'Aeroplane' was represented by a bird . . . with a motor! 'Rocket' was an arrow on fire. The ideogram for 'peace' was somewhat more complicated; a woman under a roof (that was *their* opinion!). Two trees meant 'strong'; the sun in a tree represented the 'Orient'; an insect bite in a mouth signified the verb, 'to command'; a large sheep meant 'beautiful'; a woman and child stood for 'good'. The sun and moon juxtaposed might be mistaken for 'eclipse'; in fact, it meant 'brilliant'. I was soon out of my depth - not so the Chinese, who were all able to read these characters no matter what their language or dialect might be.

My five languages were no more help to me in China than they were in Indonesia. Therefore I launched once again into 'Operation Minimum Vocabulary', making an effort to acquire the following words and phrases: 'I am French'; 'I am hitch-hiking around the world'; 'car'; 'straight ahead'; 'I am going to . . .'; 'hello'; 'thank you'; 'tired'; 'ill'; 'salt'; 'how much?' (indispensable); 'I am not American'; 'it is too expensive'; and . . . 'I love you' (useful). Luckily, I had a retentive memory, and most of the people I spoke to appreciated my efforts to communicate with them. Furthermore, with time and experience I had become downright cunning, I figured I didn't have to remember both 'hot' and 'cold' but only the easier of the two words. I'd get along just fine with 'hot' and . . . 'no hot'. Clever? Unfortunately, in China it was 'no go'. There was no point trying to put together a pocket-size vocabulary. Each Chinese word had several possible meanings which could be differentiated only by tone of voice. My Western throat proved incapable of pronouncing correctly even a single syllable.

Nevertheless, I was rarely at a complete loss. As the miles rolled by, I perfected a repertoire of sound effects worthy of a music hall act. I learned to imitate a car engine, a ship's siren, the mooing of a cow. Added to my already-acquired skill of snoring, these sounds would in theory enable me to hitch-hike by car or by boat, obtain milk, or find some shelter for the night. Since I had also retained two Chinese expressions, 'meo tchen' (no money) and 'se`sen' (thank you), I would probably be able to manage. The moment having finally come to put all this preparation into practice, I threw myself into a flawless imitation of a hen laying an egg. The Chinese watched me with expressionless faces. I tried again, this time adding a supremely subtle finishing touch to my act: I put my hand under my seat and, bending over, pretended to extract an egg. 'Cluck, cluck, cluck . . .' Nothing! People were looking at me in bewilderment, as if I had gone nuts.'Cluck, cluck, cluck . . .' Only later did I learn that the Chinese were used to eating duck eggs!

My last resort was pure mime performed without a sound. Again I met with total failure. In China, to get across the idea that you wished to eat, you had to cup your hand in the form of a rice bowl level with your chest and then, with two extended fingers of the other hand, imitate chopsticks digging into the bowl! One day I wanted to buy ten bananas, I used both hands to indicate five-plus-five; the man ran away terrified. To have made myself understood, I should have crossed my two index fingers even with my knees . . . and so forth. I also learned that it was considered bad form to say 'thank you' while seated at the table, and that dessert was served in the middle of a meal and the soup at the end!

In a country where men strolled in the street wearing silk pyjamas and where pillows were made of porcelain, one thing I did appreciate was the cuisine. It was an art that the Chinese brought to perfection, and although it was very different from French cooking, it nevertheless made me feel more at home. Another characteristic shared by the Chinese and the French was a certain notion of culture. Both peoples were convinced that theirs was the most refined culture in the world. The Chinese considered theirs to be the only culture, the true culture; in their opinion the other peoples of the world were civilized only to the extent that they succeeded in emulating the culture of the Celestial Empire.

As I was about to get off the bus in Taitung, Wun Lang, the young but rather butch woman conductor, took hold of my arm and motioned me to follow her. Where was she taking me? Naturally, I had refused to pay my bus fare, but she had not seemed inclined to make a song and dance about it. So what was this all about? We entered a restaurant, sat down, and ate dinner face to face in perfect silence. Besides smiles, we didn't have much else to exchange. Our meal finished, she again motioned me - commandingly - to follow her. I obeyed. Backpack in place, I let her lead me through the labyrinth of dark lanes that made up this dirty, unfamiliar town. Apparently she was going to find me a place to stay. How could I explain that things would go faster if I did it myself, that my personal technique was guaranteed to be rapid and efficient, that I could manage just fine on my own?

The police station! I should have guessed that we were on our way to see the police, who in Taiwan had a reputation for being very strict about regulations. But it was too late. I was cornered and was now to be given the full treatment, a tough interrogation, by an inspector from the Foreign Ministry come expressly to handle my case. The man subjected my passport to a scrutiny it had never suffered before. He read it and reread it in detail, backwards and forwards; I wouldn't have been surprised if he had produced a magnifying glass. He didn't seem overly concerned by my hitch-hiking without money. What preoccupied him was one question: had I or had I not visited Red China or the Soviet Union? Once he had been sufficiently reassured on that point, he took to worrying about me.

'Hitch-hiking doesn't exist in our country. The police will gladly provide you with a bus ticket to your next destination. Meanwhile you'll spend the night in a hotel as our guest.'

'But I can just as well sleep here on the ground, in this cell . . .'

'I won't hear of it. It would be an embarrassment for me. Miss Wun, please be kind enough to show our visitor to the Golden Dragon Hotel.'

During the days that followed, I was repeatedly surprised by the reaction of the taxi drivers to whom I made clear my inability to pay: 'Meo tchen'. They inevitably responded with a thumbs-up gesture as if to say: 'Don't worry, buddy. Just hop in and tell me where you want to go.' Concerning sleeping arrangements, it was the same thing - to the point where it became impossible for me to stretch out in the streets. I seemed to have right of access to hotels and restaurants, free of charge of course. I finally figured out why, when a Chinese man showed me newspapers in which I was mentioned. They described a penniless Frenchman being rescued by the combined efforts of a female bus conductor, a driver, and the Taitung police. The article was not very clear on the subject of hitch-hiking. Apparently, the writers hadn't really grasped the reason for my doing it. They had only picked up on one thing: I refused to pay!

Hotels, restaurants: as a matter of pride, the Chinese always treated me very well, even though I had not asked them for anything. I would much rather have stayed with families where I would have learned more about the customs and the people. Unfortunately, the Chinese of China, although generous, were also secretive and did not invite people into their homes. Chinese society was hermetically sealed. Therefore I consoled myself as best I could by attending numerous performances of the famous Chinese opera. Motionless in my seat, I let myself fall under the spell of the enchanting drama, the celestial voices and otherworldly music, the extravagant costumes, the piercing cries and clever mimicry. For hours on end the China of legend, the China of pageantry, held me in thrall. I knew that some day, in the future, I would go to Great China.

It was goodbye to the shorts, sandals and permanent sweat of the tropical countries. It was farewell to the never-ending saunas and Turkish baths. For the first time in nine months I was to experience a temperate climate and season once again. I arrived in Japan in the autumn, and with a more moderate temperature, my appetite was restored. It was none too soon either, for I had dropped to 125 pounds. I had never been so thin in my life.

Some people spend their lives dreaming. As for me, I prefer to live my dreams. Some twenty years earlier, when the first Japanese tourist office opened in Paris, I had rushed to the Rue Richelieu to dream amidst the brochures. I had been thirteen years old. Ten years later, still holding on to my dream, I had worked out an entire plan of campaign with my best friend, Jacques. In a café in Saint-Germain-des-Prés, we drew up plans for nothing less than a Paris-to-Tokyo expedition to be accomplished by way of Siberia. We spent marvellous hours calculating the mileage between stops, the number of spare tyres needed . . . Then Jacques became enslaved by a good woman and a good job, and Paris-to-Tokyo lay forgotten in a desk drawer.

And so, when I finally did set foot in Japan, I felt as if I were setting foot on the moon. I had waited twenty years to take that step, that first step into the Land of the Rising Sun. In fact, it did seem like another planet. Frightened by its first contact with the Portuguese, the earliest Western visitors, Japan shut itself off from the rest of the world in the sixteenth century and thus preserved its uniqueness. When in 1853, Commodore Perry threatened to attack if Japan didn't open its doors to trade, the sight of those three American ships belching black smoke came as a revelation. Suddenly, the Japanese realized how far behind they were, and instead of complaining - which is the case today with many nations, or at least with their leaders - they faced up to the situation with intelligent resourcefulness. They headed for Europe and came back with the best each country had to offer. It was the Meiji Revolution. Fifty years later Japan had crushed China and Russia to become the leading Asian power.

At the end of the Second World War this intelligent, skilful, tireless people drew a lesson from defeat and military occupation. The result was the Japan of today. Endowed with few natural resources (the Nipponese islands are essentially volcanic), Japan has set an example and proved that there are no poor countries, only poorly organized ones. Japan has also shown the advantages of taking inspiration from the best of what is available, whatever the source.

There were definitely two Japans, the Japan of the past and the Japan of the present. Present-day Japan was highly industrialized, with one of the world's most prosperous economies. But harmony reigned between the old and the new which was, in itself, one of the country's strengths.

The freighter from Okinawa dropped me in the port of Kagoshima. I was left to fend for myself, a stranger faced with a new currency, unfamiliar food, strange customs and a foreign language. Fortunately there were no problems hitching. The Japanese were always glad to help a European. Custom even favoured presenting a small gift to the hitch-hiker simply as a sign of friendship and welcome. To pick up a *gaijin*, a foreigner, was considered an honour. On the other hand, little charity was evident between fellow citizens, and I never saw a Japanese hitch-hike in his own country.

'The Japanese never invite foreigners into their homes', an ambassador had told me. I had the pleasure of proving him wrong, thanks to a new trick I had come up with. Each evening, I would find a table in a small restaurant and begin writing in my journal. Like all people, the Japanese were curious and . . . each time I found myself invited into someone's home. I should add, for the benefit of His Excellency, that the Nipponese generally lived in rather modest circumstances but endeavoured nevertheless to preserve a measure of pride. For that reason, no doubt, they were shy of opening their doors to an ambassador. But confronted with plain André Brugiroux, these same Japanese felt no such constraint. With such an undistinguished guest, they could be their normal welcoming selves.

This was the case with Nagakao, a young man driving a Mazda, who offered to take me to a *Ryokan* and thus introduce me to traditional Japan. In Fukushima, 200 miles north-east of Tokyo, he showed me into an old inn worthy of *Madam Butterfly*. A corridor of creaking floorboards; a thin sliding door made of light wood and rice paper; a small white room with wooden walls, of the utmost simplicity, yet beautiful and welcoming: we had entered the Japan of the past. Unlike the Chinese, who loved a profusion of colours and objects, the Japanese had mastered the art of paring things down to their bare essentials, of combining beauty with simplicity. The room was nearly empty, containing only a single low table. In a corner, a bright red bird painted on a *kakemono* scroll added a touch of colour above a typical bouquet. A small ceiling lamp of plaited bamboo slats was the final touch. A bay window opened on to a grove of bamboo. The whole setting was pervaded by an unusual peace. We entered barefoot. The *tatami* , woven grass mat, under my feet was like a caress.

At that moment, Nagakao motioned me to put on the kimono which was more practical for sitting cross-legged on the *tatami*. The servant, dressed in kimono and obi, returned with jasmine tea, the traditional sign of welcome.

'Come with me. We're going to take a bath together.'

I had already noticed that the Japanese were very clean and their clothes immaculate, but I could not help remembering my Californian adventure and the episode of the 'hot shower'. After placing our clothes in two small baskets, we entered the bath house naked. Nagakao handed me a little towel which I slung casually over my shoulder, not knowing what else to do with it. In so doing, I visibly shocked my new friend, who

was walking alongside me bent double, his towel carefully covering his
private parts. We were obviously taking a bath together, but *ofuro*,
bathing Japanese-style, was not to be a pretext for loose behaviour of any
sort.

In the bath house there was the same striking simplicity. In one
corner two stones symbolized a waterfall; in another was a small wooden
tub.

'Don't just jump in like a dirty European! Wash yourself first!'

I must admit that I found his advice somewhat surprising, but I
took the point. It seemed obvious, after all, that the Frenchman who
bathed once a week, if that, would only be soaking in his own filth -
revolting! I carefully observed my host. Seated on a stool, he splashed
himself with water from a small container which he then refilled at one
of two taps in the wall. After rubbing some soap on to his washcloth, he
went through a long soap-and-rinse cycle which I took care to imitate. It
was then time for the plunge. My friend entered the water with delight.
With complete trust I thrust in my own foot. My shriek of agony shook
the entire building. The water was boiling hot! No longer able to
contain himself at the spectacle of a clumsy, unbathed Westerner, my
samurai burst out laughing. Later on, I had the opportunity to try again,
and eventually became accustomed to the *ofuro* and even acquired a
liking for it.

Completely relaxed and dizzy with the heat, we slipped back into
our kimonos and the servant knelt to lay out our meal. Before us was a
spread of eleven little dishes containing raw fish, herbs, salted cabbage,
sweetened cucumber with sticky rice, and other items which I could not
identify. Nagakao again had a laugh at my expense, for I was incapable of
seating myself Japanese-style on my knees and heels. I had a clear
preference for seating cross-legged - the only position I could maintain
for several hours at a time.

With deep bows and a fixed smile, the servant prepared our
'bedroom' by pulling two foam mattresses out of a closet that I had not
even noticed. Laying them on the floor, she placed a sheet and feather
duvet on top of each, thereby combining Western comfort with Asian
simplicity. I slept marvellously well, and this became my favourite kind of
bed.

The next day Nagakao made a 'detour' in order to drop me off t
Aomori where the ferries left for the northern island of Hokkaido. I felt
almost embarrassed at his generosity, but he absolutely insisted on
introducing me to his country's customs and regional cuisines. To that

end he went 500 miles out of his way - something I had never encountered before.

Fascinating Japan! Every morning for ten minutes the entire nation jumped up and down. Shoulder to shoulder, bosses and employees performed the mandatory physical jerks: one, two . . . one, two. The Japanese worked with a smile, considering it a source of pleasure. While watching one of their keep-fit sessions, I tried to imagine my fellow Frenchmen or, even better, the Italians doing jumping-jacks in the courtyards of their factories. What a free-for-all that would be!

Enthralling Japan! Every day I stored up image after image, memory after memory. I wanted to see and learn about everything, both past and present. I remembered how Baudot and Séguéla had unnerved me with their comment that on a trip around the world 'nine capitals out of ten' ended up looking just the same.* I didn't agree, for every new thing captured my attention. I knew I would never get to the point of feeling blasé.

When I was not people-watching in the streets, parks and temples, I was busy studying history and tradition in the museums. But in Japan the cost of living was appallingly high. Since I was curious about everything, and since the museums were so numerous, my wallet was beginning to find my studies rather expensive. In other places I would try to get on the right side of the guard or curator by amusing him with some anecdote. A peal of laughter would seal the deal. But in Japan, museum guards - like their fellow citizens - had faces as impassive as those of Nô actors.§ It was impossible to jolly them along; they were disciples of discipline. Furthermore, in view of my meagre vocabulary, there was little chance of talking my way in either.

However, never one to turn down a challenge, I eventually managed to wangle a visit to one of the museums for free - that of Mikimoto, the inventor of the cultured pearl. As any good Frenchman would, I had noticed that the Japanese were leaving the museum by a special exit which appeared to be unguarded. I was tempted. Clop, clop, clop . . . No sooner had I slipped through the 'entrance' than the sound of wooden shoes, *gettas*, broke the silence (the narrow kimono that the

---

*Authors of *La Terre en Rond*. It was perhaps the fact that they covered 60,000 miles in eleven months in a small Citroën that left them with that impression!

§*Nô* is a form of drama performed by actors wearing masks. It moves at a hopelessly slow pace and is about as entertaining as a funeral mass.

women wear forces them to take little, jerky steps). As the girl pointed to the exit, I asked to see the director - with whom I gave the old anecdote routine a new whirl. Surprise! It worked like a charm! The fat, good-natured fellow puffed on his cigar, not believing a word but chuckling nevertheless. For my efforts I was rewarded with a delicious meal and a private guided tour. After I had told a few extra stories to the assembled staff, the director of the Mikimoto Museum asked if I was satisfied. Then he added, 'If you marry a Japanese girl, promise you'll come back for a necklace of pearls. Goodbye, French *samurai!*'

Encircled by mountains carpeted with magnificent forests lay the city of Kyoto, which had been the capital of Japan for ten centuries and which was still the nation's cultural centre. You could explore Kyoto for ever, and never get tired of it. There were endless things to discover: palaces, towers, innumerable narrow streets and old wooden houses; and most especially temples - glorious temples.

'I bet you don't know where to sleep?'

'I'd thought I might try my luck at the university.'

'What a funny idea! You'd do better to come to my house, but first let's go and have dinner.'

Yoshihiro had spent three months in Paris and spoke French rather well. He picked me up right off the street, for he was young and much-travelled. We hit it off immediately. He parked his Nissan in front of a first-class restaurant. The menu was centred around lobster and fried vegetables and, in a word, was *oishi* - excellent. My frayed sweater and scruffy shoes looked a little out of place, and I could not help feeling self-conscious - especially when the bill came to a steep 2,850 yen.

At nightfall we drove to a quiet neighbourhood. We reached Yoshihiro's home and entered through a gate at the back and crossed a courtyard, part of which was given over to a miniature garden of dwarf pines, *bonsai* trees, chrysanthemums and moss-covered stones decorated with cactus. A small spring spouting from a stand of bamboo splashed into a black-bottomed pond in which swam graceful goldfish with delicate petal-shaped fins. A door slid open to reveal a small but ultra-modern kitchen equipped with the latest electrical appliances. And Etsuko, whom I caught sight of immediately, was delightful. She smiled as if she had known me all her life, and right away I felt a close rapport with the sister of my new friend.

In accordance with custom, we took off our shoes before stepping on to the *tatami* of the living room where Mr and Mrs Sawabe greeted me in pure traditional style. They bowed. I did the same. They bowed again, and so did I. How many times was I supposed to bend over in this way with hands at my sides and a fixed smile on my face? How deeply did I have to bow? Apparently the one who bowed last was considered the politest. But that was the way it was: without the bows, there would be no Japan. Even at the wheels of their cars or astride their motor bikes or bicycles, two Japanese who recognized one another always greeted each other with a bow. Thus we went through a whole series of bows upon my arrival in the home of Yoshihiro's parents, but it was the grandmother who triumphed in the courtesy stakes. She greeted me on her knees, touching her forehead to the *tatami* as if I were the Mikado himself.

We gathered around a low table, seating ourselves on the floor. Etsuko, wearing Western dress, served us green tea - daintily and in silence. Then, still without saying a word, she took her place next to me. She watched me discreetly with her dark eyes. If I paid her the slightest attention, she would become confused and try to make conversation. It was not easy, as she spoke only Japanese, of which I understood practically nothing. With her index finger, she pointed timidly to the tip of her nose. What was the meaning of that mysterious sign?

'*Watashiwa* . . . Etsuko . . . me . . . Etsuko.'

Behind us, the colour television - the ever-present, ever-flickering TV set of every Japanese home - blared without interruption. No one was paying it any attention. In a recess in the floorboards under the table was a small heater filled with glowing coals. The thick table cloth reached to our knees. As a result my feet and toes were warm and cosy.

Not knowing what to do with her hands, Etsuko continually adjusted the table-cloth around her. Her fingers lightly brushed against my leg - by accident? The gentle touch startled me; without thinking I took her hand. A quick glance about me showed that conversation was going on as normal. Yoshihiro was tirelessly translating his brothers' questions. I felt good and decided that a hitch-hiker's life was not really too bad after all. Barely an hour earlier I had been in the street with an icy wind blowing, worrying about where I would spend the night. And here the problem was solved, with the extra bonus of a charming, tiny warm hand in mine!

The next morning, the light purring of a sewing machine tugged me from my sleep, The Sawabes were manufacturers of *tatami* mats, and my room was directly over their workshop. The smell of rice straw filled the entire house. It was a good business to be in: there were *tatamis* in every home, and they were replaced every three years.

Like every other good Japanese, Yoshihiro was waited on by his

sister, who never flinched from her role of docile obedience. One evening
I explained to Etsuko, who never seemed to tire of pampering me, that
French women expected help from men, and that according to the rules
of gallantry, men should stand back and let their women enjoy the lime
light. Etsuko quickly grasped what I was saying. Thus, one day when
Yoshikiro and I had returned from a walk, my guide sat down at the table
and ordered:

'Etsuko, bring me some coffee . . .'

'Tonight I'm a French girl!' she boldly replied.

'Hey, André, you're not here to interfere with our excellent
Japanese traditions! This isn't Paris . . .'

All three of us burst out laughing. How wonderful it felt to be
surrounded by love. Being loved was perhaps the thing I had missed most
in my life as a wanderer. Of course, the essential thing was to love others;
yet my stay in Kyoto was really very pleasant. Meal after meal, Etsuko
laid out an array of dishes, insisting that I taste all the marvels of her
culinary repertoire. I was living like a king. The father, who had noticed
his daughter's new preoccupation, said to me one evening, 'If this goes
on, you'll have to take her back to Paris with you!'

To make me even happier, Etsuko decided to accompany me to the
Autumn Festival, wearing a kimono. When I saw her appear at the top of
the staircase, my heart seemed to miss a beat. She had put on her most
beautiful kimono and was wearing a lacquered wig and ceremonial make-
up. It was incredible how beautiful she was - like a geisha from an
engraving, or a *kabuki* doll. Flattered, I bowed my appreciation. Softly,
almost as if embarrassed, she laughed in the manner so typical of
Japanese women. Her kimono was made of marvellous white silk
embroidered in red. An artistically-worked *obi* was fitted closely around
her bust.

Filled with her presence, the day passed like a dream. With her at
my side, I felt as proud as a *shōgun*. Etsuko used the occasion to introduce
me to the tea ceremony, an endless series of refined gestures. My teacher
was so graceful that I complied quite willingly with what Europeans
sometimes view as a pointless affectation. We also called on her friend
Yoko, who was exhibiting a collection of bouquets. Etsuko herself held a
diploma for the Japanese floral art of *ikebana* in which sky, earth and man
are represented. Under her guidance I appreciated all the more her
friend's work with its slow evolution of motifs, forms and colours. It was
an art permeated with the poetry, delicacy and refinement which are so
often trampled underfoot in these frenzied times.

At dusk, in one of those perfectly-groomed gardens where the wave patterns of the white gravel, evocative of the sea, encouraged quiet meditation, I contemplated my own *ikebana* sitting on the steps of a temple. I liked her laughing, intriguing eyes that filled her round face with life. I thought lovingly of her delicious dimples, and the auburn sheen of her hair. I let myself be lulled by the sound of her voice softly singing an exotic melody. Etsuko spoke to me; she knew that I didn't understand her; and we both knew that it made no difference. Her fingers were so slender that I could barely feel them in the palm of my hand. Her skin was soft and smelt faintly of rice. Orient: I loved you with all my soul.

November 21st, 1970. The big ferryboat slipped slowly into Shimonoseki Bay. I was returning from a visit to the country that had invented the printing press long before Gutenberg, as well as armoured ships and the most rational alphabet in the world: Korea. None of those accomplishments had been mentioned in my school books either!

Leaning on the rail next to me was a young Korean woman with particularly Mongolian features. Her eyes were so narrowly slit that even when I talked to her, she looked as if she were sleeping! Nevertheless, some of her sisters on the *Tranquil Morn* were among the most beautiful women in the world. They were white-skinned, but much more refined and graceful than European women, outshining even the celebrated Ethiopian or Eurasian. The *chima*, a brightly-coloured bell-shaped dress falling from the bust, transformed them into characters out of a fairy tale.

Behind us was a young American couple hopelessly in love. Hearing the Japanese immigration officer pronounce my name, the American girl opened her eyes wide.

'André . . . André! You're French? You aren't the Frenchman who's doing a trip around the world?'

'Ah . . . yes, that's me.'

'Well, I've got ten dollars for you to celebrate your birthday!'

I stared confusedly at this excited stranger. She then explained that she was a friend of good old Jenny, who when I had last seen her had been supporting the strike of the Mexican Chicano migrant workers in the Delano vineyards of California.

'Jenny wrote to me that if I was going to Japan in November, I had to look for André, 'the king of the hitch-hikers'. She told me to keep my eyes peeled for a handsome dark-haired man, tall and thin, who would be wearing a little pack on his back; and to give him these ten dollars to celebrate his birthday . . .'

We must have been a strange sight as the three of us tramped through the streets of Shimonoseki, joyful and rowdy as school kids playing truant. Looking like tramps (their get-up was about as stylish as mine), we hunted for a restaurant where we could blow the whole ten bucks on one great feast. On that day, my 33rd birthday, I did something I had never done before: I scanned the menu in search of the most expensive item. Actually, the 'menu' consisted of a display window in which were presented in plastic replica all the dishes served inside. The first time I had seen those imitations, I had mistaken them for the real thing!

'The *sushi* looks delicious.'

'Forget it, it's not expensive enough.'

We settled on the *sukiyaki*, the most famous dish of Japan. The waitress, dressed in a kimono, brought us green tea, some titbits and hot little towels. Then, kneeling, she served the main dish. On the low table she plugged in a hotplate and laid out the various components of the *sukiyaki*: thin slices of fat-marbled *matsusako* beef, from cattle fattened on beer, arranged like the petals of a rose; and, in another dish, a bouquet of white onions, parsley, beansprouts, transparent noodles, and other vegetables. She then sprinkled powdered sugar into a saucepan, added the meat, poured on a generous quantity of soy sauce, and let it simmer. Using long chopsticks, she at last added the vegetables. In our bowls we beat raw eggs in which we then dipped the slices of meat and vegetable. The beef melted in our mouths like caramel pudding. Jenny, what a treat that birthday meal was, thanks to your generosity and enthusiasm! What a friend! Overjoyed and satiated, we left the restaurant in the highest of spirits after spending our last yen on an orgy of whipped cream, chocolate and fruit.

'There is in existence a stupendous force, as yet, happily, undiscovered by man. Let us supplicate God, the Beloved, that this force be not discovered by science until spiritual civilization shall dominate the human mind. In the hands of men of lower material nature, this power would be able to destroy the whole earth.'

Thus spoke 'Abdu'l-Bahá to the Japanese ambassador during his stay in Paris in 1911!

At the beginning of August, 1945, American propaganda leaflets exhorted the Japanese population to demand their government's unconditional surrender, for that stupendous force had become operational. We know what followed. On August 6th, at eight in the morning . . . epicentre at an altitude of 2,000 feet: in one flash, Hiroshima disappeared, together with many of its 400,000 inhabitants.

The flowers had long since grown back, and the city was brighter and braver than ever. Hiroshima had erased the ruins but not the memory. Of the tragedy there remained a park as green and radiant as a day of peace, surrounding a museum where the documents on display defied the imagination. The Japanese filed through with tears in their eyes. At the exit a chart, regularly updated, compared the nuclear arsenals of the 'great powers'. The death-dealing zeros stretched on shamelessly, and beside them the Hiroshima bomb was a mere firecracker. Standing in front of that chart, a summary of mankind's progress, I considered these words of Bahá'u'lláh: '*If carried to excess, civilization will prove as prolific a source of evil as it had been of goodness when kept within the restraints of moderation*'.

Chapter 10

BORTSCH ON THE LONG TRAIN

With winter coming on, I decided not to freeze on Japanese territory but to make plans for spending the cold months in India. But the prospect of crossing the Asian combat zone once again did not appeal to me in the slightest. Furthermore, I never liked retracing a route that I had already covered. Therefore, I settled on a Russian itinerary as offering the double advantage of novelty and safety from machine-guns. There were two possible solutions: to swing through Siberia and then catch a plane from Tashkent to Kabul, Afghanistan; or to take the Trans-Siberian Railway, ending up in Iran after passing through Moscow. Freewheeling tourism of the Brugiroux variety was strictly forbidden in the Soviet Union. Only some twenty cities were open to foreigners, and every detail had to be planned meticulously in advance: hotel reservations, the exact time and date of train connections, a fixed itinerary, etc.

For all those reasons I decided not to linger in the USSR but to opt for the Trans-Siberian which, for the same price, would allow me to see more of the country. After six weeks of red tape and an interminable exchange of telegrams, I was finally wrapped, labelled,and ready for the supervised expedition into the Soviet Union. 'Mama' Intourist, the single state-run agency in charge of 'guiding' foreigners on Soviet territory, left absolutely nothing to chance. Everything was planned and programmed. I was strictly forbidden to move one step off the beaten track, and obedience to the Intourist representative was mandatory. Hitch-hiking was forbidden, hotels were compulsory and I would be an official tourist like all the others. What a comedown! I would never forget it.

I received my visa with its clear indication of the precise moment - to the very minute - of my entry and exit. As I leaned on the railing of the Soviet ship edging slowly away from the Yokohama pier (and in the process snapping the thousands of ribbons linking each traveller to Japanese soil, parents and friends), I contemplated my Soviet schedule: three days by boat from Yokohama to Nakhodka,* seven days by train to Moscow, a compulsory night in a hotel (the only one I would pay for in six years of travel), and two days by train from Moscow to Akharian, Turkey. As my thumb was off duty and I had no need to worry about where I'd be spending the night, I finally managed to resign myself to the situation. For eleven days I was going to play - perish the thought - at being an average tourist on a genuine package tour. I looked round at the ship's sumptuous fittings, elaborate decor and rugged crew members. Certainly there was plenty of meat, but it came with martial music and the glum faces of fellow Caucasians. I was immediately conscious of the sharp contrast with Asia, and longed to be back there again. I was, I felt, being brutally awakened from a delicate, gentle dream.

'Mama' Intourist, having taken me in hand, now served me caviar which I spread on rye bread along with a layer of iced butter. For the caviar, even if served by the ladleful, was still costing me plenty: $265 - the greatest single expense of my trip, meaning a sacrifice of 265 days of travel. What was more, I had nearly missed out on my share of the precious black beads, for 'Mama' had mistakenly given me the visa of a Japanese.

XАБАРОВСК (Khabarovsk), December 6th, 1970. On the Amur River. It was 2.15 p.m., and that was precisely the problem. We had just missed the Trans-Siberian Express, which had been scheduled to depart an hour earlier. The Intourist representative, sporting a cap with gold letters, was furious. While awaiting word from his superiors, he confined us to a waiting room under the eye of Comrade Lenin, several pictures of whom stared down from slogan-plastered walls. On a table in the centre of the room, a pile of literature in several languages introduced travellers to socialism. An hour later, orders finally arrived! Two quick turns of a key and we were delivered - to be put up for the night in a hotel free of

---

*The Trans-Siberian actually departs from Vladivostok. However, as that city was out of bounds to foreigners, tourists coming from Japan had to disembark in Nakhodka and join the Trans-Siberian in Khabarovsk.

charge. We would be taking the Trans-Siberian Express scheduled for the following day.

I had expected to be travelling in some sort of goods truck, no doubt from having seen the film *Dr Zhivago*. I was surprised, therefore, to be *forced* to climb aboard a first-class coach in the company of all the other tourists. The coach was comfortable with four berths in each compartment (two of which were folded up during the day), heating, white sheets and pillow cases that were changed half way through the journey, daily maid service and piped music. It was Xanadu. A little old lady, a *nanushka*, who reminded me of my Russian neighbour back in Brunoy, served as our hostess. She gave us tea for free but charged four copecks for each lump of sugar. She looked very good-natured and took special care of me; no doubt the *nanushka* found me neither touristy enough nor fat enough.

Outside the window stretched a flat expanse of birch forest mantled with snow, sprinkled with clusters of large wooden huts. From time to time the smoke of our locomotive completely enveloped the fleeting, icy landscape. Many stops lasted ten or fifteen minutes, sometimes longer. I took advantage of these halts to jump down on to the platform, stretch my legs, and nose about in the stations, usually adorned with their obligatory effigies of Lenin. Sometimes I sprinted up to the locomotive for the simple pleasure of greeting the drivers and filling my lungs with fresh air. In Chita, a town marking our entrance into Siberia proper, the thermometer registered -20°F. In spite of the cosy coach and steaming hot tea, I missed Alaska where I had had to jump up and down like a madman in order to keep warm, make assaults on garages in order to get some boiling coffee, and talk my head off in order to come up with a place to sleep. In the final analysis, those few hours of luxury left me very dissatisfied. I was a fighter, a man of action; I wasn't accustomed to having things easy.

Our train consisted of fifteen green coaches. I filmed them at my own risk, as it was forbidden to photograph anything. That rule was spelt out very clearly on the Intourist pamphlet. It was even forbidden to leave our coach except to go to the adjoining restaurant car. All the same, a few of my travelling companions attempted to explore the immediate surroundings. They didn't get very far before being stopped and brought back by plain clothes policemen. I interpreted the prohibition as a personal challenge from 'Mama' that I ought to meet and enjoy. Unlike the others who had set off in groups, I made my attempt alone, heading out with an air of assurance to march the length of the Trans-Siberian

Express. After all, the worst that was likely to happen to me was to be brought back under escort to my luxurious sleeping berth. The vestibules were genuine ice boxes. Snow swept into them in drifts, and ice sparkled. In the end I was very proud of my successful exploit of covering the entire length of the convey twice in each direction without once getting called to account.

The first thing I established was that the Soviet socialist railways had apparently heard nothing about the abolition of the class system! There were still three of them. The third class didn't even have compartments, only a simple aisle flanked by wooden benches running the length of the coach. It was very rudimentary. The air reeked of garlic sausage and bortsch, red cabbage soup thickened with sour cream. It wasn't Dr Zhivago's goods truck centred around an old smoking stove, but it wasn't far off. There was an overall grimness in the dirty wood and paint. Yet, I felt revived. In this coach I felt happier than back in my own. Here beat the heart of a people, and I was quickly enveloped by effusive kindness. With the natural openness of simple people, the third-class travellers gave me black bread, onions and a kind of salami, as well as sweets, biscuits and tea. I declared to my new friends that I was for peace and friendship among peoples - to which a fat lady muffled up in black hailed me as a good Communist. Seconded by all her fellow travellers, who nodded in agreement, she spoke of her love for Lenin and all the good things he had done for his people. The conversation lasted quite a while.

Alex, a young film maker, served as our interpreter as I spoke in English. Around him were a factory worker named Bila and a soldier, both of them apparently eager to learn. The soldier had me put on his uniform jacket amid a burst of laughter. He then gave me one of his small red stars as a present, pinning it on my sweater alongside the hippy badge that Jackie the junkie had given me in San Francisco. Alex described the harsh living conditions of his compatriots: their low wages, the high cost of living, the black market. Our secret meeting went on and on - almost to the point of conspiracy. I expected to be thrown out at any minute. I realized that he and his friends were part of the new wave of youth with universal ideas which even the Iron Curtain could not prevent from filtering through. The vibrations of unity were much stronger than dogma, and we understood each other perfectly. They were saddened and shamed by the brutal suppression of Czechoslovakia, and the Vietnam War upset them deeply. I was amazed to see how well-informed they were.

Communism, which they called socialism, was like a bush fire preparing the ground for a future crop. But was that enough? Like an antichrist, it took up the same social laws promulgated by Bahá'u'lláh: equality of the sexes; work for everyone under more humane conditions; community care of the elderly, orphans and sick people; compulsory education, and so on. Unfortunately Communism used force to impose certain worthwhile things that only love and voluntary acceptance could perpetuate. For violence would only lead to more violence and suffering.

God was dead (Gagarin had not seen Him when he rocketed into space), and religion was an opiate. I was able to agree with them in so far as the religion of our dogmas, imitations and interpretations was indeed a drug that had to be given up; and the God of our narrow imagination was indeed dead. Yet, being limited and finite, man was unable to understand a thing which was limitless and infinite. God's essential nature was entirely beyond man's comprehension. God had created us in His image, but did a painting ever understand its painter?

Peace and friendship between nations was the constant refrain of these young people, but to my mind they lacked a necessary element for attaining their goal: God. For material well-being alone could not make man happy. As for brotherhood, they were right. Hadn't 'Abdu'l-Bahá said, 'We must love all beings and all things'? But he had added, 'Only then will we see the image of the Beloved'. In order to improve the human condition and make people happier, we had to grasp the means. Material well-being had no meaning divorced from the spiritual development of humanity: it became science without conscience. Little by little man's spiritual blossoming was assured by the divine breath of God. And yet, one had to want to feel it.

The hours went by. I spent the entire afternoon with my new friends. During my second visit the following day, we were approaching Novosibirsk, where Alex was due to leave us. He invited me to his home, but with great regret I had to explain that Intourist didn't allow any deviation from the set route, and that private visits were forbidden. As a consolation, I offered him some books in English and some magazines that I had with me.

'I try my best to listen to the BBC and the Voice of America despite the impossible official jamming, but it's extremely difficult to know what is really happening in the rest of the world. The books will make me very happy, but please do not bring them into this compartment. We've already talked too much together; I'm sure we're being watched. Be kind enough to wrap the books in newspaper and hand them to me on the platform.'

Back in my compartment, I gathered together all the unwanted books and magazines belonging to me and the other tourists. It was a nice little package that I slipped stealthily to Alex.

'*Spasibo*, thank you, André. I'll never forget you.'

Just as quickly he disappeared, leaving in my hand a scrunched-up piece of paper: his brother's address in Moscow. We changed locomotives, leaving behind the steam engine for an electric one. During the stop, which was longer than usual, women with droplets hanging from their noses sold hot potatoes, red cabbage salad and picked cucumbers.

Once again the Siberian landscape displayed its endless expanses outside the window: forests powdered with white, harnessed *troikas*, horses with steaming nostrils, villages of wooden houses each surrounded by a high fence, vast shining plains stretching to infinity.

As the train progressed northward, the days became shorter. I was now sharing my compartment with a woman who appeared quite wealthy, an engineer and an officer. They did not look very proletarian to me. They seemed living proof that society needed such differences in order to be viable. It was not possible to make everyone absolutely equal. We were not all born with the same capacities; and it was obvious that an army could not consist exclusively of either privates or generals. The thing to avoid was extremes - extreme wealth and extreme poverty, the notions of caste and superiority. My new travelling companions were proud of their country's achievements. They confided in me, but separately and secretly. The Red Army songs and twangy balalaika music issuing from the loudspeaker in the corridor made private conversation easier.

When the Trans-Siberian Express pulled to a halt in Moscow's railway station, I glanced at the clock: 11.55 a.m. After seven days of travelling, we were right on time - not even a minute late.* I kissed Nanushka swiftly on both cheeks, thanking her for her free tea and her four-copeck sugar lumps. The man from Intourist, his cap screwed on to his head, was already bawling out a long list of names and packing everybody into heavy Moskvich taxis. 'Mama' was definitely keeping

---

*The Trans-Siberian is the world's longest railway and covers 5,600 miles and seven time zones in a total of 98 stops. (After all, the USSR accounts for a sixth of the world's land surface). In second place is the Trans-Canadian which can be taken 4,300 miles with considerably fewer problems.

close tabs on me. In all likelihood we were being escorted to a hotel - but which one? It was like a lottery. Some Americans started complaining. I was one of the lucky ones, being put up at the Metropol, an old establishment on Revolution Square next to the Bolshoi Ballet and only a stone's throw from Red Square.

Barely arrived, I was already worrying about the next stage of my journey. The problem was that we were one day behind schedule. I asked a frowning official from Intourist what I should do, seeing I had missed my connections for Turkey. He simply indicated that it was Sunday. My fate would be decided the next day, Monday. I went up to my eleven-dollar room, which at that price was a scandal. The 'restaurant' was more like the buffet in a bus depot, and the service was appalling. The tablecloths were dirty and worn and the wait interminable. It took half an hour just to get a cup of coffee. I had worked as a waiter and I knew how long it took to serve up a breakfast. It reminded me of Prague in 1962 with Jacques: a slovenly waiter wearing a stained uniform had spilled half of what he was serving without even apologizing. Yet I couldn't blame the waiter. Whether they served one customer or a hundred, whether they left them satisfied or dissatisfied, the waiters earned exactly the same meagre amount of rubles. Even while rejecting any idea of unhealthy competition, people nevertheless needed to be stimulated in their work, especially when they had no natural vocation for serving others.

On Monday morning, 'Mama' Intourist was on her high horse. The flak I had to take! Did that stupid administration really think I was going to let myself be pushed around that way? In any case, she didn't lack self-assurance.

'Sir, the fact that you arrived in Moscow a day late is *your own fault*.' (That was a good one!) 'All the trouble in Khabarovsk was also *your fault*' (!!!) 'and your missing the train to Turkey as well . . .'

I must admit that I was stunned speechless. It took me a few seconds to react.

'But it's hardly my fault if your ship was delayed. I wasn't the captain!'

'There are no more trains for a week. You will wait here while your visa is extended; we are making an exception. As for the hotel, it will cost you an extra sixty-six dollars.'

'You've got to be kidding! I'll agree to stay longer, but I refuse to spend another copeck. You insisted on organizing my trip, on imposing your rules and your hotel, on leading me around by the hand like a child. Now you can face up to your responsibilities.'

Unable to stand it any longer, I decided to go to the main office. The directors, at least, would realize that the hassle was not at all of my making. The main office was not in the least like the travel agencies that had their headquarters on the Champs Elysées. Here, there were no beautiful posters to tempt the traveller. There was only faded paintwork into which blended the dreary faces of civil servants. No one would claim responsibility. No one apologized or tried to help. I was disgusted. Back at the hotel, Svetlana, as beautiful as Mirella, sold tickets for performances. The previous night she had found me a seat at the Bolshoi at the very last minute. Now, I asked her if she could help me out again. I loved to hear her speak French. In other circumstances . . . but I was anxious to be done with it. Finally a train was found going to Bucharest, Romania, for the same price as the train to Turkey. Obviously, such an arrangement was going to land me farther away from Kabul and India - an extra 6,000 miles to hitch in the dead of winter. Wretched Intourist!

'Since you're not leaving until tomorrow, it will be eleven dollars more for Room 4001', declared the desk clerk.

'You're getting to be a real pain in the neck! I'm not paying another copeck. You had six weeks to prepare my 'tour'. For the last ten days you've been pestering me with your prohibitions. I'll just take my sleeping bag and sleep outside. Sub-zero temperatures don't scare me at all!'

Faced with my stubborn determination, the watchdog gave up the fight. Svetlana, with whom I shared a cheese sandwich, said that actually I was very lucky.

'At least you are free to come and visit our country. Here, we haven't even the right to leave.'

Sunday, Monday, Tuesday in Moscow. I used the time to explore the city: the Kremlin, Lenin's mausoleum, various Orthodox churches (what beautiful icons!), GUM, the state department store, Gorki Avenue, Pushkin Square, Tretriakov Museum, the underground stations with their white marble walls and crystal chandeliers. In Red Square I was asked for nylon stockings and silk scarves. I was even offered fifty dollars for a record of the Beatles! At noon I would line up for a long wait at the door of some shabby cafeteria and eventually be rewarded with a meagre pittance of food. Moscow was huge, impressive and gloomy. The Russian people were reserved but I loved them with all my heart, for once approached, they proved the most cordial of the world's citizens. I sensed in them a need to know, to communicate, to exchange.

Around eleven o'clock on Tuesday night, a warden came to collect me. Destination: the railway station. The fellow kept his teeth clenched the entire time. Once I was safely aboard the train, he handed me my passport and ticket; he then stood stolidly under my window until the moment of departure.

At midnight I was in Moldavia. A man wearing a beret woke me up to verify that I was leaving the country. A customs official then emptied out the contents of my pack on to the bench. He disappeared for half an hour with my movie camera, my journal and my prayer book.

On Thursday, December 17th, 1970, the Danubius Express pulled into the northern station in Bucharest. No propaganda, no Lenin to be swallowed whole, no more Intourist. At last I could breathe. Some words of Tolstoy's surged in my mind: 'The world is in disarray; the key to all its problems is in the hands of the prisoner of Acre'.

Cobblestone streets, Parisian-style houses, churches, cafés, boutiques, people who looked at me and smiled, familiar sounds, an alphabet I could read, a language I could decipher (Romanian being a Latin tongue): suddenly I felt at home. Christmas was approaching and France, whose presence I could already feel, seemed a mere stone's throw away. I had not seen my home for six years. I now had five nephews and nieces as well as a stepmother. I was tempted to revisit my world and meet the new additions to my family, see my brothers, and also relax. The side trip could be easily accomplished. I was so close to home - forty-eight hours, or seventy-two at the most . . .

I soon dismissed the idea, for I knew full well that if I broke my journey, even briefly, I would not have the strength of mind to leave again. It would be too hard. No, it was better to head for India, where it was hot and where all my dreams were waiting.

An icy mist, a sort of hoar frost, hung in the air and enveloped the frozen, lifeless landscape. The gutters were choked with ice. My long underwear, wool socks, parka and two sweaters felt as flimsy as silk. It took all my courage to brave the biting cold into which I plunged as I left Konstanta on the shores of the Black Sea.

The border crossing into Bulgaria was deserted at this time of year, and I walked a good three miles before hopping on to a tractor, then a horse-drawn buggy, a side-car, a post office van, and finally a school bus. In Burgas I spent the night under a staircase in an apartment complex. At Stara Zagor I found myself within twenty miles of Kazanluk. Seven years earlier, when I was working in Italy, I had made an expedition with my friend Antonio all the way to that very spot. Now I had only to make a twenty-mile detour in order to say that I had come full-circle, completed a trip around the world.

Since 1519, when Magellan's Malay slave Henrique became the first man to circle the globe, many others had followed. Today, a trip around the world was no longer an exploit - even if crossing borders remained difficult. Astronauts had done it a thousand times aboard their spaceships. American Express clients managed it in a week or two (my entire six-year budget would not cover their expenses). Aeroplane pilots saw only an endless series of airports, transit hotels and clouds. Businessmen, travelling salesmen from the world of industry, technicians and reporters crisscrossed the planet. Officials and statesmen did so in style. Seamen did the rounds of the world's harbours - which meant, more or less, doing the rounds of the world's girls. But my own trip around the world was of a different kind. It was a journey through the world of humanity with all its misery and knowledge, its wisdom and generosity; and I still had many more zigzags to make before my travels were over.

At the Turkish border, a Syrian latched on to me, speaking a rather impenetrable English. He got it across that he wished to use my passport to take a Mercedes car over the border. In Asia such cars could be resold for close to their weight in gold, and thus a lucrative trade had come into being. However, for a year now, Turkey would authorize only a single Mercedes per passport. My Syrian friend, having already got one car across, was looking for a stand-in. In exchange, he offered to take me free of charge to Damascus. He introduced me to the head customs official, who was obviously in on the deal as well. I was told that since the Arabs and the Israelis were not at war at the moment, I should take advantage of such a windfall, for one never knew when hostilities might resume. In the end I refused. The customs official seemed just a little too eager; his attitude left me suspicious. What if the Syrian was setting me up for a double-cross? No, it was too risky - unfortunately, for it was very cold and a straight run to Syria would have suited me fine.

'You Ankara?'

The driver nods his head. I jump into action, tossing my pack on to the seat. With a determined gesture, he throws it out on the ground and takes off!

What was going on? It was the fourth time that I had been subjected to the same treatment. Each time it was the same story: the driver would motion 'yes' with his head and then eject my belongings.

These Turks were crazy! Later I would realize that in Turkey, nodding the head up and down was a negative sign. Another problem was chancing on drivers who wanted baksheesh. In that case I needed a rejoinder suitable to the circumstances:

'*Para yok*, no money!'

Nevertheless, the truck drivers were a cheerful lot. They sang at the top of their lungs, beat out the rhythm on the steering wheel, honked at every woman they passed, and all the while smoked like chimneys. When they were not singing, they had the radio on full blast, which when added to the noise of the engine left me at the end of the day with my head throbbing. Some of them were really very nice. I remember one driver slipping a woollen blanket over my knees as I dozed off beside him.

God, but it was cold on the high plateaux of Anatolia. The mercury was hovering near zero. Between lifts I jumped up and down like a jack-in-the-box to stay warm. My feet were planted in the snow; it was worse than Alaska. I had never been so cold before for here I wasn't properly equipped. I progressed from roadhouse to roadhouse - sordid dens always permeated by the same rancid odour in which men inhaled the smoke of narghiles and sipped sugary tea from glasses the size of thimbles.

At one such stop I met Jean, a workman from the Paris suburbs. Disgusted with industrial civilization, he was heading to India like a moth attracted to a candle - like thousands of young people of his kind. With his limited savings, he had taken off in search of a world of greater spiritual satisfaction. In his eyes India gleamed like a promised land. I did not want to disappoint him, but I felt that my own vision was different, perhaps more realistic. In the meantime, Jean was discovering with much amazement the friendliness of the Turkish people. He looked so surprised. Indeed, I had forgotten. The first realization that really hit one on leaving home was finding that others, too, had hearts full of warmth and friendship. At the outset, one saw oneself as venturing into barbaric lands - only to find, to one's complete surprise, that in the final analysis the most fossilized and inhospitable of all continents was Europe. That first discovery of mine seemed a long way away. For me there were no more foreigners. I peered straight into the hearts of people, picking up their 'vibrations'. The veils of race, colour, or custom were optical illusions. I now knew that it was necessary first to trust the ones we call 'foreigners', and then to love them. In all likelihood they would reciprocate. In this way we can build a paradise on earth.

In Turkey the coffee house was an institution on which all male social relationships were based. Everyone spent long hours seated at tables, often without ordering anything. I followed suit, taking my place with the others. Since Turks had little possibility of going abroad, they gathered around a newcomer to observe and ask questions. It was their own way of travelling.

Belching and spitting, a little old man came over to my table and proceeded to stare inquisitively at me. I had a small goatee which, in a country where moustaches - incredible moustaches - were *de rigueur*, clearly astonished him. Soon he was fingering my chin, rotating his hand and clucking his tongue to show his disapproval. Just at that moment, I saw an old woman pass by wearing a veil and bent over double under a bundle of firewood. She was dressed in baggy, brightly coloured pyjamas. I stretched my arm in her direction, and with the same movement of the wrist and the same clucking of the tongue I indicated to my Turkish 'admirer' that I found it equally strange to see a poor old lady bowed down under such a burden. The old man did not take long to catch on. He knew perfectly well that European customs were different. Lifting his arms to the sky, he emitted a long drawn-out 'Alláh'. It was Alláh's will, he wanted me to understand.

And yet, in this land of thousands of minarets, the muezzins had been silenced. Successor to the Ottoman Empire which once extended from the gates of Vienna to Persia, from the Crimea to Morocco and the Sudan, Turkey relinquished her role as torch of Islam and took the path of secularization some fifty years ago. As a supreme blow, the Latin alphabet replaced the Arabic. European dress was adopted and the Christian Sunday was declared the day of rest. The consumption of alcoholic beverages was authorized. Why this retreat on the part of Islam? Why this 'progress'? Towards what goal?

Having endeavoured to learn more about myself, I realized now that I had to devote my time to learning more about the history and cultural diversity of mankind. I knew full well that my quest was far from complete.

In Bursa, a former capital of the Ottoman Empire, stood an old and impressive *hammam*. With domes covered with glazed tiles, it was as sumptuous as a sultan's palace. The Turkish bath was an experience I could not pass up.

The various rooms of the *hammam* were crowded with men. The bath itself consisted of a large pool of hot water occupying the centre of a beautiful hexagonal room whose surrounding colonnades reminded me of Ingres's painting 'The Turkish Bath'. I observed for a moment the *habitués* as they went through their routine; then, like them, I went to seat myself on a marble bench in one of the colonnades. A stream of very hot water flowed continuously into a sculpted stone basin. The technique was to dip a small silver bowl into the basin and pour the hot water over oneself. Leaning against splendid ceramic arabesques, I carried out my ablutions amid suffocating heat. I sweated profusely. Three times I soaped myself all over, taking my time. Once clean, though beaded with sweat, I joined the others in the pool where voices jabbered all about me.

Then there was the optional massage; I felt like trying it. A group of formidable heavy weights stood waiting in a corner. I chose one with his back turned towards me; with his moustache hidden from view, he must have struck me as somehow less terrifying. No such luck! He grabbed me unceremoniously and proceeded to rub me down with a horsehair glove. It felt as if he were scraping the very bottom of my pores. It stung like hell. He then had me lie down on the marble floor, only to begin a merciless grinding of my flesh that made me cry out with pain. The session lasted more than ten minutes as he climbed on top of me, twisted me in every direction, dug his fingers brutally into my shoulders, locked my legs in genuine judo holds. When he grabbed my ribs, it tickled. Much to his disappointment, I burst out laughing like an imbecile. But then the torture and screaming resumed. Apparently, he had never had such a noisy victim, but his massage had nothing relaxing about it. To finish things off, he 'massaged' my arm so violently that I ended up with an elbow swollen to twice its normal size. Bravo! I finally understood the French expression, 'strong as a Turk'. For the next three days my body ached and I walked like a cripple. I would never again set foot in a *hammam*!

For the Christmas and New Year holidays, I treated myself to an interlude in Lebanon. There the inhabitants admired and respected France and the French. Thus I would be spending Christmas 'at home'. As an added attraction, the weather there was mild.

Seven thousand years of history, seventeen civilizations one after the other, twelve different religions: that was Lebanon in a nutshell. In the rock, as in the landscape, were to be found those names from ancient history that had seemed so forbidding when encountered in school but which suddenly took on an unexpected charm. In Lebanon two distinct communities vied with one another: the progressive Christians,who held the country's economy in their hands, and the Muslims, set in the way of Islam. Each day the loudspeakers of the minarets fought a war of decibels with the bells of the church towers in one grand, unholy din.

Carols were resounding as I arrived in Beirut, for it was Christmas Eve. In the dusky twilight, the city was like something out of an Oriental fairy tale - noisy, colourful, scented. I felt like Aladdin as I wandered through the bazaar.

My first visit outside the capital was to the ruins of Baalbek. In the surrounding desert, which had once been the granary of the Roman Empire, I came upon the first camel I had ever seen outside a zoo. It was no doubt a childish sentiment, but the sight made me extraordinarily happy. Nearby was a black Bedouin tent made of goat hair. The shaggy goats themselves were grazing amid the desert rubble. Unsure of my reception, I hesitated before approaching, but I was quickly surrounded by a band of runny-nosed urchins.

The tent was divided in two: one side for the goats, the other for the nomads. Crouched on the dusty ground, a woman was flattening out a ball of dough on a board. She flipped it about until it was as large and thin as a napkin and then baked it on a convex metal plate. Seated cross-legged in the company of a dirty little girl, a man was eating contentedly. With a noble gesture he invited me to join him. The acrid smell of the animals made me nauseous; a baby lying on a sheepskin was crying loudly. My eyes swept over the sparse décor: no furniture, a few rudimentary kitchen utensils, some jugs of water. It was dire poverty, and it existed only a few miles from the wealthy, snobbish neighbourhoods of one of the world's most sophisticated capitals. The man shared his bread and tea, and I gave the children some sweets. I wanted to ask if I could stay the night, but I lacked the courage - or the audacity. *Salaam.*

As I left Sidon, the biblical city celebrated by Homer, a jeep screeched to a halt beside me in a cloud of dust. Three strapping young men dressed in spanking-new camouflage uniforms jumped out in a show of bravado. They held Russian-made machine-guns in their hands.

'Do you know who we are?'

I looked at them blankly.

'We are *fedayeen* . . . Al Fatah.'

In spite of frequent run-ins with the regular Lebanese Army, they continued to circulate freely.

'We like war just as much as we like whisky.'

'Well, I don't drink', I answered. 'And what's more, I'm a hippy. I'm for peace.'

They dropped me off in Tyre, the last city before the Israeli border. 'Akká was not far away . . . But since the Six Day War, the Arab countries were refusing to admit tourists with Israeli stamps in their passports. It was therefore preferable to visit the Arab countries first.

Thanks to an Egyptian friend I had known in Toronto, I secured a bed in a small chalet on the road to Bikfaya, half-way between the blue Mediterranean and snow-covered Mount Lebanon. The air was mild and fragrant with the scent of pine and olive trees. War seemed nothing but a false rumour. The chalet was part of a rehabilitation centre for deaf-mute children and was run by auxiliary nuns.

I was going to be spending New Year's Eve alone, and the nuns felt bad about it.

'We're sorry, but we have been invited into town for the evening. We didn't have time to cook you a meal; we just left a little something in the refectory.'

Sisters Fouad, Janine and Marie-Thérèse had already left when I entered the refectory. I stopped short in astonishment. Near the Christmas tree were laid out all kinds of cheese from France, a variety of delicious cold meats, fresh butter, French bread - all of it imported. 'A little something', they had said. It was a real feast! Everything I had longed for every time my stomach rumbled was there like a miracle: my favourite goat's-cheese, *saucisson*, everything! France was tugging at my sleeve one last time in an attempt to lure me home.

As if fleeing from a pursuer, phantoms draped in black crept stealthily through the streets. When they stood still, I was unable to make out any shape. Since all around me I could see only men, I concluded that the women must be hiding beneath those lugubrious veils. The veils were not at all the sort that might accentuate the beauty of a woman's eyes, as in *The Arabian Nights*; no, they were mere shrouds that covered everything. It was incredible to think that in other latitudes, in Australia for example, women even displayed their buttocks . . . while here in Syria, they hid even the tips of their noses.

The Arab world was a man's world. I discovered that fact in Palmyra, a palm-tree oasis of black tents, huts and impressive ruins situated in the middle of an ochre-yellow desert - just like on the postcards. I was in the ancient realm of Queen Zenobia, and it was here that I met my first real Arabs, for the Lebanese referred to themselves as Phoenicians. I could observe them at my leisure, for they were mostly immobile. Some fingered the heavy beads of their rosaries, while others sprawled about in coffee houses, smoking narghiles. Their heavy sheepskin coats seemed to condemn them to a state of inertia. Crouched together in small groups over glasses of sugary tea, they appeared to engage in endless conversation. Only the recording from the minaret played five times a day aroused this idle world from its torpor. At the magic word, 'Alláh' they rose automatically. Each one would clear his throat, eject a glob of spittle, and make his way to the mosque. When I followed them, one man chased me off with a threatening gesture; another threw a heavy stone at me, for I had taken out my movie camera. There was not a single woman in the mosque. Was Alláh the exclusive property of men?

The desert around Damascus was planted with . . . anti-aircraft installations. The brilliant Islamic metropolis, which still intrigues the European, was now only the shadow of a city. The town was on permanent alert. There were uniforms of all sorts, gaudily painted cars and an occasional figure in an attractive, traditional costume. Many women went unveiled, but they walked with their eyes fixed straight ahead as if they were being followed. There was never any chance of their responding to my request for information. The streets were as chaotic as a circus.

I visited the Mosque of the Umayyads, the largest in the world and a masterpiece of Islamic architecture. Inside was the tomb of John the Baptist. In the immense hall of prayer, measuring more than 400 feet in length, men walked barefoot across the gigantic carpets, prayed with their foreheads pressed to the floor, mumbled verses from the Qur'án, ate or joked, laughed, argued and even slept. Suddenly Abdul, who had taken me under his wing a week earlier in Palmyra, came up to me. He spoke a little English. He greeted me with a kiss right in the middle of the mosque and introduced me to one of the *ulema* who sported the splendid beard of a dignitary.

'This is André, my good friend from France. He has told me marvellous things about Bahá'u'lláh.'

'Bahá'u'lláh is a liar! A liar!' rejoined the Muslim theologian.

'iar . . . iar . . .' repeated the echo in the immense vaulted ceiling.

The man had gone red in the face and with arms raised to heaven was now screaming, waking up most of the sleeping faithful in the process. Abdul was taken aback. His look was friendly but questioning. My arguments had impressed him. I waited for the Muslim elder's fury to die down.

'You know', I responded, 'from the Christian point of view Muhammad was a liar too!'

Priests and theologians were always more inclined to defend their own dogma and position than to search for truth. Didn't the high priests of the Temple call Jesus a liar to his face?

I was now on the road to Damascus, following in the footsteps of Saint Paul. But instead of having a vision, I made an unusual visit . . . A few miles from where the man from Tarsus had been struck blind, a painted jeep pulled up behind me. At first I thought I was simply being offered a lift, and I climbed aboard without a second thought. But when we reached the site of the small commemorative church, the jeep did not stop.

'Hey! That's where I get off! Where are you taking me? What's going on?'

Six or seven miles further on, we arrived at an isolated farm that had been camouflaged and transformed into a military camp. Seated on a metal bed, I was subjected to a preliminary investigation. After a call had been made on a hand-cranked telephone, a guard led me to a Russian jeep and I was hauled to a second camp where I underwent a second interrogation. At a third camp, this time full of equipment and buzzing with activity, there was another flood of questions. I was caught in the mesh of Syrian counter-espionage, and to top off my bad luck, my passport was at the Iraqi Embassy. I finally ended up at General Headquarters in Damascus where I was dragged from office to office, from question to question. Again and again I told the same story.

'Have you been to Israel?'

'No, but I intend to go there some day.'

'You're a swine!'

'I'm sorry, but I'm on a trip around the world. I plan to visit every one of the world's countries.'

'We hate the Jews.'

'Yes, I know. And meanwhile, the Jews are busy repeating, "We hate the Arabs". That's great if you think you're going to find a solution that way . . .'

'You ought to hate the Jews.'

'I don't hate anybody.'

'In any case you filmed . . .'

'Look, I'm sick and tired of the way you mix things up. For the hundredth time I tell you I didn't photograph anything. But if you insist, just give me five dollars and I'll leave you my film. You can then have it developed and you'll see that there is nothing - apart from a few shots of the Umayyads' Mosque . . .'

I then had to explain my papers were at the Iraqi Embassy for purposes of obtaining a visa. The argument went on and on. It was late. I was tired. I was hungry. They had emptied my pockets. What had they found? A Qur'án and a few brochures about Syria. I was left alone for twenty minutes. Then, finally:

'You can go.'

'Oh no, not so easy! Are you kidding? I haven't had a bite to eat since this morning. You might at least have the decency to make amends . . . I promise I won't tell the Israelis where I had dinner!'

My day in a prohibited military zone at least got me a shish kebab and a pudding made from rose-petal jam.

Night had already fallen by the time I reached the grey street of the Bab-Touma neighbourhood. A continuous drizzle was falling on Damascus. Ibrahim, a student, did not want to keep me at his home any longer for fear of a police raid. I was wandering about rather aimlessly when I noticed a sign in French reading Hôpital Saint-Louis'. I entered with the intention of asking my way. The orderly, who spoke only Arabic, picked up a telephone and put me through to a sister on duty.

'I'm French . . .'

Without giving me time to finish, she hung up and almost immediately appeared like a galleon in full sail at the top of a large staircase. The French hospital was run by the nuns of Saint Vincent de Paul, but Sister Elizabeth was Syrian. She took me to a large, white, immaculate room with three empty beds. I took my first shower in ten days. The sister, whose joy was contagious, treated me with touching kindness. She decided I was tired and too thin, and begged me to stay several days until I felt rested. This Syrian nun reconciled me to her people.

Since I was in the 'neighbourhood', I thought it would be nice to make a little foray into nearby Jordan. The radio reports, however, made me hesitate; since January 8th (1971) they had been warning of fierce fighting there. King Hussein had ordered an attack on the Palestinian commando camps, thereby stirring into new life the bloody operations of the famous Black September. At the University of Damascus, the students I approached clamoured noisily against the 'little king' and shouted their hatred of the Israelis to the rhythm of military marches. I was frightened and troubled by such collective hysteria. Hour by hour I followed the unfolding events, noting them in red in my journal, for there was always a transistor radio blaring in the streets. By the 12th, the fighting had become widespread.

At the tourist bureau I was advised not to attempt a visit, as foreigners were apparently being turned back at the border. The only problem was that if I did not visit Jordan now, I would never have another opportunity. Wait? But what if the conflict dragged on endlessly or even spread to other countries? I also wondered if perhaps the Arabs were exaggerating the importance of the situation - as was so often the case. I made my decision: it was now or never. After all, I had survived a worse hornets' nest in Cambodia. Why, given my luck, shouldn't I make it this time, too? At the empty embassy, guarded by soldiers with fixed bayonets, the clerk was surprised at my request for a visa, but he granted it without any fuss.

A group of over-excited *fedayeen* gave me a ride as far as Borsa, a small town dating back to Roman times, whose houses were built of black volcanic stone.

'We want to kill that bastard Hussein', spat out the commandos, armed to the teeth. Nevertheless, they warned me against crossing the border where mortar shells were exploding constantly. At the border post I asked the Syrians to let me take just a few steps into Jordan. I wanted to check the situation first to see if it was safe to continue; if I felt confident, I would then ask them to stamp my passport.

The first thing I saw was an impressive display of military equipment with pictures of King Hussein everywhere. Advancing a little further, I discovered a country genuinely at war: here, a house hit by a shell; there, a funeral cortège. Only the sky seemed serene.

A jam-packed taxi stopped. I walked over to it.

'Where are you coming from?' I asked.

'Amman'.

'Are there any problems on the road?'

'No, none this morning. The cease-fire ought to be in effect by now. We were the first to leave the capital.'

A cease-fire with commandos: was it likely to be respected? In any event, this taxi had covered the distance without difficulty. Why shouldn't I do the same? I retraced my steps and picked up my passport stamped 'Exit'. This time I had no other choice but to go forward. To return to Syria, I would need a new visa that could only be delivered in . . . Amman.

At Jordanian customs, I was eyed suspiciously. The official who questioned me thought at first that I worked for the *fedayeen*, but when he found no visa from Red China in my passport, he let me enter his country.

It was about eighty miles from the border to Madaba, a 4,000-year-old city mentioned in the Bible and celebrated for its mosaics, during which I passed through no fewer than nine controls. The police and the army were everywhere, at every crossroads, every street corner. In Jerash where the immense Roman ruins were still smoking from the recent violence, one of the King's soldiers - one of those rough Bedouin from the desert - yanked me out of a Mercedes and packed me off to Headquarters. I asked him to be a little more courteous, but he was still hot from the recent fighting. Convinced he had landed a choice prisoner, he treated me accordingly. I was in a tight corner.

Inside a dirty office, he emptied the contents of my pack on to the floor, as if it were loot. Coming across a photograph of Maggy, he immediately called over some of his Bedouin friends who responded with bursts of laughter and obscene gestures. An officer finally extricated me after I showed him an article about my travels that had appeared in Arabic in a Damascus newspaper. I was put into another taxi, and a few miles further on the whole thing started again. In Suweileh, they went so far as to dump out my belongings on the roadside in the rain. Once past the ninth check, I arrived in Madaba in the dark. I was exhausted, completely worn out by the long hours of anxiety and tension. I decided to 'turn myself in', as I had a feeling that I would be better off in jail. I was in dire need of a good night's sleep. The local police, who resembled British bobbies, were happy to put me up. They assigned me to a narrow whitewashed cell which I shared with a man who had just stabbed his neighbour.

The next day, before I had walked fifty yards, an armoured car crowned with a large-calibre machine-gun and filled with excited, victorious royal soldiers stopped alongside me. One of the soldiers jumped down. Shouting, he grabbed hold of me. He wanted to force me aboard. Unfortunately I was not prepared to go. The commandos were inclined to use such vehicles for target practice and I had no desire to serve as a bull's-eye. A second Bedouin, wearing a khaki trenchcoat that hung down to his ankles, grabbed hold of me as well. I braced myself against the vehicle in order to resist them. By chance a 'bobby' was alerted by the mob and came to my rescue. Pulling me out of the soldiers' clutches, he then debated with them over the terms of my release. It was decided that everyone would accompany me to Central Police Headquarters, a mile away. At the headquarters - where I expected the worst - I was placed to my great surprise under the protection of the police chief in charge of tourism. That gentleman arranged for me to be taken on a guided tour of the famous mosaics, while the field guns thundered in the distance.

From the top of a hill, we gazed over a biblical landscape of white rock and black goats grazing in the shade of olive trees. We could see as far as Mount Nebo, from whose peak Moses is said to have glimpsed the

Promised Land but was never able to enter it; and Mukawir, where
Salome danced to win the head of John the Baptist.

'Don't go down there', advised my guide. 'Although it isn't a
military zone, the village is still very primitive. The villagers are simple
folk who take any long-haired European like you for an Israeli. You'd
have every chance of getting killed.'

Having no desire to end up like John the Baptist, I gave in,
reluctantly. It was perhaps the first time that I had turned away from a
challenge, but I decided I was rather attached to my skin, even if I didn't
always take very good care of it.

In Kerak, on a peak rising above the Dead Sea and the site of a
Crusader castle, there were still more policemen, every one of whom felt
obliged to check me out - to the point where I decided to do everything
in my power to avoid them. Catching me in the act of hiding, a whole
crowd of people joined our game of counter-espionage, an idiotic game in
which I was always the loser. I could no longer take one step, buy bread
or sit in a restaurant without someone coming up to me and demanding
'Passport, mister?'

A hundred times the interested party would look at me sternly, then
snatch my passport and pretend to examine it - when of course he did not
even know the Latin alphabet and for the most part held the document
upside down. Eventually, totally exasperated, I took to ignoring the
demands and refusing to show my papers. That behaviour earned me
nothing but a flight on foot through the mediaeval streets that ended
only at Police Headquarters. There, dropping from fatigue, I unrolled my
sleeping bag on the carpet in the entrance and fell asleep.

At midnight two fat men in pyjamas woke me up, wanting to search
me. I sent them packing.

'Now, enough's enough! And take special care not to touch me. I
have an atomic bomb in my pack. If you absolutely insist on seeing it,
then come back tomorrow. Right now I'm sleeping.'

With that I disappeared into my sleeping bag, where I remained as
tense and motionless as a snake poised to strike. The continual
harassment coupled with my loneliness in such a hostile environment
were deeply discouraging. The next morning I ran into one of the two fat
men. He turned out to be the Chief of Police. As he placed a stamp in
my passport, he asked me, 'Is it true you have a bomb?'

Petra was a circle of pink mountains four miles across. It was a city that
had survived five centuries after being carved from the rock by the

Nabateans around 300 BC. It was one of the wonders of the world and provided me with a refreshing break.

'Which country are you from?'

'*Frantzaoui.*'

'Then you are most welcome!'

For once the greeting was different. Yet I could not feel overjoyed, for it seemed rather sad to owe this friendliness to political circumstance: '*Dogol kwayes* - De Gaulle, very good!' I did not want to complain, but people could still be discouraging even when they were trying to be kind. If you learned the name of a flower, would you then cease to appreciate the flower's beauty? If not, why did your attitude change when you learned a man's nationality?

I had finally arrived in Amman, the capital of the Hashemite Kingdom of Jordan. It was not much to look at. The iron shutters on the shops were peppered with bullet holes; many windows had lost their glass; walls were full of dents and holes, or indeed had collapsed altogether; schools had lost their roofs. Many houses stood in ruins; many police stations had been burned down. I had the impression of having just missed an immense firework display.

Carrying a slip of paper in my hand, I made my way through the streets. Three men emerged from the dense crowd.

'What are you looking for?'

'I have a friend waiting for me at this address which was given to me in Damascus.'

'We know him. He's one of us. But you can't sleep at his house. He doesn't have room. He lives in a refugee camp. Come along with us. We'll find you something.'

In the Al Ashemi neighbourhood I met a doctor belonging to Al Fatah. He had no room in the hospital, which was overflowing with wounded men, but he found me a place in the home of some Palestinian friends, in a building that had been half-destroyed by the king's tanks during the famous Black September. Before going to bed I chatted with my hosts, even though I knew in advance that nothing would come of our conversation. Ali, a student, was the most vehement.

'We don't want peace, André. What we want is war - to be able to kill them all. They stole our land. You realize that my home is in Jerusalem.'

'But after all, you've always lived in Amman. You weren't even born at the time of the Palestinian exodus. You've always lived here. And besides, the bulldozers probably demolished your house a long time ago. You wouldn't feel at home there any more.

'You must understand - my home is in Jerusalem. As soon as I finish my degree, I'm going to pick up a machine-gun. I'm a *fedayeen*. I want to be a commando!'

My morale was flagging as I returned to my room. Passion and hatred were blinding them all. My feelings of despair were feeding in part on my fatigue and on a certain measure of fear - after all, I was staying with Palestinians who had come off worst in the recent fighting and who now awaited the final assault. Was it possible that man was forever destined to create his own misery? The unity, the brotherhood, the family, the great world family of which Bahá'u'lláh spoke: those beliefs were now definitely mine. You've got to have faith, André. Keep your cool and, above all, don't give up. You're going through a bad patch, but you're on the right road.

Meanwhile, the wicked curve of misfortune was never-ending; it was becoming a veritable spiral. The police checks continued, and at El Azraq, where I had thought I would at last be able to breathe (alas, only Westerners associate 'oasis' with 'peace'), I was once again arrested as an Israeli spy, imprisoned, and finally transferred back to Amman.

'Have you been to Israel?'

It was all starting up again, and by now I knew the script by heart. Fortunately, the end of the story never varied, and I was always released.

I discovered Baghdad at sunrise. I had spent twenty hours in a truck, interminable hours of jolting through dust and suffocating heat. I hadn't really slept for the past three nights and wondered how much longer I could last. If it continued indefinitely, I was going to be tempted to quit. For several days now, I had been mulling over the same questions: 'What are you doing here anyway? What's the purpose of this ridiculous marathon?' Hopelessness was creeping in. Yet I knew that if only I could sleep - deeply, for at least eight or nine hours - I would be my old self again. So I dug in my heels and tried to take everything an hour at a time.

Sprawled along the Tigris River, Baghdad was no longer the brilliant, captivating city of *The Arabian Nights*. Iraq was steeped in the colour and odour of the earth. In front of the shops hung sheep carcasses covered with flies and ochre dust borne on the desert winds. The overall effect was piteous.

I searched in vain for the country's fabled past, for remnants of ancient Mesopotamia and the Assyrian civilization that I had learned about in school. In Mosul, located on the right bank of the Tigris directly opposite Nineveh, the ancient capital, I looked for some living trace of the terrifying warriors of the past whose martial bearing was immortalized in a few bas-reliefs. But the populace seemed concerned with neither the past nor the future.

In the cafés and restaurants only men were to be seen, and their conversations revolved not around dreams of new strategy but around much more prosaic interests.

'How much does a marriageable woman cost in France?'

I looked blank.

Happy to talk with a foreigner, the student continued, 'Here, depending on her beauty and class, we pay up to $2,500, or the equivalent in camels and goats. Some women are worth fifty camels.

'In my country, it doesn't cost anything' (I felt like adding 'before'), 'but they have to give their consent.'

'That's strange . . . and not good. Here, they are not allowed to refuse.'

Although convinced that Europeans definitely had strange customs, the student decided nevertheless to invite me to stay in his house. Since he was not married, my presence would not create any problems.* He lived in a modest room with mud walls in a typically Muslim dwelling - meaning that the house was hidden behind high walls and that his single window opened on to an interior courtyard. There we resumed our conversation. He declared himself a 'progressive', all the while making it clear that there were definite limits: he would not allow his sisters to go to the cinema, nor would he consider marrying a girl who had already kissed another man. He explained in a most natural tone of voice that once he had finished his studies, his father would buy him a woman. On his wedding day, he would lift his bride's veil and have . . . the surprise of his life. Not my idea of a good time!

The idea of the veil intrigued me for a long time. Veils were already worn before the time of Muhammad; later, the practice was especially encouraged by the Turks. The Qur'án made no mention of it but simply recommended that women maintain a certain modesty. I did not deny that in ancient times the veil was perhaps necessary as part of family law. Before the Prophet, women were treated as livestock, and it was

*Strangers are not allowed into households where women live unveiled. If they do receive an exceptional invitation, the women must be kept out of sight.

Muhammad who gave them a defined legal status. But the veil in modern times? Today an occasional young woman, more emancipated and open to foreign influences, attempted to throw off the antiquated tradition. And yet, even if dressed in Western clothes, the Muslim woman remained veiled . . . at least in her mind.

On a bus I met a tall, pretty Arab woman, Ikbal, who spoke both English and French. Here at last was a woman I could talk to in this world of intolerant, domineering men.

'I can't go with you to the museum. I'm really very sorry, but our society doesn't allow it . . . It would be misunderstood.'

No matter. Since she worked for an oil company, I would simply visit her in her office. She was wearing a skirt that was short but proper. My presence seemed to make her uneasy; I soon realized that her agitation was not a response to my irresistible charm, but rather to her own lack of an enveloping veil. My first impression was that she was wearing one anyway as she glanced warily about. Then it gradually dawned on me that my innocent social visit - which would not have raised an eyebrow back in France - was seriously in danger of jeopardizing her reputation, and the longer she sat unveiled in my presence the more agitated Ikbal became. Perhaps she should have copied some of her girlfriends, who wore miniskirts . . . but hid them under their black veils!

The Arab, like all Asians, got up with the sun. Beginning at the crack of dawn, I was able to stand at the window of my friend's room and watch an unusual spectacle unfold in the courtyard. All the women from the adjoining quarters came there to wash in the centrally-placed fountain. Since Arab women did not wear the veil at home, I was able to learn more about them from my vantage point. They were beautiful. Bluish tattoos covered their faces, hands and feet, and their dark eyes were expressive. The old women were dressed in black, but the younger ones wore dresses of shimmery cloth embroidered in gold and silver. Almost every woman had her nose ornamented with a piece of golden jewellery mounted with a turquoise stone that covered her mouth; or at the very least her left nostril was pierced by a simple gold ring. They also wore heavy earrings and intricately-worked necklaces. The children hanging on to their mother's baggy trousers were also covered with jewellery: bracelets on wrists and ankles, medallions in their hair . . . some had their fingernails painted red.

Wide-eyed but hidden from view, I gazed at the rare sight for a good ten minutes before deciding to experiment! Toothbrush in hand, I had barely stepped through the door before they all fluttered away like a flock of sparrows. I found myself alone in front of the little fountain.

Babylon was a heap of dust . . . But what struck me even more strongly, everywhere, was to witness the stagnation in which Muslim society was struggling as if under some evil spell. Such stagnation saddened, shocked and pained me, left me feeling indignant and angry. I noted in my journal that Islam was living in its own decline. For what reason? I still had a long way to go before I would have an answer.

Al Qurna, at the confluence of the Tigris and the Euphrates, was where the Eden of the Bible was said to be. In Al Qurna there was a tree - not an apple tree - which was supposed to be the tree of Adam's temptation. The story went that God inspired Adam so that he might see the difference between good and evil (the story of the famous apple); and that by instilling in him this fundamental idea, God made of Adam the first genuine man - for we now know that there were others of his species on earth at the time.

It was on the same site, 4,000 years ago, that God revealed to Abraham the oneness of God. In a nearby town called Ur, of which a single impressive ziggurat (Chaldean temple) remained, Abraham was born. It was from Ur that Abraham set out for the Holy Land, thereby pushing mankind into its first step towards the maturity that is our privilege today. From Abraham to Bahá'u'lláh, from the notion of family to a world civilization, mankind passed through stages: Moses and the tribe; Christ and the city; and then Muhammad, the veritable founder of the modern nation.

It was night when I reached Sibah on the Shatt-al-Arab, the border. Across the river in Abadan rose the flaming columns of the Iranian oil refineries. The prospect of crossing into Iran made me feel better immediately, for I was getting fed up with the endless bickering among Arab 'brothers'. A few minutes earlier, on the bus that had brought me from Basra, another fight had broken out.* It had finished up on the shoulder of the road with everyone giving his 'brother' as many kicks as possible in an effort to settle accounts. The most violent of all had been a policeman who had smashed his fist into every nose within reach.

The Shatt-al-Arab was a delta of mingled water and earth, and its crossing was strictly controlled. Since it was night, I was forced to backtrack two miles; although there had been no sign to warn

*The best of the free-for-alls was at the border between Jordan and Iraq where a crowd of pilgrims bound for Mecca was trying to storm the customs office. A Holy War, I presume?

me, I quickly discovered that Sibah was a military zone.

The Chief of Police spotted me and demanded to see my papers. It had been a while. He was surprised to find that Sibah was not mentioned in my passport as a point of departure. It was news to me. He wanted to send me back to Baghdad. I protested, for I had no desire to make a 1,500-mile detour, especially given the present state of Arab 'brotherhood'. Without any apology he began rummaging through my pack. He found my map of the Middle East which he examined carefully. Suddenly, with a face like thunder, he fumbled in his pocket for a pen and started crossing out something on the map.

'Hey, that's my map. You don't have the right to damage it!'

'What is this Persian Gulf? It's called the *Arabian* Gulf!!!'

Quick as lightning, I snatched it away from him. Then the long routine began.

'Have you been in Israel?'

The Shah of Iran was apparently a dog; King Hussein was scarcely any better. Everything was very simple: there were friends and there were enemies, and enemies were for *hating*.

'You're lucky to be a Frenchman . . .'

And if not, my poor fanatical bureaucrat? More than the hardships of the road, the hardness of heart, the spitefulness and the crass ignorance of certain human beings sent my morale plunging.

As I crossed Iran, I felt like I was in a sort of holding pattern. I didn't really manage to get myself back to normal. One reason was that I was moving fast and did not take time to unwind. But on top of that, even if the police left me alone, I still got involved in several misadventures. When I attempted to film at the scene of a flood, a furious crowd of people came chasing after me. I escaped only by wading across a river of reddish mud. Gripping my movie camera in my fist and stretching out my arms to keep my balance, I came close to slipping and disappearing in the tepid caramel ooze.

It was something of a respite in the sense that I didn't get any more tired than I already was. But my morale was low. I felt so unhappy that I questioned every stop of my southward progression. The idea of abandoning my quest was ever more compelling, even urgent. To give up would seem so much more reasonable.

From the heights of Quetta, the capital of Baluchistan, I descended into the Indus Valley aboard one of those Pakistani trucks so abundantly decorated with motifs both religious and profane, trimmed with iridescent garlands straight out of a hippy's most psychedelic dreams.

The problem of cold weather was over once and for all. I traded my parka and mittens for a superb cap from Baluchistan, embroidered with gold thread and tiny mirrors. It would protect me from the sun which had suddenly become scorching.

I had barely had time to forget the winter before the heat became oppressive - all the more so as I was heading up the Indus perched on top of trucks which crawled along at a hopelessly slow pace and afforded no protection from the sun. The road was narrow, and the pot-holes down the middle of it forced the trucks to drive with one wheel on the road and the other up on the shoulder. Thus, every passing vehicle whipped up a cloud of dust which invaded my throat and lungs. My mouth and nose felt like sawdust. The meeting of two trucks often gave rise to epic disputes. Sometimes the problem would be resolved in a fistfight which only slowed us down all the more. When added to the problems already posed by loaded camels, caravans, a multitude of pedestrians and cyclists and innumerable stops for tea or hashish, we hardly seemed to make any progress.

Aware that relations between Pakistan and India were positively chilly, that indeed a war might break out at any time, I had taken the precaution of asking for my Indian visa before arriving in Pakistan. But the consulate to which I had applied had been unwilling to make any effort and had told me to apply again in Lahore . . . Of course, when I arrived in Lahore, I found out that the Republic of India did not maintain a consulate there. I cursed the diplomatic corps which was not only holding me up but forcing me into a 400-mile detour, for I had to go to Islamabad if I wanted to obtain a visa. Given my state of exhaustion, the idea seemed unattractive at the very least.

In the capital an employee at the French Embassy invited me to stay in his home. It enabled me to take a shower - which was sorely needed, as I had hardly washed since Syria. But I didn't linger in Islamabad. I didn't want to fall into the clutches of a good bed. I was afraid that if I did, it would start me thinking and push me into making a decision at a time when I was feeling especially vulnerable. Comfort was numbing. To return afterwards to sleeping in ditches demanded a lot of courage . . .

Only one road between India and Pakistan was open to tourists. Moreover, travellers needed military authorization. Needless to say, the vehicles venturing that way were few and far between. I spent an entire morning watching in vain, ready to stick out my thumb at the first sound of a car engine. Towards noon, a Dutch couple in a large Citroën swept right past. There had been only two people in the car and the back seat had yawned emptily. And here I stood, close to exhaustion. Tough luck! Three hours later I caught up with them at the border, and quickly understood why they had not stopped for me. They had been smuggling hashish and had just got caught. I did not realize my good fortune at the time, but I really was lucky that day.

I finally reached the Indian border. I had been waiting for this moment for hours, days, weeks. I wondered if I had perhaps done too much waiting . . . At the last second before producing my passport, I hesitated. I decided to sit down for a moment and catch my breath. Before entering this country that I had been dreaming about for so long, I had to build up some energy - and take a drink, for I was wilting with thirst. In front of me stood a few shabby stalls . . .

A haunting image came back to me: A week before on the outskirts of Multan, in a place just as uninviting as this, I had asked for water. A man had plunged his bare arm into a sort of barrel so filthy that I was unable to tell if it were made of metal, wood or clay. He had handed me a glass filled with a greyish water in which were suspended particles of dust or silt . . . I was so thirsty . . . Before drinking, I listened to the voice of doubt echoing in my mind. The water was repulsive. Where had it come from? But then, considering the state I was in, did it matter? And I was so very thirsty . . . I swallowed the entire glassful without another thought. No sooner had I finished than I began to regret what I had done. I had just made a very big mistake . . .

Chapter 11

A COW IS LIKE MY MOTHER

I squatted at the side of the road and emptied my bowels of a milky, frothy mucus. It served me right for having imagined back in Pakistan that I was anywhere close to the limits of endurance. All this because of an unlucky glass of water. What was it? Simple dysentery? Amoebic dysentery? Malaria? I had no idea, and furthermore I lacked the strength to ask myself too many questions. I spent much of the day crouched over with my trousers around my ankles. There was an entire group of illnesses - infectious hepatitis, typhoid, cholera, diphtheria - that could spell the end of everything and a quick return home if it wasn't too late already. I had heard a lot about these diseases that were the scourge of travellers:

'Everybody gets sick. You can't avoid it. At first you will turn your bowels inside out; then if you've got some resistance, enough to make it through the first ten days, you build up an immunity. If not, you'd better head home - pronto!'

Beginning in Istanbul, I had met enough sick travellers to realize how serious my present situation was. I was terrified that fever might cut short my trip. With increasing anxiety, I peered warily at every glass of water and every plate of food handed to me, wondering what sort of virus was going to finish me off. I now realized that I could conceivably expire in India. I felt it inside me, in my guts. In India the risk of death was all part of the game. Although there were plenty of taboos, there was no hygiene.

I did not know whether I had touched rock bottom in Delhi, or whether there were even worse things awaiting me. But I did know that I no longer had an ounce of energy. The marathon that had begun in Bucharest - 7,000 miles and 100 lifts - had left me exhausted. I knew too that I wanted only two things: to sleep and to settle my stomach. For that I needed rupees. I heard through the grapevine that the black market paid eleven and a half rupees for a dollar instead of the official seven and a half. It was worth a try. From experience I knew there were risks involved, and that it was preferable to check out one of those shops where, under a commercial pretext of some sort, obliging money-changers handled the transaction. There was no problem in finding such dens, as children were constantly approaching tourists in shopping districts and around monuments.

'Change, mister, change . . .'

Hanging on to my coat-tails, the children pestered me, one after another. Some even hit me in order to get my attention. All of them held on tight. Further along, a young man approached me and whispered, 'Fourteen rupees to the dollar. Are you interested?'

The guy was offering too much. He must be a trickster, a cheat. But he insisted in a cajoling tone of voice, and unconsciously I listened. I was weary, listless, vulnerable, ready to do or accept anything. I was also hungry. Performing the necessary gymnastics and partial strip tease, I extracted my traveller's cheques from a secret pocket inside my trousers. He looked them over, handed them back and led me off through the crowd. I followed him to Connaught Place, where we entered a small, very quiet restaurant. Ever smooth-tongued and inveigling, he lulled me into a false sense of security by saying how lucky I was to have run into him, the most serious and advantageous of dealers. I had no resistance to offer. I felt like a fly trapped in a spider's web. In vain I told myself that I was making a mistake, that I was being cheated. I no longer had any strength to resist.

The 'money-changer' then told me to hand over my cheques. He claimed he had to examine them in his office with a magnifying glass in order to check their authenticity. He explained that he had been cheated once and asked me to excuse him for taking this precaution. Once more I hesitated before giving in. He disappeared with my cheques behind a curtain. I knew he was making a fool of me, for black market transactions were never handled in this way. But I was played out, barely awake. Ten seconds later, struck by a feeling of remorse, I pulled myself together. Behind the curtain there was no one, no desk or magnifying glass either, just a few empty crates and a door open to the street . . . I had been conned as easily as a novice, even while realizing what was happening.

As a consenting adult, I had no excuse. I could only blame fatigue, my worst enemy.

In case of loss, traveller's cheques were reimbursed, but in Delhi the procedure was particularly long and difficult. The list of lost and stolen cheques was impressive. The riff-raff of Europe and America, having discovered endless tricks for prolonging their stay in the country, lived to a large extent off such 'losses'.

The bank made me fill in a long declaration which I then had to have notarized by a lawyer and by the embassy. I also had to include a police report of the theft and a list of the numbers of my cheques. Luckily, I had kept my records up to date. These steps cost me the remainder of my few surviving dollars. The lawyer affixed a counterfeit and therefore useless stamp, taking three bucks for himself along the way. My last two disappeared into the pocket of a bar owner who gave me counterfeit coins in exchange. When I returned to the bank, I found it closed. What was I going to do without a penny to my name?

I did not even know where to sleep, where to lay my aching head. Tough luck. I would sleep on the pavement like everyone else. Before stretching out, I opened my journal and scribbled a short phrase: 'February 21st, 1971: the blackest day.'

I continued to spill out my guts into the gutter. I was on the verge of total collapse and incapable of reason. All my resolutions, and all that the road and Asia had taught me, were of no consolation. Like a groggy boxer I no longer had any normal reactions. It was as if iron chains were weighing me down. Once again I questioned my purpose in travelling around the world. Through the fog that filled my mind I questioned everything. Bitter, crushed, despairing . . . The fact that I'd been born under Scorpio didn't help much either; every thought entering my mind took a turn towards the extreme. Indifferent to the surrounding poverty, the pestilential stench, the flies crawling all over my face, I had only one genuine concern: to sleep and thus forget my solitude, my weakness, my moral collapse.

In Chandri Chowk, the shopping street of old Delhi, I came upon a beggars' den. Overwhelmed by the wave of unimagined misery I floundered in the sewer of nauseous odours. An unbelievable number of hunchbacks and cripples, lepers and down-and-outs dragged themselves through the filth. Naked children held out their hands. The noisy crowd jostled and pushed. Everyone was indifferent to the next man's fate, for each felt himself to be at least the other's equal in destitution. Street traders and animal trainers with bears and monkeys vied for the attention of passers-by. There were splendid, bright-coloured saris to be seen, but more often there were rags, or bodies clad only in dirt. Then, of course, there were the half-starved sacred cows at whose approach the crowds scattered. There were flies and more flies, loathsome and menacing. What a cesspool! What smells! Dead rats lay decomposing on the pavement, while skeletal dogs, hairless and skinless, scratched away at their own raw flesh.

I went to what in those parts was called a hospital. Without really examining me, the doctor, a dark man with a crisp manner, gave me some pills and some medicine to stop my 'colitis'. Although it didn't cure me, the medicine did give me a little more energy.

On a railway bridge I witnessed a scene out of the Middle Ages: a dentist operating on the pavement. Next to him on the ground was a dirty towel on which were strewn various decayed, broken, and bloody teeth. On the other side, he had placed some carpentry tools and dirty grey cotton. He worked Indian-style, squatting on his heels, his knees tucked beneath his chin. He was filing down what was left of the teeth of some poor fellow who sat facing him in the same squatting position. The dentist was going to install a false tooth, while some fifty curious onlookers watched the operation. I think I was the one who suffered most. From time to time, the dentist fumbled around in the patient's mouth with his grubby fingers. He would try out the false tooth and then wipe it each time on a corner of his turban. It was repulsive to see. The patient spat on the ground, without even a drop of water to rinse his mouth. I walked away; I had already seen too much.

I made a happy choice in visiting the most perfect of architectural masterpieces: the Taj Mahal in Agra, built in the seventeenth century by Shah Jahan, a prince tormented by the memory of his adored wife. The Taj completely overwhelmed me. It was a mausoleum and a poem of love, as pure as the white marble of which it was made, as alive as the fiery precious stones with which the sarcophagus was encrusted. I spent three long days listening to the nightingales in the gardens, a haven of fresh, scented air; three days in which to gaze at the dome's reflection in the waters of the large central pool. It was love expressed in stone. At night beneath the full moon, the marble radiated a soft light and the place became magic.

I wasn't cured, but my stay in Agra did me a lot of good, especially after I met some French tourists who, being homeward bound, were only too glad to get rid of their extra rupees and, even more important, their supply of medicine which turned out to include exactly what I needed.

For the time being, I was no longer a slave to my stomach and was able to abandon my grotesque and too-habitual squat.

At the Taj Mahal I regained some of my strength. It was a good thing I did, for in Benares I was going to need all of it just to hang on, to resist the havoc that that sudden, enveloping nightmare was going to wreak. Benares, the holy city of Hinduism, was the weeping ulcer of the Indian subcontinent. All the misery in the world was concentrated there on the bank of the Ganges. It was Chandri Chowk ten times over. Truly, it seemed ordained that I would never plumb the uttermost depths. Each day there loomed out of the abyss some new circumstance which dragged me even further down.

From the moment of my arrival, I was overcome with nausea. No book, film or photograph could convey the reality of that festering sore. The pungent, asphyxiating odours, dazzling colours, deafening racket and cries of all kinds left me feeling utterly numbed. It was indescribable, something that could only be experienced. It demanded direct confrontation with rotting wounds, human magma, a flood of misery that even the most delirious mind could never imagine. Resigned and impotent, an entire population - from children to the helpless aged - stretched out its hand for alms. As far as the eye could see, hundreds and thousands of beggars sat propped up against each other waiting. It was a procession of bloody, fly-covered scabs, gaping sores, infected stumps, decomposing flesh . . . I wavered between pity and disgust as the pilgrims' silhouettes slipped indifferently along the *ghats*, the steps leading to the river.

How to describe the emaciated mendicants, skeletons with roving eyes; the holy *sadhus* draped in coarse, saffron-coloured cloth, their plaited hair hanging to their heels; the half-naked men covered with ashes, the 'V' of Vishnu or the three lines of Shiva streaked on their foreheads; the cripples dragging themselves across the asphalt which was melting in the sun; the host of pallid creatures dressed in rags or completely naked; the blind men grinning at nothing . . . With pierced ears and noses, ring-studded toes and heavy anklets which rubbed thick calluses on their legs, the women moved about impervious to their surroundings but weighed down by their poverty - for their trinkets were all they possessed. There were also a few Westerners whom drugs had reduced to human wrecks; betel chewers who sent endless streams of red spittle flying to the ground; and everywhere, invalids awaiting death. At Manikarnika Ghat, bodies were burned continually, day and night. The most fervent desire of every Hindu was to be cremated in Benares and to have his ashes thrown into the Ganges. It was hoped that in such a manner the cycle of reincarnations might be stopped.

For some ten years the youth of Europe and North America, claiming to be hippies, had been flocking to India, ruining in the process the relationship existing between Indians and humble travellers of my own sort. Traditionally, the *gurudwaras* (Sikh temples) lodged and fed their guests for as long as they wished to stay. But the hippies had overstepped the bounds by making themselves too much at home. They had smoked too much and made love too much - to the point where the temple doors had been closed to all Westerners. Nevertheless I decided to try my luck, since I didn't feel up to sleeping on the streets of Benares.

In the Luxa Street temple, they decided I was not a real hippy. I was accepted and given a rope bed, a *charpaie*. In the morning, however, I got myself thrown out by walking about with a razor in search of an electric socket. A bearded man wearing a turban threw his arms up in the air, then dashed off to alert the manager who sported the same dark beard. The latter cried sacrilege and with a peremptory gesture showed me the exit. I had been thrown out because I had wanted to shave. If only I had known earlier what I learned on my way out . . .

Founded in the fifteenth century by Guru Nanak, the Sikh religion sought to reconcile the polytheism and basic tolerance of Hinduism with the monotheism and relative fanaticism of Islam at a time when India was divided between the two religions. One of Nanak's successors was beheaded by mistake; to avoid any further confusion, the Sikhs decided to make themselves recognizable by no longer cutting so much as a hair. When their beards became too long, they divided them down the middle and tied the two ends together on top of their heads, hiding the knot under a turban.

Although by now my intestinal tract afforded me some respite, I was nevertheless worn out by the slightest exertion. Moving about was difficult because it had to be done at such a reduced speed. Added to that were the problems of stifling heat and an inadequate diet.

In Dahnbad, tired and covered with sweat, dirt and grease, I met Mr Mukherjee. Struck by my state of exhaustion, he took me to his home - something which was extremely rare in India where the overwhelming poverty seemed to have made people insensitive to each other's fate. His wife, a true disciple of Ramakrishna, welcomed me with a warm heart. 'Worship God in your fellow man', the Master had said. Both of them were tactful and extremely kind, and devoted to serving humanity. It had been a long time since I had heard such spiritual language and breathed such tranquillity of the soul. The encounter lifted my morale immediately. As soon as love made its appearance, everything became brighter. The trees seemed greener, the birds more joyful . . . Here at last was the India I had been waiting and searching for, in such eager expectation and for so long.

'You are *ramta sadhu bahata neer*. In Hindi that means the wandering saint "Flowing Water".'

It was not the first time I'd been taken for a *sadhu*. My goatee and emaciated features had often earned me that flattering epithet. But why 'Flowing Water'? My host explained that if I still looked so young, it was because I was like the water that flowed and renewed itself incessantly - unlike the stagnant water of ponds and pools. It was true that when one was only passing through, there was no time for hatred or desire. The metaphor pleased me very much.

Mr Mukherjee bought me a rail ticket to Calcutta. In the immense railway station, three times the size of the ones in Paris, the trains never arrived on time. When on railways, sacred cows still had priority.

A friend of Jenny's was living in Calcutta. I decided to visit her, since until now Jenny had always provided me with reliable addresses. However, after living amongst the poorest of Indians - in the face of whose abject poverty I appeared so rich - I was quite unprepared for the dramatic contrast.

'My stocks are on their way up. I've never made so much profit in so short a time. Did you happen to win at the races last Sunday?'

The villa reeked of opulence. Rita, Jenny's friend, had not yet arrived and her husband had not known how to refuse me entry into his home. He sat before me sipping coffee and chatting with a friend every bit as fat and rich as himself. My presence was an obvious embarrassment to them, my impoverished state in particular. But they pointedly ignored me, while making a lavish display of their wealth. It was out-and-out provocation. Rita's husband had gone to school in England and had the disdainful air shared by those Indians who spoke English well. I had difficulty in keeping my temper until Rita came in. As soon as she arrived I took my leave. A street-sweeper showed me a little patch of ground next to his hut. That would be enough for me.

I was not the only one sleeping under the stars, for half a million disinherited souls lived on the pavements of Calcutta. The most deprived ones, naked as babies, had not so much as a piece of cardboard to place between themselves and the ground. Listless children with matchstick limbs and bloated bellies languished in the dirt like giant spiders. In the morning hundreds of these poor souls trudged through the mud for hours

on end at the municipal water pumps. Each awaited his turn to moisten
the soya flour distributed by the government. Using a finger, they mixed
the water and flower in a tin can and then gulped down this 'meal', their
daily allowance. A woman quenched her baby's thirst with water from a
puddle . . .

Such a diet, failing to meet the minimum nutritional requirements
to sustain life, had created a human sub-species. '*A man is not fit to do
service for God with brain or body if he is weakened by lack of food. He
cannot see clearly*' ('Abdu'l-Bahá). Contrary to certain local beliefs, the
spirit could not compensate for the absence of protein.

Towards noon, a truck of sad repute patrolled the streets of the city:
it was the municipal hearse briskly gathering up all the inert bodies. I was
careful never to sleep on too long after sunrise.

From now on I was going to live on the railway. Stations would take the
place of Sikh temples. Getting around would be easier by rail than by
road and, all things considered, I would end up paying less. In the end I
covered 10,000 miles for just fifteen dollars.

Every foreigner who looked even slightly young carried a student
card. Since my passport described me as a student ('student' looked more
impressive - or at least less questionable - than 'hitch-hiker'), I had one
of my own. Everything was set, and all I needed in order to travel half-
price was to fill out a form requesting a reduction - which here was called
a 'concession'. The procedure was easily accomplished except in Bombay
and Delhi where the number of 'students' was overwhelming. The
authorities in those two cities were not easily taken in, knowing full well
that two cards out of three were forged, or indeed were not even student
cards at all but rather tickets to a concert series, or youth hostel permits.
As a result, in both Bombay and Delhi one 'foreign student' out of two
was simply refused his concession.

But that sort of hassle was nothing compared to the effort required
simply to obtain a ticket in India. The queues at the third-class ticket
counters in the stations were so long that it often took hours to work
one's way up to the window. There was a real danger of getting smothered
or trampled to death. I therefore turned to the rather disreputable
practice known as the *sahib* system, which meant taking advantage of my
skin colour to enter the ticket office by the employees' door and buy my
ticket directly without losing any time. With a rail ticket in hand, my
worries disappeared, for I was now entitled to sleep in the waiting rooms.
I usually spent the night in the second-class hall. Since *sahibs* always

travelled first class, the controller did not dare to check my ticket if he found me one class down. The first-class waiting room was too carefully watched, while the third-class room was the equivalent of sleeping in the street . . . At least it was comforting to know that in almost every city, I could count on finding a room equipped with toilets and showers where I could relax and sleep underneath a ceiling fan.

The actual travelling by train was somewhat less easy than entering a second-class waiting room with a third-class ticket; in fact, it could be even harder than obtaining a ticket by the normal non-*sahib* procedure. Before the arriving train could come to a full stop, the third-class coaches would already be under assault. With marvellous agility, the passengers climbed aboard, some through the doors and even more often through the windows, like an army of monkeys. Because of my backpack, I was condemned to wait until the train had come to a halt before entering the coach via the door.

Nevertheless, it was easier to board a train in India than it was to get off one. The opposing currents were not always of equal force, and the weaker one tended to be pushed back. The situation often ended in a general free-for-all on the steps of the coach. Inside, the battle continued over the few available seats, while heavy, sharp-cornered trunks came flying through the windows, propelled by energetic coolies standing on the platform. At such moments, it was more dangerous than ever to 'lean out of the window'. I always had a hard time making my way through the crowded corridors, jammed as they were with bags, baskets and bundles. The luggage racks were not reserved for suitcases but rather for the most agile passengers who stretched out on their perches and contemplated with cynical grins their less lucky fellow travellers. As the train pulled away from the platform, a few people always jumped out of the window: they were the scalpers who occupied seats on arriving trains in order to auction them off to the highest bidder.

Little by little, people got seated. They squeezed together as much as possible, with eight or more sharing a bench intended for four. Not bad! My presence was unexpected. A *sahib* in third class? It meant that I always got at least the corner of a trunk to sit on.

When my neighbours spoke English, we conversed. Our discussion was punctuated with 'Atcha, atcha', a typical expression which did not mean much by itself but which was suited to any occasion, always accompanied by a nod or shake of the head.

'Atcha, atcha, this trip is going along very well, *sahib*. Atcha, atcha, you see how everything is working out. There is a place for everyone.

Atcha, when I think there are some people who criticize this country . . .'

I concluded that everything was relative. You never got to know your own country unless you left it. Otherwise you had nothing to compare it with.

I frequently spent a night or two on the train. Since I was incapable of sleeping in a sitting, squatting or standing position, a space to lie down in was an absolute necessity. I had noticed that no one ever claimed the small area under the wooden benches. Was it somehow taboo?

'Legs up, gentlemen!'

Doing a little spring cleaning, I cleared the space of water jugs, small bags, litter and pieces of sugar cane chewed down to the fibre. I proceeded to spread out a nylon sheet on which I unrolled my sleeping bag. Then, going through all sorts of gymnastics which provoked laughter and comments, I got into bed. I used my pack as a pillow to make sure that it would still be in my possession the next morning. It was impossible to make the slightest movement, yet the space was sufficient. In spite of the echo of the wheels close to my ear and the chaotic goings-on in the compartment, I never took long to fall asleep, so great was my exhaustion at the end of the day.

I was occasionally awakened by a kick from a heel; it would be some new passenger who had not realized there was anyone sleeping under his seat. In the morning I would pinch the bare heel nearest to my nose. The heel would disappear, accompanied by a scream. In an immediate reflex, the travellers would all bend over to look, and I would see their heads appear upside down, wide-eyed, framed between their knees. A *sahib*! Unexpected to say the least!

In Madras I abandoned my sleeping bag for a light mat of woven straw and a piece of coloured cloth that I used as a blanket. For the next sixteen months I would sleep the hard way - on wood, cement, or stone - and became so used to it that never again was I able to tolerate a bed that was even the slightest bit soft.

Pondicherry: I vaguely recalled the name from my school days. The former French port still retained a colonial air. Around the Place du Gouvernment, the central square shaded by huge trees, tidy streets with French names led off in all directions. Composed of pastel-coloured houses and tropical vegetation, the city dozed at the edge of a long straight beach and overwhelming heat.

Bit by bit Pondicherry was becoming the property of the Aurobindo Society, an ashram founded in 1920 by Sri Aurobindo. At the time of my stay, this centre for the study of integral yoga was headed by Aurobindo's wife, a Frenchwoman whom everyone called 'Mother'. She died in 1974.

Whenever I had heard yoga mentioned, I'd pictured the universal cliché of a skinny, contorted man staying in some improbable posture for hours on end. But I was determined to get the whole story. What if I too attended one of those yoga schools, called ashrams? I was certainly in the right place; India was full of them. The Beatles with their guru Maharishi Mahesh Yogi had launched the trend in Europe. Ever since, an entire generation of young people from the industrialized countries had flocked to the various more-or-less authentic yoga centres in quest of the supernatural or the spiritual or just inner peace. Aurobindo was one of the best known centres. Fifteen hundred people lived in a great spiritual laboratory, striving to achieve an integral perfection, to be in harmony with the universal consciousness. In order to be admitted by the 'Mother' the aspirant had to undergo a trial period, a year of preparation at his own expense.

In 1967, the members of Aurobindo had begun to build an international, futuristic city without money or police. Its citizens would be those individuals who had attained a level of perfection permitting them to live apart from the problems of today's society. Everything had been planned so that the community would be self-sufficient. But this dream city was still little more than a building site. A central plaza in the shape of a lotus, the beginning of a farm, a maternity ward, a few houses: that was the extent of it for the moment.

'Auroville will be the first model city. In the future the entire planet will be covered with Aurovilles', a young woman explained to me.

'That's marvellous. But excuse me, did you say that these cities would have no police. Human nature being what it is, how do you expect to manage?'

'The wrongdoers will be expelled!'

I was still perplexed. Expelled by whom, since there would be no police? And expelled to where, since there would be nothing but Aurovilles? To the moon, perhaps?

On the threshold of a spiritual awakening, the world still had a long road to cover before attaining such a state of perfection. What was needed, surely, was not dreams but a willingness to come to grips with reality. Otherwise, there would be only chaos. Auroville was no doubt an excellent thing, a rare experience for those who took part - a handful of Frenchmen, Americans and other people in search of inner truth. But it did not seem to me a solution for the woes of the world. It was not a perfect city that would create perfect citizens, but rather a community of perfect citizens who would no doubt create the city of their dreams.

My state of perfection and my patience (I would never have had the forbearance to spend a year awaiting 'Mother's' benevolence) being less than ideal, I headed instead for another ashram located in Lawspet, two miles from Pondicherry.

A large green building set on a plateau of red earth continually cooled by the ocean breeze, surrounded by trees, flowers and silence: Ananda Ashram. The period of study usually lasted from three to six months, but at the time of my arrival, a special one-month course was about to begin. Ashrams were generally free, but this one asked for a 'voluntary donation' of eight rupees a day. An American woman wearing a sari introduced herself as Meenakshi Devi (otherwise Barbara Tomscha) and showed me around the school. I met the swami, the school's spiritual master. My donation having been made in advance, she then took me to my room. However, I never actually slept there, for I preferred the coolness of the roof terrace and the protection of a few palm fronds.

There were a good twenty of us yogi apprentices of both sexes and various nationalities. Swami Gitananda, a portly figure with flowing beard, radiated health. He talked to us in a strong voice in very pure English - the English of Canada, where he had spent quite a bit of time. He was a good speaker. An orthodox Hindu, he often referred to the *Bhagavad-Gita* (a sacred book of Hinduism constituting part of the famous Mahabharata epic) and to Krishna and he believed in reincarnation. Each of the thirty days passed to the same rhythm:

5.30 a.m.: Wake up. Very weak tea. Wash. We are taught to gargle and clear our throats noisily.

6.00 a.m.: The first lesson of the day, lasting a good hour, takes place on the roof just as the sun appears over the horizon. It is a class in *hatha yoga*, consisting of the famous postures that Westerners call 'yoga', but which are in reality only a preparation for the real thing. A healthy mind in a healthy body: such could be the definition of *hatha yoga*, of the *asanas*, *kriyas* and *mudras* (corresponding to the postures, circulatory activities and exercises for glandular control, respectively). We exert ourselves, each on his straw mat. Enthroned on a small podium, the swami explains·in great detail each new position but never actually performs in front of us. His corpulence prevents any demonstration. An American pastor named Rick is his chief disciple. He has been an apprentice for the last three years. Thin and limber, he puts into practice the teachings of the swami. Despite my own thinness and years of physical exertion, I am not very supple and have some difficulty in doing the exercises. I come out better on the *pranayama*, the aim of which is to regulate breathing in order to obtain control of the *prana*, the vital force contained in air. These latter exercises do me a world of good; I shall continue with them in the future.

7.30 a.m.: Glands regulated, lungs expanded, magnetic circuits co-ordinated, we form a circle, sitting cross-legged on the tile floor of the refectory. Between our knees is a bowl of gruel sprinkled with brown sugar and a glass of water: breakfast.

9.00 a.m.: We gather again on the roof for *inana yoga*, or learning how to relax. The swami draws on a blackboard, asking us to transform ourselves into hollow tubes, radio transmitters, ant-hills, triangles . . . all this using only our solar plexus. He asks us to surround our bodies with imaginary circles radiating outwards from the navel, growing gradually larger. I try manfully . . .

12.30 p.m.: Lunch. Raw vegetables. The menu never changes: one cucumber, one carrot and one tomato. Nothing else. To savour them, I feel like adopting the rabbit postured so well described by the fat and flabby swami during the morning's first lesson. How does he manage to put on weight?

3.00 p.m.: After a nap, *raja yoga* exercises of concentration.

5.30 p.m.: We are served a dish of fruit: dinner. It gets increasingly hard to bear. I'm always hungry. I'm used to eating light meals, but not to this extreme . . .

7.00 p.m.: Last session: the *satsangha*, by starlight. The swami delights us with his philosophy. The *shishas* (students) ask questions afterwards. Then after an interval of silence, we chant mantras in unison. Om, om, tam, tam: the measured litany rises softly in the calm of the night, like a last prayer.

In spite of this rather busy schedule, I still found time to go to the library and deepen my knowledge of yoga. There were numerous kinds of yoga, just as there were numerous masters and schools of thought, but I did not believe that every disciple was capable of attaining ecstasy. Nevertheless, yoga remained an excellent means of controlling oneself. It was discipline that led to personal liberation, that helped one to surpass one's sensory perceptions and the limits of one's reason and intellect. I even thought that *hatha yoga*, the basis of yoga, should be taught in our schools. It got one in shape through relaxation. In that way it was the opposite of gymnastic exercises which, while developing strength and muscle tone, were nevertheless physically strenuous.

I didn't feel that I had wasted my time at the ashram, but yoga had its limits; and moreover, the venerable swami with his brilliant gift of the gab had a true 'Leo' personality. He reminded me more of an opportunistic merchant than a holy man. When a fashion came along, he knew how to take advantage of it. Something of a curiosity, he was famous for his ability to stop his heart and for having such complete control over his muscles that he could pull his private parts up into his lower abdomen without laying a hand on them . . . Soviet doctors had made a special trip to attend the performance!

In good Indian fashion, he had married young and had four children. He had then ditched his family to meditate and become a saint. He was proud of the fact that he had not had a nocturnal emission since leaving his wife. He maintained that the sperm was reabsorbed by the body and had no need to find its way elsewhere. The force, called shakti, would instead feed into the spirit and thus, according to him, a man could preserve all his energy. I thought he was overdoing it. At fifty-nine years of age, he claimed to be a wrestling champion and a lieutenant-colonel in the British Navy. He also claimed that he had been wounded by forty pieces of shrapnel during the last World War (was I to attribute the absence of scars to the miraculous effects of yoga?). He had gone round the world nine times and practised surgery for thirty years in Canada. He was first and foremost a charlatan but nevertheless had a certain verve. As a vegetarian, he insisted that it was useless to consume 'second-hand' protein, since even the cows themselves turned to vegetation for their own needs.

His pupils were divided into three groups. First, there were those who revered him as God the Father, kneeling deferentially at his feet and taking every word he said as gospel. Wild-eyed, haunted by visions and basically unbalanced: such were Ron, David, Brian, Linda, Sergio, Alwyn. Then there were the straightforward devotees who formed a respectful majority. They believed everything but without going overboard: Meena, the lovelorn secretary who for the last three years had not left the swami's side; Rick, the king of *hatha yoga*; Eschwari, a young Indian woman who had been healed by the swami; Terry, Meena's sister, who had been fasting for sixteen days just to heighten her perceptions; Maria from Switzerland; Nathan, a Dravidian Indian; Nori, a silent Japanese. I was part of the third group, the sceptics: Kabir, a Brahman; Tom, a Swedish Maoist; Patrick, a Frenchman who was not at all involved, preferring instead his French cigarettes and clandestine steaks; his girlfriend Mireille, who didn't understand a word of English: she, at least, was out of the swami's reach; and finally there was Janos, a Canadian of Latvian origin who suspected the swami of fraud. Janos was my buddy. The swami predicted that he would be murdered within four days of his leaving the ashram. It gave us a good laugh.

Back in shape thanks to the *pranayama* exercises but sceptical about the idea of ecstasy on the cheap, I decided to leave the ashram a little before the end of the course. The first thing was to head for a restaurant in Pondicherry and treat myself to a good steak, French fries, and crusty French bread.

I had planned to go to Ceylon, but at Rameswaram I met with an obstacle: the ferry wasn't operating any more. A revolution had broken out and all communications were affected. It was genuinely difficult to plan a trip around the world. For months now I had been at the mercy of violence, political whims and disputes between Great Powers. Since revolutions had a way of ignoring timetables, I didn't wait around but chose to head north to Bombay and Nepal. If the problems in Ceylon resolved themselves, I would come back later.

In the hills of Mysore, the thin mountain air revived me. I made the acquaintance of Raghuram, a 32-year-old intellectual who reflected all the contradictions of modern-day India. He detested Hindi, the official language, and promoted Kanarese, his own mother tongue and one of the 850 languages spoken in India. Wearing a *dhoti*, a white piece of cloth wrapped around the waist, I visited the coffee plantation belonging to my host. He was a progressive landowner and extremely concerned about his workers' welfare. He had also organized a strike against the slaughtering of cows.

'A cow is like my mother!'

I couldn't entirely agree; yet I did wonder what benefit there was in killing those skeletal animals. They should at least be fattened up first. As a planter, my friend belonged to the *shudra* caste, the lowest; although the system had officially been abolished, he explained that a Brahman, a member of a superior caste, would never accept a dinner invitation to his home for fear of contamination. In keeping with tradition, his father had chosen his wife for him. He claimed to be happy with her; it was simply that they never conversed. A very simple woman of little education, his wife took care of the children and stayed in the kitchen with her sister. I saw her from a distance.

Bangalore: I walked down the wide avenues with a determined step, indifferent to the press of the crowd. Where was the Chamrajpet neighbourhood? A last ray of sunlight struck the tips of the roofs where excited monkeys leaped about. If I could not find Eschwari, I might have to spend the night in the streets. Pushed on by my rebellious instinct, my taste for non-conformity, I quickened my pace even though it might be getting me into trouble.

'May I help you? *Atcha, atcha.*'

'Miss Eschwari. Is this the right place? I'm a friend of hers from Pondicherry and would like to say hello.'

I had met her at the ashram. She had been without a doubt the most studious and devout of the swami's *shishas*. She had crowned him with flowers and kissed his feet with a fervour that could well have seemed shocking in the West. Meena, the secretary in love with the swami, had been jealous and had her expelled; but Eschwari had known how to leave with dignity. A magnificent woman, dressed in her most beautiful sari, she had given us dates and raisins on the evening of her departure and then sung for the last time with deep emotion, without bitterness. I remembered the last words of her brief farewell speech: 'I ask all of you to forgive me for the small offences I may have committed.'

Eschwari's father hesitated. He wondered whether he should let me in or call his daughter to the gate. By arriving in this way, I had offended against the social niceties, and the poor man found himself in an uncomfortable situation. He disappeared. A few minutes later, Eschwari came to open the gate and graciously invited me into a room furnished with a modest sofa, a table in the corner and a radio. Her father, mother, brothers, sisters and a woman servant were all present.

My hands pressed together in front of my chest, I bowed my greeting in the approved manner. They all watched closely. I was the *sahib*. Eschwari broke the silence by relating what she knew of my adventures. I blessed her, for she obtained her father's permission for me to sleep on the veranda. I stayed there three days and felt fulfilled, for I had been deploring my lack of contact with the local people. The appalling poverty which made individuals insensitive to their fellow men prevented me from having any true experience of an Indian household.

In any case, one room was out of bounds. It was the one reserved for worship, the *puja*. I caught a glimpse of a statue of Ganesha, a chubby god with the head of an elephant, protector of writers and learning. There were also portraits in washed-out colours framed by wreaths of fresh flowers: they represented Shiva, Krishna and Lakshmi. Small candles and sticks of incense glowed dimly.

I saw Eschwari only in the evening, as she was not allowed to show me around the city during the day. Her profound happiness set my heart aflame. With long black hair framing delicate features, she was very beautiful, but her femininity, her sensual presence, did not affect me; she seemed transfigured by her purity. We talked for long hours in the living room under the continual surveillance of her father sitting on the sofa and her mother crouching in the doorway of the kitchen. Lively and intelligent, Eschwari had truly achieved her own revolution, but without becoming a rebel. Being a clear thinker, she inevitably felt the weight of sundry taboos; nevertheless she thought it too early to overthrow the entire order.

I listened more attentively to her than I had ever listened to the swami. I was enchanted. Her father and mother had faded into two anonymous shadows. She stood before me leaning against the table, and I was at her feet. Her black skin (she was of Dravidian extraction) shone in the dusk with a very soft golden light. Her spiritual force inspired me with visions that only the third eye could perceive. It was a magnificent moment. I thought of the aureoles of the saints depicted on the walls of our churches, of the halos that at times surrounded them.

'I too would like to take a trip around the world, but I will travel in my next incarnation instead. In this one, I lack the courage . . .'

As I talked with Eschwari, I was sure the day would come when Indian women would receive justice at last. It was imperative. A balanced world depended on it.

New Delhi, Calcutta . . . Bombay. Once again I found myself in the street amidst thousands of miserable souls for whom the street was their only home. For weeks now I had been living in these streets, but I still hadn't got used to it, especially at night. I could not sleep soundly without walls around me. It was psychological, of course.

Malabar, a hill covered with enormous flowering trees, the most beautiful place in the city, attracted me in particular. It was situated at the end of Marine Drive, the Copacabana of Bombay. But first impressions were misleading, for vultures and crows glided slowly overhead, filling me with a sense of foreboding. Hidden behind the foliage, eight towers stood in silence . . . The Parsees, the last descendants of the Zoroastrians driven out of Persia in the thirteenth century by the Mongol invasion, exposed their dead in these towers. The job was quickly done. Birds of prey picked the bones clean in less than twenty minutes. It was probably more efficient than fire and certainly faster than worms. This ultimate sunbathe was the climax of fourteen

days of ceremony. Only the undertakers had the right to enter the sacred
site and to accompany the deceased. By talking my way around two girls,
I managed to enter the funeral hall, the last stop before the tower, but I
was not allowed to go any further. The Parsee world, which still
maintained the sacred fire of the god Ahura-Mazda in temples decorated
with Assyrian lions, was impenetrable, a closed world if ever there was
one. People were born Parsee; nobody ever became Parsee. Only a Parsee
man could marry a Parsee woman.

'*The truth of religion resides in moral value, not in the external
expression of imaginary values*': thus spake Zarathustra. But the breath of
his word had lost all its force - a breath that nevertheless inspired the
Persian kings of the world's first empire, a breath which appealed for
social justice, which illuminated the reign of Cyrus the Great. But the
Parsee religion, like every other religion, was in need of renewal. Lord!
How obvious this need for regeneration seemed when I compared the
contribution of Parsee morality to world history with what it had become
today.

May 18th, 1971: I had been in India for nearly three months. Now I
had been refused an extension of my visa, which left me with no choice
but to leave the country and go to Nepal. *Atcha, atcha*!

Ever since the hippies had declared Kathmandu to be Paradise on
Earth, the trucks leaving the border town of Raxaul had instituted a toll
system. They demanded ten Nepalese rupees (seventy-five US cents) to
drive their passengers up the 120-mile ascent to the capital. It was ten
rupees or nothing. Impossible to negotiate. They were all in cahoots.

I made the trip with a Canadian on his way back from Israel and
several yellow-skinned Nepalese. Dangerous hairpin bends zigzagged
8,000 feet into the clouds. We climbed through tall green pines, lulled by
the perpetual murmur of rushing streams. The air was cool. When we
began to descend through terraced fields into the famous valley, the
Himalayan Range appeared, filling the horizon. Snow and clouds blended
into each other. The Kathmandu Valley was to the mountains what Bali
was to the sea. Both were jewels where nature's handiwork and human
skill competed in beauty and daring.

Only recently opened to foreigners, Nepal was the only country in
the world where the government itself sold drugs. It was a monopoly like
any other - like the cigarette industry in France. The country's great
speciality was hashish cake, an experience I was going to try.

At the end of a narrow street, I selected the Cabin, a dimly-lit den
born of the American invasion. Overflowing with colour like a San

Francisco night-club, cranking out the same old Jimmy Hendrix hits, dens of this kind infested the city's streets. They kept the Americans from feeling homesick - for even when travelling, Americans were incapable of leaving their own country behind. Stiv, a young Nepalese whose carpet I shared, accompanied me - if discreetly. A thick cloud of blue smoke was floating just above the crowd of heads, and an acrid smell stung my throat and eyes. The room was crammed with young people, silent or uproarious, each in full 'trip'. A *shillom*, a clay pipe in the form of a long narrow egg cup and filled with burning hashish, circulated among strangers. The shallow-skinned man sitting next to me lifted it delicately over his head in his cupped hands. Several times he invoked the name of Shiva, then with a characteristic grimace inhaled three times before passing it on to me. Stiv showed me how to hold and smoke the *shillom*, a new experience for me.

I was handed a menu that was partly American-style (hamburgers, steaks, fried chicken) but only in part, for the local specialities were listed as well: hashish cake, marijuana pudding, ganja coffee . . . One cake for a rupee seemed a very cheap 'trip' indeed. Anxious to appreciate my meal to the full, I decided to swallow the cake first in order to sensitize my taste buds. It was the sort of cake that might be served at a ladies' tea party. It looked quite innocent, and I ate it in one mouthful. Stiv said that I would have to wait, that the effect was slower than when you smoked. A quarter of an hour later, nothing had happened. I was convinced that the amount had been too small and I ordered a second. Things then started to happen very rapidly. The honey cake that I was nibbling on while waiting for my order seemed incredibly sweet. My palate was much more sensitive than normal, and each crumb was a morsel to be savoured.

That stage was very quickly left behind as I began losing all notion of reality. How long had I been in this smoky den? Why was I here? My stomach suddenly caved in, as if struck by a tidal wave. The walls seemed to capsize, and panic overwhelmed me. My head was spinning, and although I knew some fresh air would do me good, I was incapable of getting up. I felt nailed to my bench. Three times I fell back with a thud. How could I get outside? How could I get through that door over there that formed a forty-five degree angle with the floor? If I bent over to get through, would I fall down? With Stiv's help I managed to get up, but I was surrounded by a swirling circle of fire. From my feet it surged upwards and struck the nape of my neck in a shower of sparks. Then it subsided. I was being tossed about on the crest of a wave which was on the verge of swallowing me up. A stream of images flashed through my mind at breakneck speed: a thousand Buddhas, a thousand birds, a thousand identical flowers repeated in vivid colours. Enough to drive me crazy.

'Stiv, please . . . make me come down!'

'What are you talking about, André? You're here on the road next to me. I assure you . . .'

'But listen, I tell you I'm gliding . . . like a bird above the roof tops. I can see it all very clearly.'

I extended my arms like a tightrope walker on a shaky wire. I was nervous and afraid of falling. The path that led back to Stiv's place seemed endless. What if a strong draught caught hold of me and carried me off to the Himalayas? I had already seen birds suddenly swept away on the wind.

Back at Stiv's, I vomited four times before sinking into an abysmal sleep on a gyroscopic floor. The morning after was dreadful. I had a splitting headache, a blurred mind, a weakened body and a queasy stomach. I hated being in such a state. I was now firmly convinced that alcohol and drugs served only to brutalize mankind. I could understand why some people got themselves involved, but by the same token, I could assure them that there were other means of attaining exaltation. The walking corpses of the drug addicts, coughing and spitting their way down the roads of India and Nepal, were daily evidence. They thought they would get 'high', 'fly', 'take a trip', but each time they came back down to earth again, a little lower than before. Their's was a false euphoria which in the end amounted to slow suicide, as Mex and Jackie's lives constantly, painfully, reminded me. All the evidence seemed to prove that the elixir of exaltation was not to be found in drugs. Genuine spiritual intoxication was altogether different: '*Think not that We have revealed unto you a mere code of laws. Nay, rather, We have unsealed the choice Wine with the fingers of might and power*' (Bahá'u'lláh).

I was sure of my path now. The more familiar I became with Bahá'í writings, the 'higher', more intoxicated I felt. The experience with the hashish cake had been a final proof for me. I had discovered what I was seeking, the real treasure at the end of my road: the choice Wine of the Revelation.

In Kathmandu's Durbar Square, the hippies blended perfectly with the kaleidoscope of colourful local costumes; Nepalese with powerful bare legs bowed beneath loads strapped to their foreheads. Indifferent to the crowd of curious onlookers, a stark naked *sadhu* made his way across the square. He had apparently come up from South India, for he was very black. A strange vision: he was going through life with his right arm raised. He probably belonged to the cult of Shiva whose followers went through life stripped naked, finding shelter in caves and forests. What was he doing in the city? Perhaps he was hunting for a new hide out or searching for *soma*, the sacred liquor through which men came into contact with the gods. In his left hand he carried a trident - a symbol of divinity - resting on his shoulder. From its tip dangled a little bundle of some kind. His hair was the colour of dirty hemp and reached down to his heels. With the inevitable red dot between his eyebrows representing the third eye, the *sadhu* had a proud bearing. There was a single, incongruous touch of coquettishness: around the tip of his most sensitive part he wore a ring on which small bells tinkled with each step. Every traveller in quest of his destiny, his divine homeland, had his own very personal style . . .

The road to Tibet passed through American, Russian and Chinese zones of influence. At the border were red flags, guards in identical blue overalls, and a large portrait of Mao against a Himalayan backdrop. But the Roof of the World refused me entry. Just as in Hong King and Macao, the Chinese did not want anything to do with me. I had wanted to visit Tibet in order to get to know the Tibetan people. Fortunately, I was able to meet some on the Nepalese side of the border. They were refugees.

'We fled when it became impossible to practise our religion. We left by night with only a little money and food. After an exhausting three-month march at altitudes of over 10,000 feet, we reached the Indian border. For the last eight years we've been in Nepal.'

They welcomed me warmly even though they had very little in the way of material goods. No sooner had I arrived than I exchanged a pair of shoes I had found on the boat going down the Amazon for a large man's earring decorated with a piece of turquoise. As jewellery it had no particular value; yet I treasured it as a family heirloom that had been worn every day for generations.

Not one of those faces, tanned by the altitude to a rich mahogany, failed to smile at me. A very bright ten-year-old named Chemi took me by the hand to show me around the camp and to visit the workshops where woollen carpets were woven. In the spinning shop it was the hour of prayer. The wheels continued to turn as the women chanted mantras. In the centre of the village was a pile of stones around which old women circulated twirling their prayer wheels, managing to pray and gossip at the same time. I was surprised that it wasn't the Americans who had come up with such a gadget: one that would save time and still get you to heaven. Throughout the village, printed banners waved from the tops of tall bamboo poles. They were prayer flags intended for the gods and wandering spirits. At the entrance to the temple, a kind of large suspended drum caught my attention. Again, it was a prayer wheel. With every turn a bell rang. So many rings, so many prayers . . .

An old shoemaker stopped me as I passed by. Taking out a needle, he sewed up the torn pocket on my trousers, then walked away without a word. What love there was in that wordless act of kindness.

The monsoon finally drove me from this fascinating country, this Tibet where I had spent several days without ever leaving Nepal. I took one last look at Annapurna, which would soon be engulfed by big black clouds. Then, my ten rupees paid, a truck carried me down through pouring rain. Behind us a landslide swamped several bends of the road in heaps of mud.

Calcutta . . . The monsoon had turned the city green, but it had not swept away the filth or provided a cure for the greatest misery in the world. The streets were flooded and cholera threatened. Once again I was plunged into the reality of the waking nightmare that was India. Today's news flash was the war in Bangladesh. Five million Bengalis had sought refuge in India, fleeing the vengeful bloodletting of the West Pakistanis. The refugees were a product of our modern-day madness. Some 50,000 of them crowded together at the end of the runway of Dum Dum Airport, twelve miles north of Calcutta. Like human livestock, they were huddled under long tarpaulins. With resignation in their faces, deprived of any comfort (had they ever known what comfort was?), men and women waited without knowing what they were waiting for. Deafened by the infernal racket of planes taking off and landing, they queued in their hundreds. Each person held a pink card in his hand and waited for his ration of rice, a few onions, some *dhal* and salt.

A Bengali with large, tender, sad eyes gestured to me to come over. A young teacher, he had fled with his wife, his little daughter and several members of his large family.

'They are hunting Hindus now. The Pakistani army held us at gunpoint while our Muslim neighbours plundered our family's five houses. They stole everything we had. It was appalling. I can't bear to see my family in this wretched state.'

The man who had lost everything then offered me a mango. His gesture moved me deeply, for I knew that fruit was practically non-existent in the camp. I begged him to give it to his daughter instead.

'Cholera is rife inside the camp. There have been 225 cases confirmed already . . .'

At the dispensary an Indian doctor was writing out a long order for medicine. He railed against all the red tape which could not be bypassed even in this case of extreme emergency. Each day the crowd of refugees grew larger. The British had set up a field hospital, and army planes were making daily deliveries of sanitary fittings. Volunteer nurses with syringes of vaccine in hand gave injection after injection. My last haunting vision was of a skeletal man dressed in rags. In his arms he held his granddaughter who had just died of cholera.

When I reached Colombo, Ceylon (now Sri Lanka), I was exhausted in every way. Physically I could hardly continue. My second crossing of India had almost been the death of me. My head was spinning dizzily, my throat burned and my legs would no longer hold me up. A worsening fever forced me to wear warm clothes, which seemed the crowning misery in such a climate. Finally, I had just been involved in a traffic accident. My driver, trying to avoid a child who had fallen off a bike, had swerved and rammed his truck into a tree. My hands and face were cut and bruised. It was nothing serious, but it seemed just one more misery.

My morale was no better. Travelling through India from north to south, witnessing its all-embracing poverty and its crowds of barely-human people, weighed heavily on my spirits. The malnutrition, the lack of hygiene, the heat, the permanent aggressiveness on the part of those unhappy souls to whom even I seemed very well-off: the accumulated misery of it all bore down on me.

Ceylon was an immediate contrast. Clean and green and flourishing, it gave me the strength to go on. Feeling a little constrained by the circumstances, I showed up at the *Alliance Française* in Colombo, worried about the kind of welcome I would receive. I distrusted not only consulates, but also the mentality of certain Frenchmen living abroad. Their attitude was often 'every man for himself'. But in the state I was in, I needed help and so I steeled myself to ring the doorbell. It was a lucky thing I did. Daniel Carillon, the young director, greeted me with infinite generosity and took care of me for five days.

No sooner had I begun to feel better than the call of the open road dragged me from Daniel's comfortable home. My dread of being coddled was pushing me into a carelessness that I knew I would suffer for sooner or later, but I could not help myself. As long as I could stand, I would press on. There was no particular merit involved; it was simply the way I was made: stubborn and obstinate to the last. A Land Rover loaded with bananas and sacks of rice picked me up in Matale.

'I'm a wholesale grocer. We're going to drop off these goods', said Nazed, the Muslim driver, as if to apologize for the lack of comfort. He then turned to his Buddhist companion and winked. Both of them burst out laughing. Religious differences did not seem to come between them, and the sight of their obvious closeness comforted me.

We were crossing the Central Province through dense jungle. My high-spirited comrades pestered me with endless questions about my trip, but the atmosphere was relaxed. Suddenly Nazed turned to me.

'Do you want to see how precious stones are smuggled?'

'Why not?'

A few miles further on, the Land Rover swerved sharply to the right and left the asphalt for a dirt track as rough as a washboard. I was jolted with every pot-hole. It was a rough ride, but what did it matter? Hitch-hiking had taught me always to expect the unexpected. No conducted tour, no scheduled transport - bus, boat, train or plane - could offer the same advantages. Although the track was a long way from anywhere, there was a surprising amount of traffic. I said as much.

'Those are gem dealers. They come to do business with the local people. There's a lot of competition because the profits are enormous . . . But you haven't seen anything yet. All these guys are only amateurs . . .'

From time to time huge lizards at least a yard long would waddle swiftly across the track which was becoming increasingly narrow and difficult. We drove for over an hour through the rain forest amid shrieking parrots and scampering monkeys. After fifteen or twenty miles the Land Rover came to a halt by a wood cabin which looked surprisingly out of place. My two companions transferred the rice and bananas to the cabin, while two guards offered us spicy yams with fresh coconut and dried fish. Nobody was in a hurry, and we lingered over cups of tea. I didn't ask any questions, but I was curious to see what would happen next.

After a bit, Nazed and his friend headed off into a thicket, following a path which was barely visible. I did my best to follow them. Suddenly, out of nowhere, a man joined us and we pushed on another mile through the dense undergrowth, pushing aside branches and roots. I wondered how they managed to avoid getting lost, for the path had petered out completely. We finally came out into a clearing where the forest had been burned. The smell of a wood fire hovered in the air above mounds of red earth. There were at least fifty holes in the ground, each testifying to the labour of the nearly-naked miners digging under a burning sun.

'You get it?' asked Nazed, proud to show us around his clandestine operation.

He commented at length on the various stages of extraction.

'I have eighty guys working for me. We split fifty-fifty, half for them and half for me and my associate. Of course I feed them as well. That's why I came here today. I have the stones polished in Colombo and get them aboard a boat heading for Hong Kong.'

'Isn't your little business dangerous?'

'Not really. The government's too weak to interfere much. Of course the police have their suspicions, but in the jungle they've got to find me first. You noticed that guy who followed us a while back? He's a guard, one of several. They give the alert and everyone disappears without a trace.'

'But even so, what about the traffic? All the cars?'

'Don't worry, we've got ready-made alibis. I own a wholesale grocery store in Tamale, so it's natural for me to deliver food to the farmers. My buddy has a little plantation in the area, complete with five elephants to work the land. So of course he's got to come and look around from time to time to make sure everything is going well!'

The next day, on the road to Dambulla, three men in a large Austin stopped to pick me up. In the back there were coconuts, fresh vegetables and sacks of rice.

'You're French? And you're going around the world I ? We might have something interesting to show you . . . How would you like to visit a jewel smugglers' camp?

'You're kidding . . . Do they really exist?'

Night and the monsoon had blotted out the landscape by the time I reached Nuwara Eliya, and the wind at this 6,000-foot altitude was biting. The gale forced me to go about knocking on doors, and I was finally admitted into the youth hostel. The room they gave me looked like a prison cell. Paint was peeling off the dreary walls, the metal bed could only be referred to as basic. A dim lamp merely added to the gloomy atmosphere. I was cold and my teeth were chattering. I could no longer control the feverish shivers running down my spine, and my legs were so weak that I could do nothing but sit down on the bed. Then I noticed a bathroom scale and I stepped on. The scale registered only 121 pounds. I was shocked! To make sure that the scale was working, I weighed my pack, which normally weighed about twenty-five pounds. No, there was no mistake. I really did weigh 121 pounds.

HEALTH ALERT: I wrote those two words in red ink and capital letters in my journal. I had never been plump, but had usually carried about 145 pounds on my 5'9" frame. In other words, I had always been slender but had taken care not to get really thin, for my weight was a kind of barometer of my general state of health. After a few months of travelling, once the exertion had begun to take effect, I had dropped to 135 pounds; then, in the tropics, I'd gone as low as 125. But until now I had not worried. This time, however, I had broken all records and the situation seemed ominous.

I caught my own gaze in the spotted, cracked mirror which hung over the wash-basin. I saw the dark rings round my eyes, my prominent cheekbones. I had trouble in recognizing myself. Was this gaunt-faced stranger really me? I ran the tips of my fingers across the skin of the stranger's face. It felt like parchment. I suddenly realized that my whole trip might have to be abandoned, for it was more than possible that the inside of my body was just as ravaged as the outside. To assess the damage, I stripped naked. The spectacle was sobering: nothing but skin and bones, not an ounce of fat, no buttocks. I placed my foot on the edge of the bed, and the loose flesh on my thigh dangled from the bone like washing on a line. My ribs were like guitar strings, while my stomach was swollen like a balloon. My skin was covered with little red spots which had made their appearance back in Nepal. I was not in any pain, but I could see that my vitality had been sapped.

I hated feeling sorry for myself and watching helplessly as my morale plunged. Over the last few months such moments had been recurring much too often, and I didn't like it. If only I could have got out of that morgue-like room and gone for a walk. But it was dark and raining, and the wind was freezing cold. A jumble of curses poured from my mind: I cursed my diarrhoea and my fever; I damned my forced vegetarianism and all the wretched taboos that were slowly destroying me. But finally I had no choice but to acknowledge the consequences of four years of physical hardship and a more-than-Spartan lifestyle. There were no miracles. Although I could have expected it, the balance had tipped when I'd accepted the glass of water that Death - disguised as a Pakistani - had held out to me four months earlier.

For more than a week now I had been having difficulty in digesting food, and despite twelve or thirteen hours' sleep every night, I still felt no better. I considered the alternatives, and realized I could never let myself die in such a place. I was a fighter and had no desire to hitch-hike my way into the hereafter. I would simply have to reduce my activity. I was going to start taking care of myself, and for me that was already a radical change in style. Eat more? This was not exactly the moment to start, as the only things I could keep down were bananas and gingerbread. The rest of the food was burning with spices.

As in New Zealand, socialism was rather well developed in Ceylon. As medical care was free, I had myself examined. The doctor's verdict fell with the finality of a prison sentence: I must stay put for at least two or three months! He might just as well have told me to jump out of the window. But no, there was no question of my staying. As long as they didn't chain me to the wall, I would continue. But I promised myself that I would change my rhythm and see a doctor more often.

The newspaper *Lankadipa* had just come out with an article about my trip. I couldn't decipher any of the beautiful Sinhalese script, but a blown-up photograph confirmed what I had seen in the mirror: it was a face out of a concentration camp, its emaciated look accentuated by the shoulder-length mop of hair and severe goatee framing the mouth. In Moscow someone had called me *Kristus*. 'Cristo, Cristo', people had yelled at me already in Colombia. Now the resemblance was perfect. I really did look like Christ in the Garden of Gethsemane.

Without forgetting that I was only André Brugiroux, just one insignificant person amongst the teeming millions of the world, I thought of those men called Prophets. They sought in the solitude of the desert to draw nearer to God. I began to long more and more for my own journey to resemble their quests.

On the ferry back to the mainland, I was quickly reabsorbed into the atmosphere of India. Squatting men and women relieved themselves in front of occupied toilets. It was an India of nausea. I rediscovered the insanitary crowding, the harassment, the half-starved sacred cows, the trains that could pass for monkey cages, the fighting over seats, the nights spent under benches - *atcha, atcha . . .*

I wanted to head straight for Kashmir, 3,000 miles due north; but I could not miss out the city of Ahmedabad where Gandhiji, as Mahatma Gandhi was affectionately known, launched his grand ideas of independence and development for the Indian nation. In 1930 the 'naked fakir', as Churchill disdainfully called him, made his first protest march, walking 300 miles with eight companions.

Gandhi's great notion of non-violence had given me a false image of a country in which daily fights and quarrels were in reality far more common. Aggression was in the air and India was even at war with her neighbours. Yet, to my eyes, Gandhi remained a pure soul, one of those men who saw the light before anyone else did. '*I cannot allow a sacred text to override my reason*', he used to say.

He paid for his lucidity with his life but did not die in vain. For India continues to inspire our world, thanks to him and to a group of enlightened Indians who emerged at the turn of the century. '*The night has ended. Put out the light of the lamp of thine own narrow corner, smudged with smoke. The great morning that is for all is dawning in the East.*' Thus prophesied the mystical poet Rabindranath Tagore. '*Things must be viewed each day with a new spirit, without preceding accumulation*', said Krishnamurti. '*The bee buzzes only until alighting on a flower. It becomes silent when it begins to suck the nectar*', stated Ramakrishna. He also claimed that all prophets foretold the same God: '*All rivers lead to the ocean*'. His disciple Vivekananda preached the necessity for union between East and West; Gandhi: non-violence; Tagore: the coming of a new age; Krishnamurti: the duty to discover things for oneself; Aurobindo: peaceful coexistence between materialism and spirituality.

When the sun rises, its first rays touch only the highest peaks. As summits of mankind, these thinkers and chosen ones captured a ray from the thoughts of Bahá'u'lláh. These philosophers were among the first to scent the new perfumes without recognizing their source. Each one reflected in his own way a part of the light, but none possessed the original intensity of the Persian. The valley was still profoundly asleep, but there could be no doubt that the sun would reach its zenith and enlighten all men.

Was Afghanistan going to be the death of me? Overcome by the heat and drained by endless diarrhoea, I had tried to squat down at the foot of a tree. Everything had begun to spin and I had collapsed. It seemed to mark the beginning of the end - the first of my stations of the cross.

I had not eaten for two days, and for some twenty-four hours my distended belly had been spilling out a stream of rotten, stinking water. The previous night in Pakistan I had found shelter at the police station in Landi Kotal but hadn't slept a wink. I had spent the night going back and forth between my bed and the latrine. I had left a trail behind me, for I could no longer control myself. With my shorts soaked and my legs streaming, I had looked like some putrid fountain. The cops had eventually thrown me out. Without a shred of dignity or self-respect, I had headed off in the direction of the border, five miles distant. But first I had had to squat again while curious bystanders gathered round to laugh. Taking advantage of my crouching posture, a pedlar had come up to me and held out an assortment of coloured bottles.

'Hey, mister! Opium, cocaine, morphine? Here take some. No pay. Free country! That good for worries. Forget, for free.'

As if I had not been forgetting myself every other minute . . .

'Get the hell out of here! You hippies are always singing the same tune. I see hundreds of guys like you, Mister Globe-trotter, every single day.'

The small-time provincial schoolteacher, promoted to director of the French school in Kabul, had not yet adjusted to the rise in rank which he certainly would never have achieved back in France. It had gone to his head, and he felt free to gallop around on his high horse. It was summer and the school was closed. How could I have dared to ask for a corner of the courtyard to sleep in? The poor man saw hippies everywhere and confused them with hooligans, addicts and layabouts.

For hours the barren rock had been pink or red. All day long I had been bouncing up and down on top of an old truck loaded with stones. I was packed in like an upright sardine with a large number of extremely dirty Afghans from whom emanated a strong smell of sheep. It was impossible to move so much as an arm; at least there was no danger of falling off. The sun was sinking fast now, and a man had started asking for money. He was collecting baksheesh for the owner of the truck. Voices were raised; there was apparently some disagreement about the price to be paid. As the discussion heated up, shouts broke out and turbans were flying. A free-for-all began on the moving truck. I wondered how they managed to hit each other at such close quarters, but fists were flying nevertheless. Twice I had to duck to avoid a blow. I tried to make myself inconspicuous. Soon I was going to have to explain that I was only hitch-hiking (I wasn't going to back off), and my own fur would begin to fly.

The driver stopped the truck: not because of the fight (there was such a racket inside his cab that he hadn't heard a thing) but simply because it was time for prayer. At the same moment all the buses in the country would be doing exactly the same thing. A truce was called and everyone jumped down. Hands and feet were cleansed in a nearby stream, and the bowing towards Mecca began. Foreheads touched the ground in rhythm to chants of 'Alláh, Alláh . . .' Across the stream a tribe of Kuchis, nomads from northern Afghanistan, were setting up their camp. The tents weren't up yet, but red-veiled women covered with jewels had kindled a fire for the kebab. Shepherds were rounding up goats and sheep whose heads were painted green or purple, and camels snorted in disdain as the sun disappeared. Their prayers finished, everyone climbed back on the truck. As soon as we were in motion, the fighting resumed.

Ten minutes later the 'cashier' got round to me. Just as I had expected, I was unceremoniously tossed out. I finally reached the valley of Bamiyan seated atop a heap of coal. The coal truck dropped me off, and a minibus rented by a group of Frenchmen picked me up and took me to the two giant Buddhas carved from the cliff which formed the heart of this principal tourist area of Afghanistan.

Even in summer the nights in Bamiyan were cold, for we were 9,000 feet above sea level. With only a piece of cloth for a blanket, I was totally unprepared. I scrounged around in the dark in the grounds of the Intercontinental Hotel in search of some shelter against the cold. I could see some arches at the end of a flower garden. It was not ideal, but the temperature would be a little higher than elsewhere . . . and then, too, I was getting tired of running about in circles, of jumping up and down and slapping my sides to keep warm. Ever since the time I had lain down on a colony of giant ants in Mexico, I had been careful to examine any potential sleeping place. So now I lit a match . . .

A wild scream pierced the night. I leaped to my feet and my blood froze. A bayonet was pointing menacingly straight at my nose - so close that I had to look at it cross-eyed. At the other end of the shiny blade was a gun, and at the end of the gun was a half-crazed soldier. Forgotten, the match burned down to my fingers, while the man went on pointing his deadly weapon at me as if determined to bore a hole between my eyes. I was utterly panic-stricken; the man was still screaming like an attacking savage. I had my back to the wall and was incapable of making the slightest move. Yet I had to come up with something if I didn't want my epitaph to read, 'Killed accidentally in Afghanistan'.

'*Touristi franza, touristi franza!*'

I blurted out those two words in a spasm of desperation. They burst out of me like a last cry for help. The blade stopped moving. Gingerly, I began to breathe again. Then, with an almost imperceptible movement, I slipped my head and then my body out of his direct aim. He seemed to have calmed down. Signalling me to turn around, he jabbed his bayonet into my back and started shouting again. He was a dead ringer for Gengis Khan; even Hollywood could not have come up with anything better. In the end I got away with nothing more serious than a good scare and a night spent shivering in the middle of a stony field.

'Did you hear those screams last night?'

'I sure did. It woke me up with a start!'

'I was sure they were cutting somebody's throat; but the doorman didn't seem to know anything about it. Whatever it was, this place doesn't feel very safe . . .'

'That's precisely why I never leave the group. I've read that it doesn't take much to get yourself knifed around here.'

At least my little adventure had enlivened the conversation in the Intercontinental Hotel. The tourists were hardly reassured to know that there were still real savages around.

But the big-dollars-and-air-conditioning set were not the only tourists to have invaded the area. There were also hordes of young people - many of them rather nice - who had come from Europe. In particular there was a crowd of French kids following in the tracks of the Paris-to-Kabul car rally which had started the fad in 1970. Now people were doing Afghanistan the way others did the Loire Valley or the Normandy beaches. The young of Europe had found themselves a meeting place in friendly surroundings. They were to be seen in all the little restaurants which lined both sides of the village's single street. Patched-up cars with splendid itineraries painted on their sides were parked one behind the other like a desert caravan. Some of the young people were indeed examples of everything the jumped-up schoolteacher in Kabul had railed against.

Most of the *chaikhanes* or village tea-houses had an empty room at the back where anybody with a sleeping bag could stay for next to nothing. In those back rooms - like everywhere else - hashish circulated freely, and I was offered it - and declined it - at least twenty times a day. I shared my room with four bodies, four human wrecks. With hollow eyes, glassy stares, sunken cheeks and sallow complexions, they hacked and coughed endlessly. They looked like corpses; only the gleam of the *shillom* passing from hand to hand gave them a semblance of life as they puffed. Lying on smelly bedrolls in the semi-darkness, they sipped hot tea in tiny glasses. Among them was a frighteningly thin French girl who sickened me with her incessant coughing; yet another victim of that drug of misfortune!

So, having made a partial concession to the 'philanthropist' of Kabul, I was going to have a marvellous time in the company of other young people belonging to the true movement of non-violence and universal love. I was really happy to see that the American-born wave of spirit had crossed the Atlantic and was now breaking on our own shores. Emmanuel, Antoine and Grégoire squeezed together to make room for me in their tiny Renault. They were fervent leftists and veterans of the student upheavals of May, 1968. But now they had progressed beyond the limited horizons of politics, violence and Maoism to join the new youth - still a minority - that had been touched by the light of Bahá'u'lláh. They seemed extremely happy. I could have been happy, too, except for the sickness unleashed by that deadly glass of water which continued to gnaw and devour my body from within. I was still losing weight.

In Mazar-i-Sharif in northern Afghanistan, the idea of death began to haunt me once again. As before, I was losing my will to go on. I shuffled about among the unsanitary hovels. Dusty sheep carcasses dangled above pools of blood. As flies drowned themselves in the drying red puddles, wasps attacked the greenish livers spread out on market stalls.

I no longer drank anything but tea - *siah* or *sabz*, black or green - served in pots which were old but artistically patched up. I was at the end of the line. When I reached the magnificent Blue Mosque . . . I didn't give a damn. My head was empty and everything spun about me. It was evening, and I was not sure if I could make it without blacking out again. By a stroke of luck the head of a school, as if to prove there were some good schoolmasters around, invited me into his office. While he was out getting me something to eat, I dozed off, plunging into a dizzy sleep. I felt myself falling, falling into a bottomless abyss.

At dawn a cleaning lady wanted me to get out. I was far from feeling cured and motioned her to let me sleep. She shouted at me and called over three fellows who seized me by my arms and legs and dumped me in a hallway. My pack came tumbling after. I sank back into sleep, but the old woman soon woke me again with whacks of her broom. I crawled wretchedly away on all fours, dragging my pack behind. Finding a deserted courtyard, I stretched out in the dust.

The walls of the school seemed to dance about me, and a black veil fell slowly over my eyes. There was a taste of earth in my mouth. I breathed deeply of that earth which attracted me now, which was waiting for me, for my hour seemed near . . .

Chapter 12

THE LAND OF BAHÁ'U'LLÁH

The streets were deserted; Shiraz was still asleep. The chilly night air had frozen the puddles of water. My companion Mansur looked at his watch. It was 6.45 a.m. We were on time. Leaning against a fountain in the middle of a small square, a man dressed in Western clothes watched us approach. When we were about ten yards from him, he walked away with a slow stride. Without a word we followed him in the strange morning silence. For a last lingering moment, darkness clung to the outlines of things. In the maze of the old city, we walked alongside the high walls which hid homes and courtyards from sight. We continued for a good ten minutes. Not once did our guide turn around, for he wasn't supposed to know us.

Iran was the cradle of my new religion. I was making my first pilgrimage, but I was undertaking a sort of investigation as well. For even if I had been won over by the words of Bahá'u'lláh in Alaska, even if I could testify to the strength and power of the Bahá'í Faith in America, Australia, China, Japan and India, I still wanted to keep an open mind and see for myself how the oldest Bahá'í community in the world was working. My insatiable curiosity, along with a certain scepticism, compelled me to verify everything before I could accept. I wanted not only to learn about the history of my faith, but also to analyze it and see if everything held together.

Certain precautions were necessary, because Bahá'ís had suffered repression for several months now, and had to be very careful. Contrary to the teachings of Muhammad, Islam - like Christianity - was showing itself capable of a cruel fanaticism. In a country which had been a model of religious tolerance twenty-five centuries earlier under Cyrus the Great (whose reign was about to be commemorated with great ceremony now in 1971), Bahá'í's were now forced to keep a very low profile. The situation had been like this for over a hundred years.

We were going to a house which had witnessed the first phase of what I considered to be the most important event in the history of mankind. As I wound through the labyrinth of lanes, I remembered the words of certain men of the seventeenth and eighteenth centuries who had had a presentiment of the views to which I now adhered. Fénelon had said, *'Whoever prefers his own glory to the feelings of mankind is a monster of vanity'*. Montesquieu added: *'If I knew something which was useful to my own motherland but detrimental to Europe and mankind, I would regard it as a crime'*. Those men and others like them had been among the world's first *cosmopolitans* - citizens of the world who wished to work for the happiness of *all* people. Like the first rays of light at the break of day, these philosophers had been touched by the birth of a new age that had begun with the American and French revolutions. I thought also of Samuel Morse who on May 24th, 1844, sent from Washington to Baltimore the famous telegraph message extracted from the Bible: *'What hath God wrought?'* (Numbers 23:23). One day earlier, May 23rd, far to the east in Persia, a 25-year-old man renowned for his beauty, refined manner, exceptional piety and noble character proclaimed himself raised by God to the rank of Báb ('gate' in Arabic). He said he was the forerunner of a greater spiritual teacher whose coming was imminent. History was starting over again: Elijah, John the Baptist, the Báb . . . The great dawn promised in all the sacred writings was lighting up the sky of mankind.

The young kid from Brunoy had left home wondering what was so special about Charles de Foucauld, St Francis of Assisi and Mahatma Gandhi. Now he in turn was discovering what he had been seeking for so long. The magnificent treasure of his quest had infinitely surpassed his own poor imaginings. It was a precious response, an inestimable reward, after a fourteen-year odyssey. People, things, events, the world: they were all falling into place, and his life was taking on a definitive meaning. *God existed*: He had kept His promises.

After passing through a series of low doorways, going down several staircases and following a long winding hallway, our guide stopped in front of a wooden door. He glanced about furtively before knocking discreetly with the tips of his fingers. My heart was beating with apprehension and emotion.

'*Alláh-u-Abhá*.'

'*Alláh-u-Abhá*. God is all-glorious.'

I answered the man who had just opened the door. Mr A showed us into a cold living room and, in accordance with local custom, served small glasses of sweet tea, refilling them several times. Mr A was a descendant of the Báb, who himself had been a descendant of Muhammad. He explained that he had been forced to wall up the doors and windows of his house after numerous attacks by the Muslims.* He then told me about the memorable evening of May 23rd, 1844.

'In those days, certain theologians had singled out the year 1844, and a veritable end-of-the-world fever took hold in the West. In Persia belief in the imminent appearance of a divine messenger was especially widespread among members of the Shaykhí sect.

' "*Behold, all these signs are manifest in Me!*"

'The Báb first announced his mission to one of the distinguished masters of Shaykhís, Mullá Husayn, just two hours and fifteen minutes after sunset on the fifth day of the month of Jamadiyu'l-avval in the year 1260 of the *Hegira*,§ and the announcement took place in this very house. "*This night*", declared the herald of a new age, "*this very hour will, in the days to come, be celebrated as one of the greatest and most significant of all festivals.*"

'After a few days of reflection, the pious and learned Mullá Husayn was firmly convinced that the long-awaited messenger had really appeared. Not long afterwards, many of the Shaykhís shared his enthusiasm and celebrated the Báb's coming. They called themselves Bábís and the young prophet's fame quickly spread throughout the country.'

'That's what the history books refer to as the Bábist Revolution', added Mansur, whose ancestors, followers of the Báb, had had to flee to the island of Bahrain in the Persian Gulf where his relatives still live today.

'The Báb's convincing eloquence', continued Mr A, 'his inspired writings, his knowledge and wisdom, extraordinary courage and reforming zeal, raised the hopes of a people which had fallen into the

*In 1979 this sacred dwelling was totally destroyed by fanatical elements.

§The flight of Muhammad from Mecca to Medina in 622 AD marked the point of departure for the Muslim calendar (1,260 lunar years = 1,222 of our solar years).

deepest decadence. But persecution began immediately, for hatred had fired up the orthodox Muslim groups.'

We crossed a courtyard and entered a second smaller patio enclosing a square pool filled with water. In one corner were a well and a large orange tree that had been planted by the Báb himself. On the ground floor of the house were the rooms where his mother and black Ethiopian servant had lived. Upstairs, the room of the proclamation was bare. Painted green and decorated with beautiful plaster mouldings, the room had a wall of stained glass opening on to the patio. On the floor lay a single carpet that could only have been woven in Persia. We communed in silence as Mr A chanted the new verses, and the melody filled my heart with joy and happiness. Flooded with colour as the light broke through the stained glass windows, the room seem transformed into a palace from a fairy tale.

'André, you're absolutely insane! You're so skinny it's downright frightening. There's no question of you leaving in that condition. I'm going to take care of you. As a matter of fact, I've already made an appointment with a doctor for tomorrow.'

The long journey from Afghanistan to Shiraz had nearly killed me and Mrs Ghadimi, a determined native of Brittany, had decided that she was going to get me back into shape. She moved me into the guest room of her brand new villa in Elahiyeh, a stylish neighbourhood of Tehran, and personally supervised my food and rest. Her husband, an extremely cultivated Persian, was a successful self-made man. He spoke flawless Russian, French, English and Arabic. One of his ancestors, five generations back, had heard about Bábism from Mullá Husayn himself. In the face of incessant persecution, his father had taken the whole family to seek refuge in 'Ishqábád in Russian Turkistan, where the first Bahá'í House of Worship had been built. The young Youssef had been fifteen when the Bolshevik Revolution forced his family to return to Iran. His six brothers had gone off to all four corners of the world to proclaim the advent of Universal Peace.

The doctor I went to see was a specialist in problems of the digestive tract. He tried to reassure me despite my 115 pounds (never had I weighed so little) and swollen abdomen. In the laboratory, they discovered a whole zoo inside my stomach! My fouled-up digestive system and shrunken stomach were destined to be the big losers of my trip around the world. For the rest of my life I would have to bear the consequences of six years on a diet that was by modern standards unhygienic and by Western standards grossly inadequate.

Shah Reza Avenue divided Tehran in two. The northern section was in full swing and conformed to the contemporary image of modern Iran. To the south, however, could be found the old conservative Persia with bearded mullás, overloaded donkeys and veiled women. It was of course old Tehran that interested me more, and I spent long hours wandering its streets. I visited the basement of the Markazi Bank where the Shah's fabulous treasures were kept. The room where the crown jewels were displayed was like Ali Baba's cave. Gold, silver, rubies, turquoises, sapphires, diamonds and amethysts glittered in the carefully controlled light. Everywhere there were heaps of precious stones among which could be found the largest cut diamond in the world, the largest pearl in the world, the largest uncut ruby and thousands of delicate pearls from the Persian Gulf, along with pieces of jewellery and precious objects.

But to my mind, all the precious stones of that legendary cache were still only stones. More valuable was the treasure lying at the bottom of a well in the neighbouring garden.

'You can kill me as soon as you like, but you cannot stop the emancipation of women', said Táhirih to the Mullá who had locked her up. In August 1852, she was strangled by soldiers and thrown into the well. Endowed with a rare beauty, and a courage as exceptional as her intelligence, the renowned poetess Táhirih had seen the Báb in a dream. Inflamed by the new divine verses, she showed so much enthusiasm and strength of conviction that all who listened to her were amazed. In an age when women were not supposed to converse with men, she defended her ideas against the most learned of men and finished in triumph each time. Arrested by order of the government, she was stoned, shunned and hounded from city to city. Though threatened with death and separated from her children, she never weakened in her determination to fight for the rights and freedom of her fellow women.

In the summer of 1848, at a meeting in Badasht of the most fervent Bábís, Táhirih entered the room dressed like a queen but minus her veil. By appearing unveiled, she had cast aside centuries of tradition, of male oppression and female submission. Her act of sacrilege provoked such a reaction that one of the men present slit his own throat, others fled, and still another tried to kill her. The woman who had been called 'the pure one', whose very shadow nobody had dared set eyes on, now appeared radiant, beautiful and strong before them.

Actually, the prophecies of the Qur'án had just been fulfilled. The 'trumpet' had sounded (Qur'án 74:8, 6:73), and a new era had been proclaimed. Equality between men and women was on its way to becoming a reality. Nicolas, the French consul at the time, the Comte de Gobineau and many other personalities spread the news of Táhirih's noble act. Sarah Bernhardt asked Catulle Mendes to write a play about Táhirih's life. He in turn nicknamed her 'the Persian Joan of Arc'. But what surprised me most was the way in which these events, so earth-shattering in their day, had been completely forgotten. Today they were virtually unknown, both in the West and the rest of the world as well.

In the heart of the city's poorer district, I repeated the clandestine expedition of Shiraz. Thanks to Mr K, a friend of the Ghadimis, I was granted permission to visit a house whose whereabouts were a secret (for security reasons) shared by very few of the Bahá'í's in Tehran. It was the house where Bahá'u'lláh had been born.

The dwelling had obviously belonged to a rich and respected family. Luxurious for its period, the house had courtyards, gardens, pools, an impressive number of rooms and, most surprisingly, was equipped with air shafts for summer ventilation and a triple bathroom. Here, too, the outside doors had been blocked. We went in silence to visit a spacious, empty room decorated with marquetry, small recesses and stained glass. This was where Bahá'u'lláh had been born. Bahá'u'lláh: *Glory of God*; the greatest name; the promised one of all ages, of all legends and all peoples; the long-awaited educator; the channel of a marvellous grace surpassing that of any previous dispensation. Bahá'u'lláh was the Kalki Avatar of the Hindus; the Sháh-Bahram of the Zoroastrians; Maitreya or Amitabha, the fifth Buddha; the Lord of the Jewish armies; the returning Mihdí of the Shi'ite Muslims; the returning Christ of the Sunni Muslims and the Christians.

All prophets, including Christ and Muhammad, came to prepare mankind gradually for the great day. Bahá'u'lláh laid the foundations for world unity and inaugurated the glorious age of peace and happiness - often referred to as the Kingdom of God on earth - that had been promised by all his predecessors.

I was truly overwhelmed to find myself in this dwelling, for I knew that my quest ended here. Throughout my travels, I had read and meditated on Bahá'u'lláh's writings, and I had understood that his teachings led to the full flowering of mankind. Like him, I knew that human beings could no longer continue to live as they were doing today, ignoring or cursing, or attacking or even destroying their fellow men. Expansionism and nationalism were the worst fruits of man's egotism.

'He was twenty-two when his father died', explained Mr K. 'The government wanted him to succeed his father in the foreign ministry, as custom dictated. But Bahá'u'lláh declined the offer, and the Prime Minister said, "*Leave him to himself. Such a position is unworthy of him. He has some higher aim in view. I cannot understand him, but I am convinced that he is destined for some lofty career.*" ' Bahá'u'lláh boldly embraced the Báb's cause, and for that he was beaten and imprisoned. Only his aristocratic status saved him from being killed. Locked up in a dreadful dungeon in Tehran, he received the revelation to his mission: "*Verily, We shall render Thee victorious by Thyself and by Thy pen. Grieve Thou not for that which hath befallen Thee, neither be Thou afraid for Thou art in safety.*" Along with his entire family, he was then exiled to Baghdád, where he made the official proclamation of his mission in 1863. After forty years of indescribable suffering as he was driven from exile to exile, from Constantinople to Adrianople, he ended his life at Acre [now 'Akká] in Palestine, in a fortress-prison of the Ottoman Turks.'

'Now I understand', I said, interrupting Mr K, 'what Jesus meant when he said: "*For as the lightning cometh out of the east and shineth even unto the west so shall also the Coming of the Son of man be*" (Matthew 24:27). Bahá'u'lláh indeed came from the East and went to the West.'

'Exactly. He died on May 29th, 1882, having written a hundred works as well as a series of brilliant epistles in which he proclaimed to the entire world the imminence of a universal civilization.* Do you know that Napoleon III of France was the only sovereign to receive two messages from Bahá'u'lláh? Certainly he was the worst of the heads of state: scheming, fickle, hypocritical, shallow, drunk on his own glory. It is said that he threw the first message on the ground, saying, "*If this man is God, then I'm God twice over*". In 1869, the emperor received a second message sent from the prison-fortress of Acre: "*It behooveth thee not to conduct thine affairs according to the dictates of thy desires . . . For what thou hast done, thy kingdom shall be thrown into confusion, and thine empire shall pass from thine hands . . . We see abasement hastening after thee, while thou art of the heedless . . .*" Of course, Napoleon III was then at the zenith of his reign and paid

---

*Epistles to Queen Victoria, Pope Pius IX, Kaiser Wilhelm I, Czar Alexander II, etc. The Bahá'í Publishing Trust (see p 90 for addresses) has published these amazing letters, which shed new light on contemporary history, under the title, *The Proclamation of Bahá'u'lláh*. Copies of these letters were sent to all world leaders in 1968 in commemoration of the hundredth anniversary of their first appearance.

no attention to the warning. And yet, one year later, he lost his throne . . .'

The days were going by a little too slowly for my taste in my 'manor house' in Elahiyeh, despite the extreme kindness of my hosts. All the luxury and exquisite decor, the cosy comforts and delicious crêpes that Mrs Ghadimi cooked for me helped restore my health but could not cure my itchy feet! I was like a wolf whose only desire was to return to the forest. I was not completely cured, but I felt much better and had put on some weight. So why stay on another day? I had never let either the mirage of comfort nor the harshness of misery alter my pace.

To get myself in training again, I headed out on a 6,000-mile tour of Iran. To my great surprise, my hitch-hiking went perfectly. On the shores of the blue Caspian Sea, I was picked up by a tank truck which was bumping its way at fifteen miles per hour along a rutted track. The driver was both a Muslim and a Communist, and although he only spoke Persian, he managed to tell me everything he disliked about the government and the British.

'*Shoma amrika'i?*' (You American?)

'*Nakher, faransavi*' (No, French).

'You Catholic?'

'No, Bahá'í.'

There was a stunned silence. Had I said something wrong?

'Bahá'í, very bad!'

'Me, very bad?'

'No, you very good, but Bahá'í . . .'

It was obvious that he was having a hard time understanding how a foreigner could be led astray by what he had learned to regard as an accursed sect. The illiterate common people everywhere had a tendency to swallow anything their mullás or other religious leaders told them. The latter, feeling their position threatened, their prestige undermined and their jobs shaky, had no hesitation in slandering the new truth by spreading the most scurrilous lies about it. But there was nothing new in that: the same thing happened in Jesus Christ's time. It was not long before my visit that the xenophobic, narrow minded mullás of Iran had been trying to stop cinemas from being built and to prevent legal changes requiring children to attend school. Fortunately their power seemed to be waning.

My driver dropped me off in Astara in the province of Azerbaijan, right on the Soviet border. It was a pitch black night. Walking along what seemed to be the main street, I looked about in the darkness for a quiet corner to sleep in. Suddenly, before I realized what was happening, I found myself in a military cell. I did not understand much, but since I was being given some shelter by force, why ask questions? I had barely dozed off when I was awakened by . . . a Frenchman!

'What are you doing here?' he demanded.

'That's what I'd like to know. They grabbed me off the street and tossed me in jail for no reason.'

'Listen, it's all a misunderstanding. They thought you were trying to sneak across the border. Maybe you didn't notice, but you weren't very far from the Russian barbed wire. They're going to let you go, so why don't you come with me? I'm an engineer. I live in a hotel and I've got an extra bed in my room. It won't cost you anything . . . Come on, don't be a fool. If you stay here, you'll find yourself in front of a military tribunal tomorrow. They don't mess around.'

In the space of two or three minutes I had passed from the dark cell of an army barracks to luxurious Room Six of the Astara Inn - where Podgorny had recently stayed. Bob, the manager, was enthralled by my stories and set a two-pound tin of caviar down in front of me. I used a soup spoon to heap it on to pieces of warm toast as thickly as sandwich spread. The meal that followed was no doubt the same as the one that had been offered to the Soviet head of state: grilled sturgeon, enormous quantities of fried chicken, fruit, ice cream . . . accustomed to meagre rations, my stomach was in a state of shock.

On September 15th, 1971, I arrived in Tabriz, the capital of Azerbaijan, and once again I made a hit. Wherever I went, everyone stared at my shorts, and the comments were always the same: 'Mini-jupe, mini-jupe!' (miniskirt).* After a long stroll through the bazaars of Tabriz, I stopped in a pastry shop to treat myself to some pistachio ice cream. Next to me three long-haired Americans were conversing in loud voices. I was astonished to realize they were talking about me.

'Did you read all that garbage in the paper about the guy going around the world? They must think we're complete idiots to believe that bit about a dollar a day. That's impossible!'

'For sure! That guy's all hot air.'

'We could do the same thing . . . if we wanted to. The papers are all

*Shorts are frowned upon in many countries and impossible to wear at all in Latin America. In Asia, those who wear them are considered hippies.

alike. They'll print anything if it's likely to sell. They don't give a damn about the truth . . .'

What point was there in arguing with them? I could have shown them my calculations and told them how I organized things, how I only changed the bare minimum and arranged to have my money sent to me in dollars and in a dollar zone - which in itself was no easy feat. Of course it meant playing banker and budgeting carefully, but I had had such a tough time saving up my money that there was no way I was going to waste a penny of it.

A Bahá'í friend named Parviz invited me to dinner. The carpet was covered with generous platters of rice, meat, sauces, fresh vegetables, fruit and yogurt. What a feast!

'How many guests are coming?'

'Just you and me'.

'But there's enough here for fifteen!'

I discovered just how lavish Iranian hospitality was. In France every hostess calculated exactly the right amount of food and usually insisted that every last bit should be eaten. If nothing remained, it was proof of her culinary talents. In Iran, on the other hand, finishing off a dish was an insult and meant that the host had not provided enough. Generosity was not to be measured.

A land of contrasts, Iran could be both hospitable and cruel. My friend Parviz came from a Bahá'í family that had known the early Bábí era, a time not so long ago when twenty thousand Bábís were massacred. Their supreme sacrifice merely proved the resilience of a cause that no one could any longer deny. I do not want to repeat the story of the abominable butchery which took place in those days, for others have already done so.* I simply want to try to explain why those 20,000 martyrs were able to sacrifice their lives; and why, thanks to my own faith, I was able to pursue my journey in spite of repeated obstacles.

Being a Bahá'í is not an inherited state, like a title passed on from father to son. Children brought up in Bahá'í families cannot declare themselves to be Bahá'ís before the age of fifteen - for the first principle of the faith is the importance of each individual's personal search for truth. Everyone must understand things from his or her own point of view and feel them with their own heart. Being a Bahá'í is above all a matter of free choice. And that simply means, in the words of 'Abdu'l-

---

*For a detailed record of such accounts, see *The Bábí and Bahá'í Religions: Some Contemporary Western Accounts* by Moojan Momen.

Bahá, 'to love all the world; to love humanity and try to serve it; to work for universal peace'.

With Parviz I visited the 'Alí Sháh Mosque, a monumental fortress with walls thirty feet thick. The Báb had been imprisoned in one of its towers for forty-one days after the population of Tabriz had given him an ecstatic welcome despite an official ban. I could not help making the comparison with Christ, who had received a triumphant welcome into Jerusalem one week before his Crucifixion. 'Hosanna, Hosanna', the people had cried.

'That's where the Báb was shot in 1850', said Parviz, as we passed the horribly anonymous parking lot of a government building.

I continued my pilgrimage alone. I visited various holy sites in Kermanshah and Rezaiyeh, as I followed in the footsteps of the Báb and Bahá'u'lláh. Everywhere the Bahá'ís welcomed me with extraordinary kindness. I felt that there were no longer any barriers, that we all formed a single family. The great universal family was about to become a reality. Christ had implied as much in the only prayer he ever dictated himself: 'Thy Kingdom come . . .'

As I observed these people whose skin colour, customs and social position were all so different from mine, but who nevertheless surrounded me with so much affection, I realized that rifles were finally useless; that black power was simply hatred of white power; that so long as there were reds and whites, one side would always consider the others to be bad guys, and vice versa. But the reality was altogether different. Only the power of Love could regenerate mankind. No matter whether it was an old rug merchant or a young refrigerator salesman, an architect or a poor craftsman, the welcome everywhere was the same: simple, touching, sincere. The oldest Bahá'í community in the world was functioning perfectly. When we attained that perfection all over the globe, our earth would indeed be a Paradise. My sojourn among the Bahá'ís put me back on my feet. I even gained eighteen pounds! Like a phoenix, I had risen from my ashes and was ready for a new departure.

One evening Mr K took me with him to the Park Hotel. In the bar, he introduced me to a fat little man dressed in a white kaftan and sandals. The man was - more or less - the new ambassador from North Yemen where a seemingly interminable war had come to an end, allowing the country to open its doors to the rest of the world for the first time. It was an opportunity I had to jump at. The only catch was that no consulates had as yet been opened and it was for that reason that my friend Mr K had insisted on introducing me to His Excellency.

In the course of an innocuous conversation, the ambassador explained that to trim down his tummy he had been doing a lot of walking, but that blisters had been an unfortunate side effect. With that, His Excellency exhibited his sore foot. It provided a perfect opportunity for me to be of service and thus obtain a visa.

'Your Excellency, if you will allow me, I can quickly rid you of that mean little blister with just a needle and some alcohol.'

We went to room 504. After lancing the great man's blister, I presented my petition. His Excellency immediately asked to see my passport. Was he going to give me a visa on the spot? No, he wished to ensure that my passport didn't contain an Israeli stamp as evidence of any visit to the land of the sworn enemy.

'So, it's a fine idea you have, to come and visit us . . . A very fine idea, young man. You'll have your visa whenever you want it, for just four dollars. But first I must reread my instructions concerning the procedures to be followed ‑ forms to fill in, photos, fingerprints and so on. You understand? Come and see me in two weeks.'

I was overjoyed by his reply, for the delay seemed very short compared to my experiences in the consulates of Kuwait, Saudi Arabia, Qatar and Bahrain. Sometimes it seemed that the entire Arabian peninsula was slowing me down.

'But certainly, Sir', they would tell me. 'You are most welcome to visit our country. Just come back in six months . . . a year . . . two or three years . . . *Inshá'lláh** . . .'

In contrast, a mere two weeks seemed like tomorrow. Actually, I had to wait a bit longer since, as a matter of principle, His Excellency liked to be cajoled. But sensing that the resistance was not as strong as elsewhere, and assisted by my good friends the Ghadimis, I decided to play along. We arranged a meeting in the Riviera Bar. When we arrived the ambassador had already downed copious quantities of gin and tonic never prescribed by the Qur'án. Wagging his head and beaming in delight, he shook my hand for a long moment. He was quite visibly drunk. Having just bought some caviar and grapes, he was about to return to his hotel to drop them off.

Quick as a flash, Mr Ghadimi suggested we should all meet there when he had finished his drink. He then kept him interested with family photos and a long story about his children, in the hope that we would be invited up to Room 504 of the Park Hotel. It was an effective strategy. Once inside his

*An Arabic expression meaning literally: 'God willing'. It signifies that all things rest in God's hands and is used very frequently to signify doubt and impossibility.

hotel room, having had considerable difficulty inserting his key into the lock, the ambassador told me to go ahead and open his diplomatic bag. Then, as he became increasingly hazy, he explained rather vaguely how to stamp the visa in my passport. It was certainly the first time I had ever given myself a visa! Finally, grabbing a pen,His Excellency, with wavering hand, granted me a three-month stay and made it all official with a magnificent signature. He didn't ask for a photograph, passport number or the reasons for my visit, and I didn't fill in a single form. With great courtesy, His Excellency walked us back to our car. Crossing the hotel terrace high above the city lights, he took me in his arms and hugged me warmly. On the verge of suffocating, I was forced into action. Applying a judo technique, I lifted him off the ground and swung him round three times. So much for protocol! As a last token of friendship, we thumped each other enthusiastically on the back. Then, with his arms raised to the heavens and his mind floating in clouds of alcohol, he watched us take our leave.

Thanks to black gold, Kuwait had emerged from the sands some ten years earlier. But in spite of its ultra-modernity, the city appeared dirty and dilapidated. Big American cars cruised along immense avenues lined with ugly concrete blocks. There were almost no trees, and the desert wind sent fine sand swirling across the asphalt roads. Two-thirds of the people in the street were foreigners. Their presence gave the crowds an interesting diversity of appearance.

I asked a Syrian shoe salesman for directions and a glass of water. The man looked about surreptitiously, then took me by the arm and pulled me into the back of his shop.

'Poor wretch!' he whispered, as if we were two conspirators.'Don't you know that today is the first day of *Ramadan*? No one is allowed to drink or eat from five in the morning until six at night. Do you understand? No one! If you do, you get hauled away by the police, and spending *Ramadan* in jail is no picnic. So don't go peeling a banana in the street. Being a foreigner doesn't make any difference. All the restaurants are closed until tonight . . . But never mind. Actually you're in luck. You see, I'm a Catholic and whenever I feel like lighting up or having a drink, I hide out back here. But I'm very careful. Here, drink.'

The country was nothing but a monotonous sweep of overheated sand broken only by an occasional torch of flaming natural gas. At night the crescent moon seemed suspended in the orange-coloured sky. It was a strange vision.

Saudi Arabia also earned her living from oil and, as a result, had made considerable steps towards modernization. Today, for example, when they cut off hands, they give them an anaesthetic. But the staff in the embassy were preoccupied with their own concerns and didn't give a damn about anything else. They turned up late for work and were scornful towards foreigners. I was refused a visa for reasons of *Ramadan* and a no-visitors policy.

The plane jolted and hiccoughed to a stop in front of a rusty corrugated iron shed. Battered by the winds in a wild landscape of purplish-blue peaks, the shed served as the customs post for North Yemen. The poor dishevelled official didn't know what to make of my passport with its unfamiliar, illegible print. But catching sight of His Excellency's flowery signature, he motioned me through as if all had been made clear.

The ancient realm of the Queen of Sheba was still buried in the Middle Ages. There was widespread poverty and a total lack of hygiene. Though it was not the first time I had been in such a situation, I always found it difficult to get used to. The narrow, winding streets were strewn with rubbish. Donkey carts and flocks of sheep kicked up clouds of dust. People in rags ambled about amid mangy dogs, lice-infested urchins and smooth-talking charlatans trying to sell something. Yet I liked San'a. The country was untouched by tourism, so people left me alone. I could not be mistaken for an American, because nobody knew what an American was. No Hilton, no Coca-Cola, no neon signs. I had never before seen a city so authentic, so unspoilt. The local architecture was unique. The houses were shaped like towers, several stories high and were built of light-coloured brick, clay or stone. Oddly-shaped windows with white frames, coloured glass and carved wooden shutters adorned the façades.

In the street, I passed men wearing knee-length 'skirts' and the inevitable turban. Often they went barefoot and carried rifles slung over their shoulders. Around their waists dangled the terrifying *djambia*, a dagger with a curved blade. The Yemenis, though armed to the teeth, had fine features and seemed very friendly. Sometimes their wives accompanied them, carrying heavy loads on their heads and wearing two veils, one of which was black with large red circles and fell to the waist. For once I had no trouble filming Islamic women. On the contrary, the men even laughed and tried to have their pictures taken as well. I was the only tourist among these people from a bygone age, but I didn't feel in the least afraid. Everyone greeted me.

'*Sadir, sadir!* Friend, friend!'

To my astonishment I didn't attract any crowds, nor did the children throw stones at me. That in itself was a surprise in a Muslim country.

Nejab, a young Yemeni student whom I had met on the plane, invited me to his house. The room in which he received me was on the top floor of a tower, just under the roof garden. The furnishings consisted of carpets and cushions, like a nomad's tent. In the middle of the room, on a hand worked copper tray, stood two water pipes. Rifles, daggers and cartridge belts hung on the wall. After introducing me to all the men of the house, he served me coffee - the famous *moka* native to the region. Unroasted beans and pieces of dried husk floated in the murky water.

Nejab was eighteen years old and had just been married by his father to a young girl whom, of course, he had never seen before. He was still in the middle of his honeymoon. Like a good Muslim, he not only did not introduce me to his wife, but went so far as to hide her away. One afternoon, however, as I was going down the stairs after my nap, I inadvertently came across Nejab's mother and young wife without their veils. As they sat cross-legged, chatting in the sun, I contemplated the scene, delighted to have transgressed a custom which I had found incomprehensible and exasperating. Since I made no attempt to conceal myself, they quickly noticed my presence. Immediately the mother turned her back and hid her face in her hands. At the same time, without losing a second, her daughter-in-law pulled her dress over her face.

The city of Hodaida, 7,000 feet lower on the shores of the Red Sea, was incredibly dirty. The whole place stank and seemed on the point of being abandoned to the flies. The sheikh Sinan Abu Lohume welcomed me into his court and asked me lots of questions. He put me up at the best hotel in town and left orders that I was to be fed in spite of *Ramadan*.

'I will serve you in your room. That way you won't risk having your throat cut', explained the hotel manager.

In late afternoon, I had fun watching the goings on in the restaurants which by 5.30 would already be full. Seated and impatient, the customers would slowly turn their spoons about in bowls of millet, as they waited for the cannon shot that would release them at six o'clock sharp. Immediately, all the heads would dip simultaneously, and the city would be filled with an amazing concert of slurping noises.

Ramadan turned life upside down in many countries but was in essence nothing more than a farce. It meant upsetting the normal daily schedule but had nothing to do with a true fast. The Yemenis got around the problem by sleeping during the day and working at night. While the letter of the law was observed meticulously, the spirit had definitely departed from the corpse of the old religion.

South Yemen provided a change of scenery and especially of atmosphere. Barbed wire, machine guns, barracks and sandbags marked the border. My pack was emptied out into the dust and a soldier inspected every last item. Actually, I didn't have much left, only the bare necessities that I could not do without: my straw mat and a sheet for sleeping; my movie camera; my journal and a pen; my prayer book; a map along with some books and brochures on the region I was currently visiting (when their accumulated weight reached seven pounds, I'd send a package home); my razor whose cord had been stripped of its plug so that it would fit any outlet in the world; a compact mirror: my nail clippers; half a comb; soap and a miniature towel; toothbrush and toothpaste; aspirin; a sweater; an anorak; swimming trunks; a pair of underpants and a pair of socks for the sake of hygiene (the rest of my clothes were on my back). Some time before I had stopped lugging extra clothes around. Instead, I would wash before going to bed and put on the same outfit the next morning. Whenever I left a cold region, I got rid of my warm clothes a few at a time. I didn't have a single cooking utensil, not even a knife (looking around for one to borrow had made me new friends). My only other piece of equipment was a long shoelace which I used at night when I felt less than safe. I attached one end to my pack and the other around my wrist as a simple precaution. Everything I had was wrapped in plastic to protect it from dust and rain.

The inventory was soon made, yet the customs search went on and on. As a welcome, it had a familiar ring; the camp-like atmosphere could only have been inspired by the Soviet Union. As soon as I entered the country, I felt the vibrations were far from good and that freedom was surely under threat. In fact, both China and the USSR were present and involved in an endless little war of influence. The USSR provided the barbed wire and the secret police, while China was responsible for the lack of butter, soap, etc. In South Yemen, Public Enemy Number One was Saudi Arabia (Israel had been relegated to second place). As my stay there had been so brief, there was no Saudi stamp in my passport. I was therefore authorized to enter the socialist paradise of South Yemen and to visit the capital, Aden. The Rock was splendid and the Indian Ocean a sparkling green, but the British-built city was now almost derelict. Only three or four Russian or Chinese freighters were moored in the bay which had once been visited by 750 ships each month. The radio, the newspapers, the graffiti on the walls and the crowds in the street all reviled the British.

Yet nothing seemed to have been done since independence. Goats roamed the hallways and stairwells of tall buildings which had been ransacked and pillaged down to their doorknobs (people used chairs to barricade the doors). The electrical wiring had been torn out of the walls, and public areas were covered with trash and excrement. At the tourist office I was given propaganda brochures but no advice, no useful information, no recommendations. Everywhere there was the same look of neglect, the same filth. Countries which pointedly called themselves 'socialist' all seemed to have something very sad about them.

Perched on top of the Rock, about to leave Arabia, I reflected on everything I had seen since arriving in Turkey. One question had been troubling me for a long time: how had it come about that the proud world of Islam which had once proclaimed at sword point the existence of a single God and which had refused to tolerate compromise - how could that world find itself today at the mercy of people who claimed that God did not even exist?

Once again, I turned to the Bahá'í writings to find the answers. Bahá'u'lláh explained that the development of mankind was dependent on certain enlightened souls who were, in fact, the guides and true educators of mankind. Moses, for example, alone and unaided, managed to free his people from Egyptian bondage and to lead them to the Promised Land, which then became under Solomon's rule the most renowned of nations. Famous for their military strength, but also for their skill, their art and their highly developed civilization, the Jews inspired Greek philosophers like Socrates and Hippocrates who made special trips to Jerusalem. But decline and dispersion followed when Titus captured the city.

All alone, like Moses, Christ succeeded in reconciling such implacable enemies as the Greeks and the Romans, the Chaldeans, Egyptians and Assyrians. Using only the power of the Word, he nurtured individual consciousness and prompted the humanizing of moral standards.

Equally alone, Muhammad united the savage and plundering tribes scattered throughout Arabia to create the last of the world's great civilizations: Islam. The famous technology so dear to Westerners had its roots in Muslim learning. The astonished crusaders, and later the questioning minds of Renaissance men, brought Muslim mathematics, art and science to the shores of a Europe shrouded in darkness.

Behind every resurgence of human civilization, there had been a soul with a prophetic mission, based on divine power. Any objective thinker was immediately aware of the chasm which separated Moses, Christ and Muhammad on the one hand from Alexander the Great, Caesar and Napoleon on the other. Furthermore, didn't the essential divisions of history correspond to the civilizations known as Christian, Islamic, Buddhist and so on?

Bahá'u'lláh explained history, but he also prophesied: '*Soon will the present-day order be rolled up and a new one spread in its stead.*'

We are living at a time when the world is feeling both the death throes of a declining era and the birth pangs of a new one. Everywhere the signs of new faith, brotherhood and universality are emerging, and the chains of prejudice, chauvinism and selfish materialism are breaking. That is the conclusion I came to as a result of my long journey. I feel that we are now living through the worst moment in the history of man, but I also believe that we are surrounded by hope.

Revelation is progressive and never-ending. The advent of a Prophet marks the starting point of a new era which, like the sun, will reach its zenith and then decline. Another sun will then rise, and history will continue. And yet there is a single sun, a single divine Word. Only the risings, the Prophets, the rebirths are multiple. There is only one God, and His teaching is continuous and gradual. '*I have many things to say unto you but ye cannot bear them now*' (John 16:12). Thus, there is only one religion, only one ethic. Having been prepared little by little since the dawn of history, the human race is now on the threshold of attaining that which has been promised us from the beginning of time: the unity of mankind which will give birth to universal peace and social justice. The age of stumbling beginnings and preparations is giving way to the age of accomplishment.

Chapter 13

'BROTHER' IS AN AFRICAN WORD

Djibouti: a miserable stretch of burning sand somewhere near the mouth of the Red Sea. I was about to begin my fifth year as a solitary hitch-hiker. It was funny, but by this stage I would be very reluctant to accept any travelling companion. I had conquered fear of myself, the fear of solitude; I was free. And then, too, I was never really alone. At times I needed other people to talk to, and someone would inevitably show up. In fact, there were evenings when I was eager to get off on my own again. The trip had been such an ordeal that I didn't think I would ever have the energy to do it again. Yet no amount of money would have made me change my style of travel, for I was doing exactly what *I* wanted to do. The price was high but so were the rewards.

In the centre of town, on Menelik Square, the tourist office stood shaded by an arcade. Inside was Naguiba, a hostess who combined exquisite manners and a French education with unfailing kindness. She wore an astonishing short, bright yellow dress with a revealing neckline. What a change! For over a year, since first setting foot on Turkish soil, I had hardly seen or talked to any women. They were always veiled, hidden, sequestered . . . I was enchanted to meet her. Furthermore, delightful Naguiba revived the poet in me, the lover of everything beautiful - something I had never ceased to be. I wanted to talk to her all day, to learn all about her life, her land and its customs. But alas! Beauty was also a Muslim.

'I'm not allowed to go out without a chaperon. This isn't Paris, you know. What did you expect?'

'Isn't there some way we could go for a walk, just a little stroll?

Couldn't we talk . . . somewhere else?'

'You're crazy. I have to go straight home after work. And believe me, they know my schedule.'

So I ended up spending long hours in the tourist office where I was actually one of the rare visitors.

As the days passed by, Naguiba began to confide in me, despite the restrictions. I sensed she was unhappy. Her religion, the treatment it meted out to women, and the local traditions and customs all weighed heavily on her. One evening she related a shocking story. She told me about the 'sewed-up' women who had been 'circumcised', a custom still observed today in Eastern Africa. I already knew that many women in Africa underwent 'operations' to remove the clitoris, but I had no idea that in the eastern regions of the continent, things were carried a step further . . .

'When she's between six and ten years of age', explained Naguiba, 'a young girl is set upon by a group of married women who pin her down and hold her still. Then against her will, the poor child is subjected to the most barbarous of rites. As she struggles helplessly, one of the women begins by ripping out her clitoris, often using her fingernail. Then another old witch starts slashing the girl's labia with any knife that's handy. It's horrid. When two wounds have been opened, they are pulled together and clamped shut with thorn needles which are planted directly into the genital lips of the screaming child. Then they cover everything up with resin. During the two weeks needed for the graft to heal, the girl is bound from hip to knee. The whole process takes place without the slightest pretence to hygiene or anaesthesia. Infection often follows. It's atrocious . . .'

Totally nauseated, I lacked even the strength to ask Naguiba to stop right there.

'This barbaric custom turns the wedding night into a horrifying butchery. Before he takes possession of his bride, the husband first performs a bloody operation with a razor blade or a piece of sharp-edged flint. A beating often goes along with it, and the whole scene is anything but erotic. Each time the woman gives birth, the wound has to be completely reopened . . .'

I couldn't believe my ears. And it was being recounted with simple resignation by this pretty *Afar*, so lively, so . . . tempting. To assault one's wife with a sharp-edged piece of flint . . . How utterly repulsive! Catching my concerned expression, Naguiba anticipated the question that I was about to ask.

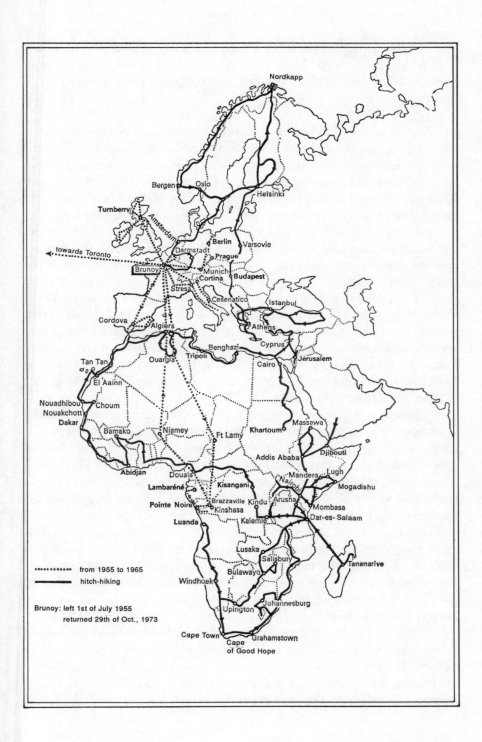

Nordkapp

Bergen — Oslo
Helsinki

Turnberry
Amsterdam

towards Toronto
Berlin
Varsovie
Darmstadt
Prague
Brunoy
Munich
Budapest
Cortina
Stresa
Cesenatico
Istanbul

Cordova
Athens
Algiers
Cyprus

Tan Tan
Benghazi
Ouargla
Tripoli
Jerusalem
El Aainn
Cairo

Nouadhibou
Choum
Nouakchott
Dakar
Massawa
Bamako
Niamey
Ft Lamy
Khartoum
Djibouti
Addis Ababa
Lugh
Abidjan
Douala
Mandera
Lambaréné
Kisangani
Mogadishu
Pointe Noire
Kindu
Nairobi
Brazzaville
Arusha
Kinshasa
Mombasa
Luanda
Kalemie
Dar-es-Salaam

Lusaka
Salisbury
Tananarive
Bulawayo
Windhoek

Johannesburg
Upington
Cape Town
Grahamstown
Cape
of Good Hope

•••••••••• from 1955 to 1965
———— hitch-hiking

Brunoy: left 1st of July 1955
returned 29th of Oct., 1973

'Don't worry. I managed to escape it. I was very ill at the time, so I only had to go through the first operation . . . So André, if during your trip you meet some sad, frightened, uncommunicative women, you'll understand why.'

My real tour of Africa began in Ethiopia where dire poverty, repulsive filth and strong pungent odours blended with the people's heart-warming friendliness, generosity and noble character. In the crude, smoky *toucouls*, where a baby sleeping on the straw attracted more flies than the calf lying next to it, I felt at home, even when surrounded by poverty and nakedness. I shared their poverty with joy: I loved them as they were.

In 1972 Ethiopia was under the thumb of the emperor. His power was based on the clergy - who frightened children away with fly-swatters, insisted that the earth was flat and mumbled their prayers in *Gueze*, the sacred language of the Abyssinian gospels of which they understood not a word. The country was one of the most ancient Christian lands, but it was just as deeply rooted in ignorance as most of its Arab or Asian neighbours. Once again, there was a great contrast between the people and their leaders. One day I stood about outside the gates of the Imperial Palace to watch His Majesty leave for work. Each day a fleet of huge Mercedes drove ceremonially along the half-mile separating the palace from the government buildings.

'New Flower', the capital Addis Ababa, was a mixture of modern skyscrapers and indescribable slums. So that His Majesty should not be upset by the sight of the latter, tall wooden fences painted a cheerful green masked the reality. How could such things still exist? How much longer would men insist on hiding misery behind walls? As long as people continued to go naked while their leaders paraded about in a Mercedes, the entire world would find no rest. I knew that absolute equality for all was simply impractical, and belonged to the realm of Utopia. 'Abdu'l-Bahá said, '*Even if equality could be achieved it could not continue; and if its existence were possible, the whole order of the world would be destroyed.*' Nevertheless, it was vital to abolish the extremes. '*The best beloved of all things in My sight is Justice*', said Bahá'u'lláh. Love was not enough. Society had to be founded on JUSTICE.

1964! What was that year doing on the calendar? I had just turned thirty-four, and the date had been November 11th, 1971, just one week before. Yet I was looking at an up-to-date calendar; there was no mistaking it. The problem was that Ethiopia, like Russia, Bulgaria, Romania, Czechoslovakia and other countries, had retained the Julian

Calendar, ignoring the reform instigated by Pope Gregory XIII in the sixteenth century. So suddenly, I was seven years younger! As for the Jews, they were already in 5732, and the Muslims were back in 1390. What a mess!

Friday was the Muslim day of rest, Saturday the Jewish Sabbath and Sunday the Lord's Day for Christians. As a result, shopkeepers in some countries worked only four days a week. How could people talk about understanding each other when they clung to such outmoded systems? In Jerusalem, for instance, each page of the calendar carried five dates: Gregorian, Coptic, Hebrew, Julian and Hegira. How could anyone keep track of them all? To bring everyone into line with everyone else, including the Hindus and Buddhists who of course have their own systems, the Bahá'ís propose a universal calendar which is completely new and not derived from any of the existing ones. The main advantage is that nobody would be forced to accept a traditional system used by his neighbour. It would mean just one less source of contention.

On February 6th, 1972, I entered into a no man's land bristling with thorn bushes and baked by a relentless sun.

'Just walk straight ahead in that direction, and you're bound to end up in Somalia', said the District Commissioner of Mandera, the last group of huts under Kenyan jurisdiction.

It was the first time I had crossed a national boundary with no barbed wire, customs or suspicious interrogations. In my travels from country to country, I had developed a genuine hatred for borders as well as for their corresponding consulates. But this time there was nothing but sand as far as the eye could see. Nevertheless, it was a little too early for celebrations.

I was in a country of nomads, of huge Somalis wandering unhindered through an immense and empty wilderness. Surrounded by sand, camels and Muslims, I had the feeling of being back in an Arab country. My pack was sticky on my back and my forehead dripped with sweat. I had not had it so hard for a long time - and all this simply to reach an 'Alláh-forsaken' place, this Somalia which discouraged tourists and went to great lengths to avoid granting them visas. But it took more than that to discourage me, especially now that I had learned my way around the maze of red tape.

Mogadishu, the capital, was accessible only by sea or air. There were no roads linking it to Addis Ababa, Dar es Salaam or Nairobi. You had to be completely crazy to attempt what I was doing, but this Nairobi-

Mogadishu foray represented a kind of challenge. Without having overestimated my capabilities, I had to admit that the going was rougher than I had expected. My progress was slow as I went from patch of shade to patch of shade, from palm tree to palm tree, from hamlet to village, from siesta to siesta. Mandera was the halfway mark, and by the time I reached it I felt I had achieved something.

In this mechanic's graveyard, I managed to ride a little way with two American millionaires who were on safari in a Land Rover driven by an experienced guide. They acted as if they were still back home in Houston, Texas. At one point we stopped to eat. I watched, entranced, as the guide dashed about setting up umbrellas, stretching out a large tarpaulin on the ground for the comfort of our lady and gentleman, producing a table, chairs and a camping buffet. Nothing had been left out: there were china dishes, elegant stemmed glasses, luxurious silverware and an immaculate tablecloth. It was absolutely incredible, something I had never seen before. Dressed in my shorts, seated on the sand in the shade of a baobab tree, I observed the unfolding scene with increasing astonishment. Perfect in his role of well-schooled butler, the guide chased away the mosquitoes with a can of aerosol spray and winked conspiratorially at me.

The American man was in his fifties and sported an impressive belly. He had fitted himself out in one of the chic stores in Nairobi and looked very much at home in his sand-coloured trousers, safari jacket and colonial helmet which must have been brought out of mothballs for the occasion. He was ready to shoulder single-handedly whatever might remain of the White Man's Burden. His wife was decked out for a night at the opera. Weighed down with diamonds, she sparkled from head to toe. As great ladies should, she wiggled just a little before sitting down. They made a charming pair. I could just imagine the bush camp which was being prepared for them complete with water, electricity, air-conditioning and ivory tusks as trophies . . .

If I had arranged my trip through a travel agency, I would no doubt have been spared the frequent police checks, compliments of the new masters of Somalia. They were definitely the chief inconvenience of my chosen method of travel. The troubles I had experienced in Jordan and Iraq were starting up all over again. Whenever I showed up in a village, I was immediately taken for a spy or a counter-revolutionary - automatically.

'What's that thing there?'
'Can't you tell? It's a grenade!'

I had been stopped in Lugh, on the bridge which spanned the Juba, a lovely green ribbon of water in the ochre-red desert. There and then they searched through everything I had, even examining in detail every page of my journal. One of the policemen finally discovered a strange item. He held it up in his hand, looking thoroughly anxious. Escorted by eight men in uniform, I made a royal entry into police headquarters. The chief and his assistant wanted to take the object apart. I strongly protested.

'In that case, make it work', they insisted. 'Prove to us that you can use it to shave.'

'That would be really easy, guys', I retorted. 'But you don't have any electricity!' And they let me go.

I spent the whole day looking for a vehicle to give me a ride, and I could not move a step without being shadowed by the police. At least that made it easy for me to volunteer for a night in jail. That was one thing off my mind. The next morning they were friendlier towards me. Unfortunately I provoked a riot in the market-place, and the excited crowd dragged me by the ear back to my previous night's hosts. Surprised to see me again, the police locked me up to get me out of the hands of the mob. I had no idea what I had done. An hour later I learned the charges: I was accused of having urinated alongside a hedge bordering a goat pasture.

'But that hardly seems like a major crime!'

'Yes, Sir, it is. Here we don't do it STANDING UP!!!'

At last I reached Mogadishu and the sea - and not a moment too soon. There were a few green trees, white houses on white dunes, and wind off the ocean. But the charm of the setting was destroyed by the atmosphere which prevailed in town. The revolution had nationalized everything and made a virtue of suspicion. Propaganda was everywhere; cinemas showed only technical or political documentaries filmed in Russia. Policemen chased vagrants through the streets, beating them with truncheons. I had never seen so many police stations. Sandwiched between two photographs of workers on a bulletin board devoted to the merits of productivity was a slogan which proclaimed 'Muhammad was the world's first scientific socialist'. I had a hard time believing in the reality of this country and wondered how long its people - so proud, indolent, easy-going and accustomed to wide-open spaces - would endure the yoke of a police state.

On the third evening of my visit to Somalia, my friend Qudrat, who was putting me up, invited a few friends for dinner. Sultan, who had lost his job when the new régime had taken over, was the first to leave. No sooner was he outside than the police picked him up and interrogated him for over an hour about the presence of this French tourist.

'We want to know what he's doing here.'

'But I've already told you, he's taking a trip around the world . . .'

'You're lying. We already know what he's up to. He came to take pictures of naked girls and publish them in foreign magazines!'

When I think that I had not even brought my camera to Somalia! Experience had taught me much, and I had developed an instinct for taking appropriate precautions before entering certain countries. Poor Sultan got off the hook by promising to spy on me and not to breathe a word.

The following day he told me that they had even offered him money, no doubt in the name of the anti-corruption campaign which was a sacred tenet of scientific socialism. He also said they had shown him a schedule of everything I had done since setting foot in the city. As we walked about, Sultan discreetly pointed out the hiding places of the policemen assigned to follow me. He said there were no fewer than 10,000 men working for the Secret Police, and that they kept an eye on everyone including each other.

What bothered me most about the situation was not so much the spy-counter-spy atmosphere, but the fact that I was cut off from all contact with the people. Any attempt at conversation was treated like an exchange of secret codes and messages. I wondered how the Soviets, who preached friendship among peoples, would ever achieve their goal. Barbed wire certainly did not have the same appeal as the flower leis of Tahiti.

I was planning to cover Africa from one end to the other.

'Your tribe?' a Kikuyu asked me, rolling his large, round eyes as he filled in a form.

The fact that I was leaving Somalia did not mean that my troubles were over. The African continent was three times as large as the United States and fifty-four times the size of France. It posed tremendous problems for the traveller. The north was completely cut off by the Sahara desert; the rain forest of the Congo basin restricted access to the centre. Aircraft, of course, could make short work of such obstacles, but for the poor pedestrian like me they seemed formidable barriers indeed. There were only two long stretches of asphalt road. In the north, one of them linked Mogador in Morocco to Cairo in Egypt. In the South there was a gigantic 'V' extending from Nairobi, Kenya to Luanda, Angola, passing via Cape Town. It was on that road that I set my speed record as a hitch-hiker: 2,500 miles in three days.

Aside from the two main roads, tarmac surfaces were virtually nonexistent. The railways were essentially for transporting mineral ores from mine to port. Only rarely did they link two urban areas and in any event they were unreliable. The rainy season was another major obstacle, as were the continual variations in climate and temperature. Many Africans were constantly at risk from sickness, and just as in South America and Asia, a variety of endemic diseases lurked in wait for the traveller: amoebic dysentery, malaria, sleeping sickness - to name only the commonest ones. My swollen abdomen was still my major worry and a constant reminder to stay away from the water. To avoid catching malaria, I swallowed quinine tablets twice a week. For the rest, I relied on luck. Otherwise I would have had to travel with the entire contents of a pharmacy on my back, and that was out of the question. As for wild animals, the most ferocious (and potentially dangerous) was still the mosquito!

Like Asia, Africa was a land of quarrels and conflicts. The traveller had to pay attention not only to transport problems and disease but also to the political situation in each country he passed through. I needed to know that it was unwise to show up at certain borders with visa stamps from South Africa, Rhodesia (now Zimbabwe), Angola or Mozambique in my passport. I arranged instead for those problem visas to be stamped in a temporary passport (one of the half-dozen I went through) that I later exchanged in Malawi, a country which maintained good relations with everybody.

When I undertook my Africa tour - from November 1971 to February 1973 - all traffic was cut between Angola and Zaïre, Zambia and Rhodesia, Mozambique and Tanzania, Chad and Sudan, Kenya and Somalia, Ethiopia and Sudan . . . Both Guineas were inaccessible: one because of its régime and the other because of its war. Fighting was also going on in Chad and Sudan, and civilians were advised to avoid the border between Uganda and Tanzania. In the past it would have been possible to visit the entire continent with two passports: one British and the other French. But today Africa was a patchwork of some sixty nations, and that meant almost as many visas. Only in the former French colonies was I, as a citizen of France, allowed entry without a visa. In order to visit the three independent countries of Botswana, Lesotho and Swaziland with the least amount of inconvenience, I passed myself off as a subject of Her Majesty the Queen. Three times I lied convincingly:

'What country are you from?'

'France.'

'Oh, Fransse, uh Fransse . . . Is that part of the Commonwealth?'

'Of course, Sir!'

I beg the pardon of my fellow Frenchmen and of all patriots who might be shocked by such unscrupulous tactics. But with a little white lie, I was able to escape enormous administrative complications. For all of the above reasons, my African itinerary bore no resemblance to an organized trip. I ended up passing through Tanzania five different times; it became a sort of staging post.

But Africa, for me, was above all the people, the black 'brother' with his open heart, his uncalculated simplicity, his spontaneous kindness, his candid good nature. 'Brother' is an African word. Never had I felt so safe as when I found myself in the heart of the jungle, in a remote village with those people some called 'savages'. Whenever they saw me approaching, my indigenous brothers would offer me a chair (in a country where everyone squatted on the ground), bring me water and ask after my welfare. Was I sure I didn't need anything? I was not just 'received' but actively welcomed everywhere. Everyone wanted to share their food or give me a corner of their hut to sleep in. I had never felt so much warmth, friendship and brotherhood. They never made me feel that the colour of my skin was any different from theirs.

I spent long months among the common people - not only because the world of the white man (and respectable black) was financially out of my reach, but simply because that was where I felt at home. Without any doubt, it was among my African friends that I met the people I had been seeking, the people I loved. It was here that I discovered to what extent we are all one, in spite of ethnic or tribal differences. I would never have believed when I began my travels how completely I was going to sweep away all prejudice. From now on I would be able to draw aside those futile barriers of illusion like a thin curtain to discover the realities of the human heart. I learned that every person was simply '*my unknown self, rendered visible*' (Khalil Gibran), that in every face we had to seek out our other self, the reflection of God. Our differences then appeared both necessary and beautiful. I even finished by wondering if what was left of civilization was not to be found in the heart of the Congo, where human relationships were still intact.

Although it seemed to me that I had discovered in Africa men of pure heart, brothers who could take their place as citizens of the global village for which I yearned and prayed, I also realized that the road to Eden was still very long and winding. It still required a great effort to clear the path, because in Africa more than anywhere, I saw how overgrown it was with old habits and customs, ancestral hatred and fanatical tribalism and nationalism. Man is, first of all, a slave to his own habits against which it never occurs to him to rebel.

Sitting beside some road or track, I often thought of my father who even after years away from his home province, never really felt comfortable in the suburbs of Paris. He continued to wear his wooden clogs, drink soup from a bowl and cut his cheese with a jack-knife, eating it cupped in the palm of his hand just as he had done back in Auvergne when he paused for a bite to eat beside his plough. When I was a child his habits had embarrassed me, because no one else seemed to do things that way. Even then I had asked myself the same question: why were ancestral habits and conditioning so tenacious?

In Mombasa, on the sun-drenched coast of Kenya, I again tried to understand why half the women walked about bare-breasted while the other half sweated under heavy black veils. Didn't the women, constantly in contact with one another, find the situation a little incongruous? It might have been understandable for someone unaware of alternative ways of dressing, thinking, living; but when the comparison was there to be made every day? Hundreds of times I puzzled over that question, and nowhere more than along the Arusha-Nairobi road, one of the most picturesque on the continent, with its wild animals posing against the backdrop of Kilimanjaro. Masai were everywhere, tall reddish-haired warriors, almost naked, decked with glass jewellery and carrying bows and arrows. They stood impassively at the roadside while a steady stream of buses rolled by carrying crowds of tourists who with their tortoise shell glasses and clanking baubles were every bit as colourful. Leaning on their spears in the midst of their flocks, what could those tribesmen be thinking of those strangers shooting at them with Instamatics, movie cameras and intrusive flash bulbs? Men without clothes and men who had just walked on the moon observed each other like animals in a zoo. Face to face, did any one of them realize how vast was the distance separating them?

And yet, they needed only to take a first step, then a second, in order to approach one another. It was essential that they make the effort. Aboriginal man could no longer dwell in his little corner of the bush, indifferent to modern technology. He had to learn to distinguish what was best in others and to accept it for himself. Familiar with the tenacity of old habits and taboos, we understood how long it could take for new ideas to take root in people's minds. Nevertheless, it was time for everyone to acknowledge the reality of every other person's existence and to stop despising them or holding them at arm's length. As contacts increased among people, sharing, co-operation and solidarity would become inevitable. Technical man, for his part, had to relearn the meaning of human relationships.

On my feet, with my thumb stuck out as usual, I wondered if I wasn't dreaming, for an endless convoy of trucks was passing me by without ever stopping. The drivers had moon-like faces and seemed to be oblivious to my extravagant, theatrical efforts to attract their attention. All dressed in the same blue caps and tunics, they were obviously Chinese, working to build the railway through the forest from Dar es Salaam to Lusaka. They were intent on linking the two capitals, 1,200 miles apart, without having any contact with the lands and peoples they were linking.

'No, a trip around the world is too much like hard work', said an African, who had been loosely holding my hand for the last ten minutes.

I protested, for I was impatient to reach Lusaka where Rúhíyyih Khánum, Mrs Rabbání, was currently staying. A 61-year-old Canadian woman, she had been travelling through Africa in a Land Rover for the past three years, together with her Iranian companion, Violette Nakhjavání. Both of them were in the service of Bahá'u'lláh. Rúhíyyih Khánum was the widow of Shoghi Effendi, who had been named Guardian of the Bahá'í Faith by 'Abdu'l-Bahá, the son of Bahá'u'lláh. She was also the author of *Prescription for Living*, the first Bahá'í book that I had stumbled across back in Alaska. That book had been a real starting point for me.

When I arrived in Lusaka the whole town was talking about Mrs Rabbání's lectures.

'What an intelligent woman! What knowledge! She's extraordinary . . .', exclaimed a Greek engineer who had picked me up.

'Yes, that's true, but what is even more extraordinary is her message!'

The first person I met was Mr Agahi, a Bahá'í from Iran who was a lowly technician in a radio-television workshop, although in his own country he had held a very senior post. He was happy to greet another Bahá'í and embraced me warmly, as was the custom in his country. One of his companions, a Nigerian, was amazed at our effusive friendliness.

'Have you known this Frenchman for a long time?' he asked.

'No, it's the first time I've ever seen him.'

'Why, that's absolutely *incredible!*'

Unimaginable. There lay Bahá'u'lláh's true miracle, the miracle of unity between men, between two complete strangers. Today, that miracle was being repeated throughout the world at an ever-quickening pace. Unity was on the march despite the scepticism of a disillusioned humanity.

It was Mr Agahi who introduced me to Rúhíyyih Khánum at a dinner. I chatted at length with that great and dignified lady who, despite her tiredness, gave me her full attention.

'I wonder how you manage to hop from country to country like that! Personally, I have tremendous difficulties with all these visa problems.'

'Yes, ma'am, I also get fed up with all those useless complications. It gets me down, but I hang on.'

'André, the world is very sick. It's reaching boiling point. Tell me, after all your ordeals, you seem to be in pretty good health.'

'Yes, but I'm tired. My stomach gives me a lot of trouble, and I take longer to recover than I used to. This trip has been very hard, but I don't suppose yours has been any easier. I can't imagine how you do it. Two women alone in a car. What do you do when you break down or have a flat tyre?'

'Oh, you know, there's always someone to help us out, at just the right moment.'

'Here you're back in civilization!' spouted off a squat little fellow with a wry, arrogant grin. Dressed in shorts and a white shirt with golden epaulettes, he had bright pink skin with a sprinkling of freckles. It was the skin of an Englishman; the man was a Rhodesian immigration officer.

It was my first contact with 'White Africa'. In the time it took me to cross the bridge over the Zambezi, at the spot where the roaring Victoria Falls plunged into a magnificent canyon, I passed from the disorderly Zambian night into the daylight of British efficiency. Victoria had all the charm and neatness of an English city, with its immaculate manicured lawns and flower beds. Everything was very orderly and freshly painted. What a change after the cheerful, easygoing style of Black Africa! Here everything was in its place - including the Blacks, which was exactly where the drama began.

Every city in Rhodesia was divided into four parts: there was a neighbourhood for the Whites, one for the Blacks, another for those of mixed blood, and one for immigrants from Asia. The African, who was normally so light-hearted, who loved to live and laugh, chat and have fun, had become in this country a cautious creature. He was reserved, respectful and submissive to a degree that broke my heart. The easy rapport, the communication was gone. As the days passed, I felt the atmosphere grow tenser. From Bulawayo to Salisbury, from the ruins of Zimbabwe to Matopos Park, the border official's words echoed endlessly in my mind: 'Here you're back in civilization.' For heaven's sake, when would it ever end? I wondered how long I would be able to put up with such selfishness, stupidity and ignorance.

The atmosphere was even more ominous in South Africa. One evening, hunger had sent me out on a search for some cheap little eating place. I stopped in front of a fish and chip shop, a modest wood structure with a single door. I was gripped by feelings of anxiety. What should I do? I had been warned that being a foreigner made no difference; the slightest mistake could mean six months in jail, without trial, in the name of the Immorality Act or the Communist Terrorist act. I stood for a long time in front of the building, wondering whether or not its sole door was intended for Whites. It was a dilemma, for everything was divided into *Blankes* and *Nie Blankes*. Finally I decided that since I was white, I ought to have the right to enter anywhere. Inside a number of Africans were waiting at the counter to be served. Instinctively, I took my place at the end of the queue. At that very moment, a white man entered. Passing ahead of everyone, he was served immediately and left just as quickly clutching his greasy little package. Putting out of my mind any feelings of shame, I left the line and did as the other white man had done. I had no desire to wind up in jail, so I would conduct myself according to the law. I had not noticed at first that there were two frying pans for the fish and two baskets for the chips. Two oils, one for the Whites and one for the . . . That's what *apartheid* was all about.

It was sickening. Every public building and most shops had two doors, even if there was only a single counter inside. Beaches, taxis, trains, buses and public lavatories were all split in two. The best of everything was always reserved for Whites. There were even public benches for *Blankes* and *Nie Blankes*. Never mind watching where you step - in South africa you watch where you sit too! It was shameful; it reminded me of Hitler . . .

It was exactly the same story in South-West Africa where the Whites were about as liberal as their South African neighbours. On the outskirts of Upington, at the edge of the Namibian desert, I spent an entire day waiting under a burning sun. Finally, a police car stopped for me. We did not exactly hit it off. Before I could say a word, the policeman, like all the other drivers who had picked me up in southern Africa, began discoursing on the familiar topic which throbbed as painfully as a toothache: *apartheid*.

'I pick up all hitch-hikers except Communists.'

'How can you tell at a glance who's a Communist and who isn't?'

'I can feel it as soon as I start talking to him. If he is one of those dirty Commy bastards, he gets out pretty damn quick.'

'So, if I understand you correctly, I'd better watch what I say . . .'

Actually, there was no need for me to talk. He did enough for us both. Speaking in a tone which discouraged debate, he told me how White Africa was the last stronghold of the Western world. According to him, any difference of opinion or any original idea was of Communist inspiration. In fact, everything he said was merely intended to justify an ultra-repressive system which put into effect laws against nature. In a thundering voice, he continued:

'I'm in charge of the Ovambos' territory, and I'm a dog-trainer besides. I teach my dogs to go for those filthy *Kaffirs* if they so much as raise a finger. Bunch of lazy slobs. Do you realize they even dared to go on strike? Believe me, they stink and they're good for nothing. You have to keep them separated from the Whites. And for that, you can count on me. You know, we've succeeded in crossing three breeds of dogs, and the results are fantastic. They're the best ever for tracking down those black monkeys . . .'

'Excuse me, Sir, but it seems to me you're not being very logical. You claim that mixing different species of dogs gives good results, but at the same time you want human beings to stay separated for ever. If I get you right, you're saying that in your country, dogs are superior to people?'

The policeman was speechless, his mouth hanging open. I said nothing more, because it was in the middle of the night. I felt that if I continued he was quite capable of dumping me in this Bantu territory which was out of bounds to Whites.

For almost thirty years now, racism had been legal and constitutional. The most cynical touch was that the Dutch Reformed Church gave its approval to *apartheid*, supporting its position with a biblical verse: '*Cursed be Canaan, a servant of servants shall he be unto his brethren*' (Genesis 9:25). I wondered by what feat of intellectual agility the Afrikaners had determined that Zulus, the Xhosas and the Asian

immigrants were all descended from Canaan. Long after Genesis, hadn't
Christ as founder of their Church suggested we love even our enemy? Had
Calvin stayed silent about loving our neighbour? The worst of it was that
this same Dutch Reformed Church counted many Blacks among its
members! Of course, religious services were held at different hours, there
being no question of mixing Whites with the sons of the servants of
servants.

It was a shameful country in which an American, because he was
white, was considered 'European' (to his great indignation); in which
Indians and Pakistanis were baptized 'Bantu'. The Chinese were also
given low status, but the Japanese were treated as officially white,
'European'. As for dark-skinned celebrities from abroad, if their visits to
the country were unavoidable, they were billed as 'honorary Whites'
which enabled them to stay in decent hotels and to move about as they
wished.* What a marvellous *Republick* it was, where a black doctor could
not give orders to a white nurse, where a white ambulance could not
transport an injured Black, or vice versa. I wondered if any other country
had laws as iniquitous as this. After 8.00 p.m., for example, Blacks were
not allowed to move about the city, which meant that servants and
cleaning ladies had to leave their bosses' homes early, there being no
question of their living under the same roof. Therefore, when white ladies
and gentlemen wished to entertain in the evening, they had to do the
serving themselves, a situation which they never stopped complaining
about.

In Grahamstown, in Cape Province, I spent long hours on the edge
of town waiting for a lift. I was in a neighbourhood reserved for Bantus,
and everything was very shabby compared to the white population's
magnificent villas which would even be the envy of a real European. The
Xhosas passed me by in silence as if I didn't exist. That was what
infuriated me. I cursed this system which transformed human beings into
shadows. I was sure they must be wondering what I was doing in their
neighbourhood, sitting on the grass with my backpack. I called to a
woman in a house nearby and - to her great surprise - asked if I might
have some water. She was visibly shaken to see me drink from a glass that
she had handed me. When I thanked her, she made no sign of
acknowledgement, not even a smile. She did not trust me. A while later, I

*In *The Geopolitics of Hunger*, the eminent anthropologist Josue de Castro reminds us that
'*In the light of modern anthropological findings there exists no superiority or inferiority of race.
What does exist are biological variations conditioned by environmental differences.*'

went up to a Bantu man selling pineapples. The man was surrounded by a group of children, but when I tried to pat one of them on the head, they vanished like a flock of birds.

Paradoxically, it was in the car of a black man that I left that neighbourhood of pariahs.

'Well', I said, 'at least you don't hold a grudge. You even give rides to Whites.'

'I'm happy to help you out. I like everybody. Actually, though, you're lucky: if I'd had my wife or daughter with me, I would have been obliged to respect the law.'

In the suburbs of Johannesburg, the gold capital, I visited Soweto, the Bantu area where 600,000 black 'servants' lived. Neatly-aligned little houses built of brick and corrugated iron had replaced the former slums. Only one shack had been preserved as evidence of the progress that had been made and of the kindness of the white man. Two fruit trees were planted in front of each home; the Bantu was expected to cultivate his own garden. Playing fields, playgrounds, theatres, inexpensive stores, churches: nothing had been left out, not even the high fence surrounding the entire compound which barred access to Whites, except for organized visits. These new neighbourhoods were certainly much better than the old slums, but the effort to help the natives was in reality nothing more than a sham. The *Blankes* were using material gains to veil the horror of their crime against humanity. Considering the enormous profits they made from exploiting the Blacks, they clearly had the means to dole out a modest share of the takings. Yes, the Bantus were better dressed, better housed, and better paid than the Blacks in neighbouring countries. They even had schools and a health service. But the fact remained that the Whites were a hundred times better paid and had a hundred times more freedom. They were sitting pretty. It sickened me. In spite of my best efforts, the black population rejected me, from habit, from fear:

'Yes, boss; no, boss . . .'

'But I'm telling you I'm not your boss.   I'm your friend, your brother . . .'

'OK, boss . . .'

In Jo'burg, a great maze of reinforced concrete, a white man picked me up before I even stuck out my thumb. He started in with the familiar speech on *apartheid*, but he had a friendly air and the tone was different.

'I've got a good factory, and I have to admit that my Blacks work better than the Whites. At any rate, I've been sending my money to London, and I'm ready to take off at the first sign of trouble. Believe me, it won't be long. It's all going to end in bloodshed. It isn't hard to understand why *apartheid* can never work. Our economy has made tremendous strides, but not because of the separation of the races. On the contrary, we've progressed because everybody has pooled their efforts. If the Blacks stopped working, everything would fall apart. Granted, they're in need of our technology, but still . . . There are five times more Blacks than Whites and they own only thirteen per cent of the land - and not the best land either. We educate them, and that's a good thing; but we just can't keep hoping that things will continue the way they've been. No, I tell you, sooner or later it's going to end in bloodshed. The ones to blame will have been the Boers, who are even more pigheaded than the English. I tell you, it's going to end in a blood-bath . . .'

'When is the next train to Kabalo?'
    'I don't know, Sir . . .'
    'I'm not asking you the exact time, just the day . . .'
    'And I'm telling you, Sir, I don't know', replied the stationmaster in Kalemie with a gesture of resignation. I would just have to wait.
    Eight years earlier, mercenaries had blown up all the bridges on the only road crossing the Kivu province in Zaïre. Since they had not been rebuilt, I was condemned to wait for a hypothetical train here in Kalemie, formerly Albertville. Abandoned on the shores of Lake Tanganyika, the city was a pitiful sight. The Belgians had left in 1960, and nothing had been done since the secessionist fighting of 1964. The church near the station still bore its bullet marks, and the Flemish inscriptions had been ripped away. The arrogant military police had enthroned themselves in a former bank which still had broken windows. Policemen and soldiers were the only people in town. Not a single worker was to be seen, not a carpenter, not a bricklayer. The shopping district was in shambles and the old colonial villas were only awaiting the next storm before collapsing entirely. Nothing had been repaired or maintained.
    Isle-de-France couldn't conceive of a *muzungu*, a White, sleeping out in the open and offered me his mud hut. Chickens and ducks flapped about in the courtyard as a young girl squatting on a mat prepared the manioc. Two other girls were doing their hair, carefully plaiting antenna-like braids, while a transistor radio blared out a scratchy and never-ending African 'cha-cha-cha'. In a corner some adults were playing cards with a nonchalance unknown in the West. Amid the banana trees, palm trees and bougainvillaea, the heat and earthy smells, the hospitality and

the gaiety, I rediscovered the easy-going atmosphere I had known in the French Congo fourteen years earlier. This time, however, I was here by choice as a brother and a friend, not as a colonialist.

Little by little, the good humour and carefree nature of the Africans won me over. Why worry, after all? Some of the Frenchmen who had been called in to restore the railway network gave me a free ticket.

'I wish you luck', one of them said. 'Here you never know when you're going to leave or when you're going to arrive!'

On a Wednesday I finally boarded a second-class carriage, ready for the first 190-mile stretch from Kalemie to Kabalo. I shared it with an African couple and their seven children, all close in age.

'We're going to have to stop at seven', the man confided. 'My wife can't breast-feed any longer, and I'm lumbered with warming the bottles myself. That's not living!'

The other compartments were all jam-packed, for whenever the Zaïrians went anywhere, they took along everything they owned. They didn't travel; they moved houses. Overflowing packing cases, bundles, basins, hotplates, bicycles, families: where did all the paraphernalia come from? And where was everyone going? The train chugged through Pygmy country all day long. Exhausted, I finally reached Kabalo only to learn that the connection for Kindu in the north had just left. That wasn't too surprising, since of course there were no fixed timetables. Once again I was given the same excellent advice: wait. What else could I do for a week? Kabalo was nothing but a depot. The airport was closed, the roads could no longer be used, no boats ventured on the Congo River . . . No, the train was definitely the only solution. All day long, I listened to the endless hammering that was supposed to put two locomotives resembling museum pieces back into working order.

I had quickly seen everything there was to see in the area: the abandoned river port with its rusty cranes, the empty rancid-smelling warehouses. I always ended up returning to the railway station which had not had a thing done to it since the departure of the Belgians. All its windows were broken, the paint was chipping off the walls, and the whole structure was on the verge of collapsing under the dust. The waiting room was a foul-smelling but peaceful bazaar. Everyone was waiting. I now understood why the local people took along all life's necessities when they travelled!

Trains, stations and most villages offered nothing in the way of restaurants or hotels. Therefore, such services were organized only haphazardly. Columns of smoke rising in the torrid sky meant that food was being prepared on little stoves or over a fire improvised between two stones on the station platform. Hens clucked and goats milled about on the tracks. In the shade men chewed on sugar cane, spitting out the pulp without a worry in the world. Everybody seemed happy and in good spirits. Their contentment was contagious and, indeed, seemed almost unbelievable in a country as poor as the land of the Kivu. The province was in a morass of stagnation despite the triumphant political slogans. It was true that Blacks now occupied the homes of the Whites, just as the orators had promised at the time of independence. But it did not look as if they would be staying there long, for the houses were beginning to crumble. It could be safely assumed that all the fuses had blown long ago and that the plumbing was out of order. The entire family was generally grouped together in the living room around a central fire whose smoke blackened the ceiling. The windows had not been cleaned in twelve years; only the broken panes - which of course were never replaced - let in any light.

These few cynical observations should not be allowed to mislead. Although I deplored the state of abandonment found in most African countries, I also sympathized very deeply with the plight of the inhabitants. Paradoxically, it was in Canada that I became fully aware of the dilemma posed by colonization. During my military service in the Congo, I really hadn't noticed anything untoward. I had been part and parcel of the dominant clique. In my own way, I had been a master. It was in Toronto that I came to understand the importance of collective freedom and to realize how unbearable it was to feel colonized. I identified strongly with the French Canadians, whose resignation was painful to witness.

To me, the idea of a superior, dominant race was intolerable. After being stripped of their own culture by the white man - first as slaves and then as a colonized people - Africans today were free but remained prisoners all the same of the civilization called 'modern'. Western civilization was already a source of tremendous difficulties in the West; imported wholesale into Africa, it could not fail to cause even greater problems among people who were unprepared and culturally dissimilar. Wherever they might be, people were entitled to the utmost liberty, dignity, respect, and justice. At the same time, I sincerely believed that progress could hardly be avoided or prevented from spreading, for progress is mankind's vocation. Co-operation was needed, therefore, in order to avoid a one-way, authoritarian system. As long as we are incapable of putting the right person in the right place regardless of colour, nationality, sex or fortune; as long as we fail to understand that we have to work for the good of the whole human race and not just for our own group or party, as long as our values and attitudes don't change, the majority of people will be doomed to poverty, and the ridiculous modern-day chaos will persist. We no longer had any excuse, for we possessed both the knowledge and the means.

From time to time, one of the ancient locomotives would belch streams of white smoke through a thousand orifices. With a diabolical screech, the wheels would turn a few times before coming to a halt for no apparent reason. Once again the hammering would begin. On the sixth day, a parade of porters carrying logs on their heads dumped their loads into the tender. Departure was in the air. The next day the carriages were hooked together, but no sooner had this been done than the interminable waiting resumed. All they had done was to move the train - along with our boredom and impatience - to a new location.

The third-class carriages were totally bare, mere boxes without benches or luggage racks, like windowless prison cells. There was only one 'luxury' carriage divided into first and second classes. Even there the seats were ripped open and rusty springs protruded. There was no glass in the windows, and the toilets were out of order. If I wanted to move around during the trip, I would have to watch my step, for the floor was little more than a succession of holes gaping above the tracks. The travellers awaiting departure snoozed in the shade of the carriages. The heat was suffocating and the sky a leaden grey. There wasn't a breath of air. How could the men bear it in their sweaters, raincoats, ties, scarves and trilby hats? On the platform, women in nightgowns were breast-feeding their babies. Some were already pregnant again; others carried *mtotos*, infants, on their backs while swarms of children romped in the dust at their feet.

At last the ancient train got under way. The steps and roofs were jammed with people. The journey of 270 miles was destined to take twenty-one hours.

In Kindu, I left the railway and caught a boat going down the Congo River. With the help of an obliging policeman, I boarded the *Delbeque* which passed only once every ten days. The boat was already overflowing with passengers, and I had to hide out in a storeroom until we had sailed.

Ubundu (formerly Ponthierville) was overgrown with weeds and scrub. Once again I camped out in the railway station, over which a flag waved upside down. I gave a piece of stale, mouldy bread to one of the railway workers for his chickens. No sooner had I turned my back than he gulped it down himself. We covered the last stretch of railway from Ubundu to Kisangani at a top speed of four miles per hour. Branches tapped against the windows. Forty-five miles down the line the train which seemed on the verge of expiring, rattled us across the equator. The other people in my compartment were curious to know what I was up to. They were convinced that my trip was very 'serious', and they wanted to know how much my government was going to pay me when I returned. It had never crossed their minds that I could be there on my own initiative, with no axe to grind.

I jolted my way to Buta on a truck, feeling shaken almost beyond endurance - especially given the fact that I was once again suffering severely from diarrhoea. In Buta I literally climbed abroad a narrow-gauge freight train, riding with two black primary school teachers on top of a tanker without railings. All night long, I forced myself to stay awake so as not to tumble off. Still later, I travelled in a diesel locomotive. The two engineers were a pair of clever rascals who made a tidy sum from taking along clandestine passengers. They had disconnected their two-way radio and stopped whenever they liked to pick up passengers, watch the girls or drink some Zaïrian 'whisky' - a banana alcohol with a rather soapy taste. Finally, I had to resort once more to the endless bone-shaking of a truck. Aching all over, I simply had to grit my teeth and bear it. There were several rivers to cross in the region and unfortunately the Belgian ferries had sunk long ago. The only thing left was to cross on a precarious assemblage of dug-out canoes propelled by paddles . . . Maybe that was the 'authenticity' that President Mobutu liked to talk about!

Nouakchott was a sorry-looking concrete jungle which had emerged too hastily from the sands for the sole purpose of providing a capital for newly-independent Mauritania. With lighter-skinned Moors, sand, camels, characteristic tents and furnace-like heat, it was definitely desert country. The Sahara stretched out before me as far as I could see. It was true that the desert today was no longer impenetrable. But to hitch-hike across was no simple matter, especially since all the trucks and jeeps heading out over the three tracks demanded high prices for passengers.

It seemed I would have to pay to get across or I would never get across at all. But I could not give up just yet. These desert drivers did not realize how stubborn I could be. Besides, now that I was an experienced hitch-hiker, I had begun to enjoy such situations. I was going to take up the challenge, and pay later only if there was no other way. I had all the time in the world; that was my principal strength.

Hardly a day passed without at least one truck heading north out of the city, but very few of them were going all the way to Bir Moghrein, the half-way point on the way to Morocco. I would therefore have to do the trip in smaller steps, progressing from village to village. I lay in wait for an entire week, checking out every rumour, bargaining tirelessly, and all in vain . . . until I finally found a truck carrying flour to Atar, 270 miles to the north. A week of palaver had not been too high a price for a free ride. At sunset I hoisted myself up on to the sacks of wheat flour, and immediately realized why the driver had agreed to take me. There were exactly fifty-two of us perched on top of the truck. With fifty-one paying passengers, the driver was doing very nicely. Once I had squeezed in among the *caftans*, I was packed as tightly as a sardine in a can. There was no chance of stretching or wiggling so much as my little toe.

We drove at night, supposedly to avoid the heat. But we had barely left Nouakchott when a burning wind heavy with sand came whipping out of the desert to engulf us in its choking dust. I soon began to miss the heavy rains of Central Africa and the Cameroon which had done so much to slow me down. After Akjout the track followed the dry river beds known as wadis. I was soon so sore from being jerked and jolted about that it began to feel as if someone were hitting me. It reminded me of a certain ride in Liberia when I had shared the back of a Land Rover with a male goat. All night long the little beast had trampled all over me in his efforts to mount a pretty she-goat on my other side. As his tether was too short to reach her, I was the one who suffered - and what a stench!

The following morning I was blue from head to foot from the dye of the Moors' clothing. Now I understood why they were called the Blue Men. I continued on to Choum perched on the roof of a jeep under the fierce midday sun. The rock, thorns and sand, the gold, purple and ochre of the landscape: everything danced in the waves of heat. It was at least 120°F and the wind was scorching. I finally had to close my eyes in pain. By the time we arrived, I was knocked out - I had a severe case of sunstroke and had lost all feeling in my legs.

From a chance conversation, I learned that it was dangerous to continue towards Bir Moghrein because of local fighting. So I decided to jump on an ore train going to the city formerly known as Port-Etienne. There I stood a good chance of finding some boat to get me to El Aaiun, the capital of the Spanish Sahara. I hadn't planned on detouring so far to the west, but it was better than dying in the middle of the desert.

Around ten o'clock at night, the longest train in the world emerged from a tunnel and chugged to a stop. The tunnel had been dug through the one and only hill in the region as if for the sheer fun of it. Couldn't they have built the track around the hill? No, because Madrid had refused to yield a single square inch of its land, and it just so happened that the other side of the hill was Spanish territory! As a question of national sovereignty, it was ludicrous. In order not to violate a barren border by even a hundred yards, men had spent months hollowing out a long tunnel in the desert - and in this heat! Ah, national sovereignty! The sacred cow! And when you think that in the olden days, the spot where two explorers happened to meet became the official border! The mile-long convoy of ore-laden trucks pulled by three diesel engines did not, of course, accept passengers. But I wasn't the only one to scramble up on to the pyramids of rock.

What a night! It was ten hours of genuine torture which I wasn't likely to forget in a hurry. I had never imagined how difficult it would be to spend time on a constantly shifting pile of jagged stone. But once the train was moving, there was no way I could jump off. Whatever would I do in the middle of the desert? I had vaguely heard tell of Mauritanians losing their lives on such trips. Now I could easily believe the stories as I watched pellets of ore weighing several pounds shake loose from the top of the pyramid and crash down against the sides of the car. A fine dust burned my eyes, filled my nose and ears and clogged the pores of my skin. The wind was still whipping the sand up as well. The stars were invisible in the laden sky. And then there was the heat . . . I could not recall ever having spent a more dreadful night. Bruised and filthy by daybreak, I looked like a coal miner greeting the dawn.

The last awkward stretch before getting back on asphalt was the distance between El Aaiun and Tan Tan, Morocco. There were two major obstacles: firstly, there was no road; and secondly, the border was simply closed. To my mind, borders were out of date. Perhaps back in the days of mule trains or stagecoaches the concept was defensible; but today, with jumbo jets and Sputniks, I really could not understand the need for them. Notions like the Berlin Wall were totally beyond my comprehension, and they were not restricted to Berlin. In Scandinavia the borders had been abolished and people could circulate freely from country to country. That did not mean, however, that Norwegians considered themselves to be any less Norwegian than before. Accursed human invention! Here, both countries were in a turmoil because

Madrid and Rabat were constantly bickering over phosphate mines that both of them coveted. So, once again, I was stuck. As I wandered around El Aaiun, I mulled over the situation. Then I met Miguel, a sergeant in the Spanish Foreign Legion, who insisted that the rupture between the two countries was only 'official' and in no way affected the smuggling trade. Twice a week, convoys from both sides of the border met in no man's land and carried out their transactions. Miguel took it upon himself to find me a seat on one of the trucks . . .

At dusk, we stopped near a miserable heap of sheet metal only vaguely resembling a pair of huts. We had tea inside and then slept, sheltered from the wind and sand. When I woke up the next morning, I was astonished to find an armada of trucks parked back to back. Fresh fruit and vegetables were being exchanged for manufactured good from Spain. Business was business, and the trafficking was being pursued with all the arrogance of impunity. There were even Spanish soldiers present . . . as customers!

After a few hours, the trading was finished and the 'enemies' separated - but not before they had arranged the next gathering. At least fifty red Bedford trucks were taking off in the direction of Tan Tan. The hardest thing was to find a driver who would give me a ride without demanding a *matabish* - a tip.

The track stretched on endlessly. The sun all but obliterated the two narrow lines of shadow which showed where the tyres of earlier convoys had passed. I could not stop drinking and mopping up the perspiration. We passed a number of abandoned cars and then, crossing an area of particularly soft ground, came upon a Citroën and a Renault stuck in the sand. Red as beetroot, the occupants were out pushing with every bit of their remaining strength.

'Damn', one of them was yelling, 'we haven't even made a mile yet in this blasted sand . . .'

Poor kids! I thanked my lucky stars that I was on foot. The truckers would pull them out, but it would cost them plenty. For towing a car out of the sand and into town, the truck-drivers charged an amount equal to the price of the car! That explained all the abandoned wrecks along the track.

At sunset after the evening prayer, big fires were lit and thorny branches shrivelled in a burst of joyful crackling. The embers would be used to cook the meal. Sitting on the sand, gazing at the slowly darkening sky, I listened to the silence of the desert. The scent of mint tea perfumed the air. It was a moment of rare serenity; I forgot everything else as I stared up at the night sky. Somewhere behind me, the moon was emerging slowly and silently like a great luminous orange. God, how beautiful the night sky could be when one had travelled so far to contemplate it. How close the Loved One seemed, and how distant and vain the struggles of humanity . . . My heart was at peace, and my thoughts danced lightly. I remembered how at the other end of this desert, whose sand was now trickling through my fingers, beyond the land of the Pharaohs, lay the *Qiblih* of my journey: Haifa, in the Holy Land.

My companions were getting ready for bed. My friends - I no longer recognized any foreigners. My home from now on was wherever I lay down my head. At the moment it was this sand, still warm from the heat of the day. The entire earth had become my country and all humanity my fellow citizens. *Yá Bahá'u'l-Abhá.* God was truly glorious.

Chapter 14

A DOOR OF HOPE

*'So powerful is the light of unity that it
can illuminate the whole earth.'* - Bahá'u'lláh

From Mount Carmel, the Shrine of the Báb dominated the Bay of
Haifa like a lighthouse, guiding the steps of Bahá'í pilgrims and visitors
alike. The remains of the Báb had been buried there in 1909, almost
sixty years after he was martyred. The Shrine of Bahá'u'lláh is in Bahjí,
behind 'Akká, on the other side of the bay. The biblical prophecies had
come true: 'A *door of hope*' . . . '*to which all nations will flock*'. And
Bahá'u'lláh could not be accused of having chosen the site in
accordance with the Scriptures, for he had been brought there as a
prisoner and exile.

February 12th, 1973: on that unseasonably beautiful and mild day
I climbed the 'Mountain of God', and a feeling of grace made me forget
all my worries and tiredness. I could hardly believe that I had finally
attained the summit of my journey. Ever since Alaska this site, which
was so very sacred to me, had become a goal or, in military terms, a
target. I breathed more deeply and more intensely than anywhere
else.Everything seemed more beautiful, more genuine. The birds sang
more joyfully and the sky shone with a purer radiance. I was filled with
gratitude. In spite of all the troubles, the obstacles and detours, I had
found the spring at which I would drink for ever the elixir of
overflowing life.

The faces around me were beaming, but in their eyes I could
also read an intense emotion. Only minutes earlier we had all
been strangers, but now we were suddenly brothers, conscious

that we were experiencing one of the most important moments in our lives. A few people wept quietly.

'Akká was today little more than a small tourist town lapped by the waters of the Mediterranean, a pleasant place to visit. Yet the site had a terrible history. It had been what Bahá'u'lláh called the 'greatest prison', a prison-fortress where the Turks had incarcerated the most dangerous criminals in their empire. It was said to be so unhealthy that a bird flying overhead risked falling dead to the ground. This abominable citadel was now a museum dedicated to the Israeli heroes of the *Hagana*. In one of its cells Bahá'u'lláh was locked up for two years. From there he sent his epistles to the world's leaders and wrote the *Kitáb-i-Aqdas*, the Book of Laws according to which the world will become *'one fold and one shepherd'* (John 10:16).

*'The face of him on whom I gazed I can never forget, though I cannot describe it. Those piercing eyes seemed to read one's very soul;power and authority sat on that ample brow. . . . No need to ask in whose presence I stood, as I bowed myself before one who is the object of a devotion and love which kings might envy and emperors sigh for in vain!'** This portrait of Bahá'u'lláh sketched by the eminent orientalist E.G. Browne of Cambridge University came to mind and accompanied me through the splendid gardens of Bahjí where Bahá'u'lláh was buried. I also thought of my Bahá'í friends scattered all over the world: the Van Brunts far off in Valdez, Alaska, who were the first to show me the path that led to what I now believed to be the Truth; the Ghadimis and other members of the Iranian community; and also those Bahá'ís in Africa and Vietnam, the entire network of friendship. Here was truly a will to love springing forth on all the continents simultaneously. Bahá'u'lláh said, *'Religion is, verily, the chief instrument for the establishment of order in the world, and of tranquillity amongst its peoples'*. I now believed those words, for no political alchemy could create a society as beautiful and pure as gold from weak individuals made of lead. Until God's kingdom was established in men's hearts, neither spiritual nor political unity would be achieved and no problem or crisis would admit of a lasting solution.

The unification of mankind and its religions; the reconciliation of religion and science; the establishment of world peace and universal justice; the adoption of an auxiliary language which could be understood and spoken by everyone; the emancipation of women; the abolition of

*This is the only written description of Bahá'u'lláh by a Westerner. Professor Browne had the privilege of meeting him at Bahjí in 1890. See A *Traveller's Narrative*, pp XXXIX-XL.

domestic and industrial slavery; respect for human rights and liberties; the right to universal education: with so many problems facing the world, I could hardly believe that people still did not want to listen to Bahá'u'lláh's message, revealed a century before in this obscure corner of the East. When he had listed these problems - well ahead of his time - the prisoner of 'Akká had also offered the necessary solutions, drawing up a coherent plan which today is becoming more and more timely and necessary. Yet, in spite of this beginning, none of the world's leaders is prepared fully to acknowledge the truth of his writings. In Paris in 1911, 'Abdu'l-Bahá, his son, stated: *'Concentrate all the thoughts of your heart on love and unity. When a thought of war comes, oppose it by a stronger thought of peace. A thought of hatred must be destroyed by a more powerful thought of love.'* Divine revelation is the greatest of revolutions.

'You have no strength left, young man.'

I grunted and strained, but could not close the heavy-springed hand press. Yet I had to convince the doctor from Tel Aviv that I was capable of going to a kibbutz. To tell the truth, I was exhausted. The nine days of my pilgrimage to Haifa had revived my spirits, but physically I was at the end of my tether. The 45,000 miles of my African marathon had sapped my remaining energy. This time I was really worn out, and I would have to stop.

The doctor examining me was as skinny as I was. He informed me that with my thirty-five years I was just within the limit for acceptance on to a kibbutz.

'Frankly, you're not in the best of shape!'

'But surely I have enough strength to pick oranges and grapefruit?'

A little surprised, the old man wrote out a health certificate for me.

I had chosen Tsuba Kibbutz on a hill in Judea, just outside Jerusalem. In Tsuba I would not have any picking to do, for no fruit was grown there. I must admit that I had no desire to knock myself out climbing trees, getting scratched all over and repeating the same twist of the wrist for weeks on end.

I had forgotten what it was like to have a room with four walls, a bed, the use of a hot shower and copious, regular meals. I shared a room in a wooden chalet with an American Jew. As soon as I arrived, I found myself in the grip of a strange new sensation, a feeling of security, comfort and carefreeness. Although life in the kibbutz struck some volunteers as spartan, to me it seemed idyllic. Still it felt odd to stay put, to be fed and lodged like a respectable citizen.

Tsuba lived up to my wishes, for there was a feeling of truly living, an ambience from deep in the past. Two hundred adults and about as many children lived there together. Neither rich nor poor, the kibbutz was twenty-five years old, the same age as the State of Israel. It resembled a family camp, and it was up to me to blend into the community.

At 6.30 each morning, I woke up and·slipped on blue overalls and boots. Each of the twelve volunteers was assigned a different task, and no one dared refuse. The first two days, I was in charge of feeding some 5,000 white hens cackling and fluttering in their cages. As I pushed along my cart full of grain, I thought how long it had been since I had last worked. That had been on board the freighter bound for Tahiti. On second thoughts, I had worked an entire day in Haifa, weeding the garden of some German nuns to pay for my stay in their convent.

On the third day I left the chickens to become a builder's labourer, helping with the construction of a kindergarten. There is nothing heavier than cement to cart around, and by evening I was so exhausted that I felt ready to drop. Luckily, the foreman was away the next day, and the three Arabs I was working with offered to relieve me so that I could go and rest. They became my first friends: Abdullah, Abed and Jamil.

Finally, on the fifth day, I found a cushy job more suited to my flagging strength. I was assigned to take care of the 400 cows and calves. Six of us worked together, and the atmosphere was one of close comradeship. My companions were surprised to see such expertise on the part of a suburbanite, but I had immediately recaptured the skills learned long ago during summers spent with my aunts Alice and Jeanne. With genuine pleasure I breathed in the familiar smell of the barn. I fed the animals, led them to the milking machines, cleared out the straw, distributed the hay, weighed the calves. The time seemed to fly past. What I enjoyed most was playing midwife. There was a calf born almost every day. Some days there were complications, and we would have to help the cow to give birth. We tied a rope round the emerging front legs of the calf, and then two or three of us would pull with all our might. It was not particularly appealing, but it was life in the raw, with all its beauty and strength. A calf with a big white spot on her muzzle was baptized 'Andrea' in my honour. For some time to come she would keep my memory alive in the kibbutz that I loved so very much.

Hebrew was the common language, but fortunately two of my companions spoke to the cows in English, two others in Spanish and the last in German. I struck up a friendship with Yanoch, a tall, athletic and permanently optimistic Chilean. We formed a team, and when work

allowed, would lie back on the straw and talk about his country or about
the war . . . the accursed, omnipresent war that was responsible for a
permanent undercurrent of tension in Tsuba.

'You can't imagine our emotion when we conquered Jerusalem in
1967. The entire population rushed to the Wailing Wall. I remember
being pushed aside by a *hasid* who couldn't get there fast enough. You
know the *hasidim*, those guys with beards and side curls who are always
dressed in black and bent over their Scriptures? They're a fanatical sect,
believing the Messiah and not the army will recover their land for them.
They refuse to carry weapons, but they throw stones at ambulances on
the Sabbath because it is forbidden to work then. They don't even carry a
handkerchief on the Sabbath. Anyway the *hasid* who jostled me was
dashing headlong towards the wall with his big black hat crammed down
over his eyes and both hands clutching the hem of his ghetto frock coat.
When he started flinging himself against the stones, I stopped him with
my machine-gun. "Where are you going so fast, when you didn't even
help us fight? Aren't you ashamed?" The sickly-looking fellow was
suddenly uneasy but retorted, "You think you conquered the Wall with
your gun? It wasn't you. It was a miracle!" '

Then Yanoch burst out laughing in his loud, carefree voice. Like
many Israelis, he didn't believe in God, but that did not prevent him
from feeling thoroughly Jewish and more at home in Israel than
anywhere else.

In addition to the friends I had made, I also had a family. Indiani
from Burma and his American wife Suzanne decided to 'adopt' me, as was
the custom on the kibbutzim with newcomers. They had travelled a lot
and didn't have the typical kibbutz mentality, which could at times be a
problem for the foreigner. They were the ones who really taught me to
love Tsuba. We spent long hours in each other's company and frequently
ate our meals together.

Purim, Pesach . . . white tablecloths and candles: the time of feasts
had come. My friends told me all about Israel, and I used my free time to
study the subject as well. I learned how to praise this life, this strong
friendship so unique on earth. I felt good, indeed too good . . . to the
point of realizing that the comfort and security of the kibbutz were slowly
enveloping and isolating me. Each morning I would repeat to myself,
'André, you're letting yourself get sluggish. These days of "pigeon bones"

*In *The Wolf and the Dog*, a fable by La Fontaine, the wolf is offered a reward of 'chicken
bones and pigeon bones, not to mention many a caress' if he will wear a collar. The fable
symbolizes the eternal dilemma of attachment versus freedom.

are going to have to end. Remember you're a lone wolf.'* In less than eight weeks, I had got myself back in shape. I had gained a pound each week and had now reached a normal weight of 140 pounds. In truth, I had rarely been so fat. It was time to leave. I had accumulated enough energy for another six months of travel through the last European countries that I had not yet visited.*

For the last time on the last morning, I dipped a large ladle into a bucket filled with yogurt. After treating myself to four fried eggs, I went to pack my belongings. Farewell to the cosy tranquillity and abundant food of the kibbutz! The road was waiting, rolling out its silver ribbon, beckoning me to follow it. At its end the sun awaited me, the midnight sun of the North Cape. It was a meeting I couldn't miss.

But before heading off towards Norway, I was going to travel all over Israel and the occupied territories, from the Golan Heights to the Sharm-el-Sheik at the tip of the Sinai peninsula, from the banks of the Jordan to Gaza. Hitch-hiking was hardly a piece of cake in the land of the Hebrews at that time. It took somebody as crazy as me to go hitch-hiking around a country at war, for nobody would pick up a 'civilian' when there were so many soldiers in competition. At some crossroads, the military police used their authority to keep the hitch-hiking organised. The result was that I was continually being pushed aside until I finally figured out the magic word: 'Tourist!' Tourists were even admitted into military trucks and patrolling jeeps! But there remained one more major annoyance: there was no place to drop off my pack when I wanted to visit a city. Everybody was afraid to keep an eye on it in case it was a terrorist bomb!

As I left the biblical land of milk and honey, I could not help regretting that man had turned it into a powder keg. 'We want peace, but the Arabs don't.' That's what I had been told from the moment I arrived. When I had been on the other side of the border, eighteen months earlier, I had heard a similar refrain: 'We want peace, but the Jews don't'. Thus, it was with a somewhat bitter smile and a half-hearted wave that I bade farewell from aboard my boat bound for Piraeus. It was a land of violence in which men on either side of the Jordan greeted each other with an ironic call for peace. *Shalom* in Hebrew, *Salaam* in Arabic: Peace, which everybody talked about but which apparently nobody really wanted. The world had arrived at an ultimate contradiction. Then I thought of the day promised by Bahá'u'lláh when people will finally

*In Skopje, Yugoslavia, I finally came full circle.

consider themselves as citizens of a common mother country, the earth, when all will be as members of the same body.

No, I was not without hope as I remembered the words of Bahá'u'lláh to the historian Edward Granville Browne: 'these fruitless strifes, these ruinous wars shall pass away and the "Most Great Peace" shall come'.* I believed in joyful tomorrows, in days of never-ending peace that would be shared by everyone, to the four corners of the earth. Six years of thumbing along every manner of road and track in every kind of weather had taught me the truth of that conviction, until little by little it had become my deepest article of faith.

Beyond our horizon, momentarily obscured, the sun was always shining. Soon, it would shed its warm light over all people. That radiant and benevolent heavenly body was symbolic of the great happiness and brotherhood awaiting us - awaiting me too, like the midnight sun.

Shalom!

---

*A Traveller's Narrative, p XL.

APPENDIX

Summary

1955-1973: eighteen years of adventure around the world, six of which involved uninterrupted hitch-hiking through five continents (1967-1973). In all, 250,000 miles or ten times the circumference of the globe, but comprising ONE SINGLE TRIP AROUND THE WORLD.

Over 200,000 (four-fifths) of the 250,000 total miles were covered for free by hitch-hiking (not forgetting that two-thirds of the globe are covered by water and that hiking by sea has become practically impossible today, in spite of many rumours to the contrary).

Total number of countries visited: 135.

Budget For Six Years' Hitch-Hiking

Total Expenses:

Living (meals-washing-lodging)	$1,017
Transport (when paid for)	$ 983
	$2,000 *total costs**

Average Daily Expenses:

Lived (bed & board) on an average of $0.4943 per day

Total daily expenses (including transport)*: $1 per day

Excluding Miscellaneous Expenses:
  Visas, souvenirs, books, museums,
  clothes, replacing stolen money,
  medicine, bank charges, postage, etc. $2,000
Films (one movie camera,
  220 reels of 8 and super-8 film) $1,000

MY RECORDS

Number of rides (cars, boats, planes): 1,978
Longest ride: Australia, 1,600 miles
Second longest ride: Peru, 1,409 miles
Speed record: South Africa, 2,500 miles in three days of hitch-hiking
Highest point slept at: Andes, 15,746 feet
Lowest temperature: Alaska, -49°F
Highest temperature: Australia, 150°F
Normal weight: 143 lbs. Lowest weight: 115 lbs.
One paid night in a hotel (forced by Intourist): Moscow
Longest wait at the roadside: 3 days in Patagonia
Number of passports used: 6
Number of journals used: 7

ITINERARY

I — BEFORE LEAVING HOME

1 FRANCE
2 SWITZERLAND   to buy goods during the war
3 LIECHTENSTEIN   passed through
4 AUSTRIA   skiing
5 BELGIUM   scout camp – travelling down the River
                          Meuse in a rubber dinghy
6 WEST GERMANY   scout camp
7 LUXEMBOURG   scout camp

II — PREPARING FOR THE ROUND-THE-WORLD TRIP

DATE	N°	COUNTRY	KM	LENGTH OF STAY	
30 JUNE 55	8	GREAT BRITAIN	6 000	15 months	
1 OCT 56	9	REPUBLIC OF IRELAND	370		15 days
22 JAN 57	10	SPAIN	3 840	10 months	
12 NOV 57	—	WEST GERMANY	400	3 months	
14 FEB 58		*flying from Paris to Pointe-Noire*	6 400	—	
	11	ALGERIA	—		1 day
15 FEB 58	12	CHAD	—		1 day
16 FEB 58	13	THE CONGO	3 200	21 months	15 days
16 APR 59	14	GABON	1 740		8 days
	15	ZAÏRE	400		3 days
	16	CABINDA	480		2 days
29 NOV 59		*flying Pointe-Noire to Paris*	6 400	—	
	17	CAMEROON	—		1 day
30 NOV 59	18	NIGER	—		1 day
1 DEC 59		*hospital in France after skiing accident*	—	9 months	
2 JUL 60	19	MONACO	10		1 day
11 SEPT 60	—	WEST GERMANY	2 730	25 months	
24 AUG 61	20	EAST GERMANY – Berlin	360		2 days
23 AUG 62	21	CZECHOSLOVAKIA	300		5 days
15 DEC 62	22	ITALY	7 430	22 months	
2 JUNE 63	23	THE VATICAN	—		1 day
16 AUG 63	24	SAN MARINO	—		1 day
4 SEPT 63	25	SAN LEO	—		1 day
28 MAY 64	26	YUGOSLAVIA	3 380		9 days
13 JUNE 64	27	BULGARIA	860		6 days
14 FEB 65		*flying the Atlantic*	6 620	—	
	28	CANADA	7 830	33 months	7 days
7 OCT 66	29	U.S.A.	1 250		3 days
		TOTAL	60 000	12 years 5 months	

The journey was broken up by a total of one year spent in France

III — HITCH-HIKING JOURNEY AROUND THE WORLD

DATE	N°	COUNTRY	KM	TRIPS	AVERAGE COST PER DAY IN US$	LENGTH OF STAY (DAYS)
25 NOV 1967	—	CANADA	80			—
	—	U.S.A.	6 720			13
8 DEC	30	MEXICO	2 280			10
18 DEC	31	GUATEMALA	380			1
19 DEC	32	EL SALVADOR	330			1
20 DEC	33	HONDURAS	160			1
21 DEC	34	NICARAGUA	380			—
	35	COSTA RICA	565		Journey from Toronto to Iguazu, Brazil by converted taxi 20,815 km, 83 days $1 per day	2
23 DEC	36	PANAMA	605			7
30 DEC		*by boat across Pacific to*	2 020			3
2 JAN 1968	37	ECUADOR	380			3
5 JAN	38	PERU	4 280			26
31 JAN	39	BOLIVIA	1 015			10
10 FEB	40	ARGENTINA	1 220			2
12 FEB	41	PARAGUAY	400			4
16 FEB	42	BRAZIL	6 350	3		27
15 MAR	43	URUGUAY	520	1		4
19 MAR	—	ARGENTINA	3 000	5		36
24 APRIL	44	CHILE	700	9		3
27 APRIL	—	ARGENTINA	780	5		11
8 MAY	—	CHILE	1 500	—		7
15 MAY	—	ARGENTINA	100	—		2
17 MAY	—	CHILE	4 200	8	An adverage of 50¢ per day	40
26 JUNE	—	PERU	4 700	32		37
2 AUG	45	COLOMBIA	—	—		4
6 AUG	—	BRAZIL	2 700	3		21
27 AUG	—	COLOMBIA	1 100	—		12
8 SEPT	—	ECUADOR	800	—		5
13 SEPT	—	COLOMBIA	1 900	1		3
16 SEPT	46	VENEZUELA	2 460	10		8
24 SEPT	—	COLOMBIA	500	3		10
		flying across Caribbean	700	—	—	—
4 OCT	—	COSTA RICA	270	2	0*	7
11 OCT	—	NICARAGUA	220	2	0	—
		flying from Managua to	1 700	—	—	—
	—	MEXICO	9 000	58	—	90
9 JAN 1969	—	U.S.A.	2 600	12	75¢	5
14 JAN	—	CANADA	3 200	14	0	22
5 FEB	47	ALASKA	6 380	17	75¢	43
20 MAR	—	CANADA	1 600	6	—	7
27 MAR	—	U.S.A.	6 080	58	—	51
17 MAY	—	MEXICO	5 700	10	25¢	17
3 JUNE	—	U.S.A.	640	8	—	15

Zero indicates free accommodation and meals through friends, resoursefulness or circumstance.

DATE	Nº	COUNTRY	KM	TRIPS	AVERAGE COST PER DAY IN US $	LENGTH OF STAY
18 JUNE 1969		*by boat in the Pacific*	6 400	1	—	10
28 JUNE	48	FRENCH POLYNESIA	3 400	7	40¢	75
11 SEPT		*by yacht in the Pacific*	1 150	1	$1	8
19 SEPT	49	COOK ISLANDS	20	—	49¢	11
30 SEPT		*flying the Pacific*	3 000	—	—	—
One Day Lost Crossing International Date Line						
1 OCT	50	NEW ZEALAND	6 300	135	$1	52
22 NOV	—	*boat across Tasman Sea*	1 900	—	—	2
24 NOV	51	AUSTRALIA	16 000	61	67¢	62
25 JAN 1970	52	*flying via TIMOR*	2 000	1	—	—
	53	INDONESIA	1 000	5	26¢	32
26 FEB		*boat across Java Sea*	1 000	—	—	2
27 FEB	54	SINGAPORE	80	5	50¢	7
6 MAR	55	BORNEO *and boat trip*	2 020	2	16¢	14
20 MAR	—	SINGAPORE	110	5	—	8
28 MAR	56	MALAYSIA	1 200	11	49¢	9
6 APR	57	THAILAND	4 700	74	37¢	29
5 MAY	58	LAOS	750	5	15¢	13
18 MAY	—	THAILAND	1 440	15	—	5
23 MAY	59	CAMBODIA	1 350	4	40¢	17
9 JUNE	60	SOUTH VIETNAM	390	4	0	13
22 JUNE		*flying South China Sea*	1 300	—	—	—
	61	PHILIPPINES	5 200	53	$1	48
9 AUG		*by boat across South China Sea*	1 130	1	—	1
10 AUG	62	HONG KONG	120	5	50¢	25
4 SEPT	63	MACAO *and boat trip*	150	2	50¢	3
7 SEPT	—	HONG KONG	—	—	—	3
10 SEPT		*by boat across South China Sea*	800	—	—	1
11 SEPT	64	TAIWAN	850	18	0	15
26 SEPT	65	RYUKYU ISLANDS	1 600	—	0	3
29 SEPT	66	JAPAN	6 010	146	—	48
16 NOV	67	SOUTH KOREA	1 480	12	50¢	9
25 NOV	—	JAPAN	1 000	6	47¢	9
4 DEC		*by boat across Sea of Japan*	1 600	—	—	2
6 DEC	68	U.S.S.R.	10 730	—	$1	11
17 DEC	69	ROMANIA	810	3	50¢	2
19 DEC	—	BULGARIA	485	17	50¢	2
21 DEC	70	TURKEY	1 520	17	$1	2
23 DEC	71	SYRIA	200	1	30¢	1
24 DEC	72	LEBANON	700	40	20¢	10
3 JAN 1971	—	SYRIA	630	22	—	10
13 JAN	73	JORDAN	1 420	19	40¢	11
24 JAN	74	IRAQ	2 600	36	44¢	14
7 FEB	75	IRAN	2 300	16	33¢	11
18 FEB	76	PAKISTAN	2 500	17	13¢	7
25 FEB	77	INDIA	11 090	90	30¢	91

DATE	N°	COUNTRY	KM	TRIPS	AVERAGE COST PER DAY IN US $	LENGTH OF STAY
27 MAY 1971	78	NEPAL	700	8	52¢	15
11 JUNE	—	INDIA	3 000	—	—	7
18 JUNE	79	CEYLON (SRI LANKA)	1 800	49	10¢	26
14 JULY	—	INDIA	5 740	—	—	17
31 JULY	—	PAKISTAN	600	5	25¢	6
6 AUG	80	AFGHANISTAN	4 025	10	30¢	15
21 AUG	—	IRAN	6 515	52	0	61
21 OCT	81	KUWAIT	150	1	0	6
27 OCT	82	SAUDI ARABIA	1 600	—	0	1
28 OCT	83	NORTH YEMEN	750	4	0	6
3 NOV	84	SOUTH YEMEN	150	2	0	7
10 NOV	85	DJIBOUTI	75	—	25¢	8
18 NOV	86	ETHIOPIA	4 550	26	0	38
26 DEC	87	KENYA	2 155	7	0	13
8 JAN 1972	88	UGANDA	1 380	11	10¢	7
15 JAN	89	RWANDA	355	3	15¢	3
18 JAN	90	BURUNDI	290	2	25¢	4
22 JAN	91	TANZANIA	1 760	10	43¢	10
1 FEB	—	KENYA	1 640	6	20¢	5
6 FEB	92	SOMALIA	1 160	4	0	12
18 FEB	—	KENYA	1 520·	8	50¢	6
24 FEB	—	TANZANIA	1 535	11	—	4
28 FEB	93	ZAMBIA	1 370	8	20¢	5
4 MAR	94	RHODESIA	1 660	9	15¢	13
17 MAR	95	BOTSWANA	715	8	16¢	3
20 MAR	96	SOUTH AFRICA	1 045	12	49¢	5
25 MAR	97	NAMIBIA	1 800	7	0	5
30 MAR	98	ANGOLA	2 865	10	15¢	6
5 APR	—	NAMIBIA	1 610	4	—	1
6 APR	—	SOUTH AFRICA	3 530	50	—	22
28 APR	99	LESOTHO	290	5	15¢	4
2 MAY	—	SOUTH AFRICA	1 635	20	—	13
15 MAY	100	SWAZILAND	170	2	29¢	3
18 MAY	101	MOZAMBIQUE	1 780	6	54¢	6
24 MAY	102	MALAWI	1 450	18	19¢	7
31 MAY	—	TANZANIA	900	2	—	9
9 JUNE	103	ZANZIBAR	130	2	0	1
10 JUNE	—	TANZANIA	110	2	—	3
13 JUNE		*flying Indian Ocean*	1 500	—	—	—
	104	MADAGASCAR	1 645	10	50¢	22
5 JULY		*flying Indian Ocean*	1 500	—	—	—
	—	TANZANIA	1 250	—	—	5
10 JULY	—	ZAÏRE	1 880	9	45¢	16
26 JULY	105	CENTRAL AFRICAN REPUBLIC	1 300	3	46¢	8
3 AUG	—	CAMEROON	1 300	10	64¢	5

DATE	N°	COUNTRY	KM	TRIPS	AVERAGE COST PER DAY IN US $	LENGTH OF STAY
8 AUG 1972	106	NIGERIA	930	8	56¢	5
13 AUG	107	DAHOMEY	180	3	75¢	2
15 AUG	108	TOGO	50	1	40¢	1
16 AUG	109	GHANA	1 050	5	52¢	4
20 AUG	110	UPPER VOLTA	760	2	0	3
23 AUG	111	MALI	1 000	2	0	7
30 AUG	112	IVORY COAST	1 450	10	50¢	11
10 SEPT	113	LIBERIA	600	3	50¢	4
14 SEPT	114	SIERRA LEONE	480	3	0	4
18 SEPT		*flying to*	700	—	—	—
	115	THE GAMBIA	50	3	65¢	1
19 SEPT	116	SENEGAL	660	8	80¢	10
29 SEPT	117	MAURITANIA	1 235	4	25¢	8
7 OCT	118	RIO DE ORO	1 520	1	0	5
12 OCT	119	THE CANARY ISLANDS	200	2	83¢	9
21 OCT	—	RIO DE ORO	80	1	—	2
23 OCT	120	MOROCCO	2 000	10	60¢	23
15 NOV	121	CEUTA	10	—	0	1
16 NOV	—	MOROCCO	840	7	—	4
20 NOV	—	ALGERIA	3 350	28	66¢	27
17 DEC	122	TUNISIA	1 335	15	30¢	10
27 DEC	123	LIBYA	2 765	11	40¢	9
5 JAN 1973	124	EGYPT	1 045	—	68¢	19
24 JAN	125	SUDAN	2 210	1	15¢	10
3 FEB	—	EGYPT	1 570	—	—	5
8 FEB		*boat on Mediterranean*	600	—	—	—
	126	CYPRUS	410	9	35¢	4
12 FEB		*fly Mediterranean*	250	—	—	—
	127	ISRAEL	3 600	78	47¢	82
4 MAY		*boat on Mediterranean* (via CYPRUS)	480	—	—	1
5 MAY	—	TURKEY	5 470	51	50¢	30
4 JUNE	128	GREECE	4 315	52	79¢	33
7 JULY	—	YUGOSLAVIA	840	7	$1.25	2
9 JULY	129	HUNGARY	445	7	$1.07	7
16 JULY	—	AUSTRIA	185	1	$1.14	6
22 JULY	—	CZECHOSLOVAKIA	230	—	—	1
23 JULY	130	POLAND	755	10	57¢	7
30 JULY		*ferry on Baltic Sea*	900	—	—	1
31 JULY	131	FINLAND	2 235	31	65¢	18
18 AUG	132	NORWAY	3 250	26	$1.44	18
5 SEPT	133	SWEDEN	470	—	72¢	9
14 SEPT	—	ÅLAND	1 030	5	57¢	3
17 SEPT	—	SWEDEN	620	6	—	3
20 SEPT	134	DENMARK	150	3	40¢	13
2 OCT	—	WEST GERMANY	450	4	—	1

DATE	Nº	COUNTRY	KM	TRIPS	AVERAGE COST PER DAY IN US $	LENGTH OF STAY
3 OCT 1973	135	THE NETHERLANDS	400	10	54¢	12
15 OCT	—	BELGIUM	250	4	0	10
25 OCT	—	WEST GERMANY	500	4	0	2
27 OCT	—	FRANCE	510	12	0	2
29 OCT		*home in BRUNOY*				

TOTAL DISTANCE: 340,000 km (211,180 mls)

DISTANCE TRAVELLED BY FOOT: 11,970 km (7,440 mls)

NUMBER OF RIDES: 1,978

AVERAGE COST PER DAY OVERALL: 49¢

TOTAL LENGTH OF TRIP: 2,165 days

O N E W O R L D
Books for Thoughtful People

MAIL ORDER

The Valley of Search
A PERSONAL QUEST FOR TRUTH
by Angela Anderson

This is the candid, highly readable account of one woman's quest for spiritual consciousness. Sharing with readers all the joys, frustrations and lessons of the journey of a lifetime, this down-to-earth, humorous and uplifting story will touch the hearts of many seekers.
192 pages, softcover, £6.95, US$11.95

Accents of God
A TREASURY OF THE WORLD'S SACRED SCRIPTURES
M.K. Rohani

This attractive, large format gift edition presents six profound selections of major significance from the sacred writings of Hinduism, Judaism, Buddhism, Christianity, Islam and the Bahá'í Faith. The passages chosen for this special anthology highlight the common basis of mankind's spiritual heritage, and explore the eternal truths enshrined in these traditions.
86 pages, hardcover, £10.95, US$18.95

Achieving Peace by the Year 2000
by John Huddleston

In this insightful analysis of the causes of war and barriers to peace, the Chief of Budget & Planning at the IMF examines the psychological, moral and practical issues and puts forward a twelve point plan for establishing a lasting peace.
160 pages, softcover, £3.50, US$5.95

Science & Religion

by Anjam Khursheed

A fascinating account of the conflict between science and religion in Western society, reviewed in the context of the latest discoveries in modern physics. It highlights the link between this conflict and the present state of the world.

144 pages, softcover, £4.50, US$7.50

The Way to Inner Freedom

by Erik Blumenthal

In this popular book, the author explains that freedom is an inner quality dependent on our own conscious choices, and presents a simple, step-by-step programme of self-discovery and self-education.

144 pages, softcover, £4.50, US$7.50

The Promise of World Peace

The Universal House of Justice

This is a perceptive critique of the key global issues confronting us today, which challenges a number of contemporary myths about human nature. Packed with facts, charts and photographs.

192 pages, 100 photos, softcover, £8.95, US$14.95

Drawings, Verse & Belief

by Bernard Leach

This beautiful, cloth-bound gift edition combines the author-artist's delicate visual images and delightful verse with an impassioned profession of faith, to provide a rare insight into the personality of a great master craftsman.

160 pages, 82 illustrations, cloth, £12.95, US$19.95

The Hidden Words

by Bahá'u'lláh

An unusual and inspiring collection of spiritual teachings which will appeal to people of all religious persuasions and those who seek a spiritual life. Lucid in style and rich in imagery, these exquisite meditational verses explore the relationship between God and man.

112 pages, softcover, £3.95, US$6.95

To Understand
& Be Understood
by Erik Blumenthal

Written by an internationally respected Adlerian psychotherapist in a warm, anecdotal fashion, this book offers down-to-earth, workable advice for successful, caring relationships in all spheres of life.

160 pages, softcover, £4.50, US$7.50

Creating a
Successful Family
by K. & S. Khavari

Focusing on equality and consultation in the home, it outlines a new approach to family life designed for the families of today. Gives practical advice for shared decision-making, problem-solving and building a strong family.

256 pages, softcover, £6.50, US$11.95

Contemplating
Life's Greatest Questions
AN ANTHOLOGY OF BAHA'U'LLAH'S
WRITINGS WITH COMMENTARY
by M.K. Rohani

Here are the enduring questions that each of us must ask if we are to explore our place in the scheme of things. Discussed, debated and meditated on throughout humanity's eternal quest for knowledge and understanding, these questions - and their answers - shed light on the meaning of our existence and our relationship with the divine. This book explores these questions in the light of the writings of Bahá'u'lláh, sharing with readers new insights and an inspiring vision of spiritual life.

96 pages, softcover, £4.50, US$7.95

A Study of
Bahá'u'lláh's Tablet
to the Christians
by Michael W. Sours

Considered one of the most significant letters of Bahá'u'lláh, founder of the Bahá'í faith, its passionate and moving appeal offers fresh insight into the meaning of a spiritual life and the personal quest for the Kingdom of God.

224 pages, softcover, £7.95, US$13.95

The Inner Limits
of Mankind
by Ervin Laszlo
A spirited and provocative examination of contemporary values and
attitudes by a leading systems scientist and philosopher. The author
argues for the emergence of a new globally-oriented, environmentally-
conscious, spiritually aware, thinking person.
160 pages, softcover, £4.50, US$7.95

Name _____

Address _____

_____ Date _____

Send all orders to:

Oneworld Publications
185 Banbury Road
Oxford, England OX2 7AR

Quantity	Title	Total
	Sub Total	
	Postage & Handling	
	Total	

Payment by: ___ Check/Money Order
___ Mastercard/Access
___ Visa

Credit Card No. |__|__|__|__|__|__|__|__|__|__|__|__| Exp. Date _____

Signature _____

Please add 15% to cover
postage and handling (min. £1/$2)